Courting Change

The Story of the
Public Citizen Litigation Group

Books by Public Citizen

Worst Pills, Best Pills—A Consumer's Guide to Avoiding Drug-Induced Death or Illness
By Sidney M. Wolfe, M.D., and Public Citizen's Health Research Group
Pocket Books (To be released in 2005)

Whose Trade Organization? A Comprehensive Guide to the WTO
By Lori Wallach and Patrick Woodall
The New Press (2004)

Women's Health Alert
By Sidney M. Wolfe, M.D., and Public Citizen's Health Research Group
Addison-Wesley Publishing Co. (1991)

Who Robbed America? A Citizen's Guide to the Savings and Loan Scandal
By Michael Waldman and Public Citizen's Congress Watch
Random House (1990)

Freedom from Harm—The Civilizing Influence of Health, Safety and Environmental Regulation
By David Bollier and Joan Claybrook
Public Citizen and Democracy Project (1986)

Retreat from Safety—Reagan's Attack on America's Health
By Joan Claybrook and the staff of Public Citizen
Pantheon Books (1984)

Over the Counter Pills That Don't Work
By Public Citizen's Health Research Group
Public Citizen (1983)

Representing Yourself
By Kenneth Lasson and the Public Citizen Litigation Group
McGraw-Hill Ryerson (1983)

Pills That Don't Work
By Sidney M. Wolfe, M.D., and Public Citizen's Health Research Group
Warner Books (1980)

Public Citizen
1600 20th St. NW · Washington, D.C. 20009
202-588-1000
www.citizen.org

Courting Change

The Story of the
Public Citizen Litigation Group

Barbara Hinkson Craig

Afterword
By Alan B. Morrison

Public Citizen Press
Washington DC

ISBN: 1-58231-031-9
Library of Congress Control Number: 2004093222

Book and cover design by Kristy I. Jackson

Public Citizen Press
Washington, DC
First Edition
2004

Printed in the United States of America

To the men and women of the Public Citizen Litigation Group,
who can look in a mirror and feel good about their lives,

And to our grandchildren, Hannah and Julia Craig
and Cameron and Aislinn Gilmour,
who, it is hoped, will one day understand
and be thankful for what you do.

Contents

Preface

This book is about the Public Citizen Litigation Group and a small group of men and women who chose to spend all or part of their legal careers making a difference rather than simply making money. It is about the process of litigating in the public interest, which, as the reader will discover, is about a lot more than just lawyering. And it is about the results and importance of the litigation battles they have won and lost.

There is a long tradition in the United States of policymaking by litigation. Like lobbying, campaign contributions and media campaigns, litigation is another weapon in a public policy battle. Business and industry have long understood this, as even a cursory review of federal case law will show. Individuals and smaller, less organized or less politically powerful interests rarely had the financial wherewithal to go to court. Then, along came the American Civil Liberties Union (ACLU) and the National Association for the Advancement of Colored People (NAACP). Both groups quickly learned that litigation was crucial to the advancement of their interests. It was not long before other groups sought to mimic this strategy. In the early 1970s, a number of public interest law firms were formed, bringing new players into the policymaking-by-litigation game.

In the early 1990s, I added a seminar called Policymaking by Litigation to my courses at Wesleyan University in which the class studied the many groups that litigate in the public interest. There were a few books on the ACLU and NAACP but surprisingly little available on groups like the Environmental Defense Fund, the Natural Resources Defense Council, Public Advocates, the Women's Legal Defense Fund, and the Center for Law and Social Policy, to name just a few. Students did original research to learn about each group they had chosen to study—a great learning experience. In the summer of 1994, I was invited to teach my litigation seminar at Johns Hopkins University's Center for the Study of American Government in Washington, D.C. One day that summer, I met with Alan Morrison, whom I'd come to know during the writing of my earlier books on the legislative veto. Over lunch, I asked: "Why has no one written a book about your Public Citizen Litigation Group?" A dangerous question it turned out to be, since his response was that I should be the one to do just that. It is fair to say that I had no idea what I was getting into when agreeing to take on that task.

i

To begin with, at that point the Litigation Group had handled more than a thousand cases, the files of which were stored in hundreds of boxes at an off-site warehouse. At the time, records about which cases were filed in which boxes were sketchy at best. This was a tight-budget group with few support staff available for the niceties of maintaining filing systems. Each attorney was responsible for keeping track of his or her own case files. Some of the attorneys were amazingly well organized; others were quite the opposite. When I would begin the process of searching through a box of files, I might find items in folders accurately labeled; more often I faced a box filed with a mishmash of articles, documents, letters, scribbled notes, old pencils and even a empty coffee cup here and there. Fortunately there were no vermin. I had warned Alan from the start, one dead rodent and I'm out of here!

For help in dealing with this mountain of material, I turned to my Wesleyan students. Without their aid this project would not have been possible. Over many years, my seminar students assumed the responsibility of reviewing the case documents and researching the history, politics, technology and law surrounding the issues involved. Each of the one hundred cases or so that I selected for further investigation has been organized, explained and researched by these enthusiastic helpmates. This enormous treasure trove of research can now be found in twenty boxes of files turned back to the Litigation Group, where they will be available for future researchers. I am sure that anyone who refers to these student-products will be amazed at what these undergraduates accomplished. Give a young person a challenge and you will be amazed at what is produced! To each and every student in my Policymaking by Litigation Group seminars from 1995 through 2001, I give heartfelt thanks for all this hard work. And to the many who continued on with the project as individual research assistants (one wonderful young woman even took on two cases after graduation), I give special thanks.

Before I began the box stage of the project, though, I had to determine which cases were the most important to research—which among them would be most useful to describe just what the Litigation Group is about. There was only one way to do that: ask attorneys of the Litigation Group for their assistance. Thus, the project began with interviews of present and past members of the Group. The current crew and those who were still in the D.C. area were easy to find. Though they were incredibly busy, all willingly made time to talk with me. Some were much harder to find and reach. With the generous aid of several research and travel grants from Wesleyan University, though, I was ultimately able to talk to almost everyone who had served with the Group for any significant time (a year or more). In the end, these interviews covered nearly fifty (ninety-minute) tapes, all of which are now stored with the Public Citizen Litigation Group.

Digging through files and interviewing dozens of fascinating professionals, though overwhelming at times, turned out to be the easy part; figuring out how to package the amazing assortment of cases and people into some sort of manageable framework that would allow a reader to understand what the Litigation Group does and why was the real challenge. Though I do not always agree with the policy aims or results of the Litigation Group, I firmly believe that the role it and other public interest litigation groups play is a critical one in our system. Government cannot work fairly if only the powerful have access and sway. Having groups like the Litigation Group in the courts does not "level the playing field," but at least it makes it a little less tilted.

From the start, I wanted to write a book that young people, like those in my courses, and the reading public would find engaging and perhaps inspiring. This is the audience I hope to reach. If people do not understand what groups like this do and how important it is for them to counter the well-financed powerful interests, how will such groups maintain the support necessary to continue doing what they do?

Originally, I had planned to write the story of the Litigation Group's first twenty-five years. Herein, however, is just the first decade (1972-1982), though a few cases lap over into the mid-1980s. Time and length made carrying the story further unrealistic. There is so much more to tell and so much data organized and interviews recorded that I hope some other writer will see fit to continue the story in the future.

My apologies to all those who gave so willingly of their time, but whose stories did not make it into the book. Most especially I want to thank Con Hitchcock, whose instruction on the complexities of so many cases and issues was invaluable (having that see-through glass office had its negatives: it was so easy to pop in). Also, my apologies and special thanks to Eric Glitzenstein (whose stories were great, and how could I not get to the love story); to Brian Wolfman (who had so many thoughtful reflections, at least one of which made it in, but sad to miss all those great class action cases); to Patti Goldman (I traveled all the way to Seattle for an interview but did not even get to that great airports case); and to Mike Tankersley (whose long, long battle throughout the 1990s to preserve White House computer records for the future is a story worthy of its own book).

To all my family and friends—daughter Linsley Craig, Anne and Bernie Cramer, M.J. and Ron Boster, Jenna Dorn, and Anne and Alan Morrison, who provided bed and board and transportation around town for my many research trips to Washington, D.C.—my special thanks. Thanks also to Johns Hopkins University's Center for the Study of American Government for hiring me back to teach my seminar for a full semester in the fall of 1995 on Thursday nights. With funding to travel to D.C. every week that fall, I was able to do an enormous amount of research on Thursday afternoons and all day Friday (with a few weekends added in when my teaching responsibilities at Wesleyan made that possible). Thanks also to the Political Science Department at the University of Connecticut, which invited me to give my seminar course to a small group of graduate students who tackled some really difficult union democracy cases. And, as noted above, Wesleyan University provided an ever-changing supply of bright and eager students as well as several small travel grants and two $1,000 research grants that funded numerous trips. Two full-semester sabbaticals also provided by Wesleyan University (Spring 1996 and Spring 1999) were devoted entirely to writing. In addition, I want to thank Betty Seaver, my friend and the editor of my three other books, who helped with the early chapters here. Sadly, funding was not forthcoming to continue her services to the end. Hopefully, after years of her fine editing, some has rubbed off. As should be obvious from this litany of thanks, this project was a low-budget, volunteer-dependent and significantly self-funded effort—much like the organization it describes.

I most particularly want to thank Joan Claybrook and the leadership of Public Citizen and its staff, whose generous support and efforts in the end made this book a reality. Thanks especially to Public Citizen Communications Director Booth Gunter, who edited the text and took charge of the production process. Thanks also to Angela Bradbery and Shannon Little for their editing, fact-checking and proofing assistance, and to Kristy Jackson for designing the book text and cover. Other Public Citizen staffers who helped prepare the book for printing include Achamma Kallarakal, Brendan O'Dell, Paul Levy, LuAnn Canipe, Valerie Collins and Jeffrey Vinson.

When I retired in 2001, thirteen chapters were completed, but no publisher was to be found. It looked as if years of work would mold away in a cardboard box. Then Alan Morrison contacted me last fall, saying Public Citizen would get the book out if I would be willing to put some finishing touches on it. Since I now live on a boat, then located in Bucas del Toro, Panama, this was quite a daunting task, but I agreed to try. Fortunately, I was able to spend three months in the States writing. Shipping all those research boxes to Panama (to say nothing of where to put them on a 44-foot sailboat) would have been more than just a challenge. Still, the two final chapters were finished aboard, with the only problem being getting the final product back to the U.S. With the book now done, my husband Bob Gilmour and I will continue our life's dream of sailing to distant shores, safe in the knowledge that the Litigation Group will persist in trying to make our political process fairer for all. With children and grandchildren a'plenty, we are thankful, indeed, that there are some players in the political game who are motivated and rewarded by something other than "what's in it for me."

Finally, I want to thank my mother, Barbara Lorraine Hinkson, who provided a place for me to write in peace and quiet at her home in Florida (that should explain why this Connecticut-based author chose January-June for sabbaticals). Most of all, though, I thank her for being my best supporter: always ready and eager to listen to me ramble on about cases; always there with comments and reactions after reading my day's writing; always willing to leave me alone when the fingers were flying over the keys. Every writer should be blessed with a mom like mine!

1

Ralph Nader Goes to Washington

This is a story about lawyers. In particular, about the Public Citizen Litigation Group, the public interest law firm founded by Ralph Nader and Alan Morrison in 1972. The attorneys of the Litigation Group—forty in all, as of 2004—could have become rich along with most of their law school classmates. Instead, they chose to try to make a difference by devoting all or a part of their legal careers to serving a cause at the expense of their own pocketbooks. Financial sacrifice is not a concept often associated with lawyers in a country where lawyer-bashing has become a national sport, a greedy shark the cartoonists' shorthand for the profession. In that sense theirs is an unusual story. What makes it compelling, however, is the nature of their cause: to make big organizations—whether governments, corporations, unions or the professions (medical and legal in particular)—more open, more honest and more accountable to the little people they represent, sell to, employ or serve.

Theirs is not an agenda that aims to serve a specific slice of the American people as, say, the National Association for the Advancement of Colored People (NAACP) serves the interests of African-Americans, or the AARP promotes the well-being of senior citizens, or the U.S. Chamber of Commerce lobbies for business interests. Rather, the lawyers of the Litigation Group work for the interests of anyone who votes, buys a product, is employed or who purchases a service—in short, nearly every one of us. Making a difference for so many over such a large set of issues is a daunting goal, but one they have pursued for more than thirty-two years in more than a thousand cases filed in federal and state courts with more than forty ruled on by the Supreme Court.

The story begins in the 1960s—a time of civil rights demonstrations and anti-war marches; of sit-ins at lunch counters and in the offices of college presidents; of the trial of the nation's most trusted baby doctor and a prominent minister for acting to thwart the draft; of three tragic assassinations—Kennedy, Kennedy and King; of hippies with long hair, beards and beads; of free love and noisy music; of bra and draft card burnings; and of Ralph Nader and the consumer movement. Hindsight paints the entire country in chaotic upheaval. The fact is that the vast majority of the then-160 million or so Americans did what people have always done: they worked, got married, raised kids, ran

1

errands, took vacations, vegged-out and mostly ignored the political goings-on about them. Still, there was something about the political atmosphere then that made activism more likely and more likely to succeed.

From the vantage point of the twenty-first century it is hard to understand fully the 1960s and the movement-style politics that developed then. First came the civil rights movement, then the antiwar movement, the open-government movement, the environmental and consumer movements, and the women's movement. For a time the economy took a back seat to other concerns in public discourse and action. There was a national mood of hope, a mood that gave rise to the belief that there was, or could be, knowledge enough to solve our problems, money enough to pay for the solutions, and will enough to put them into operation. Oddly, given the present state of mistrust of and disdain for the ability of government to do much of anything, then government was expected to provide the solutions. Few believed that the solutions would be easy to come by, but many believed in the possibility. Citizen activism mushroomed, the media paid attention, and government policymakers and private powers responded—at least on the surface, at least for a time. Why and how did this activism come about? Why the 1960s?

The depression of the 1930s and war years of the 1940s were well behind us. The 1950s saw steady national economic growth. Then came the election of John Fitzgerald Kennedy in 1960. It was as if we had turned a corner and were setting out on a new road. Our leader, a young man with his sights on a future of infinite possibilities, had a special talent in words and their presentation. For many, the JFK charisma made what he said compelling, just as there was a magic about his administration that turned Washington, D.C., into Camelot. His was the voice of hope to millions who felt left out of the postwar economic prosperity and the voice of conscience to many who had enjoyed its fruits. The message: the nation depends on the actions of each and every one of us as involved citizens. "Ask not what your country can do for you," Kennedy charged, "ask what you can do for your country." Whether his words were symbol over substance, whether his leadership would have brought the same (or better, or worse) action from our government are questions made moot by the shots fired in Dallas on November 22, 1963. His legacy was more the creation of a receptive climate for action than any specific substantive accomplishments. It was, nonetheless, a legacy that captured the imagination of a generation.

Kennedy's successor, Lyndon Baines Johnson, wanted to address the problems of poverty and inequity. His new position provided the power base, and his long legislative experience in Congress gave him the critical political know-how. The receptive national mood, combined with the resolve of a people brought together by mourning, gave the new president a unique moment in which dramatic change was possible. At center stage in the political drama were civil rights because of the decades-long activism of organized groups and leaders representing the African-American community—groups like the NAACP and leaders like Martin Luther King Jr. among many others. The Civil Rights Act of 1964 and the Voting Rights Act of 1965 were the first legislative accomplishments in the new president's agenda. Dozens of other initiatives addressing housing, health, safety and welfare issues, known collectively as the "Great Society Program," soon followed.

U.S. involvement in the Vietnam conflict (Kennedy's other legacy) would soon dampen the national unity and destroy the political power of Johnson as well as the potential for success of his "Great Society." The mounting public dismay over the war, and the role of the United States in it, was a major cause of more movement-style politics as citizen activism against the war brought millions of sideline watchers into the political game. Activism's success became contagious and spread to concerns beyond the war, which led to many of the new "social regulatory" programs enacted during the Nixon presidency (1969-1974). The new programs addressed air, water and land pollution; workplace safety; product safety; and equal employment opportunity. Ralph Nader caught the activism bug and went to Washington, D.C., where he fathered the consumer movement that became the major catalyst in the creation of many of these new programs. If Nader had come on the scene in 1954 or 1984, instead of in 1964 as he did, the consumer movement might never have gotten off the ground. But the timing was right and Nader came, fought and stayed. How this one man spurred a movement is integral to the story of the Litigation Group.

After arriving in D.C. in mid-1964, Nader found work as a consultant to Assistant Secretary of Labor Daniel Patrick Moynihan. His charge was to write a critique of the federal highway and traffic safety program. It was a topic of considerable interest to this thirty-year-old Princeton University and Harvard Law School graduate, one to which he had been trying to bring public attention for some time in his writings and letters to officials. What most concerned Nader was the link between the design of automobiles and the nature and severity of injuries suffered in accidents. Contrary to the "nut behind the wheel" theory then in vogue, it was the car, not the driver, that was often at fault. Lives could be saved and injuries avoided by changes in car design. Proof lay in the studies of engineers and academics, but nothing was being done about it. Nader wrote and published articles on the problem, yet no one listened—not to the experts, not to him. Not yet.

Soon after arriving in Washington, Nader was asked by a small publishing house to write a book about dangerous cars. The publisher had never heard of Nader, but had turned to him at the suggestion of the man he had first approached, who was too busy to take on the project. Nader tackled the challenge with what is his now famous vigor (some would say—most often those who are the target of his attacks—fanaticism). In little more than a year the manuscript was finished and published as *Unsafe at Any Speed*. The book is an exhaustive analysis of the design defects of the automobile in general and of General Motors' Corvair in particular. It is also an attack on the failure of the auto industry and its government overseers to do anything about the defects that had caused thousands of unnecessary injuries and fatalities. Nader's information came from dozens of engineering studies and traffic accident analyses conducted by academics, the industry and the government. He took what was known to insiders and presented it in a way that others could understand. He was not a discoverer so much as a packager. Reading the book thirty years later, one is struck by how tame it all seems.

Nader contended that engineers within the companies, as well as those in academia, had known for years about the role of design defects in causing horrific human suffering. More damning was the charge that they knew how to fix them. Yet these professionals had done little either to force change in the industry or to bring the problem to public attention. The root causes of the inaction, Nader argued, were profit considerations; the absence of, or failure to enforce, professional norms of responsibility in the engineering community; and the co-optation by the industry of the government agencies and the congressional committees responsible for traffic safety. What he described was a cozy "iron-triangle" relationship. It was a relationship that had been described during the 1950s and early 1960s in the academic literature of political science, economics and the law as the norm, not the exception, in economic regulatory arenas (airline routes and fares, maritime shipping rates, agriculture subsidies and so on). Nader's book was hardly the first to note the power of the iron triangle, but it was the first to land the message on the front pages of the nation's newspapers and on television and to get it on the best-sellers list.

Unsafe at Any Speed was not written in the usual muckraker style. There are no graphic details of blood and gore, of maimed and dead bodies to horrify the reader and galvanize an outcry for reform. Rather, the book reads like a scholarly analysis—hardly a page-turner. It is not surprising that, when the book was published in the fall of 1965, it made barely a ripple despite the publisher's promotional efforts. Besides its style and its unknown author, part of the reason for slow sales no doubt was attributable to media resistance. As Nader's publisher later recalled, the response of one newspaperman when asked that his newspaper review the book was, "With all our automobile advertising? You must be crazy."

If General Motors (GM) had sat tight and waited for *Unsafe at Any Speed* to vanish into the dark hole of unread, unheard-of books—the fate of most published works—the phenomenon that became known as "Naderism" might never have occurred. But the giant decided to swat that pesky fly. GM hired a private detective to "get something" on Nader. The apparent aim was to use the "something" to discredit Nader and thus make his charges suspect as well. Wrong fly.

In January 1965, Nader stopped by the Senate Subcommittee on Executive Reorganization to promote his auto safety concerns. Just a month before he arrived at the subcommittee door, Senator Abraham Ribicoff, a Democrat from Connecticut and chairman of the subcommittee, had decided to hold hearings on the federal role in highway safety. That he would decide to do so is not surprising. President Johnson's call for action on a laundry list of public problems had created a climate for what has become known as entrepreneurial politics. Members of Congress and their staffs were entrepreneurs too—searching for problems to expose so that they could get publicity; searching for topics for new legislation so they, like the president, could get public credit. Nader's expertise came at just the right moment. The Senate committee staff persuaded him to help them put together ideas and questions for the subcommittee to use in the hearing and also scheduled him to appear as a witness. Little did Nader realize how serendipitous his connection to the Senate committee would prove to be. Nor did he realize how serendipitous a meeting with another member of Congress (or, to be more precise, an aide to that member of Congress) early the next year would also prove to be. The member of Congress was Representative Jim Mackay, a Democrat from Georgia; the staffer was Joan Claybrook, who would become one of the most important Nader deputies.

Like Nader, Claybrook had also come to Washington, but her arrival was the result of winning an American Political Science Association Congressional Fellowship, one of the first four women to win this award. "When LBJ met with the congressional fellows for the academic year 1964-65, he looked around and asked, 'Where are the women?' " says Claybrook. As a result of this, the Civil Service Commission sought out women to encourage to apply for the next year. Following her graduation from Goucher College in 1959, Claybrook had gone to work doing policy research for the Social Security Administration in Baltimore. When Claybrook came to D.C. in the fall of 1965, she decided to begin her fellowship on the staff of Representative Mackay. One of her first tasks was to set up a meeting between Mackay and Nader. Mackay had just read *Unsafe at Any Speed*, which had sparked his interest in introducing auto safety legislation in the House. "I chased Nader down and he came and autographed his book for the congressman," Claybrook recalls. Then Mackay put her to work researching the best approach for setting up an auto regulatory bill. There was a lot of action throughout 1966 in Congress on auto safety both in the House and the Senate. Nader buzzed around Capitol Hill from office to office and committee to committee, pressing for the strongest possible bill. He stopped regularly by Mackay's office to work with Claybrook in fashioning the legislation.

In early 1966, just after his book came out and while he was preparing to testify before the Senate Commerce Committee on the auto regulatory bills, a friend told Nader that a private detective had come by claiming to be investigating him for a potential employer. The man had asked some pretty strange questions about Nader's sex life, alcohol and drug use, and whether he was anti-Semitic (Nader's parents were immigrants from Lebanon, which apparently prompted the last query). What was going on? For some weeks Nader had suspected that he was being followed. His friend's warning, together with confirmation from other friends around the country about similar encounters with the same private investigator, convinced him that he was right. After a private eye questioned a Senate guard about Nader while following Nader into a Senate office building, Ribicoff's staff called the auto companies to determine whether they had hired the detective. All denied any involvement—except GM, which said "no comment." Ribicoff was outraged. This was the sacred ground of the Senate, and harassment of a witness who was to testify before Congress was a violation of federal law.

In a firestorm of indignation, Ribicoff attacked the automotive company on the floor of the Senate. Then he called the president of GM, James M. Roche, before his subcommittee to be questioned about the incident. This was an event sure to attract considerable news coverage—the chastisement of one of the nation's most powerful capitalists. Before his public spanking was over, Roche, though continuing to deny emphatically that his company had done anything wrong, publicly apologized to Nader for the investigator's actions. Charles McCarry, author of *Citizen Nader* (a 1972 book which is generally thought to be none too sympathetic toward Nader), wrote:

> General Motors proceeded with its investigation on the assumption that there must be something wrong with Nader. "You have come out," Ribicoff told him at the hearing, "with a complete clean bill of health and character, with nothing derogatory having been adduced." Ribicoff and his colleagues certified Nader to be what most people thought had vanished from the American scene: a man of flawless virtue. ... All Nader had, when he went into the hearing room was brains and anger. When he walked out, he had a constituency.

Following the hearing, sales of Nader's book soared. Requests for speaking engagements poured in. Nader willingly obliged, carrying his message of corporate power misused, and beating his drum around the nation to arouse citizens to action. This gangly, awkward, perpetually rumpled, cerebral young man pressed cause after cause against the most powerful interests in the land. He collected his speaking fees and used the money to further his causes. He settled an invasion-of-privacy suit against GM for its private-investigator fiasco for $425,000 ($284,000 after attorneys' fees, a significant sum in those days) and used the proceeds to finance new organizations to join him in his fights. The corporate powers hated him. The much-ignored vast middle class, especially the young, applauded him. Elected politicians embraced the scandals he exposed for their own purposes—sometimes for grandstanding, occasionally to act upon. The media lapped it up. An American hero was thus created.

Nader's message was straight from *The Little Engine That Could:* if we think we can get up that mountain, we can. "Almost every significant breakthrough has come from the spark, the drive, the initiative of one person. You must believe this." These were standard lines in a Nader speech intended to fight the lethargy in our society bred by the sense of individual powerlessness—problems are too big, the powerful too powerful. The media had turned him into a powerful engine; his speaking fees, settlement and book royalties provided the

6

fuel. Nader chugged on.

On September 9, 1966, less than six months after the Senate Commerce Committee hearing on auto safety, with Nader at his side, President Johnson signed into law the National Traffic and Motor Vehicle Safety Act. It was quite a milestone. The act created the first major safety regulatory agency since the Food and Drug Administration (FDA) had been established in 1906. The "milestone," however, was not quite what Nader had hoped or pressed for. During congressional debate and action on the auto safety bill through the spring and summer that year, lawyer Lloyd N. Cutler, chief lobbyist for the Automobile Manufacturers Association, lobbied hard to soften many of the strongest provisions. With Nader on one side and Cutler and his colleagues and the big auto companies on the other, a compromise was finally reached—a compromise that gutted what Nader considered the most critical provision of the bill: criminal sanctions for executives who knowingly allowed their companies to build cars that did not meet federal safety standards. Even with the incredibly advantageous circumstances created by the subcommittee hearings, his book's popularity and Nader's persistent public badgering to stiffen congressional backbones—and the media coverage of it—Congress would not impose jail sentences on auto executives. Still, it was a law that for the first time took the power to decide how safe cars would be from the manufacturers and gave it to a federal agency. Even without criminal penalties, strong standards with civil enforcement penalties would force auto companies to improve car safety.

Responsibility for turning the law into effective action went initially to a new agency within the Department of Commerce. But the new agency, eventually called the National Highway Traffic Safety Administration (NHTSA), was soon transferred to the Department of Transportation. After completing her fellowship, Claybrook went to work at the agency responsible for implementing the new law. "Starting a new agency was a real trauma," Claybrook recalls. The traumas were not just about what to do about auto safety either—much of the struggle had to do with establishing independence and power within an existing department. Being on the inside was not easy, especially for a strong auto safety advocate.

Nader fully understood that the legislative battle was only round one for car safety. He turned to pressing the bureaucrats, Claybrook included, for a vigorous implementation of the provisions that did pass. But Nader was a lonely voice against Detroit and its car manufacturing allies from around the world (and Claybrook was a staffer, not a power player, in the agency). Cutler and his phalanxes of assistants were a constant presence during the agency deliberations, asserting the combined might of the auto companies. When the first set of auto standards was issued in 1967, Nader publicly attacked. The agency had "not compromised with the industry. ... They had surrendered to it." The standards were "a fraud on the American people." Nader was disappointed and disgusted, but not derailed.

During the next few years Nader chugged on up mountain after mountain, exposing an array of dangers and fighting for federal action on them: the risk of leakage from old and failing gas pipelines; the despicable conditions in the 20 percent of meat-processing plants which were not subject to federal regulation; the illness known as byssinosis (lung disease caused by exposure to cotton dust) in the textile industry; the electrocution of hospital patients caused by faulty equipment. The news reporters loved it all. Nader provided great copy —a juicy story right away and promises of a continuing saga to report as the crusader fought on.

Nader's *modus operandi* was to call a press conference to detail harm being done and to furnish exhaustive statistical and technological evidence of abuses knowingly perpetrated by an industry. To follow up on the diagnosis, he would lay out a specific remedial plan. Then he campaigned to force action. He was the rational analyst, the policy innovator and the policy promoter rolled into one. His approach was a sharp contrast to the "expose-and-run" tactic of most investigative journalists. Even the people's representatives in Congress more typically played the game of exposé for media visibility, not for lawmaking or corrective oversight of the executive branch. Indeed, as Nader would soon learn, even when Congress actually passed a law, it needed constant oversight to ensure it was implemented in the public interest. And, as he was learning from the auto safety issue, getting the government bureaucrats to implement Congress' promises effectively, even when they were reasonably clear, was more than a full-time job.

Nader's campaigns and their constant play in the press led to his being cast as the people's delegate, "our" tribune, national ombudsman. His every waking moment and nearly all the earnings from his book royalties and speaking engagements were devoted to his causes, or as they were soon dubbed— Nader's crusades. Skeptics abounded. Religious saints, maybe (and even they were rare), but political saints? Two decades later, commenting on this disbelief, Nader asked: "Is it so implausible, so distasteful, that a man would believe deeply enough in his work to dedicate his life to it?" Such devotion is surely rare and just as surely perplexing to the forces subject to his crusades. Nader could not be bought off, could not be scared off, would not give up, would not go away.

For a while the powerful were caught off guard. It did not take long, though, for them to devise strategies to fight back. Madison Avenue-crafted public relations campaigns, hordes of Washington-based professional lobbyists and (despite the campaign financing law of 1974 that eliminated some of the worst abuses), money, money and more money poured into re-election chests of members of Congress (legalized bribery, Nader dubbed it). It did not take long, either, for economic issues to reemerge as the driving force of national politics; the mounting debt (driven by the Vietnam War and implementation of LBJ's Great Society programs) combined with the oil shocks of 1973 and 1979 (which led to huge oil price increases that sent inflation spiraling upward) saw to that. The window of opportunity for social reform was shorter than anyone then imagined.

The logical first step for the rational analyst was information-gathering. He chose as his target the regulatory agencies that made up the government's apparatus for overseeing the private business sector. These agencies were the citizens' supposed bulwark against capitalist power when and where it went astray. They included the Federal Trade Commission (FTC), the Interstate Commerce Commission (ICC), the Securities and Exchange Commission (SEC), the Civil Aeronautics Board (CAB) and the FDA.

But even though the political climate was receptive, Nader found early on that he needed help. One person could make a difference, but it would take many more to really change the world. What he needed to accomplish this goal were expert investigators. What he could afford were students who would either volunteer or work for poverty-level wages.

During the summer of 1968 he hired seven Yale and Harvard law students to study the FTC. He also created an organizational structure for this research effort and called it the Center for Study of Responsive Law. Nader saw his mission as training other leaders, not creating a following. To that end, he employed at the Center (as it soon become known) recently minted lawyers, economists, political scientists and doctors to be the leaders of the student researchers. He was looking for people with the gift of outrage and the dedication, imagination and brilliance to channel that outrage into action. As he once described it, "We are looking for tigers." John Schultz, a 1968 Harvard Law School graduate, was tagged as the first tiger. His job was to lead the FTC study.

Activities on college campuses in the late 1960s had awakened much outrage and commitment to action. Many students had joined the civil rights movement, participating in marches and voter registration efforts in the South. The antiwar movement was heating up, especially following the 1968 trial of the "Boston Five" in which Dr. Benjamin Spock (of baby book fame), the Reverend William Sloan Coffin Jr. (the Yale University chaplain) and two other leaders were found guilty (one was acquitted) and sentenced to two years in prison for conspiracy to counsel, aid and abet violations of the selective service law (their violations consisted of collecting draft cards from students and turning them in to the Justice Department as a protest of the war). Though the verdict was later overturned, it set off a firestorm of protest on campuses. Student activists around the nation, but especially in the more liberal Northeast, barricaded college presidents' offices and closed down classes in protests against the war, demanding among other things, that ROTC be abolished. Students, at least some of them, were showing themselves to be not easily cowed by adults, even those in positions of power. The seven students who would soon become known as "Nader's Raiders" had something more than outrage, brains, confidence and courage—they had the Nader name, which could open doors and command media attention.

The FTC had been created in 1914 to protect the consuming public against the excesses of industries that had grown powerful in the post-Civil War period. The populist movement of the turn of the century and the trust-busting campaign of President Theodore Roosevelt challenged the old rule of *caveat emptor*—let the buyer beware. The citizen alone was no match against big industry. The framers of the Constitution believed that the government they were creating had to be designed to prevent it from becoming tyrannical; separation of powers, checks and balances, and federalism were their solutions. When the people discovered that business and industry could also become too powerful, only the national government appeared to be of sufficient size and strength to rein in capitalists when the profit drive, insufficiently countered by the discipline of a competitive market, led to corruption and greed.

The literature of the academic field that studies the theory and behavior of public organizations has long recognized the life-cycle imperative of bureaucratic organizations, that is, of organizations like the FTC that do not face the market's profit-and-loss discipline. Public agencies are not funded by sales of products or services; rather, they must secure a share of the taxpayer-funded budget. Budget-making, which is the province of elected legislators, is about who has political clout. At inception and in its first years, a public agency is more likely to have the necessary political clout; the public demand and support that led to its creation normally lasts for at least a while. Thus, it is free to spend its time and energy pursuing the goal for which it was created. This makes it an attractive workplace for enthusiastic supporters of the agency's mission. As time passes, and the public's attention fades, the agency is forced to become its own defender in the political process. The private powers (businesses, industry, trade groups, farmers, the medical community) that are the object of the agency's regulatory power press for less regulation (or more favorable regulation) in the agency, to the president and in Congress. The agency has to spend more and more of its time on defending its actions, adapting to power politics and obtaining its share of the budget; less and less is available for the primary goal of protecting the public interest. The employees who signed on because of their commitment to the agency's goal get discouraged and leave. More and more of the remaining workforce is made up of what the experts call "conservers," those who have job protection as a higher priority than pursuit of the agency mission. The agency suffers from goal displacement; it becomes increasingly more concerned about self-preservation. *Let's keep it quiet, let's keep it peaceful, let's keep our jobs.* The rule of action becomes inaction. *Don't rock the boat!*

The FTC was by 1968 well into the old-age phase of this bureaucratic cycle. Indeed, by the time of Franklin D. Roosevelt's presidency (1933-1945), its presidentially appointed leadership had become little more than a patronage dumping ground for appointing big contributors to well-paid non-jobs. The commission's reputation was such that it earned the nickname "the Little Old Lady on Pennsylvania Avenue." Nader's Raiders jumped into the FTC boat and rocked away. Using the newly passed 1965 Freedom of Information Act, they demanded to see the files and budget documents and to interview the commissioners and top civil service employees of the agency. The FTC hierarchy was not thrilled, but it responded. No doubt the nature of the times and of the attackers provided a strong incentive for cooperation, however reluctant. All the banal traits of aged bureaucracies, which the Raiders found in abundance, were exposed in a report that was released on January 2, 1969.

A few weeks later Richard Milhous Nixon was sworn in as the thirty-seventh president. Nader's public visibility and power at that point were soon apparent. The new Republican chief executive clearly felt compelled to respond to the Raider's report on the FTC, though he wasn't quite prepared to embrace the students' findings as the final say in the matter. He moved swiftly to commission the "big boys" in the American Bar Association to do a "professional" study. The bar's credentialed experts found many of the same problems and recommended many of the same solutions. Nixon's appointee as chairman of the FTC, Caspar Weinberger, immediately began to implement many of the reforms suggested by the bar and the Raiders.

The David versus Goliath strategy had worked. A bunch of students had set the FTC boat a-rocking and forced the highest officers in the land to take action. Determined to replicate this success, Nader hired more Raiders for the summer of 1969 and more young attorneys and professionals for the Center staff. Soon the small squad of activists would become a battalion.

2

Creation of the Nader Network

By the summer of 1969, the new president's honeymoon period—that six months or so of a first term when the people and the media are usually a bit more generous, a bit more hopeful, a bit more forgiving than is the norm—was pretty much over. Many who had voted for Nixon had done so because of his promise to end the war in Vietnam. After six months, the end did not seem any closer, and the antiwar mood was rapidly spreading from the activists to the general populace. The Republican Party had regained control of the executive branch, but its ability to pursue a more conservative agenda was initially cramped by a public still in a demanding frame of mind and a Democratic Congress. Citizens seemed to want those in Washington to do more, not less, to solve the nation's problems. At this point, the cost of the promised solutions was not fully known or understood, and the corporate backlash against regulation had not fully materialized. Nader and his growing popularity was both a driving force and an indication of that citizen demand. Ever the politician, Nixon swayed with the breeze, working with Democrats in Congress on a virtual flood of new legislation, much of which was touched by Nader. Washington bubbled with activists and activity. Nader was very much a part of it as he moved to expand the size and reach of his Raiders and the Center.

Author McCarry describes the aura of the first Nader headquarters:

> The Center for Study of Responsive Law was housed on Dupont Circle during 1969 and part of 1970 in a crumbling brick mansion, gabled and turreted and dotted with unwashed windows. This first headquarters of the Nader organization had an air, at once tacky and vibrant, that suggested the zany righteousness anarchists and certain young lovers have in common. Inside, the Raiders roosted—aware, as one of them said, that they were the elite of a whole generation in search of a means of expressing a sense of honor. Ralph Nader, by his example of public emotion and rigid loyalty to a set of principles they believed to be their own, was giving them the means.

Reuben Robertson, a Yale Law School (1964) and a London School of Economics (1965) graduate, was one of Nader's new recruits for the Center in the spring of 1969, just before the second summer of the Raiders. There are dozens of stories to be told of the second-year recruits and the battles they waged. Robertson's is typical and useful to tell here for two reasons. First, he went on to become part of the Public Citizen Litigation Group. Second, his activities while at the Center illustrate a point about Nader that is often missed.

After law school and his year in London, Robertson spent three years as an associate at one of Washington's largest and most prestigious law firms, Covington and Burling. There he learned much about the techniques of law but found the practice he was putting them to not really gratifying. The world around him was seething with frustration and anger—cities were burning; civil rights supporters were marching; antiwar demonstrations were gaining in strength and numbers. It seemed that he should be doing something more useful. When Robert Kennedy challenged President Johnson for the Democratic presidential nomination, Robertson grabbed the opportunity to work full time on Kennedy's campaign in early 1968. Then Martin Luther King Jr. was shot on April 4. Somehow his decision to join the Kennedy campaign became even more important. Just two months later, on June 3, 1968, Kennedy fell to another assassin's bullets.

Robertson, like hundreds of other Kennedy workers, had to deal with his anger and sorrow and move on. A call from a friend led him to a position on the legal staff working on civil rights litigation for the Federal Highway Administration in connection with discrimination in employment on federal highway projects. (Title 7 of the 1964 Civil Rights Act mandated equal opportunity in all federally funded projects.) By 1968 the interstate highway building projects were 90 percent federally funded, yet in many sections of the country local construction unions effectively fenced minorities out of highway construction jobs. It was not as exciting as a presidential campaign, but it was considerably more satisfying to fight for equal opportunity than to fight for the financial gain of big businesses. Unfortunately, the opportunity was short-lived. In November 1968, Richard Nixon was elected president, and when John Volpe took office as the new head of the Department of Transportation, Robertson saw that his innovative civil rights litigation would have less support.

Early in 1969 a friend of Robertson's introduced him to Nader. Robertson told Nader of his interest in working on public issues and asked for advice on how to get an organization started. The answer: "Come work with us." Robertson did. By June he, like each of the other Center staffers, was teamed up with a group of law student volunteers. Each team was to study a different government agency. Robertson's interest in transportation led him to choose the Civil Aeronautics Board (CAB). It was, as he says, "a little agency in its own nook." Virtually no one representing the public interest had ever been involved in the agency's actions. If ever there were an industry-captured agency this was it. Its rule of action was to take care of the airlines—keep competition out and

13

protect the fare structure. Robertson describes his first encounter with the Board:

> Nader and I went out one day to the Civil Aeronautics Board to introduce ourselves. We said: "We just want to say hello. We are citizens and we are going to have a group of other citizens working with us this summer studying your agency." They were stunned. They were staggered. Nader's Raiders were going after them. We were ushered right into the chairman's office where we met with him and his executive assistant. Their apprehension was palpable. They were sure Nader was going to "do something" to them. Did we confuse them! Nader played "good cop." He was perfectly agreeable and charming. I played "bad cop" demanding that we be given access to this and that; saying that we were out to see if there was any bribery going on here. We were just pulling their chain to see what they would say or do. Our act clearly flustered them. As we walked out of their office and got on the elevator we could hardly contain ourselves. When the doors shut we burst into gales of laughter. ·

The CAB then, like the FTC, had a reputation as a dumping ground for political hacks. For the Raiders it was an ideal situation. Everything the agency did seemed to illustrate what was wrong with government. There were so many pent-up complaints and so much repressed frustration among many of its civil servants that, as soon as it was known that Nader was interested, the legendary sieve of Washington bureaucracies turned into a waterfall. By the end of the summer Robertson and the Raiders had ample evidence of what was wrong with CAB. In Nader style, the evidence was quickly packaged into a public report.

Robertson's story is similar to many others that resulted from the work of Nader recruits. Their investigations expose problems; the problems require action; others must become involved in the effort (in Robertson's case, members of Congress, the media and the courts); if action is taken, an organization must be put together to follow what happens next; the creation of an organization leads to more investigations being undertaken; and the cycle repeats. The pattern illustrates the lessons Nader learned in his first years: (1) individual action matters, but the creation of permanent organizational structures and development of experienced players is critical to long-term success—a team, not a lone wolf, is key; and (2) information and reason matter, but it usually takes more to force the system to act. These realizations led to the formation of the state-level Public Interest Research Groups (PIRGs) to harness the energy of college students to educate the public and develop public support for government action. The importance of the media to issue visibility was well understood from the beginning. It was clear that public interest advocacy would require long-term commitment and a many-faceted strategy.

Robertson's account continues:

> During our study I personally became very interested in what the CAB was doing. Fundamentally important to me was the understanding that the staff of the agency were basically decent and honorable people. But, day after day they hear only one point of view. Naturally enough, after a while they are persuaded by that view. The airline people were also basically decent—they were just trying to run a business in a noncompetitive atmosphere of a huge club, sort of like the national baseball league. They all had to get along and figure out how to mollify the regulators. The regulators were smart and able but erratic and unscientific. No one bothered to ask why they were doing what they were doing and whether it was working. Suddenly, when we came along, someone was asking.

Robertson filed a number of Freedom of Information Act (FOIA) requests with the CAB during the fall of 1969 and winter of 1970, demanding access to data about the rate-making process to, as he puts it, "ring their bell." The agency was finding it harder to follow its standard operating procedure: secret meetings with airline representatives to negotiate acceptable rate increases. From his position at the Center, Robertson pressed for information and "literally made fun of them."

Then Robertson linked up with a staffer of Representative John Moss, a California Democrat who was interested in airline regulation. During a CAB administrative hearing, Moss and several other members of Congress pressed the agency to open up its rate-making sessions to allow for citizen participation and charged that failure to do so would negate the legality of any fare increases granted. When the agency denied the request, Moss, who had been the chief sponsor of the FOIA in the House, and thirty-two other members of Congress members sued. Robertson then worked closely with the representative's staff on the case.

This case was one of the first instances of many to come in which members of Congress sued the executive branch to enforce the law. Before long, the Litigation Group attorneys would be representing members of Congress in many similar challenges against the executive branch.

"When the appeals court ruled against the board in *Moss v. CAB*," Robertson recalls, "it came as a terrible blow. They had fully expected to win." The opinion was highly critical of the CAB. "[I]gnoring the general public's interest in order to better serve the carriers," the court admonished, "is not the proper response to the difficulties supposedly created by outdated or unwieldy statutory procedure. After all there is more to rate making than providing carriers with sufficient revenue to meet their obligations to their creditors and to their stockholders." The decision forced an internal reevaluation of CAB's role, which was called the Domestic Passenger Fare Investigation. When the investigation was announced, Nader and Robertson created the Aviation Consumer Action Project (ACAP) with Robertson as its co-director, staff, secretary and janitor. One of ACAP's major purposes was to gain a platform from which to speak on the consumer's behalf, "to go and yell and scream and ask embarrassing questions at the proceedings," Robertson says.

In the spring of 1970 one of the CAB's congressional protectors, Senator Howard W. Cannon, a Nevada Democrat, held subcommittee hearings to address the airlines' major problem: they were losing money. Could Congress do anything about it? Robertson managed to get on the witness list. "I was listed as a consumer representative, and I expect they assumed I would be beating the drum for tougher regulation," Robertson remembers. "To their surprise, I said: 'Abolish the CAB. Set the airlines free.'" The senator and airlines were taken aback. Was this a Naderite talking? "They thought we were all commies or socialists—always for government power, always against industry." It is a mistaken view of Naderism.

Nader has always sought the best minds he could recruit. He has tried to enlist those who share his belief that to protect the general public, or at least give it a fighting chance against the power of large entities—whether corporations, governments, unions or professionals—the individual cannot fight alone. It is not that he is anti-capitalist or anti-government or anti-union or anti-doctor or anti-lawyer. His fear is the fear of the framers of the Constitution: unchecked power. Long historical experience has shown that the bigger and more monopolistic the power, the higher its probability of abuse. "[Nader's] real message," writes James Fallows, author and former aide to President Carter, "is not after all that corporations are bad or government is bad but that if you have a supine populace, then everything else will be bad because unchecked power will be abused." Nader wanted innovators and activists, not those who were blindly obedient to some philosophical creed or to their own notions of how to fight. Robertson found, as have others, that Nader is open to reasoned argument and evidence on how best to achieve a goal. Robertson believed that consumers would be far better served if fares were set by a competitive market than by an industry-dominated agency and/or an agency that approached the economics of regulation as irrationally as the CAB. He gives an example of its irrationality:

> One phase of the Domestic Passenger Fare Investigation had to do with elasticity—a key issue in any marketplace pricing question. If you raise the price what's going to happen? What if you lower it? How will price affect consumer demand? CAB in its wisdom went through an elaborate proceeding with all sorts of professional economists and airline experts and they finally came up with a formula to apply: elasticity equals 0.7. I was incredulous. Did they mean at all points on the chart? At all points on the curve? Let's say we

16

increase the shuttle fare from Washington to New York to a million dollars. That would mean demand would decrease by a factor of only 0.7? Or if we decrease the fare to $10, the demand would increase by a factor of only 0.7? It was nonsense! What it amounted to was a confession that regulation of fares to balance profit and demand was a job that could not be done. Once you could show that after all this effort this was the best they could come up with, it sealed their fate.

If fares could not be rationally set, it was obvious that they were being set by some other method. That method was all too clear: pressure politics. There was no doubt that the airlines were, and would continue to be, the loudest and most constant voice in the agency rate-making process. There did not seem to be any way to assure a balanced voice for the public interest; Robertson and Nader alone could not provide that. Even if the CAB's rate-making hearings were open to citizen participation, few citizens would have the time, money, expertise or incentive to participate. Regulators would continue to be bombarded by airline lobbyists' demands. The airlines were not really free-market capitalists at all; they did not want a competitive market, they wanted protective government regulation on their terms, for their advantage. It was not an approach that would be likely to serve the interest of the flying public. Government regulation is key to many public interest problems where there is little to no incentive from market forces for the private sector to act responsibly (on such matters as health and safety and environmental protection), but in this case the market was apt to be a better public protector.

Knowing what should be done is one thing; getting it done, another. Implementing solutions to the problems exposed in the summer 1969 studies of the CAB and several other agencies proved to be much more difficult than the Raiders' experience with FTC the summer before. The reasons were many. They were asking now for more action on more fronts, and their forces were spread more thinly. They had lost the advantage of surprise, which their first exposé had enjoyed. Media attention to their efforts was spread over more issues and more players. The Republican administration had settled in and become more resistant to their agenda. Agencies and the powerful interests they regulated now paid more attention to them and had learned how to counter their attacks. And other issues were vying for the political center stage—especially the Vietnam war, but also women's rights and the environment. It took until 1978, and the concerted effort of Senator Ted Kennedy and his legislative aide, Stephen Breyer (who would become Supreme Court Justice Breyer in 1994), to get action on airline deregulation. Nader and Robertson, along with other ACAP staffers, were there throughout the long effort. There is little doubt that organizational structure and permanent players were critical to sustaining such a protracted battle.

Courting Change

* * * * *

Sidney Wolfe first met Ralph Nader at a meeting of the Medical Committee for Human Rights in 1966, a group that had provided medical support for the Mississippi voter-registration marches in the early 1960s and was by then working on a variety of public health issues. Wolfe recalls that "Ralph and I were the most outspoken people there. I was impressed by him and from that point on volunteered nights and weekends consulting and in the next years overseeing some of the Raider projects at the Center."

Wolfe, a physician, had come to Washington, D.C., in the summer of 1966 to join the National Institutes of Health (NIH) as a researcher in the National Institute of Arthritis and Metabolic Diseases. His undergraduate and medical degrees were both earned at Case Western Reserve University in Cleveland, Ohio. The move to NIH was in his own words, "his Canada," his way of avoiding military service. By the mid-1960s young doctors were being drafted in increasing numbers to deal with the heavy casualties from the war that was heating up in Vietnam. His antiwar stance was balanced by a strong sense of social responsibility, especially directed toward his own profession. Working with Nader was a way to serve his conscience. Unlike Nader, though, he was trying to balance his crusading with a full-time job and a family that included four young daughters.

As a volunteer at the Center, Wolfe wrote a letter to the Food and Drug Administration (FDA) in March 1971 demanding that the agency act immediately to recall the existing supply of intravenous fluids. Studies had shown that nearly half the national supply was contaminated and of significant danger to patients to whom they might be administered. In typical Nader fashion, the letter was backed up by evidence and released to the press. This was definitely the sort of issue that would play big in the media and arouse a large and angry public reaction, which in turn would prompt, it was hoped, a fast government response. It worked. Within days, the company that had distributed the contaminated fluids voluntarily recalled them.

As a result of publicity on the intravenous fluid issue, "a lot of people started calling Ralph and/or me." Wolfe recalls. "'Oh, you think the intravenous fluid thing is a problem,' they'd begin, 'let me tell you about this.' Then they would go on to describe some preposterous example of medical malfeasance." Evidence of dozens of specific medical-related problems poured into the Center. Most had been the subject of considerable research; information actually was not in short supply, but follow-up action was.

One of the incoming calls came from employees in a West Virginia plant who suspected that they were suffering from mercury poisoning as a result of exposure in their workplace. They wanted Wolfe to check out one of their co-workers who had been hospitalized. No one would listen to them—no one in government, no one in the union, no one in management and no one in the hospital in the company-dominated town. Wolfe took great care to ensure against potential conflicts of interest (after all, he was an employee of a government agency and was volunteering in his off hours for a group that was attacking government agencies). In May 1971, he took vacation time to travel to West Virginia, where he indeed found evidence of mercury poisoning in the hospitalized worker.

Congress had created the Occupational Safety and Health Administration (OSHA) in 1970 to mitigate workplace hazards. Nader had worked on the legislation with a Center staffer, Gary Sellers. Wolfe's request to OSHA for an inspection of the plant was perhaps the first of its kind. He encountered resistance, but eventually the agency complied and found substantial violations at the plant.

Increasingly, he was finding that, although he enjoyed research, was free to follow his interests at NIH, and published frequently, his work at the Center attracted him most. He talked about starting a group to monitor health issues with Nader, who offered to fund the venture. The Health Research Group (HRG) was born.

But, Wolfe admits, he was "too cautious to completely cut loose from what was by then six years of academic medicine. My initial inclination was to give it a trial run." There was precedent for lawyers using their skills for public interest work on a full-time basis. A virtual explosion in the number of such groups had occurred between 1968 and 1971 with the help of the Ford Foundation and other philanthropic groups. But there was "zip, zero, nothing in the way of precedent for this sort of venture in medicine," Wolfe notes. "My only model was research, so that is what I adopted." He explains:

> If there is a problem there will be evidence. If there is good evidence of the problem then something should be done about it. If a scientific remedy can be found it should be applied. It is as simple as that. ... We do not need to deal with the questionable issues, the ones where the evidence is inconclusive: there are more than enough of the clear problems to address. In choosing what to do we select only projects we can do something about, where we can make a difference by changing things, where our efforts will help a lot of people. We look for problems where the injury is or will be serious—like cancer, not a rash. There is never a problem having a full plate to choose from.

Wolfe cut back at NIH from seventy to forty hours a week and put in twenty to thirty hours at HRG; by the fall of 1971 he was aboard full-time: "Once I decided to leave NIH, I was committed. I knew HRG would be my life's work." He decided that HRG would have three missions. The most important was to monitor the FDA's regulation of the safety of the food supply, prescription and over-the-counter medicines, and medical devices. This has accounted for more than half of HRG's workload. The second mission would be to push OSHA to live up to the portion of its legal mandate having to do with the protection of the health of workers. The third: holding doctors and hospitals accountable to the public. For a while HRG also monitored the newly created Consumer Product Safety Commission, "but it was so moribund, such a disaster" that Wolfe deemed the effort of no use. And because there were numerous other groups working on environmental issues, he decided to leave that area to them.

In June 1972, Wolfe testified at a congressional hearing about OSHA's first year. His assessment directly challenged the rosy picture painted in "The President's Report on Occupational Safety and Health" (released in May that year), which was being touted by OSHA as proof of its great success. One of Wolfe's major targets was the watered-down OSHA-approved warning labels and signs in asbestos production plants about the dangers of breathing asbestos dust. It was nothing more, he believed, than capitulation by a government agency to industry powers once again. Corporate America was getting away with mass murder, literally. In his testimony, Wolfe leveled a scathing attack against the government's failure to protect its citizens and against the profit-driven homicide perpetrated by some corporations.

> As more data concerning occupational health and safety is accumulated, the problem begins to display many attributes of a civil war. The annual casualty rate is 14,000 deaths from injuries and accidents alone. Probably more than 50,000 workers die unnecessarily each year if black lung disease, silicosis, byssinosis, asbestosis, bladder cancer, and a myriad of other occupationally-caused diseases are also included.

> Although the data is not complete, the casualties, or "body counts" seem to be derived almost exclusively from one party in this civil war. From the ranks of the eighty or so million workers in this country have come virtually all of the above-mentioned fatalities and, in addition, millions of victims who are injured or disabled as a result of being in the workplace. If more conventional weapons were used in this battle, the eighty million workers would have little difficulty in ending the conflict in which the opposition consists of a relatively small core of corporate executives.

> However, the "weapons" are not conventional. Coal dust, cotton dust, asbestos, mercury vapor, benzene, lead, punch presses, mine cave-ins, are but a few of the literally thousands of physical and chemical hazards which constantly threaten the lives and health of American workers. Further adding to the insidious nature of these weapons is the fact that some of them (such as those causing cancer) do not show their effects until many years after the initial exposure. Nor is the armor conventional. Whereas the workers are down

in the mines, in the clouds of dust or toxic fumes ... the corporate executives are away from the scene of battle, protected by both distance from the dangers and by well-ventilated and separated offices.

Wolfe was determined to change things. Over the next thirty years, nearly all of OSHA's major actions to protect the health of workers on the job resulted from HRG petitions, which were often followed by litigation, lobbying and public education undertaken in conjunction with Public Citizen's other divisions. The course has rarely been easy or swift, nor is the war anywhere near finished, but many battles have been won along the way. When asked if he gets discouraged, whether endless war doesn't wear him down, Wolfe responds: "There is nothing to get discouraged about. If I'd selected lots of losing battles to wage, then I probably would get discouraged. But almost everything we have worked on has sooner or later resulted in a better situation, not always the best, but usually considerably better." Wolfe acknowledges that the campaigns sometime go on for years before resolution and that many unnecessary deaths and injuries happen in the interim. "But I think about the lives saved because change has finally come as a result of our efforts—if we had not acted these too would be lost." Wolfe's attitude is the difference between the old half-full, half-empty glass. It definitely takes a half-full sort of attitude to stick with this kind of work. It also takes boundless energy, and Wolfe, like most of the other Nader team players, has energy aplenty. There is a vibrant intensity that telegraphs his commitment, concern and determination. HRG quickly developed into a small, close-knit team with "Dr. Sid" as its long-term captain.

Over the past thirty years HRG has worked on hundreds of issues. One of the first major concerns was Red Dye #2, an additive used in many manufactured foods that scientific studies had shown was a carcinogen (a cancer-causing substance). On November 12, 1971, HRG filed a petition with the FDA asking the agency to ban the dye. After four years of scientific and legal wrangling, the FDA agreed to ban the use of the dye in foods. HRG played a major role in exposing and forcing action on asbestos poisoning, and publicized and aided in the legal initiatives against the health risks of the Dalkon Shield (a birth-control device) and the silicone gel breast implant. It took years of HRG effort, but the government finally required printed warnings about the dangers of toxic shock syndrome, a rare but often fatal bacterial infection associated with the use of tampons, and of the danger in giving aspirin to children because of Reye's Syndrome. HRG was successful in forcing OSHA to issue a regulation mandating that workers be told the identity and dangers of toxic substances with which they come in contact. In each instance, HRG had to resort to the courts to accomplish its end, and in each instance the group worked hand-in-glove with the litigators at the Litigation Group.

Sometimes litigation was not possible or was unsuccessful, and HRG turned to other strategies. When the responsible government agencies refused to make public the information they had on disciplined doctors, HRG published the information in its own book. When the FDA refused to require drug companies to include package inserts adequately describing a drug's side effects and naming other drugs that should not be taken at the same time, HRG published the information in *Worst Pills, Best Pills,* which became a best-seller and a major source of funding for Public Citizen. Over the years HRG has published many other books providing information that the government or industry has failed to make available to the public. And over the years, Wolfe has become a television celebrity appearing on major talk shows to promote these books and HRG's causes.

* * * * *

Similar experiences by other Nader-recruited and Nader-funded crusaders led to the creation of other organizations in the early 1970s. The result, derisively christened "Nader's Empire" by its detractors, began to take shape. To be the public's watchdog over the National Highway Traffic Safety Administration, the Center for Auto Safety (CAS) was formed. The Public Interest Research Group (PIRG) was created in Washington, D.C., and later dozens of state-level and college-campus chapters were brought into being with Nader money and inspiration and the commitment of hundreds of young professionals and students. Organizations of progressive scientists, engineers and economists sprouted as the result of a single or a few dedicated individuals energized by Nader's call to action—providing advice, testimony, evidence and support where experts were critical. Public Citizen, what one author dubbed the "Mother Spider" of Nader's advocacy groups, was created in 1971 with the money Nader raised in response to newspaper ads and a fundraising letter he sent out (more than $1 million from some sixty thousand contributors) to act as an administrative center for activists working on a variety of fronts. Public Citizen's Congress Watch division was organized by Nader and Joan Claybrook in 1973 to monitor legislation and to lobby Congress. The Public Citizen Litigation Group was brought to life in 1972 by Nader and Alan Morrison.

Dozens of other Nader-created, Nader-inspired and Nader-allied organizations were outside of Public Citizen. In 1989, *Forbes* magazine scathingly attacked "St. Ralph and His Web of Interests," likening the organizations to John D. Rockefeller's Standard Oil Trust. The article's inaccuracies and misrepresentations aside, the notion that the dozens of public interest organizations that it listed as connected in some way to Nader somehow added up to a secret trust comparable to the old Standard Oil Trust bordered on the ludicrous. The impossibility of fitting the pieces of the public advocacy universe Nader helped spawn into a neat organizational chart with clear lines delineating the power/mission relationships among the parts and to Nader was seen by the *Forbes'* authors as proof of a nefarious motive behind the confusion.

Not so. The haphazard and confused result was not designed.

22

Creation of the Nader Network

The growth of the organizations depended on which willing individual with what agenda burning in his or her belly happened to cross paths with Nader, or which of his own many ideas and issues he was able to find someone to pursue. Limited funds was a given, but combined with high expectations and an ever-expanding number of causes to pursue, penny-pinching was necessary. Nader's frugal ways are legend. Stories of his admonitions to use both sides of every page of paper, to reuse paper clips, to avoid telephone calls when a stamp would do, abound. His miserly salaries (only half jokingly referred to by some recipients as "slave wages") are the subject of much wonderment—how does he get his troops to work so hard for so little? But, if you don't have a lot of money and you have much you want to do, you can't create big organizations, so you go for small; you can't create plush workplaces, so you go for bare bones. Every penny must count. Nader's strategy was to find the best people; give them charge over their own structure; allow them independence to develop their own agenda; provide funding (slim though it may be) and support so they can focus on their primary task; and expect a high return on your investment. Independence and freedom to focus on a goal passionately held helps people to stay employed at wages far below what their talents would otherwise command. Nader was empowering and enabling his workforce to perform the task at hand and choosing the troops carefully to ensure incentive and drive.

Nader's organizational arrangement of many loosely allied entities with overlapping roles also reflects his oft-expressed apprehension about the negative aspects of large and/or monopolistic organizations. In part, his fear is grounded in a recognition of the goal-displacement tendencies of the bureaucratic aging phenomenon. What Nader understood from the start (and what has long been understood by bureaucratic scholars) has become well recognized by most of the world today—large organizations of all sorts (government, business or nonprofits)—inevitably become stagnant, inefficient, resistant to innovation, unable to adapt to change. By the 1990s, most of corporate America was embracing a leaner, more empowered, more flexible organizational strategy. Philosophy and limited resources set Nader on this approach from the start.

Nader understood another tendency of large formal organizations: power leads to corruption and corruption harms the least powerful. Author McCarry describes Nader's concerns:

> He believes that the whole long process of concentrating the powers of the human race in institutions has been a mistake. Nader thinks that structure, no matter how it begins, is likely to be employed against the public interest and cites the trade unions, with their humanistic origins and their parochial end, as an example. He dreams of new kinds of power. "We've got to have sources of power that will rise to the occasion," he argues. "Somehow unstructured power, *ad hoc* power, initiatory democracy, whatever you

want to call it, is less likely to be abused and more likely to be continually nourished."

No one has yet found the blueprint for designing such entities, though Nader seems still at the drawing table. But by 1970 it had become clear to Nader that an organization of some sort would be necessary to fight the battles in his endless war against corrupt powers in society. Still, he was determined somehow to build organizations that could and would stay perpetually young, vigorous and focused. In his brief remarks to the gathering in celebration of Public Citizen's twenty-fifth anniversary in 1996, Nader spoke of Public Citizen's beautifully renovated new headquarters. "Do not become too comfortable here. Do not become complacent. Do not let this measure of success blind you to reality. Resist these temptations." It was a call to remain alert, to stay nimble, to not stand down from battle readiness. The old dingy offices with rickety furniture and absence of amenities had served as a constant reminder to the troops that they were still in the trenches. To fight the powers they were up against, they needed a sense of constant urgency. His early apprehension about the dysfunctional tendencies of organizational structures remains, and his effort to prevent the aging process from infecting the organizations he helped create continues.

But it is not just size and structure that make for innovative, energetic organizations. In the end it is all about people. Nader's description of the sort of person he seeks:

> It's tough ... to get the full range of qualities for this kind of work—
> the value system and the sense of equity and the stamina, the hard
> work and the inability to get discouraged or despair, the ability to
> subordinate personal problems to professional dedication, the ability to square your work with your spouse, the ability not to be
> tempted, the ability not to make blunders. The ability to work with
> people and not have ego problems. ... And to be smart, even brilliant.

His dream is to find hundreds, thousands, even millions of citizens, who are able and willing to do what he does. It is definitely daunting to find many specimens of the human animal who could live up to his standard. Total dedication to "the job" exists, of course. All those eager, hungry young professionals clawing their way up the corporate ladder or onto the partnership list or into political office or even into the hierarchy of many religious orders are proof of that. Power, wealth and prestige are the rewards that seem to motivate such devotion; a sense of equity and a value system are rarely a center component or end product of the quest. Nader cannot offer such rewards, and his ends demand the even greater commitment to equity and values. Nader has lived his life in single-minded pursuit of his causes, without avocations, without wife, without children, with many devoted associates but few friends to serve. Some priests and monks exhibit such self-denial. Would there be many of the professionally trained experts Nader needed who would do likewise?

Metaphors of war abound in descriptions of Nader and Nader organizations. It is no wonder that this is so. In war it is the fear, the immediacy, the common purpose, the common enemy that binds the troops and volunteers of the underground, that blots other concerns and responsibilities from the personal screen. Dedication to this sort of cause at the expense of all other concerns, even family and friends, is highly valued in our society. Nader offers the opportunity to do something that matters. Looked at as a short-term commitment—a year, two, maybe even four or five—total self-denial for the bigger cause seems a reasonable compromise. The numbers of applications for the Peace Corps and VISTA (Volunteers in Service to America) illustrate the willingness of many citizens to serve such causes. But Nader's message is that this war will never be won, that eternal vigilance is the necessary price if keeping power in check in a capitalistic democracy is the goal. Trench warfare or selfless service forever is a much harder sell. Short-term draftees, especially if they give total devotion to the battle, are useful, but it takes a critical mass of long-term, experienced players to build an organization's reputation and to provide the continuity and expertise (both substantive and political) that can compensate for inadequate wealth in the war to protect the public against big power when it becomes corrupt.

The genius of Nader's organizational structure is its ability to provide the sort of alternative rewards that seem tailor-made for attracting the particular talent he needs. The crusading general may need to be single-minded, but the very informality of the structures he set up for his troops allows them the flexibility to have a life too. Not surprisingly, those who exhibit the commitment to the value system and the sense of equity he demands are usually individuals who are sensitive to the needs of others in their lives—spouse, children, parents and friends. The long-term players in the Public Citizen Litigation Group are a fascinating assortment of complex and interesting individuals who have families and time to be fathers, mothers, lovers and friends. They share with Nader a belief in a fairer system, a commitment to try to make it so, the intelligence to work effectively, a willingness to work hard, and the resilience not to give up. What they do differently is to balance a commitment to those ends with other values—to have a life beyond their role as "public citizens."

The Nader-style organizational structure provides other rewards as well. The small work groups and informality enable comradeship and team spirit to flourish. The connection to the other Nader groups provides kinship to a larger team making the unbelievable forces lined up against them seem a bit less intimidating. Perhaps it is what they are doing that provides the greatest of rewards. It is something they believe matters, that they believe will make a difference. And, to top it off, it is fun! As one long-term Litigation Group attorney who has had many far more remunerative offers explains, "I just can't imagine doing anything else that would be so much fun." After two decades, he still looks forward to going to work every day. As author Robert Fulghum once suggested: "So often doing good involves a kind of grimness. ... If we could just figure out how to have more fun at it, maybe more of us would join the ranks of those who seek after justice and mercy." Hundreds of hours of interviews with those who have worked at the Public Citizen Litigation Group yielded a common denominator: "It's such fun doing what we do!"

For most of us, understanding Nader is difficult, in part because so few of us could imagine walking in his shoes or sustaining his seriousness of purpose at what seems to be the expense of all else in life. Many times his detractors have predicted an end to his influence on public affairs, certain that no one could "stay the course" for so long. Though his influence has waxed and waned, after forty years he is still the sturdy, indefatigable warrior, and innovations are still his weapons. At a time when many people in public life bend to every political wind or swim with the money flow, and when we are regularly given reports of yet another powerful leader in government or the private sector who has lied to us or ripped us off, someone who is consistent, honest and not out to feather his own nest is remarkable, indeed. We yearn for someone we can trust. It is earned trust that best explains Nader's long tenure as an influential public figure. But perhaps his greatest accomplishment has been in organizational design and recruitment of a dedicated and talented team that has multiplied his effect infinitely more then if he had chosen to tilt at the windmills of power alone.

It would take many volumes to cover the story of all the Nader organizations and the many thousands of battles they have fought. What lies ahead is part of the story of just the first fifteen years of just one—the Public Citizen Litigation Group. Since the one is very much a piece of the whole, though, as our story unfolds we will return often to these other players in the Public Citizen advocacy network that Nader spawned.

3

The Birth of the Public Citizen Litigation Group

" Some would say that public interest law is like streaking: no one knows how or whence it comes but when it does it sure gets public attention. Others would say its origin can be summed up in two words: Ralph Nader." In describing what he called "the New Washington Lawyers" in his 1972 book, *The Superlawyers: The Small and Powerful World of the Great Washington Law Firm*, Joseph C. Goulden was one of those "others" crediting Nader as the force behind the "very noisy revolution" in public interest law going on at that time. Between 1968 and 1971 Nader had inspired dozens of young lawyers to come to Washington, D.C., to work as his Raiders or at the Center or with PIRG. When reason and publicity failed, his troops resorted to litigation. The media publicity covering the legal battles, along with Nader's ceaseless proselytizing on his campus speaking tours, spread the new gospel of public interest law throughout the law schools. More and more students there wanted to be a part of his crusades and the crusades of the other litigation groups that were sprouting like dandelions around the nation. For most public interest litigation groups, the biggest stumbling block was funding. Most public interest law firms had to turn to foundations to pay the bills. Nader chose not to rely on philanthropic foundations, because he wanted to maintain his autonomy and avoid the potential of having to shift priorities to suit large donors. But Nader had his fame to aid his fundraising efforts. Few others were so fortunate.

Grants from the Ford Foundation between 1968 and 1971 had helped to nurture a host of new public interest law organizations that also employed idealistic young lawyers, including the Center for Law and Social Policy, the Environmental Defense Fund, a legal clinic at Georgetown University Law Center (which was known as INSPIRE, or the Institute for Public Representation, at first), the Natural Resources Defense Council, Public Advocates, and the Sierra Club Legal Defense Fund. The ground for this explosion in public interest law firms was laid by an unlikely player—Warren Burger, then a U.S. appeals court judge. In a 1966 case involving the Federal Communications Commission, Burger had said, "The theory that the commission can always effectively represent the listener interests ... is no longer a valid assumption." Because all employees of government agencies are paid from the public purse—from the taxes of the people—the expectation always had been that government officials would operate in the public interest. The Raiders' studies brought a very different reality to public attention. The truth was that public agencies were most often captives of the businesses they purportedly regulated, or were no longer interested in vigorously pursuing their legislative mandates, or both. If the government agency could not be trusted to represent the public interest, someone else would have to do so. Burger's words had amounted to a court stamp of approval for encouraging and enabling public interest groups to be included in an agency's decisionmaking process. However, participation in agency deliberations by submitting evidence and testimony generally turned out to be not enough. Litigation was the hammer necessary to get an agency to listen to the little voices of the public interest groups over the din of the powerful. As Nader had quickly discovered from his first Raiders' efforts, public interest participation required public interest litigation.

Nader had provided the opportunity to serve and had spread the spirit of civic duty among law students. Then the fever spread to others, who created their own organizations to fight for the public interest. The successes of the first public interest lawyers convinced the granting foundations that the strategy was a legitimate one to fund, and new innovators found financial underwriters. As public interest law firms blossomed, the big law firms were forced to expand their *pro bono* (for free) opportunities in order to attract the best law graduates. As Goulden noted, "New graduates won't go to firms without public-interest programs, and much of the work done under that banner further radicalizes the men doing it." Over the years to come, the large firms' commitment to public service waned, but many of the public interest law firms created at that time survived and even flourished.

Public interest law became a fact of life. But from its beginning a vigorous debate has been waged among legal scholars, political scientists and partisan politicians (which even spills over into the popular press at times) over the "propriety" of these self-anointed "private attorneys general" who claim to be the representatives of "the people." "Just who," opponents ask indignantly, "do these uppity youngsters think they are?" The attorney general of the United States and his or her assistants in the Department of Justice are the rightful claimants to the status of "the people's" attorneys. These so-called public interest lawyers are nothing more than vigilantes. What right do they have to say that their position equals "the public interest"? Moreover, opponents continue, if organized groups or individuals want to affect the policy process, they should go to Congress. Judges are not policymakers, and they should not be forced into that role. Nonetheless, because the Litigation Group claims to be a public interest law firm, it is worth considering the legitimacy of the claim.

In 1968, Harvard law professor Louis L. Jaffe, a leading scholar on administrative law, presented a strong defense of private litigants as representatives of the public interest and of the courts as a site for citizen action aimed at affecting public policymakers and public policy outcomes. "In democracies," Jaffe points out, "as in other forms of government, majorities are made by leaders and elites. I contend that judges, operating within the confines of the case or controversy requirement, may help supply that leadership." He continues:

> This does not require that judges as a class be any better than Congressmen, Senators, executives or businessmen. It does no more than recognize that, given jurisdiction of a case, those judges who do have qualities of leadership may have the opportunity of solving a problem which other responsible lawmaking bodies have not been able to solve, often because of the obstruction of minorities or the indifference of the citizenry. And it may happen that, because of the character of the question, the judicial process is well-suited to devise a solution (though, as was true of the reapportionment problem, it may be very ill-suited). Be that as it may, the solution is, as is true of all solutions, only an experiment. If the solution is put in constitutional terms it may be at least qualified by legislation, and it may be set aside—or modified—by constitutional amendment, later judicial decision, or popular nullification. And as is true of all acts of leadership, a judicial action may provoke, by way of reaction or reinforcement, action at the legislative level. Thus though judicial intervention may cause popular responsibility to atrophy it may, on the contrary, energize it as we have seen in the enormous legislative movement generated by the school desegregation decision.

Jaffe goes on to discuss why citizen participation through lawsuits is an important and "creative element" of our form of government and "thoroughly consistent with the primacy of majority rule." He notes, "Democracy in our tradition emphasizes citizen participation as much as it does majority rule. Citizen participation is not simply a vehicle for minority protection, but a creative element in government and lawmaking." The citizen lawsuit is not only "thoroughly consistent" with democratic principles, it is a critical form of citizen participation within the framework of majority rule. Some of his reasons, he admits, are more compelling as applied to suits against the legality of administrative and official action, in other words statutory as compared to constitutional challenges, though he clearly means to defend both.

His argument proceeds as follows. The sense of exclusion from government felt by so many citizens undercuts the requirement of citizen participation central to our democratic principles. The rapid expansion of national government powers in the mid-twentieth century (as the administrative state was constructed in response to the Great Depression, World War II and the galloping economic growth and social activism that followed) left citizens diminished, unable to participate in the complex and overwhelming procedures of the new behemoth. Much of the new government power is exercised by administrative agencies through the processes of administrative rulemaking, order-making and discretionary decisionmaking, processes heavily weighted toward the business/industrial players most affected. The economic stake and financial power of business and industry groups that are subject to government regulation is such that their regular and vigorous participation is a given. The sheer volume, complexity and ongoing nature of the processes makes individual citizens unlikely participants, however, and thus their viewpoints are more likely to be missed or ignored. Citizen voices can achieve volume by means of group participation. Without some positive effort to assure group participation (some procedural devices to enable citizen groups to participate, such as funding to enable their participation, and the ability to invoke judicial controls if they are denied access or a fair hearing), the citizen groups in all likelihood have insufficient resources (money, power, incentive, access, expertise and so on) to go it alone. It is not necessary that citizen groups represent *the one and only public interest* to participate; that there is a problem precisely defining "the public interest" is immaterial. It is enough to recognize that citizen groups should be able to participate effectively (however narrow or broad their viewpoint, however large or small their membership/support), and that they (more than, or at least as much as, the powerful organized business interests) need access to courts to accomplish this end. Again, it is a given that big business and industry resort to court whenever it is to their benefit to do so.

This sort of rationale motivated the Ford Foundation and other philanthropies to fund the establishment of new public interest law practices. Business and industry were using the law, lawyers and the courts to protect their interests, and so the less-well-off, less-powerful, less-organized interests should have access as well. Nader makes much the same argument: "I have never said the corporations shouldn't be entitled to their Lloyd Cutlers and their Clark Cliffords. The whole thrust of my argument is that there must be lawyers on both sides of a hearing room. The corporate lawyers must be constantly challenged and counter-balanced by the *pro bono* lawyers. That's what it's all about."

Nader and the other lawyers who sparked the public interest law movement were first and foremost believers in the law and the Constitution. They took literally the promise held out in the famous lines of the great Chief Justice John Marshall: "We are a nation of laws, not of men." The United States was to be ruled not by the whim of kings but by laws that would apply to all citizens equally and made by representatives of the people. What is so striking about the public interest lawyers, then, and those at the Litigation Group today, is this strong belief in the system: it can work if only the game can be made fair for all. One Nader's Raider put it this way: "We were the conservatives of the radical movements of the sixties. We did not see civil disobedience as an effective means to reach a more just system. We embraced the promise of the law, as it was supposed to be, as the best route to justice." Law as the organizing principle of society was not the problem; rather, the problem was the unfair advantage the powerful had over those in control of the law.

To Marshall's "a nation of laws" might be added, "and lawyers," for it is the legal profession that has long captured most of the positions of power when law is the game at hand—whether the game is being played in the courts, the legislature or the executive branch (or inside corporations, for that matter). And, because government action can be taken only pursuant to a law, law is almost always the game at hand.

All lawyers are trained as advocates, trained to develop and present the best defense of, or attack for, a client's position against an adversary, who is expected to counter in like fashion. With law as the game and lawyers as the prime players, it is no surprise that the game plan is mostly an adversarial one. For an adversarial approach to be fair or just or reasoned, all sides must be equally well represented. Only then can the decision maker (whether judge, agency head or legislator) make a just or rational decision. Only then is justice or reason served. If one side can hire more lawyers and experts and/or smarter and more experienced lawyers and experts than the other, this imbalance may lead to a skewed judgment. If one side is unorganized and hence not even able to "field a team," so to speak, its interests may be wholly missing from consideration. That, of course, was just the point Nader's crusades were making: the public interest, particularly the unorganized consumer's interest, is not adequately taken into account when Congress acts, when the executive branch acts, or when the courts act. And surely not when corporations act on their own.

It also had become abundantly clear, as the crusades continued, that representation had to be there at every stage of the complicated policymaking process, because the powerful would be. The true nature of policymaking is that it is never completely finished. Policies are always subject to modification by some other actor or some other branch of government almost before the ink can dry on the page of the law, the agency rule or the court order. The powerful know this. Their experts are skilled at protecting their advantage and pressing for more every time a policy decision is announced. The public interest needs its own experienced experts and lobbyists to keep the general interest at the table. Otherwise, all the legislators, bureaucrats and judges hear is a one-sided view.

The need for their own lawyers was a lesson learned from the early Nader crusades. Courts offered the only reasonably level playing field. In the two other branches, rational decisionmaking is the myth; money and power the reality. Reason, facts and fairness are not guaranteed to prevail in the courts, but at least they have a fighting chance—although it takes quality lawyers to play on these courts. Public Citizen Litigation Group attorney Brian Wolfman, who was named director in 2004, explains the appeal of the courts:

There is an enormous power in what we do, if for no other reason than this: I file a lawsuit (I might file it against a private company or a government department) and they have to answer. That is something that is completely different about dealing elsewhere; in Congress, the executive or the board room they can completely ignore you, swat you like a pesky fly, or pay you symbolic momentary attention. But in court they ignore you at their own peril, to put it mildly. And that in itself is something that makes the courts a powerful playing field. Moreover, because of the legal culture they not only have to answer, but they have to answer in a certain way and in a certain time frame. They have to answer the question you ask, deal with the specific arguments you make and the specific facts you allege. The facts are perhaps the most powerful ingredient. It is the public portrayal of the facts you present that they ignore at their peril. One reason public interest lawyers are so often hated is that day after day they are bringing out facts people in positions of power in government or industry do not want out and do not want to deal with. And, they are brought out in an arena that does not just splash them on the front page one day, bury them the next, and forget them the next. The facts go on with the suit. It is a power with which they must reckon.

Paul Levy, another Litigation Group attorney, said:

As a litigator you litigate before biased people [judges], but there is a corpus of law that confines a judge's discretion. Their prisms of ideology are filtered by the law and the discipline of writing opinions connected to that law. I have always had the sense that if I can figure out their ideals or ideology, I can craft an argument that can persuade them to my side. It is the politics of the intellect, not the down and dirty of the pressure lobbyist, where money and power, not reason, rules. Judges are not saints, but most of them, especially the lifetime appointed federal judiciary, are immune to the intimidation of money and threats.

To pursue a long-term litigation strategy, to take on the immense and powerful law firms that represent big business or the gigantic Justice Department when it represents government agencies, it would take more than volunteers, more than individual activists litigating on their own, more than Nader alone. What was needed, Nader concluded, "is a corps of such public-interest lawyers" who could follow a case "year after dreary year as it proceeds through the regulatory agencies, the Congress, the courts, the executive branch bureaucracy." Nader set out to find himself a litigating tiger.

* * * * *

That tiger turned out to be serving as assistant chief of the Office of the Civil Division of the U.S. Attorney for the Southern District of New York: thirty-three-year-old Alan Morrison. The summer of 1971 found Morrison growing restive. Up to then his career had paralleled that of many of his high-powered peers, but his curiosity about public interest law had been piqued by reading *America, Inc.: Who Owns and Operates the United States?* by *Washington Post* writer Morton Mintz and a former counsel of the Senate Antitrust and Monopoly Subcommittee, Jerry S. Cohen. The book "made it so clear," Morrison remembers, "that the big guys didn't need representation; the little guys did." Mintz had become a "tough investigative reporter" because of *Unsafe at Any Speed.* "When I read Ralph's book I began to understand," says Mintz. A "perpetual state of outrage about the injustices of society" and a lifetime of crusading journalism was one outcome of that understanding. He regularly covered Nader's activities. "Ralph's campaigns let you feel that there is some relationship between doing your job and the benefits flowing therefrom." Inspired by Nader, Mintz would in turn inspire the man who would become Nader's "private attorney general for the people."

As with so many of the Nader recruits, happenstance brought the young attorney and the consumer crusader together. A Harvard law school student, Jerry Neugarten, who had served as a Nader's Raider the summer before, was hired as a 1971 summer intern in Morrison's office at the U.S. Attorney's Office in New York. One day in a brown-bag-lunch discussion of the intern's future, the intern turned to Morrison and asked, "What are you going to do when you grow up and get a real job?" Morrison talked about the Mintz book and wanting to find some way to work for "the little people." Like Reuben Robertson, he had been contemplating setting up a public interest firm on his own. The intern offered to write a letter to Nader about Morrison, and Morrison took him up on it. "I thought if Nader came to New York sometime we might get together and chat," Morrison recalls. "But shortly after Labor Day, I got a phone call from one of Nader's folks saying they were considering setting up a public interest law firm. Would I be interested in interviewing for the directorship?"

That fall, Morrison traveled to Washington to talk with Nader. "When I came down to be interviewed by Ralph," Morrison reminisces, "I didn't even have a resume with me. Somebody said, 'You ought at least to have one.' So I said, 'give me a pencil' and I wrote out a few of the things I had done."

The son of an attorney, Morrison had grown up in a well-to-do suburb of New York City. "In 1954, when I was a senior in high school, the Korean War had just ended, but almost everybody had to go into the military, and the only questions were, in what capacity, what service, and when." He applied for and won a Navy ROTC scholarship that paid his full tuition at Yale University—a glorious sum of $1,000 per year back then. He graduated in the top quarter of the Yale class of 1959, just four years after Nader had graduated from Princeton. Law school was postponed by four years Navy service as a desk officer, public information officer and speech writer on cruisers in the Pacific and Mediterranean—the *quid pro quo* for the tuition aid. "Although the Navy was not always fun," Morrison recalls, "it was enormously educational for me and a great growing up and learning experience. It also made it a lot easier to go back to law school and a lot harder to complain about what was going on in law school. At least I wasn't told when I had to wake up, what I had to wear, and what I had to say to whom every minute of the day!"

At the end of his tour of duty, he entered Harvard Law School, graduating in 1966, eight years after Nader's graduation from the same institution. "Most of us remember law school as a tense and unpleasant experience, but Alan always says his years at Harvard were the happiest in his life," a former associate recalls. "Alan wasn't born to be a lawyer; he was born a lawyer." His record in Cambridge supports this assessment: magna cum laude, law review and president of the Harvard Legal Aid Society.

Morrison became an associate with a prestigious New York corporate law firm, Cleary, Gottlieb, Steen & Hamilton. Burt Lehman, an associate at Cleary, fixed Morrison up with a young woman who had been his wife's college roommate at Smith. Cupid's arrow struck home and on September 24, 1967, Anne Scherck and Alan were married. A year later he turned down a transfer offer to the firm's Paris branch to work in the Office of the U.S. Attorney for the Southern District of New York, "in order," as he puts it, "to have the opportunity to do more of what I liked most, litigating." A year later he was placed in charge of a government suit to recover $250 million in excess profits, taxes and interest from U.S. Steel. On the basis of his impressive work in the district court, Morrison was promoted to assistant chief of the Civil Division and given responsibility for more than two dozen lawyers. In June 1970 his first daughter, Nina, was born.

Morrison didn't put this much into his scribbled resume, but it hardly mattered. Nader measures his tigers by spirit, mental agility, acumen and energy. When he talks, Morrison's words come at breakneck speed. He tends, when he really gets going, to start a second sentence before finishing the first, leaving it to the listener to fill in the missing parts. His excitement is telegraphed in body language and in a voice that starts out deep and ends on a high pitch. (His demeanor in court is another matter; his reputation as one of the most effective litigators is well earned.) And Nader? Ideas spill out in torrents. It is easy to imagine the electricity that must have been generated between the two men that day, especially since the interview occurred mostly on the run.

Morrison waited for Nader at the Center, but it was not Ralph who arrived. Instead, Morrison was picked up by a dark-haired, lively young woman, Joan Claybrook. She announced that Nader had to give a talk at George Washington University and she was driving him there. Would Morrison come along? They could talk in the car.

Claybrook was by then working with Nader at his Public Interest Research Group (PIRG) while attending Georgetown Law School part time. After her year as a congressional fellow, she had joined the Johnson administration as a staffer in the new auto safety agency she had helped create. When the Nixon administration took over in 1969, she decided to apply to law school but stayed on with the new administration for a while, attending law school part time at night. When Nixon tapped Doug Toms to head up the auto safety agenda, Claybrook suggested to Toms that he push for NHTSA to become a separate agency in the new Department of Transportation. Toms listened and made it a condition of his taking the job. He kept Claybrook as a special assistant. "The thing Toms liked best," Claybrook remembers, "was to travel. So we set up a challenge to foreign car makers to develop experimental safety cars with great dual results. Toms got to travel, and significant innovation on car safety resulted worldwide." During this time the shootings at Kent State occurred and partisan politics was heating up in anticipation of the mid-term 1970 congressional elections. Claybrook was too "hot" as she puts it, too connected to the Democrats, to stay on as a special assistant in the Republican Nixon administration. She decided to take some time off to rest and put her attention to her law studies. Within three weeks she was immersed full time in the Senate campaign of Paul Sarbanes. So much for rest and study. For several months in the summer and fall of 1970 she worked on the campaign. After Sarbanes won, she returned to law school at night. Nader then cajoled her into coming to the new PIRG, a more activist organization created to augment the research role of the Center for Study of Responsive Law he had just set up with the money he got from his settlement with General Motors over the private eye fiasco. Claybrook quickly became a right hand to Nader, which included everything from schlepping him around (ironically, the great auto safety man never drove) to helping him implement an endless stream of new ideas. One of her first tasks was "to accompany Ralph on a trip to Japan to check out car safety at the Honda and Toyota factories where we found that the cars Japan was exporting to the United States were safer than the ones sold to their own citizens." Claybrook recollects what happened next. "Ralph found an old 1910 English typewriter and had me type a letter on this rickity old machine to the prime minister saying they ought to at least have the cars at home as safe as the ones they sent abroad. As he was leaving the country he held a press conference to release a copy of the letter. Then he flew off and I got to stay for the fireworks!" The day Morrison came to be interviewed she was doing chauffeuring duty as well as finishing law school and working full time at PIRG. Such is the charm of Nader and the enormous energy of Joan Claybrook, the dedicated activist who would a decade later become the heiress to the Nader Public Citizen "empire."

After Nader's talk at George Washington, he and Morrison walked quickly back to Dupont Circle—an interview on the run. "What Ralph wanted to know was what I wanted to do if I came here," Morrison remembers. He was prepared, pulling a folded yellow sheet of jottings from his wallet. That sheet (which he carried with him until a few years ago) listed some of the things he would like to pursue. "I had three or four ideas in mind. One was the professions. That was clearly something I really wanted to do from the start, because no one else was doing anything about the professions, especially our own profession." The bar had become a law unto itself and there were serious problems—barriers to entry that were used to keep prices up, minimum fee schedules that had the same purpose, prohibitions against advertising that hindered a young lawyer's ability to get a practice going (and kept prices up), restrictions on what non-lawyers (paraprofessionals) could do that made simple tasks (like filling out legal forms) cost more than was needed, and so on. "I felt," Morrison notes, "that as lawyers we had a responsibility to clean up our own house. Ralph was behind me from the start." No surprise there. Nader had been pushing the members of his own profession to assume more responsibility for building a fairer and safer world for some time.

Morrison's second item: a challenge to the constitutionality of the anti-lobbying restrictions of the Internal Revenue Code for charitable organizations. If they could be overturned, it would be much easier for the public interest groups to raise funds. "It is simply a fact of life," Morrison observes, "that it is always easier to get people to give to good causes if they can write the gift off on their income tax." Somehow, activating the celebrated American charitable instinct takes the carrot of a deduction on Form 1040 in April. Needless to say, Nader supported this as well.

The yellow scrap of paper had many more goals listed as potential litigation projects: going after the misuse of power by the presidency, seeking First Amendment protection for advertising, obtaining free speech for nonprofit organizations, protecting consumers, mounting antitrust actions when the Justice Department failed to act, and pursuing democratic rights for union members. On the occasion of the twenty-fifth anniversary of the Public Citizen Litigation Group in 1997, one writer noted that the list was "so ambitious it would be laughable had not so many of its goals been realized."

Morrison had some ideas about what he did not want to do, as well. "There were two things I knew I didn't want to do, not because they were not important but because other people were doing them and because I had no special expertise to add: civil rights and the environment." The Litigation Group has done a couple of cases in the civil rights area where there was a procedural issue involved or some compelling circumstance (for example, when the Veterans Administration was discriminating against a female attorney who also happened to be the mother of one of the early Litigation Group attorneys, they took on the case). It has also taken on a few environment cases when the principal focus was something else, like trade or auto safety or nuclear power. But by in large it has stayed out of civil rights and the environment. "We do a lot," says Morrison, "but we can't do everything."

One of the criticisms of Nader by 1971 was that he was spreading himself too thin, trying to do too much, undercutting his effectiveness by lending his name to too many causes—"chicken franchising," as one critic called it. But just how much this sort of criticism was really a duckblind for the position that

Nader "should get off my back" or should "save himself for my issue" is open to question. Morrison recalls a conversation to this point soon after he joined Nader's team. "Six months or so after I came, I was flying down to North Carolina to give a talk. I was sitting next to a fellow on the plane and he asked what I did. When I told him, he said, 'This is a great thing,' and so on and so forth. 'But, you know you all spread yourself too thin, you try to do too many different things.' Not less than five minutes later he said, 'You know there is one area you guys have got to get into,' and he never understood the contradiction between his two points." It was a classic expression of the budget balance dilemma: Cut the budget! But, don't cut me, don't cut thee, cut that guy behind that tree! A broad agenda, as Morrison notes, "has always been our greatest strength and our greatest weakness. There is virtually nothing that is out of bounds. We are not like some groups that are confined by their foundation grant or by their membership to a specific agenda. We will listen to anything."

Nader and Morrison clicked. At $15,000, Morrison would be taking an $8,500 annual cut, but this was a great deal better than the $4,500 Nader had been paying lawyers who worked at the Center. Nader knew, though, that if he wanted someone who would stay, he had to be a bit more realistic. Accepting the position would mean that Morrison's wife would have to give up her part-time job as a program officer at the Carnegie Corporation, which she really didn't want to leave. But, as Morrison recalls, the calculus was "if the job was right for me we'd go to Washington. We have often talked about the changes since 1971 and what it would have been like to face this decision ten or fifteen years later. But, back then the question of Anne's job was simply not discussed. Obviously that would not be the way it would happen today."

In February 1972, the Morrisons moved to Washington and the Public Citizen Litigation Group was born. More than thirty-two years later, the Litigation Group is still litigating on behalf of the "little people" against the giants. Through the end of 2003, only forty lawyers had been hired by the Litigation Group as permanent staff, of whom only six stayed less than two years. With a median stay of five years and an average stay of nearly eight years (and a few who have lasted decades, Morrison included) it has been a pretty lean operation. What follows is the story of Alan Morrison and his Merry Band of Litigators—forty men and women who have made an enormous difference.

4

Organizing the Litigation Group

The winter of 1972 inaugurated a cataclysmic time in American politics that would close off opportunity for most social activism. LBJ's Great Society programs were increasingly coming under attack as their full cost became apparent. The flood of new social regulatory programs that had been pouring from Congress was slowing to a trickle. The groundwork was being laid for a constitutional crisis that would pit Congress against the president. Mistrust of politicians and cynicism about political solutions were growing, as was the proportion of the public indicating "little approval" of business (60 percent in 1972, up from 46 percent in 1967). When Alan Morrison arrived in Washington in February to set up a new public interest law firm, the political scene showed many signs of what was to come both for the nation and for his new venture.

A heated debate was unfolding over the Nixon administration's request for a $59 billion increase in the debt ceiling, which would raise the total national debt to $480 billion. The deficit for the fiscal year was predicted to reach $25.5 billion by the end of June (the fiscal year then ran from July 1 to June 30). If the annual deficit continued at this pace, economists estimated, the nation's debt would double in just two decades. (Reality would prove even worse. By 1981 the total U.S. debt more than doubled, reaching $1 trillion, and by 1996, a decade and a half later, the debt had quintupled to $5 trillion.) The cost of the war in Vietnam, combined with the escalating costs of the new housing, health and welfare programs, was rapidly outstripping revenues from the national tax income. Some form of tax increase seemed inevitable, but, as usual, no politician wanted his fingerprints on any such proposal. At the time the nation was still under a wage and price freeze that had been ordered by President Nixon in August 1971 in an effort to bring inflation under control—not auspicious circumstances for increasing the tax bite on working Americans. The era of deficit politics was unfolding, and this would dramatically change the receptivity of Washington policymakers to entrepreneurial politics and the cries for action from the likes of Nader.

When Morrison arrived, the 1972 presidential and congressional elections were just nine months away and the Democrats were in wild disarray, with everyone but the dog catcher running in the presidential primary races: George

McGovern, Edmund Muskie, Ted Kennedy, Hubert Humphrey, Jesse Jackson, Eugene McCarthy, Shirley Chisholm, John Lindsay, Wilbur Mills, George Wallace and a number of lesser-knowns were out stumping the nation. On February 26, Muskie, the acknowledged front-runner, stumbled and lost his lead in the polls. His tears shed on camera over a story published in a New Hampshire newspaper, *The Union Leader* (a story he saw as untrue and offensive to his wife), were seen as evidence of weakness. Though Muskie won the New Hampshire primary, McGovern was a close second. After that, McGovern's campaign took off and won him the Democratic nomination. Painted as a far-left liberal by his opponents, McGovern's nomination led to Nixon's landslide re-election in November.

At the beginning of February, Nixon had announced a peace initiative, a move many cynics saw as re-election politicking after nearly three years of unkept promises and inaction. The Paris peace negotiations started with much fanfare but soon broke down. Renewed fighting broke out in Vietnam. By then, however, the president had managed to focus the nation's attention on another matter. On February 18, Nixon left on his trip "to open the door to China," a trip that commanded newspapers' front pages and lead stories on television news for the eight days he was gone. The last national draft lottery, which affected the more than two million men born in 1953, was held while he was away; March 6 "won" the dreaded first-place draw (young men born on this date would be the first drafted) and July 23 was the far more appealing last-place date.

On February 2, the Justice Department filed suit against Associated Milk Producers for price manipulation and a long list of violations of the Sherman Anti-Trust Act. The industry soon moved to protect itself by funneling money to Nixon's Committee to Re-Elect the President, otherwise known as CREEP, in hopes of influencing the administration to drop the case. The scandal that would develop from the industry's efforts to launder illegal corporate donations through Mexico became a major catalyst for the campaign finance reform act of 1974. That law provided for public funding of presidential campaigns but also enabled an explosion in the creation of political action committees (PACs), primarily by big business, the professions and unions. By the end of the decade, PAC donations would become a major source of congressional campaign funds. This mechanism, considered legalized "bribery" by some, added more volume to the voices of the moneyed in the political process and made the job of public interest groups like Nader's even more difficult.

There were many other signs of the changing times that February. Vice President Spiro Agnew challenged the use of federal Legal Services (the publicly funded legal aid program for the poor) attorneys to sue government officials. It was the opening salvo in the conservatives' battle against legal aid for the poor that continues even today. Nixon ordered a study to devise a strategy to fight mandatory school busing. Attorney General John Mitchell, who would soon figure prominently in the Watergate scandal, quit to head the

Nixon re-election campaign. News columnist Jack Anderson charged that the Justice Department's decision to settle its antitrust suit against ITT was linked to a $400,000 pledge from one of the company's subsidiaries to the 1972 Republican National Convention fund. Anderson's article implicated a White House aide in the exchange. The Supreme Court ruled that the Federal Trade Commission's power extended to prosecuting unfair and deceptive trade practices, not just to antitrust actions. The Atomic Energy Commission and fourteen environmental groups began a marathon meeting on the safety of nuclear power plants just as the Supreme Court agreed to hear a freedom of information challenge by Democratic Representative Patsy Mink of Hawaii against the Environmental Protection Agency for its refusal to release nuclear bomb test data.

In Congress, Senator Sam Ervin (D-North Carolina), chairman of the Subcommittee on Constitutional Rights, disclosed that the Army Intelligence surveillance of civilian officials from 1967 to 1970 (including U.S. senators, representatives, a Supreme Court justice and a number of state governors and state legislators) was far more extensive than previously revealed. Ervin's role in exposing this and other illegal activities by government agencies led to his chairing the Senate Watergate hearings. Senator Frank E. Moss (D-Utah) became the chief sponsor of a bill to limit the tar and nicotine content of cigarettes in light of dramatic increases in tobacco sales despite the recent law banning televised cigarette commercials. The Senate broke a Southern-led filibuster and supported new enforcement powers for the Equal Employment Opportunity Commission. It also outlawed sex-biased programs in colleges.

Also in February 1972, Anwar el-Sadat flew to Moscow to seek arms for his "holy war" against the Jews in Israel. The My Lai massacre courts martial concluded. Black communist activist Angela Davis was released from jail in California on $102,500 bond. Killings and violence between the Irish Republican Army and the British continued in Northern Ireland. Hanoi announced that American POWs would not be released until a peace accord was signed and displayed five recently captured U.S. fliers during a press conference. The long coal strike in Britain was finally settled. The California high court barred the death penalty as cruel and unusual punishment. Hijackers of an Athens-bound jetliner released 172 passengers, including Joseph P. Kennedy, the third son of Robert F. Kennedy.

All these events illustrate a political pot, at home and abroad, at full boil when Alan Morrison came to town to set up the Public Citizen Litigation Group in February 1972. His first day on the job was not auspicious—no fanfare, no headlines, not even a squib in the *Post*. "Looking back on all of the things that were going on that February makes me realize how small and insignificant we were," Morrison reminisces. "I suppose I viewed myself as a small-time player then, with no notion that we could really make a difference on any kind of grand scale. Among other things, I viewed myself primarily as a litigator (although I broadened that notion as I began to understand what it would take to mount an effective public interest law practice), and thus many of these events were beyond my field of vision." How quickly this changed.

* * * * *

One of the first things the Litigation Group took on was the ITT matter shortly after White House aide Dita Beard blew the whistle on how the administration had agreed to back off the antitrust case. Before long, Morrison's team would be representing Senator Ervin and a number of other members of Congress in their struggle with Nixon over impoundment of funds and representing Representative Mink in an action involving the drug DES. In less than two years Morrison would be challenging Nixon's firing of Special Prosecutor Archibald Cox, and his team would be involved in the nuclear power and tobacco issues. The powers in Washington would soon sit up and take notice of this bright young attorney and his corps of even younger talented recruits. At the start, though, even the other Nader organizations didn't seem to pay him much heed.

"No one seemed to be expecting me," Morrison recalls. Nor was there an office awaiting. Morrison went to Nader's Center for Study of Responsive Law, which was then at 1156 19th Street N.W. and reported in. After talking with various people, he was given a corner desk in the offices of the Tax Reform Group (another Nader organization), which were at 733 15th Street N.W. The Lawyers Committee for Civil Rights was also in the building, and it had "a modest law library which I was able to use," Morrison recollects. In June the Litigation Group moved to the fifth floor of an old gray office building at 2000 P Street just off Dupont Circle. In December 1973 it moved up to the seventh floor, its home for the next twenty-one years.

Over the next few weeks, his time was spent talking with Nader and others about how many attorneys he could hire and beginning the process of bringing in and choosing cases. He knew just what he was looking for in both searches. For lawyers, he wanted the best, brightest and most committed. For cases, those that would make it "easier for citizens and consumers to get the information they need in order to know what is going on; to get access to the decisionmaking process, especially during implementation of the law by the executive branch, which is where so many of the specific decisions about the law are really made; and to have access to the courts when the system is not working and they need help to force it to do what it is supposed to do."

Finding cases was the least of Morrison's worries. The growing number of Nader-founded organizations had plenty of litigation needs and ideas. Reuben Robertson at the Aviation Consumer Action Project was fighting the Federal Aviation Administration to obtain copies of reports about existing mechanical defects in airplanes that were provided by the airline companies to the agency and was trying to force the FAA to strengthen airline safety. Both Sid Wolfe at the Health Research Group and Lowell Dodge at the Center for Auto Safety had numerous irons in the fire for which legal help was needed. And Nader himself, as usual, was brimming with ideas about issues that could be pursued through litigation, one of which ensued from Allegheny Airlines' bumping of Nader from a Washington to Hartford, Connecticut, flight on April 28, 1972. These internally generated cases provided a critical client base for getting the new Litigation Group off the ground. But Nader organizations were not then, nor are they now, the only source for the Litigation Group's caseload.

"People write or call us or Ralph out of the blue requesting help," Morrison said. For example, within a month of the Litigation Group's founding, Lewis H. Goldfarb, an attorney employed by the Federal Trade Commission, called to ask for help in suing the Virginia State Bar and its local bar associations over a price-fixing scheme called "minimum fee schedules." Carl Stern, an NBC newsman, also called that first spring. He had been trying to get documents out of the FBI about its domestic counterintelligence operations. Stern had reason to believe that the FBI had been spying on and attempting to disrupt individuals and organizations like the New Left (an assortment of liberal activists, including many in the liberal wing of the Democratic Party), but his network would not foot the bill for a court challenge. The Litigation Group stepped in free of charge. Then a bit later, in 1977, a letter came from Rosemary Furman, a legal secretary being attacked by the Florida Bar for lending a hand to battered women by filling out legal separation, divorce and child custody forms. She wrote, "To: Ralph Nader, Re: HELP!" As the Litigation Group matured, its court victories mounted, and the unsolicited requests for its services increased.

Often the idea for a case simply "comes out of our own heads," says Morrison. "I always said if I went to a conference and didn't get at least two good ideas for a case out of it, I'd wasted my time." Litigation Group attorneys are always on the lookout for actions by any big actor (business, government or the professions) that strike them as unfair, wrongheaded, illegal or otherwise in need of redress. One of the Group's biggest victories came when the Supreme Court in *INS v. Chadha* declared the legislative veto unconstitutional. That case began when Morrison came across a regulatory reform bill being debated on Capitol Hill that would subject all rules and regulations issued by any executive branch or independent agency to potential veto by one house of Congress. The challenge to the 1985 Gramm-Rudman-Hollings deficit reduction act was generated when Nader got a call from someone on the Hill and, sputtering in disbelief, called Morrison.

Sometimes these self-generated cases resulted from careful attention to an issue area such as separation of powers or the practices of a particular profession. Occasionally, just keeping up with what was going on in society opened up a new area. In the 1990s the fairness of class action settlements and preemption issues were added to their agenda in this way. Reading new court and agency decisions and offering to take cases on appeal were common sources of cases. In the 1980s, that is how the Litigation Group's work on labor preemption and fair union representation was developed. Litigation in all these instances often meant finding a client who could meet the courts' requirement that the plaintiff have standing (that is someone who could claim some injury or potential injury caused by the party to be sued). "Client creation" is usually relatively easy for the Litigation Group. It has the Nader-founded organizations plus dozens of public interest group allies it can turn to. The pool of potential clients is considerable. And because Litigation Group clients do not have to pay, volunteers usually come forward.

Occasionally, the Litigation Group joins existing cases at a party's request or by its own initiative. Working with a Senate staffer who rounded up a number of members of Congress, including the chairs of every Senate committee, as clients, the Litigation Group wrote an *amicus* brief in a case that was being brought by the state of Missouri against Nixon's impoundment of highway trust fund money. When Americans United for Separation of Church and State (AU) was challenging an Internal Revenue Service ruling that denied its tax-exempt status because the organization lobbied Congress, Morrison—who had had this issue on his little yellow sheet of ideas—called with an offer of help, which AU accepted. It would turn out to be the first case Morrison argued before the Supreme Court.

Unlike most fledgling law firms, the Litigation Group was blessed with plenty of clients and potential clients. That is still true. The problem is, and was, choosing from among them. Morrison has many selection criteria, but he is quick to note that there is "no science to their application." He asks such questions as:

- Is the case likely to have significance beyond the parties involved? Would the substantive outcome of the case, if we win, matter? Is it important to a fairer process or a better world?

- Is the area central to the interests of the Litigation Group or some piece of Public Citizen or its allied public interest groups?

- Do we have a chance of winning?

- Will the cost of carrying on the litigation be within our means?

- Is anyone else likely to do the case, so we do not have to?

- Is there something we would rather do with our limited resources that this would prevent?

- Does the case involve an issue of such moral outrage that none of the above matter much?

"It is important to note, though," Morrison cautions, "that a negative response to these questions does not rule out a case. We always try to remember the perfect is the enemy of the good." Hence, some or all of the criteria are often ignored. A loss in court may be a strategically acceptable tactic for securing a win elsewhere; an unpopular ruling, for example, might stir Congress to act. Though another organization or attorney might be willing to take a case, neither might be as able or willing to argue it in the same way or with the same force as the Litigation Group. Sometimes a good case would be too expensive, so expertise is shared or advice is given. Even if a case is not central to the Litigation Group's goals, Morrison declares,

> it might be that it is the best of what we have to choose from at the moment. We take them as they come along, because we can't control what it is that is out there. Even with a statute like the Freedom of Information Act where we principally know the areas that need further developing by court interpretation, people just show up or situations just pop up. ... Most of all we are just trying to prevent bad things from happening or to patch up problems as they come along. There is an overarching goal, of course, of making more information more easily available to any and all citizens, but it is not possible to map out a strategic plan with any certainty with an agenda as broad as ours is. Sometimes case selection is nothing more than case doing—that is, we step in as circumstances develop.

Another reality for the Litigation Group is limited resources. Because of this (and perhaps because it results in a focus on appellate argument, the form of law practice that Morrison prefers), the Litigation Group has from the beginning avoided taking on cases that are heavily "fact specific" (those that require subpoenaing many documents or taking many depositions). Instead, its lawyers focus on questions of *the law*. Does e-mail count as an agency record that must be preserved and made available to the public (unless otherwise exempted) under the Freedom of Information Act? Does the constitutional requirement of separation of powers allow one house of Congress to veto the actions of the executive branch? Do the words "to the extent feasible" in the Occupational Safety and Health Act require that, if the technology to eliminate a hazard in the workplace is known, it must be applied no matter the cost? Fact-specific questions like whether an agency has a document or whether an agency regulation vetoed by Congress was technologically sound or whether a particular chemical is a carcinogen require the sleuth side of lawyering—investigation through gathering and sifting through documents (using the subpoena power) and interviewing people and experts (by sworn depositions). Gathering evidence such as this is very labor-intensive and expensive. With limited funds, few attorneys and little staff help, taking such cases would necessarily mean taking fewer cases. Not that the Litigation Group never takes such cases, but fiscal reality limits the number.

Organizing the Litigation Group

* * * * *

Knowing what he wanted to accomplish and how he planned to go about it, Morrison knew, too, the kind of associates that were desirable. Nader asked him "to test the outer limits of the law," so Morrison needed people who were creative and willing to stretch beyond the tried and known. Brains and derring-do, not experience, were the key. Indeed, long experience was apt to be a hindrance. Warren Bennis, in *Organizing Genius* (1998), notes that nearly all outstanding "work groups" have been made up of youngsters. For example, most members of the team that developed the A-bomb in World War II were twenty-five years old or younger. There is an advantage, he postulates, in the innocence of youth: the young do not know what they don't know yet and can thus still believe in the possibility of complete success.

Bennis gives some clues about the organizing principles that are essential for creating a group dynamic that will enable creativity to flourish. First and foremost is a good leader with a nose for talent, able to find subordinates who are bright and who will work together, or, as he puts it, "who will want to play tag in the sand box together." Egotistical loners can rarely be combined into a functioning team. A good leader acts as the curator, not the creator; the role is to enable the group to function. A good leader inspires but, most important, must be able to create a genuine and sustained sense of trust among the group members and between all of them and the leader. A good leader must be able to articulate to the group what the goal is and why it matters, and convince the group that what it is doing toward the goal is meaningful. A leader and group with all these ingredients in place will be energized and will be a force far greater than the sum of its individual parts.

Morrison instinctively acted on the basis of these principles in 1972. Almost universally, past and present Litigation Group attorneys characterize him as a brilliant teacher and leader who, once he had chosen a member of the Group, had absolute confidence that the person was capable of doing whatever the job required. It was a confidence by which the person was held to the highest standard, but the teacher side of the leader was always there to guide and to inspire—though the style of guidance was not the nurturing variety. No one accuses Morrison of mollycoddling. His style was sometimes severe and insensitive, as well as very demanding (although the passage of years has softened his approach a bit). If a team member could not cut it or deal with the style, he or she would leave or be let go. "There was no pussyfooting around, no gentle let-down," remarked one former Group member. "But," as longtime Litigation Group veteran David Vladeck says, "Alan was equally gruff and demanding with us all. He let each of us know that he would not have hired us unless we were smart enough and good enough to do what he expected. He pushed us to use the brains we had and to be the best we could be. We all understood that we were just kids up against complex issues and powerful and experienced players and that we were playing in the top courts of the land. We understood, as he did, that we had to be good, really good—better than everyone else."

Fortunately, Morrison had a good nose for talented and compatible players, so the number of recruits who left because they couldn't stand it or who were shown the door was low. The lawyers quickly adjusted into a supportive and enthusiastic team. "We all had our fingers in everyone else's pie. We'd read each other's briefs, pound one another in grueling moot courts, troop out to watch each other whenever someone had an oral argument," says Vladeck. "There was a fervency, an excitement, an ideological drive and belief that we were using the law for socially good purposes, that made what we were doing critical and meaningful."

There was also teamwork, which still prevails. "We are spared the competitive atmosphere here that interferes with friendship in many legal practices," Morrison says. "What is there to compete for here? There is no partnership. Pay is pretty much lockstep, with everyone getting the same small increase each year. Your case is your case; no senior partner is going to steal it away just as it becomes interesting. The offices are equally unimpressive."

* * * * *

But if the leader was a bit gruff, the "children" were gaiety itself. "There has never been a place where I had more fun than at the Litigation Group," Mark Lynch reminisces. He adds:

> It was an extraordinary place that attracted a rare aggregation of individuals. The *esprit de corps* and comradeship was tops. Much of it had to do with Alan's personality and leadership, and that it was small and we all felt special, and the time was right—we were all of "the generation." When someone would get hold of the advance sheets of some awful court decision, they'd let out a whoop, "Holy shit! Look at this opinion!" and run into someone's office to rant and rave. When we'd get briefs from the other side in one of our cases, we'd hoot in rage or delight and dash around to share our reaction. The great thing about it was that this sort of excitement was sustained—it went on and on, day after day.

They were young and without many other commitments or demands on their time. Most of the Litigation Group attorneys of the "Children's Crusade" generation (as they jokingly called themselves) were single or divorced and without kids. They ate lunch and often dinner together, played softball on the National Mall together, joined Yates' Gym in Georgetown and worked out and played squash together, and most weekends they'd wander into the office to work and end up going out to drink and play together afterward. They dressed in blue jeans and T-shirts (except on "suited" court-appearance days), worked in seedy offices decorated in Salvation Army seconds, and hammered out their briefs on ancient typewriters and copied them on a sometimes available Xerox machine (when Nader was not mad at Xerox and threatening to cut off funding the machine). They ran in and out of one another's offices at will. Until they built up a full library of their own, they often had to run over to Georgetown Law or to the Library of Congress to do research.

"We became closer to each other than to any other group of people in our lives," Vladeck says. But he goes on to temper the image of lightheartedness with a bit of the more serious side of what they faced:

> In hindsight that time looks all excitement and fun. But, back then, when it was the present, it was more like making your way through a maze in the dark. In many ways it was more terrifying than exciting. The odds were so against us. We had the moral understanding that we were right even though every external force seemed to be telling us we were wrong. There was this sense that we had to be constantly convincing people that their orthodoxy had to be changed. It was swimming up a very-fast-moving stream strewn with rocks and boulders. We were repeatedly asking the power establishment to give up things it held dear and to surrender power it had long exercised on its own. With a goal that demanded a reordering of the way things work—a reordering most often mightily resisted by the powerful—it is no wonder we felt under siege much of the time.

Morrison established a level of professionalism and quality of work that demanded the best. The way he saw it, they were playing ball with the big guys and had two strikes already against them. They could not afford additional disadvantage from their own mistakes. "We had to think clearer, write better, and no typos allowed," Kathy Meyer recounts. "And that was doing most of our own typing since we normally had only two secretaries for the ten attorneys to share, with 'white-out' the only correction available for mistakes. There were not many places in the public interest world that strove consciously for that level of perfection."

Their spirit and camaraderie were a way to give one another courage and confidence, a way to lighten the reality of enormous odds. They were little ants trying to move a whole grove of gigantic rubber tree plants. Levity helped them hold onto their high hopes—much as soldiers joke among themselves as they set out to storm an enemy position. Being part of the Litigation Group in those early years was an all-consuming passion. It was fun, but it was work and responsibility beyond what any law firm would entrust to a bunch of freshly minted, inexperienced, untried kids. But then, it was the kids or no one if Morrison was to pursue the broad agenda he had in mind.

Courting Change

Former Litigation Group attorney Bill Schultz recalls his first day on the job, January 3, 1976:

> I was handed two major cases. One, a challenge to the Price-Anderson Act's provision that allowed the nuclear power industry to limit its liability insurance to a fraction of what the damage in life and property would be if a plant were to have a major accident. The other, a challenge to the FDA's over-the-counter drug regulations. I was just twenty-six years old, a couple of years out of law school, and though I had clerked for a U.S. district judge, I had virtually no litigation experience. These huge cases were my cases, all mine! I would be responsible for briefing and arguing them throughout, and both would go all the way to the Supreme Court.

What other green-horned attorney could claim such a case docket? Larry Ellsworth, who came in September 1973, in his first year and a half had six arguments before the U.S. Court of Appeals for the District of Columbia—a court widely regarded as the second highest in the land because it hears the vast majority of all cases involving the federal government. Ellsworth, too, was only twenty-six when he joined the Litigation Group.

After a relatively rapid turnover of first recruits (Tommy Jacks and Ray Bonner stayed just two years; and Ron Plesser two and a half), the team was fairly stable for the remainder of the 1970s—Morrison, plus Larry Ellsworth, Gerry Spann, John Sims, Bill Schultz, Diane Cohn, David Vladeck and Paul Levy. A few came and went during that time. Mark Lynch moved on to the American Civil Liberties Union after two years, and Linda Donaldson stayed for just over two years before going to the Department of Health, Education and Welfare during the Carter administration. During most of the decade, Reuben Robertson, who was just two years younger then Morrison, had four years of legal experience (at Covington and Burling and at the Federal Highway Administration) as well as three years with Nader under his belt, was part of the Litigation Group until he left in 1978—though for some of that time he was running the Aviation Consumer Action Project as well. Arthur Fox was also a part of the team from almost the beginning until 1990, but he was a couple of years older than most and had several years of experience working as an attorney at the National Labor Relations Board. Like Robertson, Fox wore two hats, spending only a part of his time on litigation matters while also organizing and promoting a group called PROD (a dissident group of truck-driving Teamsters that was brought to life by Nader, Claybrook and Fox with the purpose of pressing for truck safety and union democracy). Ellsworth, Spann, Sims, Schultz, Cohn, Vladeck and Levy (and while they were there, Plesser, Bonner, Jacks, Lynch, Donaldson) were the "children" of Morrison and his Children's Crusade during the Group's infancy who will carry the stories through the pages ahead.

"Alan really did teach us," says Kathy Meyer, who joined the Litigation Group in 1979. "He is a great teacher, perhaps most of all because he loves his trade so much." What Morrison's "students" remember most about him are his enthusiasm, imagination, excitement and creativity. "Alan could get as much fun out of working through some arcane point on civil procedure as he did from working on the grand separation of powers issues," says Eric Glitzenstein, an attorney who joined the Litigation Group in the mid-1980s. "He has this incredible genius for seeing connections between seemingly disconnected things. We would be working over a brief in a freedom of information case and he'd come up with a concept from a completely unrelated field of law like torts."

> He is just so innovative and creative in his thinking, always willing to try new approaches to the same old problems. Sometimes they don't work, but failure has never destroyed his enthusiasm to try again and again. I remember one instance involving the silicone breast implant FOIA case. At one point we tried to introduce expert testimony but the industry objected because the experts we wanted to call were under protective court orders. [The experts had testified in an individual tort action brought by a recipient of a breast implant and had been ordered by that court not to speak about anything they knew that was the result of information in any documents subpoenaed from the industry for that case.] Alan came up with the idea of entering a motion to strike all the industry briefs from the court record unless they lifted the protective order. The adversary process requires that the court hear both sides. If we could not counter the expert testimony they relied on because of their obstruction of our witnesses, they should not be able to put their version into the record to stand alone. No one had ever done anything like this before and, lo and behold, the judge went for it.

Part of Morrison's teaching was by example. "Just watching him was an education," according to Meyer. "The way he strategized, the way he handled people, the way he did an oral argument, the way he worked through a case." But it was more than soaking up the technique of the master. Alan was into "hands-on apprenticeship. He was co-counsel on all our cases back then," Meyer notes. "It was not that he led you or told you what to do. You'd go to Alan and say, 'I've got this problem. What should I do?' And he'd say, 'What do you think you should do?' Then we'd do it and he'd deconstruct what we did word by word, line by line, showing us how to build a better brief, a better argument, a better oral. The hows and the whys were always part of the reconstruction process. We were flying but we were flying under his wing."

Moot courts are another part of Morrison's teaching process, but in these grueling marathon events everyone participates in the teaching—though in the

49

early years there was little doubt about who was the chief. Morrison insisted from the start that before anyone argued a case in court there would be a practice argument before the home team; for big or complicated cases there might be two or even three. For these events everyone would gather in Morrison's office around his hand-me-down schoolmaster desk or in the "library," their one common meeting room. The library on the seventh floor of 2000 P Street was maybe twelve by eighteen feet and furnished with a large metal table and an odd assortment of chairs. Homemade shelves covered with law books circled the room, one corner of which was known as the "Tommy Jacks Memorial Hole," where no books found a home because the shelves sloped in on each other at a crazy angle. For Jacks and Morrison, aptitude for law did not translate into an aptitude for carpentry.

The attorney arguing the case would stand behind Morrison's desk or at the end of the library table with an upturned carton as a lectern to present his or her case. But "to present" does not convey what happens in a Litigation Group moot court now—or happened then. Each attendee is loaded for bear, having read their presenting colleague's and the opposition's briefs and given thought to questions. As soon as the attorney begins the argument, the questions fly. Most Litigation Group attorneys remember their own moot courts as the scariest part of their whole time there. "It was eight or nine of your best friends, all hot shots trying to show each other up, hurling lightning bolts into your argument," Kathy Meyer recalls. But these practice trouncings rendered the actuality of court argument much less frightening. They were prepared emotionally and intellectually for the real event. Eight or nine heads had helped to work out the best answers and best strategies. It was rare that a question from the real court had not been anticipated and worked over by the moot court players.

"Advocacy is inherently a collegial process," Vladeck says. "No one has a lock on wisdom. There is seldom one right answer, one and only one way of approaching a problem." The best legal argument is one that takes into account a variety of viewpoints and, after all, most of the Litigation Group cases are heard by a panel of judges (three at the appeals court level and nine at the Supreme Court). Even when it is one judge (in the district court or in a state court), that judge's decision will most likely be reviewed on appeal by a panel. Because different heads will be ruling, wisdom dictates that different heads be consulted in building the argument to present. The oral process and rigorous atmosphere of the moot court is particularly conducive to brainstorming, allowing bright minds to interact in a fast and productive fashion. As Gerry Spann describes it, "a moot court with Alan is a process of oral thinking that puts your brain cells in motion and comes up with solutions."

"If you didn't know that we loved each other, you'd be horrified at the way we tear each other down," says Vladeck. "The tearing down is always followed by a building up," Spann recalls, "You'd argue around the flood of questions, then Alan would zero in: 'These are the problem areas of the case. These are the questions you need to worry about. This is how to handle them.'" To be *moot-courted* at the Litigation Group is to be prepared for court. For Morrison, that was a goal of the first magnitude.

Another of author Bennis' observations about what makes for a creative work group is the curatorship mode of leadership. The curator takes care of the accomplishments of others; he is the enabler, not the inventor; the builder, not the creator. Morrison had every intention of being both inventor and creator, but his style was to "share the glory along with the work," in Spann's words. The Litigation Group would be a team of inventors and creators. Morrison might be first among equals, but the rest were equals where it counted. "One of the geniuses of Alan's organization of a group of large egos," Spann continues, "was his decision from the start that if you wrote the brief, you argued the case. I don't think this was any big conscious decision on his part; it was just the way Alan is. He wouldn't want someone taking a case from him, and he wouldn't want to take someone's case either." It may have been no big deal to Morrison to share the visible and fun side of litigation with his subordinates, but it certainly is not the norm either in private practice or in other public interest law firms. Eric Glitzenstein tells about watching a Sierra Club case being argued in 1994 while he was awaiting his turn to argue. The "kid" who had written the brief was "carrying the briefcase" for the "senior" Sierra Club attorney who was arguing the case. "We may have had to carry our own briefcases, but we carried them for our own cases," remembers Bill Schultz with satisfaction.

Because Morrison chose to define the agenda of the group broadly, he was also able to give the crew much more latitude in developing their own caseloads. "One of the marvelous things about working there," Mark Lynch relates, "was that Alan let us follow our own interests." There were cases that they had to do, of course, especially if another piece of Public Citizen or an allied group needed litigation assistance. But if there were an area of policy that particularly caught the eye of a Litigation Group attorney, he or she had the time and freedom to develop cases in it. "We don't have to take cases where we believe the other side is right. We can stick to our principles," Morrison notes. "We do things we think matter, which provides a reward in itself. I have the best caseload of any practicing litigator I know!" Said Lynch, now in private practice with one of Washington's most prestigious firms, "There were very few dreary cases at the Litigation Group." Morrison could not reward with money but he could reward with responsibility and considerable independence—which wisely he did.

Morrison could also reward with flexibility. A few Litigation Group attorneys have taken a break to pursue other interests and then returned. Morrison himself has taken time off to teach at Harvard Law School, at NYU Law School, at the Richardson School of Law at the University of Hawaii and at Stanford Law School. Litigation Group attorneys have written law review articles and even books during their tenure there. Arthur Fox, who has done both, asks, "Where else could you have the time to write the book and law review articles to advance your legal agenda that I had here?" The job offers all kinds of opportunities, Morrison points out. "We testify before Congress and agencies [and] take trips to speak and bring 'the word' to the public. We can write all we want to for journals and papers and give interviews to the press without fear of antagonizing some client. We can serve on committees and take fellowships with time off to try other things for a semester or year. The job is not just what we do but how we get to go about doing it."

What Morrison wanted in colleagues in his public law firm was more of what he was himself. He wanted people who would be as excited about the game they were in as he was, and equally in love with the intricacies and possibilities of the law. Most critical, because he would have to play the role of teacher if he was to turn neophytes into seasoned litigators, his young colleagues had to possess the sort of mind that could follow his rapid-fire thoughts. "Alan has this way of communicating that takes a while to get used to," Kathy Meyer comments.

> He starts a sentence, never finishes, jumps to another idea, tunes out, and then comes back in on an entirely different topic. In Alan's mind, once he has said the first four words he knows where he is going and you should too. I remember when I first came, I used to run out of his office and madly try to write down everything he said to make sense of it all. After a while I found myself finishing his thoughts, anticipating where he would go next, jumping in talking at the same time along with him and having a conversation end with no clear completion, and feeling completely satisfied with the whole thing.

Not everyone can connect with this communication style, and a few who signed on took longer to figure it out or left in frustration. "At first I was totally intimidated by Alan," Linda Donaldson admits.

> A conversation with Alan was a unique experience. First he would talk extremely fast and then he'd be talking away and in the middle of the conversation he'd turn and walk out of the room. I was convinced for the first few months that he had developed some sort of antipathy for me. But I finally realized this was just his way. Much of what I know about litigation I know from Alan. One of the things I most remember was his way of describing the different purposes of a brief and an oral argument. He'd say, "The brief is the how. The oral is the why." The purpose of the brief is to give the judge a good theory, a good reason on which to write an opinion—it is to tell the judge how to rule with us on the law. The purpose of the oral argument is to try to get the judge to want to go

our way. It is the oral that demands setting your case in the big picture, showing the human and policy impact ruling for or against us will have. Alan would tell us to use anything in our oral we've got going for us that an average person could understand as the real purpose we are here in court. Later, when I did some private litigation work, I found these lessons to be invaluable tools for advocacy. And when I taught, equally valuable teaching points.

Another Morrison "rule for litigation" as described by Ron Plesser: "Legal writing is not a mystery; don't save the best for last!" Morrison's simple dictate was always, "Be straightforward. Tell them what you will tell them. Tell them. Tell them what you told them."

With Morrison, it also helps to have the talents of a cryptographer. Spann tells a story on this point. "Alan has this horrible handwriting that looks like little squiggly lines. One time Bill Schultz was trying to interpret some comments Morrison had made on a brief. Unable to make anything of the scrawled remarks, Bill hung the brief on the bulletin board with a note: 'I'll give 25¢ to anyone who can decipher these comments—including Alan!' To this day Bill still has his twenty-five cents!"

At the "heart of every great group," author Bennis observes, "is a dream with a deadline." It is deadlines that force the talent of genius to turn a dream into reality. Otherwise, inertia and/or the search for perfection, rather than closure, rules. The nature of fighting with the law as the weapon means deadlines: statutory or court-mandated deadlines for filing actions, court-mandated deadlines for filing briefs and scheduling orals, schedules for filing comments in agency rulemaking procedures or for appealing agency decisions.

The Litigation Group's big dream—making the system fair—was pursued by following hundreds of smaller dreams: forcing aspirin makers to warn people about the dangers of Reye's Syndrome when aspirin is given to children with flu or chicken pox; getting access to documents about car safety; stopping companies from forcing employees to drive unsafe trucks; preventing lawyers from fixing prices for procedures like house closings; making the powerful occupants of the White House abide by the law that requires preservation of all presidential documents; and more. Morrison says,

> If you like being an underdog and being an outsider, you'll do fine here. But if you need the fancy lifestyle and to be part of the "in" group in town, you'll not be happy long here. Sometimes it is a role one can enjoy for a time until finances, especially the cost of educating children, hits. Financial needs have caused some to leave for the profit world. Sometimes one partner is the money earner while the other is here pursuing the cause. We are equal-opportunity avengers and we upset a lot of people. It makes some people uncomfortable to have so many people angry at them, and sooner

or later we seem to find ourselves on the other side of even some of our best past supporters. Our power is the power of persuasion and the ability to make a compelling argument. It is not the approach of the activist who pickets. It is slow and often frustrating because it requires passion contained. But, for those who find reason and logical argument comfortable, it is the best of the best careers.

The Litigation Group team Morrison formed in the early 1970s was young. It was energetic. It had a great leader trusted by all. It had an *esprit de corps*. It had a big dream that could be chased in hundreds of different ways, allowing each member an opportunity to fashion a weapon to his or her own liking. And it had deadlines. What it lacked in money and experience and political power it made up for in chutzpah and hard work. "It was," as Bill Schultz says, "like the best of academia, with no bureaucracy and no exams to correct, and the best of the litigation world, with no bill-paying clients to be ruled by or to serve." Moreover, although Morrison might not have foreseen the possibilities that lay ahead to play in the big league, events soon conspired to catapult his Public Citizen Litigation Group into the top courts of the land as it fought a wide variety of the big and powerful, including the highest political figure of all—the president of the United States. There were many unforeseen events, but perhaps the most consequential of all was Watergate. Just four months after Morrison came to Washington, on June 17, 1972, five burglars broke into the Democratic Party's campaign office in a complex on the banks of the Potomac known as the Watergate. The revelations that followed shook the very foundations of the nation's trust in its leaders. The Litigation Group began its life as the crusader at a time when mistrust of major institutions was rampant. Timing could not have been more auspicious for its launching.

What Morrison and his colleagues at Public Citizen could not have known was that the window for social reform would not remain open for long. Over the rest of the 1970s, the Litigation Group sank its fangs into dozens of legal issues, with some notable successes and a few disappointing losses. The corporate backlash of the 1980s, however, made its battles harder to fight and even harder to win.

5

The Litigation Group Cuts Its Teeth

In hindsight, the Watergate years seem like a time of political chaos that must have consumed the nation. At the time, though, the unfolding drama moved at a snail's pace with its full import yet to be understood. Morrison was just beginning his recruitment process, with only two young attorneys aboard, when five men carrying electronic surveillance equipment and wearing surgical gloves were arrested breaking into the Democratic national headquarters office on the sixth floor of a swanky Watergate office-apartment-hotel complex on the banks of the Potomac River. The date was June 17, 1972. News reports of this bungled burglary went virtually unnoticed at first by most readers; after all, what was one more break-in in the nation's capital? But this was no ordinary crime, and these men no ordinary criminals. This was political skullduggery with politically connected actors running the show. Their attempted crime was to plant a bug in the political opposition's headquarters so they could eavesdrop on the goings-on there. They were acting like CIA agents spying against a foreign enemy; but these men were not the CIA (though some had connections to it), and their target was our own people, not a foreign enemy. It was not until that fall that the story began to unfold of the broader scandal behind this break-in that would ultimately bring down a president.

On September 15, a grand jury indicted the five for attempted burglary and attempted interception of telephone and other communications and indicted two other co-conspirators, E. Howard Hunt, a former White House consultant and former CIA employee, and G. Gordon Liddy, a former White House staff member, former FBI agent and then counsel to the Finance Committee of the Committee to Re-elect the President (CREEP). Public reaction at first was little more than a murmur of distress—mostly disbelief at the stupidity of trying such a stunt and the amateurish execution by those involved. It was just about this time that the Litigation Group got involved in a political fight of similar contours. The litigation involved an effort to get files from the FBI through a Freedom of Information request.

Information is power, as the saying goes. In the never-ending dance of policymaking, Nader had learned that the opposite is surely true: no information means no power. In 1966, a year after publication of Nader's *Unsafe At Any*

Speed, Congress passed the Freedom of Information Act (FOIA). The new law held the promise of being a powerful weapon to pry information out of government agencies, but reality was not living up to the promise. Instead, "the deeply inured penchant for secrecy" of government agencies, as Senator Ted Kennedy (D- Massachusetts) put it, held sway. Information requests from the Naderites were delayed or refused by one government agency after another, forcing Nader's volunteer attorneys and the few staff attorneys at the Center and at the Public Interest Research Group to file court challenges. Creation of the Litigation Group offered the opportunity to mount a more coordinated and sustained legal attack against agency FOIA foot-dragging. Fortuitously, just about the time that Morrison arrived on the scene, the Stern Family Trust agreed to provide funding for Nader's groups to hire a FOIA attorney full-time who would become part of the new Litigation Group under Morrison's direction. The informal communications network of the Nader world sent out a hiring alert. Ron Plesser responded.

Plesser had been a LSCRRC (pronounced lis-crick), a Law Student Civil Rights Research Council intern, assigned to the Washington, D.C., ACLU chapter while at George Washington Law School. He was also a friend of Mark Green, who by 1972 had become one of Nader's principal deputies at another Nader affiliate. After his graduation in 1970, Plesser, unlike Green, had followed the establishment route by joining a New York City corporate law firm. The lead partner there was a famous First Amendment lawyer, and Plesser had harbored a hope of getting to work on at least some First Amendment issues. No such luck. "I was just making rich people richer," Plesser explains. "I could see the people ahead of me, the junior and senior partners, all doing pretty much the same stuff I was doing, at a higher level of course, but just more sophisticated and bigger versions of more acquisitions and sales. It was not at all what I really wanted to be doing. Then I got this call from Mark telling me that they had gotten this funding to do freedom of information litigation and had just hired this great guy to head up a new litigation organization for Nader. The salary would be $12,000. Was I interested in applying?"

"Anyway, I had this friend who was into this Eastern luck thing, you know where you throw some pennies and sayings come out from the way they land. We went out for drinks right after I got the call from Mark, and I told him about the decision I faced. So he said, 'Let's throw the pennies.' So I threw them and it came out, 'The prince in purple knee bands will come for assistance and you should follow.' We looked up to see what 'prince in purple knee bands' meant and it said this meant a great leader of the people. We had a roar over it. I decided to go down and try for the job."

"On George Washington's birthday down I went to be interviewed by Nader and Morrison," Plesser continues, "It was snowing out, and Ralph arrived in combat boots, not purple knee-bands, but it was close enough. On April Fools' Day, 1972, I arrived for my first day as director of the Freedom of Information Clearinghouse. Everyone in New York was kind of amazed I did it."

Plesser was the first of Morrison's Litigation Group team in the door. For a few weeks after his arrival the two of them were still housed behind the Tax Reform Group over on 15th Street in one big room. Within a couple of months Plesser and Morrison moved to the fifth floor of 2000 P Street, where they were joined by another new hire, Ray Bonner, a Stanford law graduate who had served as an attorney in the Marines during Vietnam. The offices on P Street were an improvement, as everyone at least had his own office. And comings and goings there were frequent. Plesser faced a big demand for help with freedom of information requests from inside Nader groups and outsiders as well.

The Litigation Group fought dozens of FOIA cases in these early years, but Plesser's victory against the FBI in the case of *Stern v. Department of Justice* was a crowning moment of his years at the Litigation Group. Just as was slowly becoming evident in the Watergate affair, what Plesser uncovered in *Stern* was evidence of a government out of control, using its power against the law and the people.

In September 1971, there had been a burglary of a FBI office in Media, Pennsylvania. Some of the "stolen" files made their way into the hands of NBC newsman Carl Stern. The files mentioned an FBI activity called COINTELPRO (pronounced co-in-tel-pro), a domestic counterintelligence program that appeared to have been mounted against a radical movement known as the New Left. Counterintelligence programs are an integral part of the international spy business. The CIA, for example, might send one of its agents to infiltrate a foreign government agency or foreign private organization in an effort to spy on and/or to disrupt the activities of that organization from within. To this end all sorts of classic spy tactics are used: sowing disinformation, planting compromising evidence about leaders, disrupting meetings and so on. But what Stern found in the papers from the Media break-in was something quite different. This was not a U.S. agency attempting to disrupt the activities of an enemy nation. It appeared to be a U.S. agency spying on and disrupting organizations of its own citizens. Stern filed a FOIA request with the Justice Department, in which the FBI is lodged, seeking records about COINTELPRO. On April 25, 1972, his request was denied by Deputy Attorney General Richard G. Kleindienst. "The information you seek is exempt from disclosure ... in that it is specifically required by Executive order to be kept secret in the interest of national defense or foreign policy," Kleindienst claimed. In addition, the information was protected from disclosure as "inter-agency or intra-agency memorandums or letters which would not be available by law to a party other than an agency in litigation with the agency."

Stern wrote back asking that the material be reviewed to see if it warranted being classified and assuring the department that he sought no documents that would "inhibit the free expression of opinion within the agency." Letters went back and forth between Stern and the Justice Department during the spring of 1972. By summer it became clear to Stern that it was going to take more than asking to get the documents he wanted. His network was not willing to foot the legal bill, so Stern turned to Plesser and the Litigation Group's Freedom of Information Clearinghouse for help.

Plesser and Stern fashioned a carefully structured letter to make it clear that "no one's expression of opinion about the program or information gathered in pursuit of it" was being sought. They also clarified that Stern had "no objection to being given the answer to my queries (i.e. when the program was authorized, by whom, the nature, purpose and scope of the program, changes if any or date terminated) with all other portions of the memoranda deleted."

Throughout the fall of 1972, as the widening scandal surrounding the Watergate break-in began to surface in the press, Stern and Plesser pressed on with their efforts to get the COINTELPRO documents. Each response from the Justice Department seemed to claim yet another FOIA exemption: internal personnel rules and practices, and investigatory files compiled for law enforcement purposes, were added to the national security and inter- or intra-agency memoranda exemption claims. An incredulous Plesser wrote on Stern's behalf again to the Justice Department in October. The last letter from the department "so misperceives the nature of my request," the letter noted, "that I assume it was intended as a bit of good-natured mischief. I couldn't care less about your internal personnel rules and practices. ... I don't wish to know who worked on it. I don't wish to know what they found out. I simply want to know what—as a matter of program and policy—they were directed to do, who authorized it, when, and what changes, if any, were subsequently made in that authorization." And then, lest the Department think Stern was going to give up if they just stalled long enough, the letter concluded with the attorney general's own words on the FOIA act: "'If government is to be truly of, by, and for the people, the people must know in detail the activities of government.' In that spirit, and with that purpose, I assure you I intend to see this matter through."

The election of 1972 came and went. Despite allegations of widespread Republican campaign law violations first reported by *The Washington Post* on October 10, 1972 (spying on Democratic candidates and their families, forging letters, leaking false information to the press, using the FBI to investigate Democratic campaign workers, planting disruptive demonstrators at the national convention, stealing confidential campaign files, among other charges), Nixon was re-elected in a landslide with sixty percent of the national popular vote and a majority in every state except Massachusetts and the District of Columbia.

Soon after Nixon was sworn in for his second term, the Justice Department wrote to Stern with a final denial of his request. It was time to go to court. On January 31, 1973, Plesser filed his case in the District of Columbia, asking the court to order the FBI to give Stern the documents he had requested. It was, they knew, a long shot. The FBI was an agency the courts seemed unwilling to order around.

Through the early months of 1973, there was no word from the district court on Stern's request. Meanwhile, a cresting wave of political scandal broke over the nation's capital. On January 30, 1973, former Nixon aides G. Gordon Liddy and James W. McCord Jr. were convicted of conspiracy, burglary and wiretapping for their role in the Watergate break-in. The convictions (and guilty pleas of five others involved) did little to quiet the bloodhounds in the news media. Reporters and editorial writers sensed a trail that ran higher into the administration than these two low-level presidential aides. Roused by the continuing media coverage, a week later (on February 7) the Senate voted unanimously to form the bi-partisan Senate Select Committee on Presidential Campaign Activities, chaired by Senator Sam Ervin, to investigate what was developing into "a political spy puzzle involving espionage and sabotage implicating White House officials and financed with hundreds of thousands of dollars in secret campaign funds." The suspicion that those seven burglars had not acted on their own in breaking into the Democratic Party presidential campaign headquarters was gaining wider credence.

The number of people caught in the scandal's wake began to grow. One of the first to go was L. Patrick Gray, the acting director of the FBI—the very agency that had been stonewalling Stern. Gray resigned on April 27 following reports that he had been directed in July 1972 by White House Chief of Domestic Policy John Ehrlichman and White House Chief Counsel John W. Dean to destroy documents belonging to E. Howard Hunt (one of the seven conspirators in the break-in who had pleaded guilty). So it seems the man who was denying Stern access to the COINTELPRO documents because they might affect the FBI's law enforcement responsibilities was himself breaking the law. Three days later on April 30, 1973, White House Chief of Staff H.R. Haldeman, Ehrlichman and Attorney General Richard Kleindienst resigned. The same day, Dean was fired. Less than three weeks later the Senate Watergate committee began its televised hearings, bringing the scandal into the living rooms of millions of citizens. With the pressure on, Nixon reluctantly agreed to the appointment of a special prosecutor. On May 18, the same day the Senate hearings began, new Attorney General Designate Elliot Richardson (who had been tapped to take over after Kleindienst resigned on April 30) appointed former Kennedy administration Solicitor General Archibald Cox to become the Justice Department's special prosecutor for the Watergate investigation. Though it was not clear then, these events marked the beginning of the end for the Nixon presidency.

In mid-June 1973, John Dean appeared before the Select Committee. Under oath and a grant of immunity, reading from a 245-page prepared statement for over six hours, Dean testified that he and President Nixon had discussed the Watergate cover-up "at a series of personal meetings—the first in September 1972 and many more in late March and April of 1973." He also claimed that Haldeman had cleared with the president ahead of time the plan to bug the Democratic headquarters at the Watergate. Dean's testimony opened a Pandora's box of dirty tricks and misdeeds involving the highest officials in the land, spreading way beyond a simple office break-in. The political fallout of forced resignations and federal grand jury indictments escalated.

Court deference to the FBI is afforded in respect of the agency's critical law enforcement role. Suits against the FBI are rarely successful. But judges read newspapers too. The nation's law enforcement agencies were not in a position of much respect in mid-1973 and District Judge Barrington D. Parker showed little reluctance to take on the FBI in his order granting Stern's request for the documents to be produced. The opinion came down on September 25, 1973. Judge Parker wrote:

> The Court's *in camera* review and inspection leave little, if any doubt that the communications here involved have nothing whatsoever to do with internal personnel rules and practices of the agency. ... Contrary to the assertions of the FBI Special Agent, the documents in question do not constitute such communications. ... [T]he documents themselves nowhere indicate any relationship between Cointelpro and law enforcement proceedings. ... The information sought does not relate to detailed investigatory activities of the FBI. ... The Court concludes that the government has not carried its statutory burden of establishing that the information is covered by the seventh exemption.

Although the government usually has sixty days to appeal, the judge granted a stay of the court order to deliver the documents if the Justice Department appealed within thirty days. But this judge added an unusual hammer. If the Justice Department did file an appeal, the stay would expire after forty days unless a brief were filed by the department with the court within that time. If an appeal were filed, the judge was ensuring that it would not be an appeal for delay purposes only.

Whether the Justice Department would have filed an appeal under different circumstances is anyone's guess. But the fall of 1973 was not an auspicious time for the FBI or the Justice Department. Since his appointment on May 18, Special Prosecutor Archibald Cox had moved vigorously to impanel a grand jury to aid his investigate the Watergate affair. The U.S. Constitution and federal law provide for a two-step process in criminal prosecutions. First, a panel of citizens known as a grand jury is selected to look at all the evidence against an individual. If the grand jury votes that there is sufficient evidence to proceed with a prosecution, then the accused is indicted and tried by a different jury of his/her peers. The grand jury need not find sufficient evidence to prove guilt; it need only find sufficient evidence to suggest that guilt is a reasonable possibility. The point of this double-staged citizen control is to prevent the prosecutor from becoming a persecutor. Its aim is not always realized. As one legal expert puts it, "The grand jury would indict a ham sandwich if the prosecutor asked it to." But still, its inclusion as a constitutional mandate in the Bill of Rights reflects the fear of putting too much control in the hands of a single individual.

To prosecute anyone for Watergate-connected activities, Cox needed first to get indictments from a grand jury, and to that end he needed to bring to the grand jury all the evidence available. Following the July 13, 1973, revelation by former presidential cabinet secretary Alexander Butterfield that Nixon had recorded all conversations and telephone calls in his office since 1971, Cox had tried to subpoena the tapes for his grand jury. Nixon refused, claiming "executive privilege." Cox turned to the courts for help. When on August 29, U.S. District Judge John Sirica ordered Nixon to turn certain tapes and papers over to the court for *in camera* inspection, Nixon refused and appealed. When Sirica's order was upheld by the U.S. Appeals Court for the District of Columbia *(Nixon v. Sirica)* in mid-October, Nixon attempted to fashion a compromise that would allow him to summarize what was on the tapes rather than turn them over. He announced his proposal to the nation just a few days later on October 19. Cox fired off a response: "In my judgment, the President is refusing to comply with the court decrees. ... I can not be party to such an agreement." Cox's statement made clear that he intended to fight on using all means, including the courts, to gain access to the tapes. The next day Nixon ordered Attorney General Richardson to fire Cox. In what has become known as the Saturday Night Massacre, Richardson refused and resigned. Then Deputy Attorney General William D. Ruckelshaus was ordered to do the firing, and he too refused and his resignation was demanded. The next in line of command at the Justice Department was Solicitor General Robert Bork. When ordered to fire Cox, he complied. This action by Nixon, aimed at containing the damage to his presidency, backfired. All hell broke loose. Calls for Nixon's impeachment came from around the nation. Almost immediately, the Litigation Group filed suit against Bork for the firing *(Nader v. Bork)*. Needless to say, the COINTELPRO documents issue was hardly the Justice Department's first priority at this point. But, to Stern and Plesser, these documents were important; indeed, they were potentially more critical evidence of an administration out of control and acting outside of the law. They pressed on.

On December 6, 1973, Acting Attorney General Bork caved in. He sent an assistant U.S. attorney over to the Litigation Group's headquarters at 2000 P Street to hand-deliver two documents. [Bork was the target of another Litigation Group case at this same moment—*Proxmire v. Bork*—a court challenge to his authority to be acting as attorney general since the president had not submitted his name to the Senate for confirmation.] Twenty-four years later, Plesser recalled the moment:

> When this guy delivered the documents I was so excited I could hardly read them. I grabbed the phone to tell Carl. He was over covering the Ervin hearings so I dashed downstairs and hailed a cab. When I got to the Senate Office Building I ran in and got a guard to call Carl out. "WE GOT IT," I nearly shouted. When he

read what I handed over he went nuts. What we had was even more damning than we imagined. That night it was the lead story on NBC news. There I was a twenty-seven-year-old who had helped expose an incredible misuse of power by those in one of the highest and most powerful offices of our country. It was the first time the FBI was ever ordered to turn over documents. It remains one of the most memorable moments of my life.

And what an exposé it was. One of the documents, a single page long, was a copy of the April 22, 1971, order to all FBI agents discontinuing "all COIN-TELPROS operated by the Bureau." What this memo revealed, though, was that not only had the FBI mounted a counterintelligence action against the New Left, but that it had run five other counterintelligence programs against other groups, including what the FBI documents referred to as "Black Extremists" (later documents would reveal this target included the Black Panthers and Martin Luther King Jr., among others), as well as the Socialist Workers Party, white hate groups and the Communist Party. The other document, dated May 10, 1968, described the agency's program for "Disruption of the New Left." Excerpts from this memo show just what the FBI was up to:

> Effective immediately, the Bureau is instituting a Counterintelligence Program directed against the New Left movement and its Key Activities. ... The purpose of this program is to expose, disrupt, and otherwise neutralize the activities of the various new Left organizations, their leadership and adherents. It is imperative that the activities of these groups be followed on a continuous basis so we may take advantage of all opportunities for counterintelligence and also inspire action in instances where circumstances warrant. ... We must frustrate every effort of these groups and individuals to consolidate their forces or to recruit new or youthful adherents. In every instance, consideration should be given to disrupting the organized activity of these groups and no opportunity should be missed to capitalize upon organizational and personal conflicts of their leadership. ... You are cautioned that the nature of this new endeavor is such that under no circumstances should the existence of the program be made known outside the Bureau and appropriate within-office security should be afforded this sensitive operation.

> The Bureau has been very closely following the activities of the New Left and the Key Activists and is highly concerned that the anarchistic activities of a few can paralyze institutions of learning, induction centers, cripple traffic, and tie the arms of law enforcement officials all to the detriment of our society. The organizations

and activists who spout revolution and unlawfully challenge society to obtain their demands must not only be contained, but must be
neutralized.

Who was this dangerous New Left the FBI was out to "neutralize"? It was a
hodge-podge of antiwar activists including many college students and the likes
of Dr. Benjamin Spock (of baby book fame) and the Reverend William Sloan
Coffin Jr. (the Yale University chaplain); civil rights activists, who included
many clergy from a wide variety of denominations, as well as students and the
members and leaders of the African-American community; and political candidates and Democratic Party members (especially in the Northeast) who were
trying to break the control of entrenched party bosses and move the party in
what they believed to be a more socially conscious direction. What were they
doing? Marching, demonstrating, writing editorials, speaking at colleges, staging
sit-ins, running for office, getting out the vote, exhorting the public to adopt
their causes—all the sorts of activities that those who cannot buy the powerful
use to try to influence the powerful. What did the FBI do to "neutralize" these
citizens? After many more documents were finally released, *The New York Times*
reported:

> A tactic commonly used was to spread information "to create dis-
> sension and cause disruptions" in the organizations. FBI informers
> planted false information identifying prominent members of the
> organizations as Federal agents. Infiltrators disrupted meetings
> sometimes proposing blatantly illegal actions that caused dissen-
> sion. (In one previously disclosed case, an FBI informer actually led
> in making plans never carried out to bomb the 1972 Republican
> convention.) Agents also distributed, often anonymously, false or
> unsubstantiated damaging information about prominent leaders to
> friendly members of the press, employers, business associates, cred-
> it agencies, family members, friends, and local law enforcement
> agencies. In some instances the information alleged sexual miscon-
> duct.

Plesser and Stern were excited by what they read in the two memos, but
from what was revealed they suspected that the agency was withholding a lot
more than it was giving. The day after receiving the documents, Plesser wrote
to the FBI noting the extent of Judge Parker's order and their intent to "seek
what remedies that are available to us" unless they were satisfied that Judge
Parker's order "has been fully complied with." The remedy remaining, of
course, was to return to the judge with a motion to hold the Bureau in contempt of court. The same day, Stern wrote to the FBI asking for all documents
in the five other COINTELPRO programs that had been listed as being "discontinued" in the one-page memo Justice had turned over to them. The day

after Christmas 1973, the FBI responded to Stern's new request. "I regret to inform you," the letter stated, "that the information you requested is contained in investigatory files compiled for law enforcement purposes and thereby is exempt from public disclosure." Plesser and Stern were dumbfounded. Was the FBI nuts? It had lost in court. It had not appealed the decision. It had turned over presumably identical documents about the COINTELPRO-New Left program. What was going on? They soon received a partial explanation in a formal letter as to why the two memos had been delivered to them on December 6.

> In view of the unique issue presented by this litigation and the closeness of the issue as to whether the documents come within the Court's Order, we have transmitted them to you. In our view, although the documents come within exemptions to the Freedom of Information Act, it might very well be that the Court would determine that they come within the purview of its Order. Under the circumstances of this case and in view of the fact that the Department has decided not to appeal, it has been determined not to pursue the matter further.

Needless to say, this was not a satisfactory explanation for why the other COINTELPRO documents should be withheld. Stern and Plesser pressed on, filing an appeal with the attorney general of the department's denial of their second FOIA request. Perhaps with bigger and more critical issues to address as the damage from the Watergate floodwaters continued to rise (erased tapes, fights with the Congress over whether the tapes or edited transcripts would be provided, etc.), Attorney General William Saxbe (who had been sworn in on January 4, 1974) granted the appeal on March 6, 1974. Sort of. The Department was attempting to gloss over its about-face by claiming that it was "modifying" the denial, not "granting" the appeal. "I have decided to modify the denial, granting access as a matter of administrative discretion to part but not all of the requested material," Saxbe's letter said. "The release to you of the records now being made available, like the release of the Cointelpro-New Left records made available to you by former Acting Attorney General Bork, should not be interpreted as necessarily indicating that this Department is in agreement with District Judge Parker's decision in your recent suit." Sour grapes, self-denial or just Washington double-talk? Regardless, Stern had his proof of FBI wrongdoing, and hopefully the bureaucrats at the FBI had learned an important lesson: sooner or later you will be exposed, so think twice before trying this sort of thing again. The point of the Litigation Group's vigorous pursuit of FOIA litigation is that government can be held accountable to the people only if the people know what their government is doing.

Other COINTELPRO targets, now aware of what had been going on, moved quickly to get information on what had been done to them. On March 22, 1974, for example, the Reverend Jesse L. Jackson, president of Operation PUSH (People United to Save Humanity), called on other black leaders to join him in a class action suit to subpoena COINTELPRO files dealing with actions against black activist groups. On November 17, 1974, three months after Nixon's resignation, the Justice Department finally released all the COINTELPRO documents, and Attorney General Saxbe held a news conference to make a public apology for these past "improper activities." He also announced that FBI Director Kelley had sent a memorandum to all FBI personnel, strongly reaffirming the Bureau policy that "FBI employees must not engage in any investigative activity which could abridge in any way the rights guaranteed to a citizen of the United States by the Constitution." For this promise to be kept (as with most promises from ever-changing government leaders) it would take an ever-vigilant watchdog—a reality the Nader organizations had well learned. When Senator Frank Church soon subjected the FBI's activities to sustained public view in what has become known as the Church Committee Hearings, Nader's organizations were there to add their support for legislation to limit the FBI's power to engage in clandestine activities in the future. Still, legislation, like internal rules, is useful only if enforced, and leaving the enforcement to the agency alone invites the potential of similar problems in the future. The Litigation Group and Stern had to go back in to court against the FBI yet again in the 1980s.

* * * * *

In another Freedom of Information Act case undertaken in its early years, the Litigation Group sought access to the vice presidential papers of Richard Nixon. *Brandon v. Sampson* became the first case, among many, in which the Litigation Group raised the questions of access to and control over the papers of the highest elected officials. The genesis of the Brandon case involved a bit of subterfuge.

In November and December of 1969, an appraiser spent six days examining four hundred and fourteen thousand items of general correspondence of Nixon as vice president (1953-1961); eighty-seven thousand items from the "Appearances File" of Nixon (1948-1962); twenty-seven thousand "invitations and turn-downs" correspondence (1954-1961); fifty-seven thousand items from the "foreign trips as VP" files (1953-1961); and fifteen thousand items from files involving the visit of Soviet premier Nikita Khrushchev to the United States (1961). All but a few of these items clearly represented files created in the process of the official responsibilities of Nixon as vice president. The appraiser fixed the "fair market value" of these six hundred thousand items that filled one thousand, one hundred and seventy-six boxes at $576,000. One is left to wonder how he reached this figure, given the inherent problem of placing a fair market value on such documents and the level of scrutiny possible given the time taken (six days total spent in the appraisal means a review of one hundred thousand items per day or, assuming an eight-hour day, twelve thousand, five hundred per hour). More to wonder, why was an appraisal made at all?

It turned out that the papers in question had been transferred from the executive office to the National Archives on December 30, 1968 (after Nixon's election to the presidency, but before he assumed office) and on March 27, 1969. Deputy Counsel to the President Edward L. Morgan signed a deed of trust on March 27, 1969, which purported to make a gift of these papers to the United States. The deed included a provision that restricted access to these documents during Nixon's presidency and made clear that the president would have the ability unilaterally to change the date on which the restrictions would be lifted (just a day before his resignation he did so, extending it to 1985). Some gift!

All this effort was aimed at income tax avoidance: an effort to sneak a deduction through before the law Congress had just passed, disallowing such deductions, went into effect in July 1969. The Nixons declared this gift as a tax deduction, saving over $200,000 in that year's taxes. In early 1974, Mr. Nixon was forced to pay a $467,000 settlement with the IRS over this tax deduction and other items. It is a safe bet, though, that these shenanigans would have gone unnoticed but for Watergate.

The Litigation Group's involvement in this began in October 1973, when Robert M. Brandon, director of the Tax Reform Group (a Nader organization) and Robert L. Kuttner, Washington editor of *The Village Voice*, looked into newspaper reports about how Nixon had donated his vice presidential papers and taken a tax deduction on them. Immediately, they called the head of the General Services Administration (GSA), Arthur F. Sampson, seeking access to the papers allegedly given to the people of the United States. Their request was denied. The next day Brandon and Kuttner had a letter (officially a FOIA request) hand-delivered to Sampson requesting access to both the "instrument of trust" entered into by Nixon transferring these papers to the people of the United States and to the papers themselves. On October 16, 1973, they were granted access to two documents, labeled chattel deeds, dated December 30, 1968, and March 27, 1969. Access to the donated papers was denied because of the restrictions placed in the deed by the president. Brandon appealed again to the agency head, and on November 19, 1973, the GSA issued a final denial, claiming that the pre-presidential papers are not "records" under the FOIA. Further, he claimed that the papers were specifically exempted because the Presidential Libraries Act of 1955 gave control over these papers to a president or vice president and that since 1934, the National Archives had treated the collected papers of presidents and vice presidents as their private property, rather than as publicly owned federal records. Brandon next wrote to Nixon explaining that the GSA had wrongfully denied him access to the papers and asking him to waive the purported restrictions upon access so that the American people could study the information they contained. He never got a reply.

In the meantime, they discussed their efforts with Morrison. "It was not so much that we wanted the papers," Morrison recalls, " but we saw this as a way to challenge the legality of the tax deduction, at least in the public eye, if not for the IRS." Many people believed at the time, and still do, that the public papers of government officials, including presidents and vice presidents, belong to the government and thus to the people. Some of the papers might still be subject to FOIA exemptions, of course, but to whom they belonged appeared to Morrison then and now to be obvious. "Second," Morrison continues, "Nixon had almost certainly backdated the deed after the tax law was changed to deny him the right to get a deduction (for something he didn't pay for, let alone own). He, of course, denied it, but if the deed were backdated, the restrictions were invalid, and more important, it would prove Nixon a crook." Given the timing of the case in conjunction with the Watergate revelations that fall, the latter end was an attractive prospect for a group not particularly enamored with the Nixon presidency by this point. "The beauty of this issue compared to the mess developing over the Nixon tapes was that it was a purely factual one," Morrison says, "on which we were clearly entitled to discovery."

On December 28, 1973, Larry Ellsworth (who had just been hired in September to take over the Freedom of Information position at the Litigation Group) filed suit in federal court claiming: (1) that the United States already owned all or almost all of the papers Nixon purported to give and to restrict access to; (2) even if Nixon did own the papers, there was no valid gift since the purported deed was not signed by him or his duly designated agent, and the restrictions contained were so extensive that the transaction was nothing more than a transfer of custody; (3) that there had been no valid acceptance by the GSA because it could not accept a deed not validly executed and the restrictions were so excessive that it would constitute an abuse of discretion for acceptance as a gift. Ellsworth asked for a court order directing the GSA to grant access to the documents. After filing in court, Ellsworth sought a court subpoena to take the deposition of Edward Morgan. The administration attorneys countered with a motion for a protective order and a motion to dismiss the action. Within weeks, Morgan, who at that point was an assistant secretary of the Treasury, resigned. The issue that clearly seemed to prompt that resignation was his role in signing the VP papers' gift deed. "Nixon Papers Figure Resigns: Aide who Handled Nixon Papers Quits," was the headline on the front-page *Washington Post* article. As noted above, Nixon had to pay the tax—the gift was no gift and/or did not make it in time because of the defect in the deed (Morgan's unauthorized signature). The U.S. Treasury won, but the Litigation Group lost. The district court would not let it depose Morgan, and on April 3, 1974, granted summary judgment to the GSA. Ellsworth appealed.

Briefs and reply briefs were filed with the Court of Appeals for the D.C. Circuit during the summer and fall of 1974. The appeal was derailed for more than two years by a much bigger presidential paper issue—Nixon's post-resignation effort to secure control of all his presidential documents, using much the same tactic as the district court judge allowed to stand in *Brandon*. On

September 7, 1974, less than a month after resigning, Nixon signed an agreement with Sampson providing for deposit of the Nixon presidential materials with the GSA, but retaining "legal and equitable title" and arranging for destruction of some of the material. (After all, he had gotten away with this tactic in *Brandon*, so why not try it again? How different things might have been had the district court been more receptive to the Litigation Group's arguments back in April.) What followed was a maelstrom of suits challenging the agreement and a flood of editorials decrying the chutzpah of this dethroned president. Congress's reaction was swift and clear. Within three months the Presidential Recordings and Materials Preservation Act was passed. It provided a specific procedure for dealing with the Nixon presidential materials and clarified the government's ownership of all future presidential materials. Nixon then sued the government, claiming that the Presidential Recordings and Materials Preservation Act was unconstitutional *(Nixon v. Administrator of General Services)*. Because of the similar issues in *Brandon*, the appeals court ordered that the case be deferred pending disposition of the Nixon suit. It took until 1977 for the Supreme Court to rule against Nixon and uphold the preservation law.

On December 22, 1977, the appeals court reactivated *Brandon* and overruled the lower court, stating that "the grounds relied on by the District Court in summarily denying appellant's claim for access were erroneous." The decision to "cut off discovery and grant summary judgment before a proper record could be developed," was inappropriate because, even without adequate discovery, the appellant raised "serious questions not addressed by the District Court, about Mr. Nixon's intent to impose restrictions, the procedures followed in establishing the restrictions, and the application of the statutory exemption to the materials involved." The court then ordered the district court to allow discovery to go forward and then to consider the merits.

On remand, the district judge held a status conference (a meeting of the judge and counsel from both sides) for the purpose of establishing a schedule for discovery. Faced with the certainty of discovery regarding the circumstances under which the 1969 deed was prepared and delivered, Nixon immediately undertook settlement discussions. The judge extended the time for submitting a proposed schedule for depositions and briefing several times to allow for negotiations toward a settlement to proceed. Then on March 22, 1978, Nixon signed a letter revoking the access restrictions and opening the material for research and historical uses. Who can doubt, given the long fight Nixon put up to prevent access to his presidential papers and tapes, that the impending deposition was the key element in prompting his action here?

In light of the settlement, the Litigation Group attorney (Ellsworth had by then left the Group so it was a new attorney, Diane Cohn, who was acting on Brandon's behalf) agreed to a stipulation of dismissal. In effect, they had won just what they set out to win, though it had taken nearly five years to do so. It was a reason to celebrate. What would come next, however, was most disheartening. To get paid, the Litigation Group would have to return to court, a process that went on until May 1981.

6

Taking on the Imperial Presidency

Knowing what is going on is the critical first step in citizen control over the government. Acting on that knowledge to force accountability is the next. Morrison was determined from the start to use all the litigation hooks available for holding the government accountable to the law, the Constitution and the people. The opportunities that seemed to call out for litigation strategies against high-level administrative actors seemed to be everywhere in those first two years.

One of the first big cases the Litigation Group undertook involved the question of separation of powers, a concept that is implicit in the constitutional design of three branches sharing the power to govern. The framers intended to create a system of checks and balances to prevent the government from becoming tyrannical.

To govern under the Constitution, at least in the domestic sphere, it takes the cooperation or at least the acquiescence of all three branches—legislative, executive and judicial. (The president's power over foreign policy and national defense is, by Constitution and long practice, considerably greater.) If a domestic policy problem exists that a president believes requires a government solution, he is not free to order one on his own. Congress must pass a law for the government to have the power to act, but the law is not a law unless the president signs it (or Congress passes it by two-thirds in both houses over a presidential veto). If citizens are harmed by the executive's effort to implement a law, they may challenge the executive's actions in court. It is the courts' power to interpret the meaning of the law or the Constitution if such a case is brought before it. The president is the head of the executive branch, but he is not free to choose his subordinates on his own. Unless the office is an "inferior office," the president must secure the consent of the Senate for the people he wishes to appoint. The president takes an oath to faithfully execute the law. The Constitution does not give presidents the power to pick and choose which laws are worthy and should be followed; the expectation is that all laws must be enforced.

All these procedural necessities can be frustrating for a president with an agenda that is not shared by the Congress (or by the courts for that matter). But what was perceived as mere roadblocks by the executive were in Morrison's mind *the law* and thus a part of the critical protections for the people against the exercise of arbitrary and capricious power. This carefully wrought design for decisionmaking was created by men who well understood, as one author puts it, that:

> [D]emocracy is built on the assumption that one's rulers are not perfect. ... That is why there must be institutional checks and balances and a maximum of public visibility and accountability in the decision making process. ... Democracy is precisely about the priority of means over ends, since it rests on the belief that agreement cannot be reached over ends unless a sound deliberative process is in place.

Though Nixon's November 1972 re-election had been a landslide victory, it had not brought him a Republican Congress. Both houses remained firmly in the control of the Democrats. To pursue his agenda of cutting the size and scope of the federal government, Nixon could not count on support from Congress. One strategy he had been using for the past two years with much success was to simply refuse to spend funds appropriated by law. From 1970 through 1972, the nation was experiencing significant inflation, estimated variously at between 6 and 8 percent per year. This was quite a jump from the 3 to 4 percent inflation rate that had been the norm over the two preceding decades (though nowhere near as high as it would become by the end of the 1970s). Nixon and many economists believed that high inflation rates were being driven by the galloping growth in government spending that they attributed to the costs of funding President Lyndon Johnson's Great Society programs and to the Democratic Congress's penchant for spending on highways, environmental programs (especially sewage treatment plant construction grants to municipalities) and other district "pork" goodies. Congress passed appropriation bills. Nixon signed them into law. Then the president "impounded" some of the funds that the law directed be spent.

Congress had given presidents the power to withhold appropriated funds under limited circumstances (to effect savings when program objectives could be achieved for less than the amount appropriated by Congress or to apportion expenditures over the fiscal year to prevent year-end shortfalls, for example). But nowhere in the Constitution, nor in any law at that time, was there any grant of power that would allow a president to refuse to spend appropriated funds simply because he did not like the program or because he wanted to fight inflation. Indeed, in 1972 Congress failed to pass a bill supported by Nixon that would have put a ceiling of $250 billion a year on government expenditures and provide the president with the power to cut appropriated funds in excess of that ceiling. When the spending ceiling bill died, Nixon boldly declared his intent to withhold appropriated funds anyway. By the 1972

November election, federal courts were being flooded by cases challenging Nixon's impoundments of billions of dollars intended for a wide variety of programs, including highways, education, job training, housing, Indian health and food stamps. Though the administration was losing most of these cases in court, this did not seem to act as much of a deterrent. After hi re-election, Nixon set his impoundment ax swinging with renewed vigor.

At 2000 P Street, Morrison and his Litigation Group joined the impoundment battle. The struggle for power between Congress and the president over expenditure of appropriated funds was hurting a lot of folks. It was not just a question of which branch would win, but whether the constitutional design that set up separate branches with built-in checks and balances would continue to perform its protective purpose—to protect against any one branch or any one actor becoming too powerful and thus being able to use that power to harm the people. Over the next two and a half decades, Morrison's passion for the separation of powers and balance of powers issues would land him in the center of nearly every major constitutional struggle of this sort to come before the courts. He would tackle questions of presidential appointment power, legislative vetoes, presidential line-item vetoes, deficit reduction gimmicks and more. Morrison soon became a recognized expert on this topic. Some even call him *Mr. Separation of Powers*. The impoundment cases were where he cut his teeth.

The case that sparked Morrison's interest was *Missouri v. Volpe*. At Nixon's order, Transportation Secretary John A. Volpe had refused to release highway building funds that the law directed be given to the state of Missouri. The state had won in the district court on August 7, 1972. An appeal was filed by the Justice Department on behalf of Secretary Volpe in the U.S. Court of Appeals for the Eighth Circuit. In its argument at the district level, Missouri's attorney had focused more on the highway fund law and its mandates than on the constitutional separation of powers issue raised by presidential use of impoundment power and its potential intrusion on Congress' power of the purse. Morrison believed he could add important arguments for the court to consider about impoundment's constitutional implications. The only way to get into the case was to file an *amicus* brief. To accomplish this, though, he either had to get the permission of the litigants in the case (both Missouri and the Justice Department) or the permission of the court.

Congress has long delegated to the courts the power to make their own procedural rules. One such rule limits who can file *amicus curiae* (friend of the court) briefs. *Amicus* briefs allow interested "bystanders" who are not parties to the case to raise important information for the judge's consideration. *Amici* need not show direct injury, but not just anyone can file such a document, or courts would be inundated with excess, duplicative and extraneous material. Courts want to be certain that a brief will add new information that the litigants in the case do not raise. The litigants want to be sure the balance of power in the argument does not shift by the addition of outside players. Morrison knew these hurdles existed.

What he needed most was a client for whom to speak. The obvious client was Nader's newly created organization, Public Citizen. Given the different perspectives of Nixon and Nader, the likelihood of getting the Justice Department's approval for this client seemed remote. Morrison and Nader talked. Why not try to get members of Congress to join in their brief? After all, it was laws passed by Congress that Nixon was gutting by his impoundments, and it was the citizens in states of senators and districts of representatives who were suffering as a result. Some bigwigs could add clout to their request to file and thus perhaps persuade the Justice Department, or if that did not work, persuade the court to let them in. Morrison set one of his new hires, Tommy Jacks, to work investigating who in Congress might be persuaded to join their effort.

Jacks was, as Morrison recalls, "a tall, gangly Texas boy with long sideburns, a boyish laugh with a sort of deferential Southern manner" who had come to work for Nader after law school and a clerkship for a judge in Baltimore. He was "very savvy with a lot of good ideas." Morrison's nose sniffed the sort of talent he was seeking and hired him right after the clerkship in September 1972. Jacks did not end up staying long at the Litigation Group; the pull of Texas roped him back in just two years, and there he became a highly regarded and successful plaintiff's trial lawyer. Back in 1972, though, this greenhorn was tackling the president of the United States.

Jacks drew up a list of twenty-four senators plus six Missouri representatives and nine other representatives who might be willing to get involved in the case. One of the measures Jacks used in selecting members was who voted against the $250 billion spending ceiling that had been defeated in the Senate in 1972. Jacks then fashioned a letter for Nader to sign. Just after Thanksgiving, thirty-nine letters went out to the best prospects. "I am writing to invite you to join me and Public Citizen in submitting an *amicus* brief," the three-page Nader letter began. In the middle of the letter Nader raised an issue that twenty-five years later Morrison would bring to the Supreme Court in another case challenging line-item veto power Congress gave to President Bill Clinton:

> Finally, the Founding Fathers clearly intended to limit the veto power by requiring that the President veto only entire bills and by providing for a Congressional override; yet by impounding funds appropriated by Congress, the President may effectively exercise an "item veto," avoiding the potential embarrassment of a public veto announcement and the risk of a Congressional override.

Nader's letter included another carefully structured appeal to the audience he was attempting to persuade. "On another occasion, during a televised interview with ABC correspondent Howard K. Smith, Nixon offhandedly dismissed as 'games' hearings of the Senate Judiciary Committee's Subcommittee on Separation of Powers concerning impoundment."

With the help of Michael Pertschuk, then a staffer on the Senate Commerce

Committee chaired by Senator Warren G. Magnuson, they managed to round up the chair of every Senate committee. Leading the list was Senator Samuel J. Ervin Jr., chair of the Government Operations Committee. (While the impoundment issue was in the courts, Ervin, as already noted, was selected by his colleagues to head the Senate committee investigating the Watergate scandal.) Another who agreed to sign, Senator Robert C. Byrd, would become the named plaintiff in the challenge to the line-item veto that Morrison would bring in the late 1990s.*

In addition to the chairman of every standing committee in the Senate, the *amicus* brief included a few other senators (notably Hubert H. Humphrey) and a few representatives (including Morris K. Udall). Last on the list was the newly created Public Citizen organization. With the deadline for filing looming, Jacks set to work writing their brief. As was the norm, Jacks ran drafts and ideas by Morrison, who worked them over and pressed him to refine and sharpen the argument. One door to getting into court was closed on December 13 when the Justice Department denied their request for consent to file an *amicus* brief. The Justice Department brief was due at court on December 26 and, under court rules, their brief was due the same day. Now Jacks had another task facing him, to prepare a motion to the court to persuade the judge to let them in. They missed the deadline, but with everyone pitching in on the research, typing, editing and copying over the week between Christmas and New Year's Day, Jacks was able to file both his motion and brief on January 2.

"The issues confronting this Court overshadow any damage, albeit considerable, which has been suffered by the plaintiff [the state of Missouri] in this case," Jacks' brief argued. "Of far greater concern is the erosion of fundamental constitutional concepts, which Senator Ervin summarized when he stated:

> In this era, the powers of the executive branch have become dominant in the operation of the governmental structure. The power of the purse is one of the few remaining tools which Congress can use to oversee and control the burgeoning Federal bureaucracy. Congress is constitutionally obligated to make legislative policy and is accountable to the citizens for carrying out that obligation. The

---

*The other senators who agreed to sign onto the Litigation Group amicus brief included James O. Eastland, president pro tempore and chairman, Judiciary Committee; Michael J. Mansfield, majority leader; Robert C. Byrd, assistant majority leader; Jennings Randolph, chairman, Public Works Committee; John L. McClellan, chairman, Appropriations Committee; Howard W. Cannon, chairman, Aeronautical & Space Sciences Committee; Thomas F. Eagleton, chairman, District of Columbia Committee; J.W. Fulbright, chairman, Foreign Relations Committee; Vance Hartke, chairman, Veterans' Affairs Committee; Henry M. Jackson, chairman, Interior & Insular Affairs Committee; Gale W. McGee, chairman, Post Office & Civil Service Committee; Warren G. Magnuson, chairman, Commerce Committee; Lee Metcalf, chairman, Joint Committee on Congressional Organization; Frank E. Moss, chairman, Aeronautical & Space Sciences Committee; John Sparkman, chairman, Banking, Housing & Urban Affairs Committee; John A. Stennis, chairman, Armed Services Committee; Herman E. Talmadge, chairman, Agriculture & Forestry Committee; and Harrison A. Williams, Jr., chairman, Labor and Public Works Committee.

impoundment practice seriously interferes with the successful operation of that principle and places Congress in the paradoxical and
belittling role of having to lobby the executive branch to carry out
the laws it passes.

The attorneys at the Justice Department were not happy. Here it was just six
days before oral argument and they were faced with a thirty-nine page brief
that focused the case on an issue they were trying to avoid. With lightning
speed they filed an opposition motion objecting to the Litigation Group's effort
to broaden this case from a question about what they claimed was just a short-
term deferral of funds into a major constitutional confrontation. In a footnote
to their objection, Justice Department attorneys alleged that the Litigation
Group had stated that the reason they were asking to join was because they
believed "that appellee's (the state of Missouri) brief would be inadequate."
Jacks had a new problem; placating what was sure to be an angry state attorney. As soon as he read the Justice Department's motion on January 4, he was
on the phone. "As I told you by telephone," he wrote the next day, "I was most
disturbed ...[and] particularly incensed by the statement in footnote 1. ... We did
not even suggest in our request to the Justice Department that we desired to
file an amicus brief because of any doubt on our part concerning the 'adequa-
cy' of the briefs that would be filed by the State. ... I was surprised and embar-
rassed that the government attorney attempted to so mischaracterize our statements."

Oral argument in the case was scheduled for January 8. There was nothing
now to do but wait. Jacks got a call on Friday, January 5, from the clerk of the
court. Not only was their brief accepted, but the court was asking them to come
to participate in the oral argument (a fairly unusual request for an amicus).
Torn between excitement and terror, Jacks raced into Morrison's office with the
news. The Monday oral was just three days away and Jacks had never argued
a case in a court before. As Morrison recalls, "This was not the case we wanted to have as his maiden voyage—not with thirty-nine of the most powerful
members of the House and Senate to represent, a matter of this significance to
argue and no time to prepare him." There was barely time to get plane reservations and get out there. Morrison packed his bag and headed for Missouri. It
was then, and remains, an exception to the Litigation Group norm that the brief
writer gets to argue the case.

Morrison does not remember much about the oral argument itself, but the
memory of the event remains vivid:

The moment the court was called into session, the presiding judge
said, "Will the attorney for Senator Ervin and the others please step
forward?" A chill went up and down my spine when I realized that
the judge was talking about me and that I was representing not only
Senator Ervin, but the chairman of every single standing committee

in the Senate.

Three months later, on April 2, 1973, the court announced its ruling. It was a win, albeit by a split (2-1) vote of the appeals court panel. Morrison prepared a summary for his clients. "On the merits the Court adopted the approach urged by us," his letter noted. It also had adopted their argument for the jurisdiction and political question issues. "[O]n the question of subject matter jurisdiction," Morrison pointed out, "the statute which it relied on was argued only in our brief." Over the next two years, the Litigation Group continued to monitor the impoundment cases that were being filed around the country as Nixon and then President Ford continued to wield the impoundment ax in the name of fiscal responsibility. Where they felt it necessary, and there was the opportunity, they filed *amicus* briefs. One of the cases they were involved in that arose in neighboring Virginia (over a veto of clean water appropriations) was a big win for Jacks in both the district and appeals courts. *Cert* was granted.* by the Supreme Court (along with the impoundment case *City of New York v. Train*, which became the lead case name in the consolidated cases). This time Jacks got to argue, though he almost did not. The reason he almost did not illustrates the bizarre atmosphere of government versus the people that seemed to pervade so much of those Watergate earthquake years. The Supreme Court clerk had mailed a notice to Jacks informing him that he was to be granted fifteen minutes to argue at the oral argument. Three weeks passed before the notice was delivered to 2000 P Street. It was the U.S. mail and what seemed to be an orchestrated effort to intercept Litigation Group and other Nader organizations' mail that nearly sank Jacks' chance at oral argument this time. Although the mail story discussed next is not central to the work of the Litigation Group, it does give a flavor to what was going on in Washington at the time.

* * * * *

In the fall of 1974 (following Nixon's August resignation and thus during the Ford administration), the Litigation Group and a number of other Nader organizations began to notice a problem with their mail delivery. Letters addressed to one organization (for example, the Litigation Group) were showing up, after what appeared to be many days delay based on the stamped mail date, at other Nader offices (some at the Center, some at Congress Watch, etc.). Nowhere on the envelope was there any indication that the recipient was other than the Public Citizen Litigation Group or the attorney there or the address anything other than 2000 P Street. Some mail was being delayed an inordinately long time even when it made it to the right address (including the notice from the Supreme Court to Jacks, which was three weeks in transit). On October 9, 1974,

---

*Since 1925, the Supreme Court has had the power to pick and choose which cases to accept on appeal. Acceptance is done by granting a writ of *certiorari*, or more simply stated by granting *cert*.

the Litigation Group secretary wrote to the Central Post Office, Delivery and Collections department, noting the problem and asking that it be "checked into as soon as possible." The answer was pure bureaucratese: we've looked into the matter and concluded that it is just human error; we'll make sure it does not happen again. But, after a short hiatus, the problem began again. Morrison began to wonder if there was more to this than simple Post Office incompetence.

Then came a revelation. The United States Postal Service, at the request of certain government agencies, including the CIA, FBI and even the Department of Agriculture, routinely conducted domestic mail surveillance on citizens, entirely without their consent or knowledge. This news came via testimony of CIA Director William Colby. In January 1975, Colby told a Senate subcommittee that the CIA had been reading the mail of selected American citizens for twenty years. Included among the targets was a member of Congress. Not only were many citizens subjected to invasions of privacy, many more were subjected to a process known as a "mail covers" search. Using Form PS 2000, Postal Service agents recorded the name, address, the date and place of postmark, and the class of mail involved. This information was then forwarded on another form to the government department that had requested the surveillance. The process is called a "mail cover" search because it is just the envelope, not its contents, that is the subject of the surveillance (that such mail is sometimes opened was clearly a possibility). By law such searches were to be only for the purpose of furnishing "an investigative lead to assist in protecting national security, locating a fugitive or obtaining evidence of commission or attempted commission of a crime." Representative Robert W. Kastenmeier (D-Wisconsin), chairman of the Subcommittee on Courts, Civil Liberties and the Administration of Justice of the House Committee on the Judiciary, reacted immediately to this "threat to civil liberties" by requesting that the chief postal inspector supply an analysis of the use of mail covers for 1973 and 1974. The analysis revealed that more than thirty-five separate agencies (national, state and local) requested more than four thousand mail covers for those years. In addition, more than two hundred and fifty mail covers for national security purposes were ordered. Of course all this made its way into the newspapers.

When Morrison read the news accounts, he decided to find out whether the Litigation Group was a target. He conferred with a friend at the law firm of Williams, Connolly and Califano who agreed to act on the Litigation Group's behalf. This was, after all, a government agency interfering with the sanctity of the attorney/client privilege. It was an intrusion that was utterly repugnant to the legal community. Who knew how many others might have been (or would be) similar targets? It was a tailor-made issue to get the big guns to go to bat for them. Joseph Califano Jr. (soon to be appointed head of the Department of Health, Education and Welfare in the Carter administration), vented the legal community's ire in a February 17, 1975, letter to the postmaster general:

No lawyer who is subject to a government mail surveillance can continue to practice effectively and to represent his clients adequately. A surveillance intrudes upon the confidentiality of the attorney-client relationship by making known to government officials the identities of persons whom the attorney may be representing. It also may reveal to the government the identity of witnesses with whom the attorney is in contact, and, where the government is a party to the litigation, may result in the possible intimidation of those witnesses. Furthermore, the existence of a mail cover at least suggests the possibility that mail has been opened, particularly in those instances where the cover results in delays and misdeliveries. Where delays do occur, serious consequences may result for the lawyer who must respond promptly to legal papers and comply with deadlines imposed by the courts. The operation of a mail surveillance against any attorney plainly violates the constitutional rights of both the attorney and the client and should never be maintained on the basis of a secret request by a government official. While the practice is particularly repugnant where the surveillance is of an attorney, a mail cover on any citizen violates both the right of privacy and the right to use the mails, unimpeded by government officials.

Califano's letter asked that any mail covers on the Litigation Group be discontinued immediately and that the Postal Service provide pursuant to the Freedom of Information Act all regulations, guidelines or policy statements on mail covers and any and all records of mail cover requests made by any agency against any member of the Litigation Group or any other Nader organization.

Under attack, the Postal Service moved to quiet its accusers. Tours were offered of the mail processing centers and "all cooperation" was promised in finding the problem. The tours occurred; the "all cooperation" part was, in Morrison's opinion, a sham. One of the Service's mail cover regulations, provided to the Litigation Group under its FOIA request, stated that, "If the Chief Postal Inspector, or his designee, determines a mail cover was improperly ordered ...all data acquired while the cover was in force shall be destroyed, and the requesting authority notified of the discontinuance of the mail cover." No provision for notifying the citizen subject to the illegal mail cover search was included in the regulations.

On March 27, Califano again wrote to the Postal Service noting that, with this regulation, it was quite possible that any mail cover files on the Litigation Group might have been destroyed. Califano made many requests for further investigation and information in this letter, but little was forthcoming. Following the findings of the Rockefeller Commission that the CIA was involved for more than twenty years in covert mail operations, intercepting millions of letters annually, Califano wrote again (in July), this time to CIA Director Colby and FBI

Director Clarence M. Kelley, as well as to the postmaster general. In each letter he asked for any and all information about any mail cover or mail intercept operation of any kind with respect to the Litigation Group or any of its attorneys. The only thing that was forthcoming was an admission that a letter to Litigation Group attorney Reuben Robertson from an academic friend doing research in Russia in 1966 (which covered such critical national security issues as the fact that the friend had lost forty-two pounds, that the concerts were great and the food not, and the library frustratingly slow and overburdened with red tape) had been opened and copied by the CIA. The bad press surrounding the post office's involvement in such surveillance resulted in some fast footwork in the blame-avoidance game and a more cautious agency in the short run but little real structural or procedural change to ensure that such transgressions could not occur again.

* * * * *

Jacks did get to argue before the Supreme Court though he almost didn't for another reason: he barely qualified to join the Supreme Court Bar in time. The third anniversary of his admission to the bar, which is the minimum experience required, came just in time. In fact, it was so close that Jacks had to go to court to be admitted on the morning of the argument. Of course, to prepare for this big event he was "mooted" by his colleagues. "Most moot court presentations are disjointed and awkward," Larry Ellsworth says, "but not Tommy's. He was smooth, understated and compelling." It was a performance that was replicated in front of the real court and rewarded soon thereafter when the court ruled the impoundment power unlawful on February 18, 1975.

By that time, though, Congress had taken matters into its own hands. Angered by Nixon's continued impoundments, Congress passed a new law, the Budget and Impoundment Control Act (BICA), part of which set up a specific process that presidents had to follow for "deferring" or "rescinding" appropriated funds in the future. Before long another Republican president (Reagan) would try his hand at circumventing this law and the Litigation Group would be back again fighting the executive in court. The BICA law allowed a president to defer expenditure of some funds for a year, but the level of congressional mistrust of the executive was evident in the "legislative veto" provision also included. Deferrals had to be reported to Congress and either house could force the expenditure by voting to veto the president's deferral. The Litigation Group and other Nader organizations had been very active in pressing for inclusion of the impoundment provision in the budget act. Both Nader and Morrison testified on the Hill. "At the time," Morrison recalls, "I did not even notice this legislative veto provision in the impoundment law." In two years time, congressional provisions adding legislative vetoes to dozens of other laws would lead to one of the biggest separation of powers cases in history and one of Morrison's and the Litigation Group's biggest Supreme Court victories (*INS v.*

Chadha).

* * * * *

Despite lower court rulings against presidential impoundments, Nixon continued to use the strategy to cut spending in programs he did not support (and since the Supreme Court did not rule until after he resigned, he just kept it up). Often he got away with it since not every impoundment was challenged in court, and those that were took months or years before a court order (if one was forthcoming) forced the reinstatement of the funds. Still, this method reaped only partial results. Fresh from an overwhelming re-election victory, a determined and still cocky second-term Nixon administration moved on other fronts as well. One weapon he had was the public relations armada of the presidency and the executive branch. Orchestrating a unified administration message about the need to cut spending was the goal; the dissemination of "information kits" to all executive branch departments detailing what everyone should say was the means. Nixon's effort to create a harmonious executive chorus for budget-cutting became the subject of another Litigation Group challenge in what became known as the "Battle of the Budget"—a White House staff-orchestrated effort to use the entire executive establishment as one big public relations firm to defeat congressional proposals that would increase the president's proposed budget then being worked on in Congress.

On April 4, 1973 (just two days after the Litigation Group and its congressional clients won in the *Missouri* impoundment case), *Washington Post* reporter Mike Causey's column "The Federal Diary" led with "PR Men Gird for 'Battle of the Budget.'" He wrote:

> The Nixon administration is mobilizing the bureaucracy's extensive and expensive public relations apparatus for an attack on the "spendthrift" Democratic-controlled Congress. To make sure voters get the same message, federal writers have been given a detailed set of guidelines by the White House, telling them how to warn taxpayers of the dangers to their pocketbooks if Congress tampers with the President's budget. The guidelines, obtained by this column, tell government specialists how to write speeches warning of tax increases, and give lists of 15 federal programs to be hit, anti-congressional "one liners" to be used by officials on the banquet circuit, and examples of "horror stories" to be used in spotlighting federal programs Mr. Nixon wants to end. ... Kits called "The Battle of the Budget, 1973" were distributed yesterday morning to top agency officials and public relations aides.

What Causey was reporting was not an entirely new approach (Kennedy and Johnson had rallied the administration to push anti-poverty programs and civil rights, and Johnson had used the administration to build support for the war in Vietnam), but the apparent scope and central-control feature of Nixon's public relations campaign far surpassed what had come before. Moreover, the attack-oriented nature of the whole effort was unprecedented and definitely something that would not fly with the Democratic Congress once it was known—and in leaky Washington it was inevitable that it would be found out. As Causey noted in a follow-up column two days later, "Mandatory use of White House-approved phrases in talks and press releases indicates the administration has declared all-out war on congressmen who back programs the President doesn't and that the bureaucracy's unmatched communications resources will be used to beat Congress over the head." The campaign was organized down to the finest detail (with the "same thoroughness—and many of the same techniques—they used in the last election campaign," as another reporter noted). The man behind the kits was Ken W. Clawson, a former *Washington Post* reporter who would soon be appointed the administration's information director. On April 8, columnist David Broder joined the battle. He wrote:

> Weeks ago ...Clawson announced to the agency information chiefs that the President wanted his hold-the-line budget drive given top priority in every possible forum. Applying this doctrine, Clawson ordered a quota of one "economy" speech per week for every presidential appointee in the department or agency. Last week, the quota was tripled. ... Target areas were identified—mainly small to medium-sized cities with conservative Democratic or liberal Republican congressmen. Agency public relations men were told to coordinate their principals' speaking plans ...in order to avoid overlapping appearances and to assure maximum coverage.

Broder reported many other strategies (two editorial page commentaries per week, recorded budget messages for radio stations, etc.). The "Battle of the Budget" kits included sections on sample speeches illustrating Nixon's position on the budget, sample anecdotes showing what could happen if Congress had its way in the budget process, and pages of polls supporting the president's justifications for defense spending and his effort to cut the rest of the budget. The kits also included a number of one-liners, such as: "Now that the election is over, the old, recurring disease of 'spending sickness' is once again reaching epidemic proportions with some members of Congress." And: "This may look like a Santa Claus Congress—but it's got a bag full of bad news for the taxpayer." And this: "When one man helps himself to another man's bank account, that's called embezzlement. But when a big-spending Congressman helps [himself] to the taxpayer's income with higher prices and taxes, then it's called 'compassion.'" And this: "Some people on Capitol Hill seem to have the power of the purse mixed up with the power to declare war on the American taxpayer."

Over at 2000 P Street, Morrison followed the unfolding "Battle of the Budget" story with considerable interest. He set Tommy Jacks to work investigating what the law said about executive lobbying efforts of this sort. There were two relevant laws—the Lobbying with Appropriated Moneys Act of 1919 and section 608(a) of the current fiscal year's appropriations bill for the Treasury, Postal Service and General Government. Both pieces of legislation forbade the executive from using funds appropriated by Congress to influence any member of Congress or oppose any legislation or appropriation by Congress. Since all the money that executive branch officials can spend comes from funds appropriated by Congress, these laws amount to forbidding the president from lobbying Congress. Of course, presidents and executive branch actors always try to influence what Congress does, and, of course, Congress wants and seeks input from executive actors. But information and influencing are one thing; orchestrated campaigns, another. Orchestrated campaigns undercut the ability of Congress to get the full range of information and to hear the full range of opinions from the enormous variety of experts in the executive branch.

Perhaps what the Battle of the Budget illustrates most starkly is the different views of the executive branch. Is the executive branch like a corporation that is directed by the president? Or is it one piece of a three-part government structure in which the department heads are directed by the law and congressional oversight as well as by the president (the courts can also be included as a player here, having the power to direct a department to follow the law or Constitution)? The Nixon administration looked at the executive branch as a hierarchy with him at the top—his word, his plan, his ends were what should rule. The congressional perspective was different. The president is head honcho, of course, but he and his team in the executive branch are beholden first to the law, and the law is what Congress creates. Senator Hubert Humphrey (D-Minnesota) moved quickly in response to the *Post* articles by calling for an investigation by the General Accounting Office and an analysis of possible illegalities by the American Law Division of the Congressional Research Service (CRS), the two agencies created by Congress for this purpose.

Jacks and Morrison moved equally quickly. On April 20, 1973, Jacks filed a complaint for declaratory and injunctive relief against Ken W. Clawson. Their next action was to subpoena Clawson, the architect of the budget campaign, to be deposed. This illustrated the power of a court case. Clawson could deny news reporters' requests for interviews or simply say "no comment." But he could not deny a deposition subpoena and he would be forced to answer the questions asked and do so under oath.

On April 19, the CRS delivered to Congress the results of the investigation that had been requested by Humphrey. Eleven days later, Comptroller General Elmer Staats submitted the GAO's report. Both agencies found Nixon's budget kits to be in violation of the appropriations and anti-lobbying laws. It was great news for Jacks because these were powerful players corroborating the Litigation Group's position that the kits were illegal. Jacks' first action was to request expedited discovery. This is a request to have the court order the opposition to respond to interrogatories (written questions) and schedule depositions (oral questioning under oath) without delay. The hearing before Judge Parker (the same judge who would rule that fall for Plesser and Stern in the FBI case) did not go well. As Jacks described in a memo:

> During the hearing on our motion for expedited discovery, Judge Parker indicated that he was not very impressed with our allegations. During the course of my oral argument he interrupted me when I began to describe the unprecedented nature of the PR campaign being waged over the Battle of the Budget. He asked how old I was and indicated that, in his view, all this is pretty much old hat. If we are going to convince him that this is illegal conduct we are going to have to marshal some really compelling facts.

Nonetheless, the judge granted their request and on May 2 Morrison and Jacks deposed Clawson. It was a frustrating deposition, Jacks recalls. "We had thought that by going to Clawson we would be able to grasp everything at its source." It became clear from the deposition that the PR campaign was far more disjointed and less centrally directed than they thought. Their "dragon" was really an "octopus," as Jacks described it. "To slay the beast we must join as defendants all the PR officers in the various 'tentacles' [by this he meant all the executive departments] and initiate a rather lengthy and expensive series of depositions and engage in other types of discovery. Only by doing this can we develop the factual background necessary to convince Judge Parker that this was an extraordinary campaign and not the usual run-of-the-mill puffery on the part of the Administration." Given the Litigation Group's limited resources, this was not an attractive prospect. Fortuitously, the need to marshal those facts was made moot just a few days later when Clawson began to recall the kits, and by mid-June, the government submitted an affidavit to the court stating that the PR kits had been recalled, that all copies had been recovered, and that a decision had been made not to reissue them. Soon after this, the judge dismissed the case as moot. The president's PR effort succumbed to its own bad PR. There is little doubt, though, that the threat of the suit, and the power to get the answers from those involved that a suit allows, had hastened the demise.

* * * * *

Impoundment and budget PR kits were two of Nixon's weapons in his war to eliminate the programs he opposed, but there were others as well. From the start of his second term, Nixon moved vigorously to use his other executive branch weapons, one of which was people. Nixon sought like-minded budget-cutters to appoint to agencies he wanted to get rid of.

One of the president's prime targets was the Office of Economic Opportunity (OEO) and especially its Legal Services program (a legal aid program for the poor and a program dear to the hearts of many powerful Democrats in Congress). The goal was to kill Legal Services as well as a number of other OEO programs and then to shut down the OEO. The president sought an OEO director who would be sympathetic to this goal and on January 31, 1973, appointed Howard Phillips as acting director. The president, undoubtedly well aware that his nominee would not be approved by the Democratic Senate, did not send his name to the Senate for confirmation. Phillips took over at OEO with sword slashing. Within weeks, he ordered that no grants to Legal Services programs be approved for a period longer than thirty days; added new requirements that would delay the grant review and approval process for months; ordered that grants expiring after February 28, 1973, not be approved pending further instructions from him; fired subordinates in the agency who voiced support for Legal Services; and withdrew existing delegations of authority to regional directors who did not toe his political line. The end result was that the flow of grant money to Legal Services programs around the country slowed to a trickle, causing many offices to close down. Lest anyone miss his intentions, Phillips made them crystal clear in comments to *The Washington Post* on February 17, 1973: "I think Legal Services is rotten, it will be destroyed."

The next day Ralph Nader sounded the trumpet for battle in an op-ed piece. "The federal program providing lawyers for the poor," Nader wrote, "is heading for destruction." His article described the role Vice President Agnew had played over the past year in attacking the Legal Services program by making "wild unsupported smears [which] were widely reported in the media but subjected to no challenge as to their veracity." He then provided an example of Agnew's "bellowing." "A destitute mother of five can't get legal help with an eviction notice but a middle class dropout can get legal counseling in setting up his underground newspaper," he quoted from news reports of Agnew's statements. "The record of legal services supports precisely the opposite of what he describes," Nader continued. "Poverty lawyers have served millions of poor people in their difficulties. They have pioneered in the courts and obtained decisions which overcame local and state government lawlessness, expanded the rights of consumers, tenants and workers and advanced more just procedures to give citizens fair notice and hearing by government bureaucracies." Then he sent a warning: " [W]hat is happening to legal services will likely soon happen to other programs for the elderly, children who need day care, the mentally retarded, juvenile delinquents, the hungry."

Phillips and the president soon discovered that law and Constitution matter; that the ends they sought could not be obtained by ignoring both. Legal Services had some pretty powerful allies, not the least of which was the American Bar Association (ABA). When the ABA objected to Nixon's campaign to kill Legal Services, the White House reacted by abolishing the ABA-sponsored advisory committee to OEO, which was supposed to shield the legal services program from political meddling. Days later, a partner from Covington & Burling, one of Washington's most powerful law firms, wrote to Phillips on behalf of the National Legal Aid and Defender Association (the Washington-based national organization of Legal Services attorneys). The ten-page letter was an indictment of actions by the new OEO acting director that detailed the "damaging and imminently threatened disastrous impact on the Legal Services Program." It also requested a meeting with Phillips to determine "what action you propose taking to restore lawful order and fairness of administration" and to determine "what steps we should advise our clients to take to protect their interests." That the "steps" included the possibility of suit was abundantly clear. The February 28 meeting produced a few bones of compromise from Phillips, but the administration's goal of killing both Legal Services and the OEO remained firmly in place.

On February 23, 1973, Senator Harrison A. Williams, chairman of the Senate Labor and Public Welfare Committee, wrote to the president urging him to submit a nominee to be director of the OEO since the position was being filled by an acting director who had not received Senate approval. The Litigation Group's work on the *amicus* brief in the impoundment case was not only rewarded by an invitation to argue in the appeals court, it earned the group a lot of visibility and new contacts among the senators and their staff as well. Among these was an attorney on Williams' committee staff. When the possibility of litigation in the OEO affair was suggested, the staffer sought Morrison's advice.

Section 601(a) of the Economic Opportunity Act, which created the OEO, required that the director "shall be appointed by the President, by and with the advice and consent of the Senate." Recognizing that a president might need to fill temporary vacancies due to death or resignation, Congress had provided as early as 1792 for temporary appointment power. But aware of the potential for abuse of such power, Congress by the mid-1800s restricted temporary appointments to ten and then thirty days and restricted the actions of the temporary appointee to performance of the duties of the vacant office. In practice, a flexible interpretation has allowed for longer temporary appointments if the president has submitted a nominee to Congress but no action has been taken. But the Phillips' acting appointment was not about congressional foot-dragging. Nixon's intent to circumvent the Senate was blatant; he knew that Phillips would never be confirmed by the Democratic Senate. So Nixon figured his temporary appointee would just charge in, get the job done and leave. Senator Williams was not about to sit still for this direct challenge to Congress's constitutional power.

On March 14, Morrison filed suit on behalf of Williams and three other senators in the U.S. District Court for the District of Columbia, seeking an order for the removal of the defendant Phillips from his position as acting director.

Morrison hung the challenge on both statutory and constitutional hooks. "The attempted circumvention of this statutory mandate by the addition of "Acting" to the defendant's title cannot be permitted to stand since by this device the Executive would be able to avoid the clear intent of the law and the precedent would become a basis for avoiding the constitutional requirements of Senate confirmation of other officials in the Executive branch," Morrison wrote. He had one stumbling block in making his case, though. The thirty-day limit law applied to military and executive department officers. The OEO was neither; it was one of those "twilight zone," independent agencies placed in the executive branch but not part of any executive department. Morrison had to provide the legal logic to pull the OEO under the thirty-day limit law. To this end he combed the record of congressional debate at the time of passage and subsequent amendment of the law. Poring over dozens of yellowed pages in what was called in 1868 the *Congressional Globe* (the early version of today's *Congressional Record*), Morrison found his historical proof. "Senator Trumbull, the principal senatorial sponsor of the 1868 law that set up the temporary appointments limits, stated that it was his intention that "the bill should repeal all other laws inconsistent with it." Then quoting from the Trumbull's remarks on February 14, 1868, Morrison continued:

> the intention of the bill was to limit the time within which the President might supply a vacancy temporarily in the case of the death or resignation *of the head of any of the Departments or of any office appointed by him with the advice and consent of the Senate ...* but lest there be any misapprehension about it the second section [now 3349] is intended to be very full and to repeal all other laws on this subject, *so that the whole law in regard to supplying vacancies temporarily will be in this one act.* (emphasis added by Morrison in his brief)

Even before Morrison began to work on the court challenge, several local community action agencies (who also were being denied funds by the OEO) and the American Federation of Government Employees (the national union representing the fired OEO employees) had filed suit in the same U. S. district court. When Morrison filed his case, it was assigned to the same judge. An effort to consolidate all the cases against Phillips failed when the government objected. The other cases went ahead with argument scheduled for March while the *Williams* case was scheduled for a later date. Morrison went to work on his brief and delivered it to the court on April 12. His prognosis for winning looked particularly bright at that moment. The day before, on April 11, U.S. District Judge William B. Jones had ordered Phillips to halt his termination of OEO programs and declared past orders to break up the OEO null and void. The judge's opinion paralleled the reasoning set forth in many of the district and appeals court decisions against presidential exercise of impoundment power: the OEO had been authorized by Congress; money had been appropriated to fund its programs; presidents cannot undo authorization and appropriations law by "budget message" (Nixon had announced his intent to end the OEO in his 1973 annual budget message to Congress); the money must be spent. Judge Jones noted that "if the power sought here were found valid, no barrier would remain to the executive ignoring any and all congressional authorizations if he deemed them, no matter how conscientiously, to be contrary to the needs of the nation." The judge also noted that if the executive "wishes to abolish an agency it must submit a reorganization plan to Congress." And finally, he noted that Phillips had failed to comply with legal provisions requiring publication of "all rules, regulations, guidelines, instructions and application forms in the *Federal Register*" thirty days before they can become effective. Phillips had lost on every point raised by the plaintiffs.

The district court had ruled Phillips' actions illegal and ordered him to halt his efforts to terminate OEO programs, including Legal Services. But, as a scathing letter from counsel for plaintiffs to the Justice Department on April 27 makes clear, the court order was not having much effect at the OEO. "National and regional OEO personnel, who unquestionably are agents of defendant Phillips, have continued to enforce various phase-out instructions, in clear violation of the Court's Order. ... This indifferent (and in many respects openly defiant) response by OEO to the Court's Order is causing considerable confusion ... and damage." Stopping Phillips was going to take something more.

Now it was Morrison's turn. His goal was to chop the acting director off at the feet and have him booted out. On May 21, he stood before Judge Jones, whose order the OEO was ignoring. Jones was from Montana and quite conservative, but as Morrison recalls, "a no-nonsense judge who was not about to stand for shenanigans in his courtroom. When he concluded that the Justice Department was playing with his court for its own ends, he came down hard."

On June 11, Morrison's motion was granted. The court ruled that "defendant Howard J. Phillips is serving unlawfully and illegally in his position," and enjoined him from taking any action as acting director. On nearly every point the judge adopted the reasoning in Morrison's brief. (It is useful to place the timing of this case into the Watergate events. The resignations of Ehrlichman, Haldeman and Kleindienst, and the firing of Dean occurred on April 30, and the televised Senate Watergate hearing began on May 18. In mid-June, just after Judge Jones' ruling, Dean testified about Nixon's involvement in the cover-up. Nixon administration shenanigans were likely to be viewed with more suspicion at this point.)

"Judge's ruling plucks OEO from trash heap" and other such news headlines were triumphantly waved around the Litigation Group headquarters, and a victorious call was made to Morrison, who was speaking to a Western Massachusetts PIRG on that day. But the celebrators were quickly forced back to work. The Justice Department immediately filed an emergency motion for a stay pending appeal with the U.S. Court of Appeals for the D.C. Circuit. Delay was the game and time was working for the administration.

At that time, the federal government's budgetary fiscal year (FY) ran from the beginning of July to the end of the next June (for FY 1973, it thus ran from July 1, 1972, to June 30, 1973). That meant that if the clock ticked on for just nineteen more days, the authority to spend the money Congress had appropriated for OEO programs for FY1973 would expire, and thus the refusal by Phillips to spend those funds would result in killing most of the OEO programs. Well aware of this potential, Morrison pounded out a brief in opposition. Meanwhile, Senator Williams sent a formal letter to Nixon:

> Yesterday ... the U.S. District Court ... ordered Mr. Phillips' removal ... I therefore urge once again that you promptly submit for Senate approval a nominee qualified to be Director of OEO so that the work of this important agency may go forward in accordance with the plain intent of Congress.

The Nixon administration ignored Williams, choosing to try to beat the clock with an appeal. A week after the court order removing Phillips, Morrison was back fighting the Justice Department attorneys in court, this time before an appeals court panel of Judges James Skelly Wright, Harold Leventhal and Spottswood William Robinson III (Leventhal and Robinson were both appointed to the appeals court by President Johnson; Wright was appointed by President Kennedy. It was a potentially more receptive panel than it might have been).

On Friday, June 22, in a unanimous *per curiam* (unsigned) opinion, the appeals court denied the government's motion: "We do not believe appellant has shown sufficient likelihood of success on the merits to warrant a stay." Then, to clarify how the agency was to proceed if the district court's order forbidding Phillips to take any further actions as head of the OEO were followed, the appeals court remanded the case to Judge Jones, giving the judge the authority if he "concludes that circumstances warrant further relief, in this case" to amend his order. "In the interest of justice ... and the public interest," the appeals court explained in a footnote, "we see no reason to require the formality of a notification by the District Court, followed by a formal remand of the case to permit the entry of such amendment, under the normal procedure." The higher court judges were obviously well aware of the ticking clock and the need for speed if the lower court orders were to be enforced. They were just as obviously not about to cooperate with the administration's effort to use the budget clock to circumvent a court order.

Three days later, on Monday, June 25, Judge Jones held a hearing. The burning question was how to spend the $142 million of grants and contracts that the OEO had been holding up before June 30. The amount of money to be spent in the next few days was almost as much as the OEO's budget request for the next fiscal year. The Justice Department attorneys now claimed that the reason the agency was paralyzed and unable to act was because the court had removed Phillips. It was all the judge's fault. Was the judge supposed to believe that someone who had been flagrantly ignoring his order for over two months would suddenly be converted and obey a second order from him? An incredulous Morrison responded, "OEO's argument that it is paralyzed is an excuse for it not to do what it did not want to do—fulfill the purpose for which OEO was created." At the end of the hearing, the judge ordered the OEO to deliver by 10 a.m. the next day a list of names of current OEO personnel with grant-making power. The administration got the message: this judge was not going to let the clock run out if he could help it. The day after the court hearing, Nixon appointed Alvin J. Arnett as director of OEO and sent the name to the Senate for its advice and consent.

On June 27, Judge Jones announced his rulings. First he made absolutely clear that Phillips was out: "To re-establish [Phillips] in that position would make a mockery of the law and would exceed even the liberal bounds of equity." Then he allowed that given the emergency nature of the current situation, Arnett could serve as director while the Senate considered his nomination. Arnett might be director, but his marching orders issued from the court:

> Arnett or persons acting under valid delegations of his grant-making power ... are ordered to consider all pending applications for grants or benefits of funds ...to be made from fiscal year 1973 funds by 12:00 noon on June 30, 1973, and to notify all applicants for funds of the decisions rendered on their applications by telegram or other means to assure that the applicant knows of the decision by 12:00 noon on June 30, 1973; if any of those grants are denied, the Director shall inform the grant applicant of that decision, along with full findings and conclusions on which the denial is based as soon as practicable but in no event later than 12:00 noon on June 30, 1973.

Judges rarely issue such detailed orders to executive branch officials. Perhaps it was the blatant disregard both of the law and his own earlier order that prompted this judge to flex the judicial muscle more than usual. Perhaps the Watergate scandal goings-on at that moment also stiffened judicial resolve. At any rate, the judge's actions led to more celebrations at the Litigation Group headquarters. A bunch of twenty-somethings and their mid-thirties general had taken on the president of the United States and the bigwig attorneys at the Justice Department and won. If they could do this, anything was possible. Two months later, Morrison received a letter of appreciation from the National Legal Aid and Defenders Association. "The events of the past two months have shown that your efforts and those of your colleagues have been successful beyond belief. There is a new director of the Office of Economic Opportunity and almost all of the poverty programs are again serving their clients."

* * * * *

Morrison would soon be back in court with another temporary appointments case, this time involving Robert Bork, who had been serving as acting attorney general since the Saturday Night Massacre on October 20, 1973. But before this, Morrison and Nader went after Bork for firing Special Prosecutor Archibald Cox. "I never thought that Bork was personally to blame for the firing," Morrison notes. "Mostly he was caught in a position over which he had little control." Of course, Bork could have quit, as did Attorney General Richardson, or refuse to act and been ordered to resign, as Deputy Attorney General William D. Ruckelshaus was, but sooner or later someone in the chain of command would have obeyed the president and for the sake of the Justice Department's other critical business the need to keep some top-level leadership in place was paramount.

When the Watergate firings were reported by the news media, Nader was on the phone to Morrison immediately: "We have to do something!"

"We agreed to meet at my office on Sunday morning, along with some others," Morrison remembers, "and we got hold of the regulations establishing the Special Prosecutor Office." There they found the legal hook to challenge the action. The Justice Department had issued a formal rule published in the *Federal Register* on June 4, 1973, when Cox was appointed, that forbade his removal except for "extraordinary improprieties on his part." As Morrison well knew, the courts had long settled the question of the binding nature of an administrative rule on the agency that issued it. The Justice Department had made its rule, now it had to abide by it. As usual, the first stumbling block Morrison faced was finding a client who could get standing in court. Nader was more than willing to serve and indeed was listed as the plaintiff when they filed suit on October 29. But they were well aware that Nader's claim of injury might not survive the court's standing barrier. Basically the best he could claim was that as a citizen and taxpayer he was harmed by the Department's failure to follow the law. The taxpayer standing question was another generally settled issue, because unless one could claim a First Amendment harm (and the case law really seemed to restrict this to an Establishment Clause claim), taxpayers had no standing to sue. Morrison set out to find some clients who would be more likely to pass the standing hurdle. Again he turned to Congress. Senator Frank E. Moss (D-Utah) and Representatives Bella S. Abzug (D-New York) and Jerome R. Waldie (D-California) signed on. The addition of these plaintiffs as an amendment to their suit proved critical. It was also "a wonderful stroke of luck when we got Judge Gerhard A. Gesell for the case, as he was a man of great ability and willingness to take on people whom he believed were doing the wrong thing," Morrison says.

At the first hearing on the case on November 9 (to address whether an injunction should be issued to reinstate Cox and to decide whether the case should proceed to be considered on its merits), one of the first actions taken by Judge Gesell was to drop Nader as a plaintiff, saying he was just a "volunteer" who had no legal standing to sue. The judge also denied their request for an injunction, noting that Cox had not joined the case and that a new special prosecutor, Leon Jaworski, had been appointed and sworn in on November 5. Judge Gesell stated that he felt that "the public interest would not be served by placing any restrictions upon his [Jaworski's] on-going investigation of Watergate-related matters." But the judge did allow the case to continue, turning down the Justice Department's claim that, since a new special prosecutor had been appointed, the case was now moot. On the contrary, the judge noted that a ruling in the case could have an effect, as claimed by congressional plaintiffs in their affidavits, on consideration of bills pending in Congress for an independent special prosecutor or of impeachment resolutions in the House.

On November 14, just a few days after the hearing, the court issued its ruling in the case: "The Court declares that Archibald Cox, appointed Watergate Special Prosecutor was illegally discharged from that office." The win did not get Cox back, but it served an important purpose. Notice was given loud and clear to the president and the country that Nixon had overstepped his bounds in ordering Cox fired. The hoped-for result was that it would ensure that such an action did not happen again. Even though Nader was dismissed as a plaintiff, the case went down in history as *Nader v. Bork*.

Bork continued in his position as acting attorney general throughout November and into December. On November 20, Senator William Proxmire (D-Wisconsin) wrote to the president stating that in his opinion Bork had been unlawfully acting as attorney general since the thirty days expired on November 19 and requesting that the president either submit Bork's name or another nominee to the Senate for confirmation. A week later the White House counsel replied to Proxmire stating that the thirty-day limit did not apply to the Justice Department. Proxmire turned to the Litigation Group, whose success with the thirty-day limit issue in the OEO case for Senator Williams made them the experts on the issue. On December 6, Morrison filed a complaint asking the court to declare that the thirty-day limit of the vacancies act applied in this case and to enjoin Bork from continuing to act as attorney general. Four days later, the president submitted the name of William Saxbe to the Senate for consideration. Morrison tried to press on for a declaratory judgment as he had in *Nader v. Bork* case, but this time it did not work. He was not able to persuade the court to rule on the question of whether the Justice Department had to follow the thirty-day rule. On March 1, the case was dismissed as moot.

By the time Nixon resigned on August 9, 1974, the two-and-a-half-year-old Public Citizen Litigation Group, by then numbering seven attorneys, had made its mark in the Washington legal community. The executive branch, and especially the powerful Justice Department, had learned that, though youngsters and greenhorns they might be, they could not be ignored. These bright young lawyers had quickly figured out how to play in the big leagues. Members of

Congress turned to them for help (or were willing to cooperate with them when they requested) in reining in an executive branch that was out of control. The big legal firms of Washington, D.C., learned they were a power in court to be respected and reckoned with. Federal judges quickly came to appreciate the thoroughness of their preparation and the creativity of their legal arguments (even when they ruled against them). Throughout the Watergate scandal, they had played a visible role in well-publicized efforts to hold the government accountable to law and Constitution. But this was only a small part of their litigation agenda during those first years and explains only a small part of how their reputation grew.

7

Information Is Power

Creation of the Freedom of Information Clearinghouse as part of the new
Public Citizen Litigation Group provided a critical service not only to other
parts of the growing Public Citizen network but to dozens of other public interest groups and individuals. Prior to Ron Plesser's arrival on the scene, most
legal actions under the 1966 Freedom of Information Act (FOIA) were brought
by big businesses. Economic stake and economic resources made litigation possible for the likes of pharmaceutical giant Bristol-Myers, but it was simply too
expensive for most public interest groups or individuals. Now there was a place
for the "little guy" to turn, and turn they did. From the day of his arrival, Plesser
was inundated with questions and pleas for help.

One of the first requests came from Mal Schechter, publisher of the newsletter *Hospital Practice*. On January 9, 1970, at a Medicare-approved nursing home
in Marietta, Ohio, thirty-two patients perished in a blaze traced to flammable
carpeting and inadequate fire safeguards. Schechter asked the Social Security
Administration (SSA) for its inspection and other relevant records on the
Marietta facility and fourteen other facilities that he knew also had suffered
fires. Schechter wanted the information on these known fire incidents to provide his readership (mostly doctors serving senior citizens) with accurate and
up-to-date information about the conditions in nursing homes. The administration refused each and every one of his repeated requests over two years.

Nader had read an article by Schechter about the problems he was having,
so when he ran into Schechter at a meeting he asked: "What are you going to
do about it?" Schechter replied, "Ralph, there isn't much I can do about it
because I don't have the wherewithal to go to court." When Nader offered help
from the Litigation Group, Schechter immediately accepted and called to schedule a meeting with Plesser. On April 11, 1972, Plesser filed a complaint against
Secretary Elliot Richardson of the Department of Health, Education and Welfare
(HEW, the department in which the SSA was lodged) in the U.S. District Court
for the District of Columbia. Plesser had been aboard only eleven days, and this
was just one of several new cases already headed to court.

On April 14, a grateful Schechter wrote a letter of thanks to Nader for
launching him on "a career as a litigant. ... Whatever emerges from the courts

after the investment of cerebrum, adrenaline, and gastric pH, I reap a great psychological plus from the opportunity to associate with ... Alan Morrison, Ron Plesser and all. I would buy a used car from any of them." In what amounts to lightning speed for the courts, just three months later, U.S. District Judge Joseph C. Waddy granted Plesser's motion and ordered HEW to produce the reports for Schechter's inspection and copying within twenty days. HEW provided the reports Schechter had specifically requested. It was not the end of the matter, however. On October 16, 1972, Schechter requested access to the reports on several other nursing homes. He anticipated no problem. After all, a court had ordered production of similar reports and the SSA had complied. His assumption was quickly proved wrong.

"We must decline to comply with your request," the SSA responded. "The United States District Court, in the case to which you refer, directed the Department to make available to you Medicare survey reports on fifteen named nursing homes, and this order was obeyed. The Department has not acquiesced, however, in that ruling." The court had ruled; no appeal was taken; the Department complied. But the Department still thought the court was wrong, and it was not going to budge.

The tragic fire in Ohio that led to Schechter's original FOIA request also had prompted the Senate Committee on Aging to hold hearings during which the deputy commissioner of the SSA had admitted that more than one hundred and fifty of the four thousand Medicare-approved nursing homes were "fire-traps." He then said that this information had not been made available to the public. Members of Congress were appalled and pressed for action. In response, the SSA issued proposed regulations that called for publication of all future surveys concerning the conditions in any institution participating in the Medicare program. But the SSA was holding fast to its argument that past surveys were exempt from disclosure despite the judge's order in *Schechter v. Richardson*, an order that had specifically stated the survey reports were not exempt under any provision of the Freedom of Information Act or of the Social Security Act. So it seemed that until the new regulations were final (and that could take months or years), no surveys would be public and even then past surveys would remain secret.

The administration's rationale for refusing to release past data was that it would be unfair to make public the safety data that a nursing home provided unless the nursing home knew ahead of time that it would be made public. The law gave the SSA the power to require a nursing home to submit safety information if it wanted to be a Medicare-certified facility, but the agency also believed it had the power to withhold the data and had agreed to do so. Thus, the agency argued, the nursing homes had presumed the data they sent would be for HEW's eyes only. Behind the administration's decision to promise secrecy seemed to be a belief that, if a nursing home knew information it provided would be released, it would refuse to provide it or would provide inaccurate information (and thus the agency would not know of problems and could not try to get them corrected). But the SSA did not need to rely on nursing homes to volunteer information; it had always had the means to force compliance through legal action or withdrawing a nursing home's Medicare certification if false or misleading information were submitted. Was the agency afraid it could not force compliance or just reluctant to cause financial harm or embarrassment to one of its regulated companies? Where, Schechter wondered, was the department's concern for the elderly people who were forced to use nursing homes? It seemed to be yet another example of a government agency that had lost sight of its real mission. To get the documents he now wanted, Schechter would have to go back to court, and for this he again turned to Plesser.

The problems Schechter was having were hardly an isolated case. The SSA was not the only recalcitrant bureaucracy. The penchant for secrecy was widespread and persistent despite the FOIA's demand that public agencies make all their documents available to the public unless that Act specifically exempted a document or class of documents from disclosure.

* * * * *

Ever since passage of the Administrative Procedure Act in 1946, federal agencies have been required to publish procedures and rules in the *Federal Register* (a daily official publication of the U.S. government) and to make publicly available all final opinions, statements of policy and staff manuals, and to maintain an index of this information. But the 1946 law permitted agencies to exempt from public disclosure "any matter required for good cause to be held confidential." With this broad discretion, agencies erected walls of secrecy around their actions that frustrated the efforts of reporters, scholars and citizens to find out what was going on in the executive branch (the cozy relationship between regulating agencies and the businesses they regulated usually, though not always, meant that business and industry had fewer problems obtaining information). As the government grew in size over the years between 1946 and the mid-1960s, the frustration with executive branch secrecy also grew. In every session of Congress during that time, bills were introduced to modify the law to make more information available. These legislative efforts were vigorously opposed by the affected agencies and often by the business interests that were subject to government regulation. The activist spirit of the mid-1960s offered an opportune moment for action and standard bearers of reform were ready and waiting in Congress. The forces for open government were finally strong enough to prevail, but not without first making significant compromises to balance individual privacy concerns, legitimate government secrecy needs, and the proprietary and trade secrecy needs of business and industry. Though the stated purpose of the FOIA was to open up government, the act that passed allowed an agency to withhold access to records that qualified under any one of nine exemptions. The exemptions are listed by number with their short-hand nickname since they are usually referred to in that manner.

The last two exemptions (8 and 9) are basically special protections for banks and other financial institutions subject to federal regulation and the oil industry. Neither exemption has been the subject of significant litigation. Just what is covered by the other seven exemptions has been the subject of much legal controversy. Agencies, in most cases, argue that the exemptions should be read broadly, allowing as much information as possible to remain secret. Most often, the businesses subject to regulation side with secrecy, though openness is more attractive when it might provide information about a competitor or about what an uncooperative agency is doing. Nader and other public interest groups, as well as the press and scholars, argue that exemptions should be narrowly construed with as much information as possible being made public. The courts repeatedly have been called upon to referee this tug-of-war. At first it appeared that openness would be the rule. For example, in 1971 the U.S. Court of Appeals for the D.C. Circuit noted in *Getman v. NLRB*: "The Legislative plan creates a liberal disclosure requirement limited only by specific exemptions, which are to be narrowly construed." Subsequent courts often quoted this as precedent, but as Plesser and his colleagues soon discovered, not necessarily to reach a decision favoring openness.

The Litigation Group, with Plesser as a FOIA-dedicated attorney, was not the only party litigating under FOIA, but in the early 1970s there was little doubt that its lawyers were the prime movers and shakers. As Plesser notes, "What we did was to jump in and push for openness one incremental step after another. We poked and prodded the daily actions of government agencies toward actually realizing the laws' promised ends." When a court ruled against them, the case was appealed, and if that did not work, there was always Congress.

* * * * *

Perhaps nowhere was agency resistance to openness more incomprehensible than in the case involving efforts by Nader and Clarence Ditlow (who at that point was hired by Claybrook to work at the Public Interest Research Group but would soon move over to the Center for Auto Safety as its long-term and still-active director) to get information from the National Highway Traffic Safety Administration (NHTSA) about safety defects in cars. NHTSA was attempting to stretch exemption 3 (the other statute exemption), exemption 4 (the trade secrets exemption) and exemption 7 (the law enforcement exemption) into a hole big enough to drive nearly everything the agency did into hiding.

NHTSA is required by law to investigate safety defects in cars, whether reported by citizens or auto companies, or discovered by the agency. "Safety defects investigations conducted by NHTSA," as described by the associate administrator of NHTSA's motor vehicle inspection program, "are initiated with the transmittal of a letter of inquiry, known as an 'information request,' to the manufacturer of the vehicle containing a suspected defect under investigation.

The information request ... describes the alleged defect and *requires* the manufacturer to submit his explanation for the malfunctioning, with appropriate documentation." (emphasis added). Here was another law giving a government agency the power to force a corporation to provide safety information, data that could provide citizens with critical information necessary to protect their safety and lives. And here, again, the government agency seemed determined to keep the information secret at all costs.

On June 8, 1971, Nader wrote to NHTSA: "It is my understanding that the Department of Transportation has approximately 80 pending defect investigations. In order to correlate the work and information of the Public Interest Research Group with that of the Department of Transportation, a listing of ongoing investigations with the following information as to each investigation is needed." The letter went on to list five specific information requests: (1) the make, model and year of the vehicle being investigated; (2) the component of the car that was under investigation for defects; (3) the date the investigation was initiated; (4) the current status of the investigation; and (5) how the problem came to the department's attention. NHTSA wrote back saying it would provide information in response to (1) and (2) but would not for (3), (4) and (5), claiming that this information was part of an "investigation file for law enforcement purposes" and thus exempt from disclosure under the Freedom of Information Act .

When NHTSA finally made public its list of cars and components being investigated, the heater system of the Corvair (the car targeted in *Unsafe at Any Speed*) was one of many on the list about which Nader sought more information. Ditlow wrote to NHTSA in February 1972, this time asking for the documents involved in a negotiated settlement between the agency and General Motors to resolve the Corvair heater problems, which had allegedly caused gas and carbon monoxide fumes to leak into the passenger compartment. In response to Ditlow's request, NHTSA provided some information (that which was found in what were referred to as Books A, B, C, E and F) but not the information found in Book D, which was refused at the request of General Motors.

Plesser challenged NHTSA's refusal to release Book D (and the refusal to release information in response to Nader's requests about other defect investigations) by filing a case in the U.S. district court in Washington, D.C. The result was a resounding win for the Litigation Group and Ditlow. Judge Aubrey E. Robinson Jr. did not mince words:

> The exemption on which Defendants primarily rely ... is exemption 7, for "investigatory files compiled for law enforcement purposes." ... Although labeled "investigative" the correspondence here sought is correspondence between the agency and the auto manufacturer being investigated. There are no apparent problems with confidential sources, premature revelation of suspects and the like. And most certainly in the present case there is no problem about discovery of

the information by the subject of the investigation, since the auto manufacturer is either the recipient or the source of all the correspondence here sought. ...

This is a case where lawyer's verbiage has transformed six insignificant paragraphs into a major bone of contention. The only thing more puzzling than why Plaintiffs would want these documents is why Defendants refuse to disclose them. Of course, Plaintiffs had no certain knowledge of the contents and doubtless were incited by the great efforts expended by the Government to prevent disclosure.

To this Court the struggle over Book D seems a monumental waste of effort by all concerned, apparently motivated by GM's "request" that the documents remain confidential. Yet the agency must know by now that it cannot withhold by fiat that which the law requires be disclosed.

For Plesser it was another sweet victory, made all the more delicious by the rare scolding the judge dished out to the executive agency. The victory was destined, however, to be short-lived. Judge Robinson had relied on a February 23, 1973, decision of the U.S. Circuit Court of Appeals for the District of Columbia in *Weisburg v. Department of Justice*, which put the burden on an agency to show that withheld documents were "likely to create a concrete prospect of serious harm to its law enforcement efficiency." But four months after the district court decision in *Ditlow*, the full U.S. Appeals Court for the D.C. Circuit, sitting *en banc*, overruled and vacated *Weisberg*. The court ruled that if documents are classified as "investigatory files compiled for law enforcement purposes," exemption 7 applies. "It is not the province of the courts," the *en banc* court continued, "to second-guess the Congress by relying upon considerations which argue that the Government will not actually be injured by revelation in the particular case." If an agency said a document was part of an "investigative file," it was, period; no court review was allowed.

Perhaps it was the district court's pointed remarks about the ridiculousness of the agency's position about Book D that caused NHTSA to turn this set of documents over to Nader. But relying on the full court's overruling of *Weisburg*, the agency appealed the portion of the district court's ruling in *Ditlow* that dealt with correspondence between NHTSA and investigated parties in connection with all the other pending auto defect investigations that the Nader organizations wanted. *Weisburg* had involved a different, indeed a unique, fact situation: an effort to obtain the minutes of the Warren Commission's investigation of President John F. Kennedy's assassination. Morrison and Plesser believed that car safety data was a very different matter. Surely the public interest here was both more compelling and more critical. This was more than curiosity about a past murder: knowledge about car defects might save lives today. *Ditlow*, like *Schechter*, was headed back to court.

* * * * *

Among the many FOIA cases Plesser handled while at the Litigation Group, perhaps the most important was *Vaughn v. Rosen*. The facts of *Vaughn* are pretty dull compared to nursing home fires and carbon monoxide fume leaks, but the results of the case probably did more to advance the cause of government openness than any other case. Yet it was a case that Plesser had to argue hard to get Morrison to allow him to take.

In the summer of 1972, Robert Vaughn was an assistant law professor at American University's Washington College of Law and an associate attorney at Nader's Public Interest Research Group, where he had been directing a study of the United States civil service system. When Vaughn joined PIRG in the summer of 1970, it was just as Harrison Wellford was completing his study of the Department of Agriculture, a department described as "one of the most resistive ever studied by a Nader group." Methods of resistance, Vaughn recalls, "varied from the subtle and ingenious to the blatant and forceful." He described a weekend heist by Agriculture Department officials of most of the publications dealing with insecticide regulations from the department's library shelves, among other examples. This action followed the department's failed effort to bar Nader student investigators from their library. They had to let the students in, but they were going to make sure nothing was there for them to see. It seems a preposterous response for folks who supposedly work for the public, but it was not far from the norm. Nader once described some of the methods of bureaucratic evasion of the FOIA as: the contamination ploy, the I'm-sorry-but-it's-not-here technique, and the gee-wiz-but-the-costs-to-provide-it-are-just-too-prohibitive dodge. What Vaughn ran into with his study of the United States Civil Service Commission was more like the protect-our-sources argument the departments seemed to be advancing in *Schechter* and *Ditlow*.

Vaughn wanted access to the Civil Service Commission's final reports containing the findings of inspection teams that studied the operation of all federal departments and agencies. The inspections aimed to evaluate personnel practices for compliance with federal laws mandating things like equal employment opportunity and fair employee grievance procedures, as well as effective enforcement of regulatory responsibilities. The agency argued that if the reports were made public, the willingness of civil servants to share honestly what was going on in their programs would be compromised and thus problems might go undiscovered. Plesser needed to illustrate to the court why public access to the inspection reports was critical. An example he used later in his brief: "[I]f an inspection should find that the enforcement of a health and safety law, such as the Coal Mine Health and Safety Act, was impeded by negligent or improper use of personnel, public access to the reports would be crucial."

Plesser first had to persuade Morrison that this was a case worth taking. It helped that the plaintiff was a Naderite, but still Morrison required that a file memo defending the case be written. "Alan never asked for a file memo from me before or after that, but for this one I had to do it," recalls Plesser. Perhaps the issue of personnel studies did not sound worthy of the Litigation Group's limited resources (Morrison does not recall just why he resisted taking on the case), but Plesser has "never forgotten it and, after the magnitude of the win, never let Alan forget it either." The file memo done, Plesser was given a go-ahead and filed suit on August 31, 1972. Briefs were filed during the fall by both sides and in December, without oral argument, U.S. District Judge John H. Pratt granted the government's motion for summary judgment and dismissed the complaint. The judge provided no explanation for why he ruled. Plesser immediately appealed to the U.S. Court of Appeals for the District of Columbia Circuit. Oral argument was scheduled for June 7, 1973, before Judges Malcolm Wilkey, Spottswood Robinson and District Judge Frank Kaufman (district judges are sometimes designated to sit on appeals panels when caseload requires).

"The thing that bothered us most about the case," recalls Plesser, "was that the department had provided no factual information about the information we sought." Indeed, their statement of facts in the lower court brief, "did little more than state the policy and legal basis for not disclosing the documents ... [it did] not state in any detail the circumstances under which the documents are compiled nor ... discuss in any detail the content of the documents or how they are used." Basically, Plesser was trying to argue about documents about which he knew next to nothing. "When I stood to argue in the appeals court," Plesser recollects, "Judge Robinson broke in almost immediately, saying something like, 'You can't argue your case, can you counselor, because you haven't any information about the documents you seek?' What I did next was pause for a moment and then simply agree—'No I can't your honor'—then I sat down. I think at first Alan, who was sitting with me, thought I was just giving up."

On August 20, 1973, the appeals court announced its decision: unanimous in Plesser's favor. But what he and Morrison had won was far more than they had imagined possible. The opinion written by Judge Wilkey sent a clear message to the executive branch to do its job and stop putting the burden on the courts. After restating the facts of the case below, Wilkey echoed Robinson's point at oral argument. The government's brief "did not illuminate or reveal the contents of the information sought, but rather set forth in conclusory terms the Director's opinion that the evaluations were not subject to disclosure." He went on to note that the FOIA explicitly requires that, when the government declines to disclose a document, "the burden is upon the agency to prove *de novo* in trial court that the information sought fits under one of the exemptions." Wilkey then set out the problem created by the failure to provide sufficiently clear information about the documents sought: "In a very real sense only one side to the controversy (the side opposing disclosure) is in a position confidently to make statements categorizing the documents. ... At this point the opposing party is comparatively helpless to controvert [the government's] characterization. ...This lack of knowledge by the party seeking disclosure seriously distorts the traditional adversary nature of our legal system's form of dispute resolution." Then Wilkey got to the real issue (at least from where he sat). To compensate for this problem, the trial court would be forced to examine the documents *in camera* to see whether the government was properly categorizing the documents. This could be "very burdensome" for the trial court and would be "compounded at the appellate level. ... We could [in this case] test the accuracy of the trial court's characterizations by committing sufficient resources to the project but the cost in terms of judicial manpower would be immense." Wilkey noted that although "such an investment of judicial energy might be justified to determine some issues," in this area of the law "we do not believe it is justified or even permissible." FOIA places the burden "specifically by statute on the Government."

Next, Wilkey flexed his judicial muscles and set out a remedy for this sort of problem in the future. First, he sent the message that courts "will simply no longer accept conclusory and generalized allegations of exemption," and then he devised a process for agencies to use to assure sufficient detail. This process, quickly dubbed as a "Vaughn Index," requires that the agency formulate a system of "itemizing and indexing that would correlate statements made in the Government's refusal justification with the actual portions of the document(s) at issue. Such an indexing system would subdivide the documents under consideration into manageable parts cross-referenced to the relevant portion of the Government's justification." He went further still, giving the trial court the power to designate a special master "to examine documents and evaluate an agency's contention of exemption" in cases where the material involved was so massive as to "still be extremely burdensome to a trial court." Then Wilkey remanded the case to the trial court for action. Now the Civil Service Commission would have to provide a Vaughn Index for the material it was refusing to release.

At first blush it might seem strange that Judge Wilkey, one of the more conservative judges on the D.C. Circuit, would rule against the government and do so in such an activist manner. But here the activism was to a large extent "self-protection" for a court system that was being buried by an overwhelming growth in its case load, the result, to a large extent, of all the liberal legislative activism of President Johnson's Great Society programs and the host of social regulatory laws passed in the late 1960s and early 1970s.

Of course, the government appealed to the Supreme Court. "The court of appeals has improperly and without argument on the point, promulgated procedures which prescribe in detail the manner in which the government is to prove its right to exemptions under the Freedom of Information Act," argued Solicitor General Robert H. Bork in his petition for *cert*. This was judicial legislation, judicial activism—anathema to Bork and other advocates of judicial restraint. The Supreme Court (no doubt more swayed by the court-workload-protection logic) denied *cert*, thereby leaving Wilkey's ruling in force.

For Plesser, Vaughn and others seeking government documents, it was a breath of fresh air. Now the agencies could not stonewall by sweeping everything under a claim of several exemptions. Before *Vaughn*, agencies had little to lose in trying this ploy. Judges were simply not able to do adequate *in camera* reviews to challenge agency claims. The Vaughn Index would force agencies to provide a defense for each document withheld; indeed, as applied, it forced agencies to defend portions of documents that might be released even where other parts could be exempt. The burden was placed where the FOIA placed it. It was a win far beyond what Plesser could have imagined. But it did not help Vaughn get his documents, at least not yet. Another district court hearing and another appeal would be necessary. Indeed, it took until December 1975 to get final action and by then Plesser had left the Litigation Group. Meanwhile, *Ditlow* (the car safety case) and *Schechter* (the nursing home survey case) were also chugging along on appeal.

When HEW on November 14, 1972, announced its formal denial of Mal Schechter's request for the release of more nursing home survey reports, Plesser had a complaint filed in district court within a week. The denial came just two weeks after Congress amended the Social Security Act (October 30, 1972) to mandate that HEW make available to the public "pertinent findings" of each survey report of a Medicare-approved facility within ninety days of its completion. After the beating the SSA representative had taken during congressional hearings that spring, a regulation to provide for disclosure of future surveys of Medicare-approved facilities was issued by the administration nearly two months before the law even passed. With a determined Congress breathing down its neck, apparently the department decided that it would be wiser to be cooperative. But that cooperation did not extend further than the department's reading of what the new law would force it to do; and that, department officials were confident, would require only future reports to be released. Government attorneys took until the end of January 1973 to respond to Plesser's complaint in court, and by that point the new regulations had become effective. Of course, the government argued that the case should be dismissed as moot, but Plesser and Schechter believed that there remained critical reasons for releasing the reports of past surveys, so they pressed on. The briefing process consumed the winter and early spring. Finally, on June 1, 1973, Plesser, one Justice Department attorney and two HEW staff attorneys for the new secretary of HEW, Caspar Weinberger (with the new secretary the case now became *Schechter v. Weinberger*), appeared for a hearing before U.S. District Judge George L. Hart Jr. The transcript of the half-hour hearing is a fascinating read. At the outset, the initial remarks by Judge Hart must have been disquieting for Plesser.

Responding to the government attorney's opening lines, which described two of the specific reports Schechter wanted (current and past reports on two facilities that participate in the Medicare program), Judge Hart said: "I tell you what gives me great concern is what you report as the nature of these previous reports prior to the time that the Government put in a new method of checking. ... And you state that these reports are frequently accusatory in tone and have not attempted to present a balanced assessment of the provider's operation . ... Now, if there is a lot of information which has not really been checked and cross-checked and has not been given the people against whom it was made an opportunity to answer, has the Government got a right or anybody else got a right to come in and just get this unverified information and broadcast it?" This characterization of the reports as unverified, accusatory and lacking response from the inspected nursing home was soon shown to be open to considerable question.

When Plesser's turn came, he had the fifteen survey reports that Judge Waddy had ordered released to Schechter to use as illustrations. Based on specific problems contained in these reports, Plesser argued that, not only would there be no "unwarranted invasion of privacy" for the nursing home, there was a significant health and safety need for the information for any patients already there or considering whether to go there. This line of argument seemed to strike a chord with the judge: "Well, surely, if the information is accurate, has been checked, and the operators have been given an opportunity to reply, then it cries out for being made public, because my own experience with nursing homes and by general reputation [is that] most of them are terrible. And, as a matter of fact, from what I have seen of about two and have heard of many others, I don't know how they continue to operate."

One can imagine that Plesser tasted victory at this point; even more so when a few minutes later the Justice Department attorney, in response to a direct question from the judge, noted: "Your Honor, to be candid, I have not read all of these reports, not only the fifteen that [the department] released to the plaintiff earlier; but I haven't gone over to the agency and examined all of these hundreds of reports." When the question was asked of the HEW's own staff attorney, he too admitted he was not familiar with the fifteen survey reports Plesser was using as examples. These fifteen reports were all the examples Plesser had, as none others had been released, and he had relied on them extensively in his written brief to illustrate his argument. The opposing attorneys must have been well aware that he might refer to them in oral argument before the judge so why had they not read them? The department's staff attorney then described the "normal" process that had been followed prior to the new regulations. He admitted that the deficiencies that were initially written up "cold" as "raw data" were provided to the facility being reviewed and there was an opportunity "to answer or to correct it."

Plesser was able to make a good case for why past data was needed—that to be able to evaluate a facility one needed some historical data about its past compliance record to know if a current good review followed years of bad or vice versa.

Then the Justice Department attorney returned with a different line of argument: the Social Security Amendments of 1939. They gave the power to the administration to decide whether information should be disclosed. The Medicare Act was passed in 1968 and said nothing about taking that power away, and Congress had never in subsequent amendments to the Medicare law, until the most recent ones (the October 1972 Medicare Act amendments), directed that these reports be released. Basically the Justice Department was calling for judicial restraint and deference to the elected branch. If Congress wanted to act, it could. It did not do so until 1972, so it must not have wanted to before that. And, it was the elected Congress that was responsible for making the law, not judges. Of course, an alternative argument might be that since Medicare passed after the 1966 Freedom of Information Act, Congress might have assumed that its provisions for openness (unless a document fell under one of the nine specific exemptions) would control and that specific directions to disclose would thus not be necessary.

But the judge heard the call for restraint: "You know what? I'm afraid you're right. I don't like it, but I'm afraid you are. I will with great reluctance, grant the defendant's motion for summary judgment and deny the plaintiff's ... and I hope you appeal it." Not much solace in getting a reluctant ruling against them, but appeal they did.

More than a year later (October 3, 1974) Plesser's case was decided by a panel of the U.S. Circuit Court of Appeals for the District of Columbia. It was a win this time, a win enormously helped by a decision from the Third Circuit presenting the same legal question. The court may also have been influenced by the fallout from Watergate, as the appeals court decision in *Schechter* came less than two months after President Nixon's resignation. It may also have been swayed by the fact that the Senate had passed a bill significantly strengthening the courts' role in reviewing FOIA actions on October 1, 1974 (and the House would follow suit by an overwhelming majority—349-2—on October 7). The Third Circuit decision had noted that the claim of a "blanket exclusion on disclosure of all files, records and reports compiled under the Social Security Act ... is in direct contravention of the liberal disclosure requirement of the Freedom of Information Act." In other words, the department could not use the broad discretion to deny disclosure found in the 1939 amendment for FOIA's Exemption 3 (which allows non-disclosure if another statute specifically grants this power). Plesser did not even have to argue the case; the court simply ruled, "We agree with the reasoning of the Court of Appeals for the Third Circuit."

By this point the pre-January 31, 1973, surveys Schechter was after were not so critical, but the win here, as in *Vaughn*, was a lot bigger than one case. The administration could no longer lay claim to a vast discretion to withhold information under the 1939 law to circumvent FOIA. The SSA would be subject to FOIA and its explicit exemptions for all its files and documents. Like other agencies, it would have to defend its decisions not to disclose, not just rely on administrative fiat.

* * * * *

Like *Schechter*, the appeal in the Ditlow car safety case dragged on into 1974. By the time its appeal was argued (in February 1974) there was a new FOIA attorney at the Litigation Group. Morrison had decided to keep Plesser on but to add a new attorney to the FOIA position (using the FOIA position as an entry-level training position). For a new recruit, Morrison turned to Victor H. Kramer (formerly a partner at Arnold and Porter), who had been one of Washington's most respected corporate lawyers. But the call of "making a difference" was not heard only by young ears. Reminiscing about his decision to join the public interest law world, Kramer recalls: "With two quite young associates in tow, I was on my way to do some depositions for a very big case we were handling when I fell and broke my leg on the ice in front of National Airport. The associates went on without me and did a very credible job. I never heard a word from the clients or from another long-term client I was also scheduled to meet. No one ever called to ask how my foot was. They paid huge bills on time without a complaint, but not much else. I was getting tired of that sort of relationship."

Soon after that experience, Kramer had a call from a young attorney, Charles Halpern, "a very bright and promising Arnold and Porter associate who had left in 1969 to start the first modern public interest law firm, the Center for Law and Social Policy." Halpern had persuaded the Ford Foundation to fund his firm (the first of many grants the Foundation would soon provide to similar efforts, especially in the environmental area). Halpern asked Kramer if he would like to come help them out for a bit. Kramer took a leave of absence and joined Halpern "in a rat hole of an office with plaster falling everywhere, with no heat and these youngsters in filthy clothes, long hair and unshaven. I often wondered at the time," Kramer remarks, "why the hell I had done this!" The "kids" who joined Halpern (Joe Onek, who later became assistant counsel to President Carter under Lloyd Cutler; Jim Mormon, who later became an assistant attorney general; Jeff Cowan, who went on to head Voice of America; Bruce Terris, who went into private practice; and Patricia Wald, who was appointed to the U.S. Appeals Court, D.C. Circuit, by Carter) called Kramer "Daddy-o." Soon, and thankfully, they moved over to 20th Street just off Dupont Circle to a luxurious old mansion that had been rented by the fledgling Natural Resources Defense Council (NRDC), another public interest law firm started up with Ford Foundation money. The "Dean of public interest law," as Kramer has often been called, had "an enormous elegant Victorian dining room" as his new office there. [Twenty-seven years later, after an architectural firm completely renovated the building, Public Citizen, including the Litigation Group, would move in.]

At the end of the year, as the author of *Superlawyers* put it, Kramer "sent word to Arnold and Porter he wasn't returning; finished, just like that, tossing over a $200,000-a-year partnership and casting his lot with those goddamned kids who are always yakking about consumerism and berating Washington lawyers who 'whore' for the corporations and things like that." By that time, he had a second public interest job as well, as director of the Georgetown Law Center for Public Interest Representation, another Ford Foundation-funded venture. Georgetown had decided to create a public interest law firm within its law school where law students could spend a full semester for credit. Five law school graduates would be hired as "fellows" for a year (at the grand salary of $8,000). Kramer had agreed to become the recruiter, trainer and director of the venture and thus began what became known as "the nursery school for public interest lawyers." Kramer, like Morrison, saw the value of FOIA cases for training neophyte lawyers as litigators, and thus his fellows and the law students they led worked a lot with FOIA. It was a natural recruiting ground for a Freedom of Information Clearinghouse attorney.

Larry Ellsworth, "a shy, small-town boy, not polished, not arrogant but very intelligent and careful," and one of the early fellows at the Georgetown Law Center became the first Litigation Group recruit of many to come through Kramer's program. Ellsworth had graduated from Michigan State University in 1969 and headed to Harvard Law. While there he had been active in the Legal Aid Society, which had hired a bus to take a group of them to Washington, D.C., for one of the antiwar demonstrations. "The bus was sabotaged, we later found, out by the FBI, so we all crammed into volunteers' cars and drove eight hours straight through the night," Ellsworth said. So one of COINTELPRO's targets was now to be a Litigation Group attorney.

"Larry was a bit overwhelmed at first," Morrison remembers. "Within his first six months there he had six arguments in court." His first turned out to be the appeal in *Ditlow*. Ellsworth's recollection of his oral argument in *Ditlow* before the appeals panel of Judges McGowan, Robinson Sr. and Robb is that it was a "bloody beating."

> I got up there and I said, "Good morning your honors, my name is Larry Ellsworth."

> The chief judge looked down quizzically at this twenty-six-year-old, wet-behind the ears youngster, as he riffled around through the pile of papers in front of him on the bench and interrupted my opening line with, "What? What? Who are you?"

> I repeated my name and tried to go on: "There are two issues before the court today. The first is ..."

> At that, he interrupted again: "Counselor do we have to reach the second issue if we find against you on the first?"

> "No, your honor," I replied.

"What? What did you say," he thundered back.

So I replied, "NO YOUR HONOR."

"Well," he said, "you don't have to shout, young man."

There was little to calm the nerves or reassure the novice in this beginning. Still, there was no option but to continue. "They had scheduled fifteen minutes for the oral," Ellsworth recalls. "I was up there for forty-five minutes and never got to my carefully prepared text. I was just peppered with one question after another." When he returned to his seat, Morrison leaned over and whispered, "Well, look at it this way, Larry. Starting your career with an argument like this means there is nowhere to go but up." The appeals court announced its ruling on February 27, 1974. The *per curiam* opinion was short and blunt: *Ditlow* is like *Weisberg*; *Ditlow* loses.

Wins like *Vaughn* were offset by the losses like *Ditlow* and a number of cases the Litigation Group brought between 1972 and 1974. Even when the threat of lawsuit was sufficient to persuade an executive agency to release information, the time, cost and effort required was becoming enormous. The regular resistance he was facing in trying to get information out of the executive branch quickly convinced Plesser that other avenues of attack were needed, and as a member of a Nader organization he had an obvious place to turn for help. He began regularly meeting with Nader and the Center for Study of Responsive Law staff to discuss the need for other changes he saw from his litigation perspective.

* * * * *

Nader was already at work promoting legislative changes to the 1966 FOIA law by the time Plesser came aboard in April 1972. During the spring of 1972, Representative William S. Moorhead (D-Pennsylvania), chair of the House Government Operations Subcommittee, had been persuaded to hold hearings to address implementation problems of the Freedom of Information Act. "There are 55,000 arms pumping up and down in government offices stamping 'confidential' on stacks of government documents; more than 18,000 government employees are wielding 'secret' stamps, and a censorship elite of nearly 3,000 bureaucrats have authority to stamp 'top secret' on public records," Moorhead noted at the hearings. "These are not wild estimates. These numbers are provided by government agencies." Representatives of the Nader organizations were there as witnesses to chronicle the problems they had been having (excessive delays in agency responses to requests for information; excessive copying costs charged by agencies; and prohibitive legal costs when litigation was required) and to proffer solutions (time limits for agency action on FOIA requests; reduced or no copying costs for public interest groups; and the ability for courts to award attorneys' fees for plaintiffs who won FOIA suits against the government). It would take until fall 1974 to get amendments passed to accomplish these goals and a lot of effort by many in the public interest world (supported by many in the news media) to get them through.

In January 1973, the Supreme Court made matters worse with its ruling in *EPA v. Mink*, a case brought by Representative Patsy Mink (D-Hawaii) and thirty-one other members of the House in an attempt to get information about underground nuclear testing sites. In a 5-3 decision, the majority ruled that courts could not review the contents of documents withheld from the public under FOIA's first exemption (the national security exemption). If the executive branch said a document was to be exempt because of national defense or foreign policy needs, it was final. In a concurring opinion, Justice Potter Stewart agreed that the majority had interpreted Exemption 1 correctly, as written by Congress—that is, that there was no provision for court review of an executive decision to classify something and thereby claim a right to not disclose. But he went on to point out that the law as written was unwise at best.

"One would suppose," Justice Stewart wrote, "that a nuclear test that engendered fierce controversy within the Executive Branch of our Government would be precisely the kind of event that should be opened to the fullest possible disclosure consistent with legitimate interests of national defense. Without such disclosure, factual information available to the concerned Executive agencies cannot be considered by the people or evaluated by the Congress. And with the people and their representatives reduced to a state of ignorance, the democratic process is paralyzed." It was Congress, though, that had "conspicuously failed" here by providing "no means to question an Executive decision to stamp a document 'secret' however cynical, myopic or even corrupt that decision might have been." It was up to Congress to change the law.

With *Ditlow*, *Weisberg* and *Mink* as precedents, judges were inhibited from reviewing executive branch claims of a FOIA exemption and thus a litigation strategy became a less-powerful alternative. In the spring of 1973, Nader and Plesser arranged to meet with Senator Ted Kennedy (D-Massachusetts), chair of the Senate Judiciary Committee, to try to persuade him to hold hearings on the FOIA problems. "We went into Kennedy's office," Plesser recalls, "and the senator welcomed us and asked how we were and what we were working on—you know, beginning with a little stroking. Nader completely ignored the small talk and cut right to the chase. 'THIS' is what we're here for!' From then on it was all FOIA problems we discussed." Kennedy held hearings to investigate the problems and, along with a long line of executive bureaucrats who opposed changes and a few others from the public interest world, Plesser and others from Nader's groups testified in favor. By then, Nader had brought Joan Claybrook on to start Congress Watch as Public Citizen's legislative lobbying arm, and soon thereafter he hired another foot soldier, young attorney Mark Lynch, to push legislation on Capitol Hill.

Like so many of the Litigation Group attorneys of the 1970s, Mark Lynch was molded by the crises of the time. He had grown up in West Haven, Connecticut, and graduated from Yale University in 1966. Three weeks later, this young man who had seldom been west of the Hudson River, was in Vietnam as a volunteer with the International Voluntary Service (a private organization under contract with A.I.D. that was a precursor to the Peace Corps). His job was to teach and to help improve agricultural methods. He stayed there as a IVS volunteer until 1970. "I started out neutral on the war but soon recognized that what I was seeing on the ground was very different from the official version I read in the papers," Lynch recalls. "It was my first confrontation with the proposition that the government isn't always honest—and in a pretty massive way." From that experience grew a fascination with government secrecy that would take him first to Congress Watch, then to the Litigation Group and soon thereafter on to head the Washington litigation office of the American Civil Liberties Union. But first came law school at George Washington University. "I hated the first year of law school," he admits, "and dropped out in the spring of 1971 to return to Vietnam as a stringer for six months for *Newsweek*." He did return, though, and after a summer working for a Legal Services group in Stamford, Connecticut, on a busing integration plan, he graduated in 1973. During the spring recruiting season of his final year at law school, Peter Petkas, one of Nader's early recruits (who headed up the Corporate Accountability Research Group), was interviewing at George Washington. Lynch stopped by to say hello and ended up being recruited by Claybrook to work with Congress Watch (and he was roped into coming aboard before graduation, just as Claybrook herself had been). Quickly he was tapped to work with Plesser on the FOIA amendments.

Soon Lynch and Plesser became a well-oiled machine, with Lynch playing the role of lobbyist. Lynch's job was "to hang around Congress" and to "twist arms," tracking down members and staffers to pitch the FOIA amendments and to build outside coalitions to support the legislation. "I was the chief legal expert. My experience with actual cases and agency shenanigans could illustrate just where the problems were," Plesser notes. "Lynch would trot me out to testify or bring me along to help with legislative wording."

On March 14, 1974, just a week after the Government Operations Committee had voted to send the bill forward, the House passed its amendments to FOIA by an overwhelming majority (383-8). On May 16, 1974, Kennedy's committee voted unanimously to approve legislation amending FOIA, noting that the act had become a "freedom *from* information law with the curtains of secrecy still tightly drawn around the business of government [emphasis added]."

On May 30, 1974, FOIA legislation passed the Senate by a 64-17 vote. During debate on the Senate floor concerning the change to Exemption 7 (the law enforcement records exemption that figured in *Ditlow*), Plesser and Lynch wanted to be sure that the debate would explain precisely the intent of the change—that the government would have the burden of proving some tangible harm to a *particular enforcement proceeding* in order for the exemption to apply. "Ron had jotted down a little colloquy for Senators [Philip] Hart [Michigan Democrat] and Kennedy in the Senate anteroom," Ellsworth recalls. "Unfortunately, Ron's writing is nearly impossible to decipher." So when the senators got on the floor one began, 'My understanding is that this amendment is to overrule ... mumble ... mumble ... mumble.' " They were trying to read the scribbles but were not having much luck. Fortunately for the Litigation Group, the printed floor debate reflected just what Plesser had written—no mumbles included. Later in a case seeking access to the records relating to the investigation of former Vice President Spiro Agnew, which led to his plea of *nolo contendere* to one count of federal income tax evasion, a substantial portion of the Hart-Kennedy colloquy is quoted verbatim in the Litigation Group brief as proof of legislative intent. This little game of making legislative history is played by the big boys for the powerful all the time, and it was satisfying to have it work for their side a bit.

In October, the conference report resolving the differences in the two bills passed both houses. By this time, Nixon had resigned and Gerald Ford was president. There is no doubt that the lobbying efforts of Plesser, Lynch, Claybrook and a host of others mattered in getting these amendments on the agenda and to the floor; without this effort there would probably have been no bill in position for final action. But the shroud of mistrust and disgust hanging over the nation at the time surely provided compelling incentive for passing legislation that could prove congressional opposition to secrecy and obstruction of the public's right to know what its government was up to—especially with the mid-term congressional elections just a few weeks away.

As passed by Congress, the amendments required reasonable copying fees, with a waiver provision when the public interest was served; allowed courts to award legal fees and court costs to attorneys who won FOIA suits against the government; set a ten-working-day deadline for agency response to a FOIA request (with a twenty-working-day deadline for responding to appeals of denials); authorized a court to find that an agency employee had acted arbitrarily and capriciously in denying a request and provided for disciplinary action; and required an annual report to Congress from every agency to enumerate and defend all decisions to withhold information. In addition, the amendments specifically addressed the problems in *Ditlow* and *Weisberg*, as well as *Mink*. Courts were empowered to examine documents that agencies withheld *in camera* and to determine if an exemption was improperly claimed. [This, of course, did not help in *Ditlow* or *Weisberg*, as a change in the law does not apply retroactively, but in the future it would allow lower court judges the ability to do what Judge Robinson did in finding not defensible NHTSA's claim of an Exemption 7 exclusion for Book D.] And courts were also specifically allowed to review whether a stamp of "classified" was properly applied, with a specific note in the committee report that this provision was meant to overrule *EPA v. Mink*. The new amendments covered nearly everything Plesser and Lynch had sought.

But convinced by his Justice Department and other advisers that the executive branch could not function effectively under these new requirements, President Ford vetoed the law on October 17, calling it "unconstitutional and unworkable." By then Congress was recessed for the 1974 mid-term elections. There are so many other factors to explain the Democratic landslide in the House that November, in which seventy-four new Democrats were elected, giving the party one of the largest majorities in history—the Watergate mess, the agonizingly slow Vietnam withdrawal, Ford's pardon of Nixon, etc.—but the veto of a bill aimed at opening government by the first-ever unelected president undoubtedly contributed. How could Ford, who had begun his administration with a promise of openness, have sided "with the secret-makers on the first big test of that promise?" Senator Edmund Muskie (D-Maine) asked. When Congress reconvened in late November, Ford's veto was overridden (371-2 in the House; 65-27 in the Senate).

* * * * *

There was new law and clarity from Congress about its commitment to openness, but the executive branch did not seem to notice the change. FOIA requests continued to be denied, and cases continued to flow onto the FOIA desk at the Litigation Group. With congressional intent clear that the courts were expected to play a reviewing role, there were some significant FOIA wins for the Litigation Group, but in the case of *Robertson v. Butterfield* (which had been won in the appeals court even before the 1974 amendments passed) the highest court in the land would soon strike another blow against openness. And again, it would take congressional action to overturn a court decision.

Reuben Robertson had been a summer recruit leading a group of Nader's Raiders in their study of the Civil Aeronautics Board. Robertson also went after the Federal Aviation Administration (FAA) that year, producing a report in December 1969 that was critical of the FAA's regulation of aviation safety. The next summer Robertson and a group of student Raiders attempted to get more information out of the FAA about air safety enforcement. They had numerous meetings with FAA staff and, when they were stonewalled, filed FOIA requests to inspect agency records. Though they sought many other documents and raised other issues, the two most critical to the case ahead were Mechanical Reliability Reports, known as MRRs (summaries of reports of serious mechanical malfunctions which are required to be submitted by the airlines to FAA), and System Worthiness Analysis Program reports, known as SWAP reports (which consist of analyses made by FAA staff concerning the operation and maintenance performance of commercial airlines). These two sets of documents contained information that Robertson and Nader believed were critical for the flying public to know.

As they were attempting to get information that summer, an engine explosion and in-flight emergency occurred on an Air France Boeing 747 passenger flight. Information about the August 17, 1970, incident was not made public until October of that year, though Robertson and the student Raiders had made repeated attempts to find out about two secret FAA meetings they heard had been held during August. The meetings, convened to address safety concerns about the 747s, were attended by FAA representatives and representatives of the airlines, the aircraft and engine manufacturers and the Air Transport Association (the national trade group of the airline industry). In later depositions of those present, it was learned that the trade group participant and other industry representatives requested that the FAA keep information about the engine problems from the public and not allow any of Nader's people to attend the meetings. They feared that widespread public awareness of the actual problems would have an adverse competitive impact on airlines operating Boeing 747 passenger service planes. Following these meetings, the FAA made a decision not to ground the 747s. At about the same time, the agency formally denied Robertson's FOIA requests for access to the MRRs and SWAP reports and to the meeting data.

Information about the 747 engine problems eventually leaked, and on September 29, Robertson wrote to the agency requesting that all FAA's actions concerning these problems be made public. On October 1, the National Transportation Safety Board released to the public a letter addressed to FAA Director John Shaffer recommending remedial action for the 747 engine problems. It also included mention of the August 17 Air France incident. The cat was now fully out of the bag. In a press conference the next week, Shaffer admitted that Nader had been trying to get information about the engine problem. Then, explaining his refusal to provide it, Shaffer stated: "Nader is crying wolf, running through the streets. I have 53,000 people working on increased reliability of aircraft. What is he going to do with the information? If he had anyone with the technical ability to evaluate the problem of systems errors, I'd be happy to give him the data."

Shaffer's explanation for why he would not provide the MRRs or SWAP reports to Nader was also given in a press conference: "I think [Nader's] on the wrong track if he's really interested in mere safety. I don't know why he's doing it. I suspect he wants to review these reports, and when he gets something exciting, say 'ah ha!' If I thought he could help the cause of safety I wouldn't deny him these reports. But if we are compelled to divulge this information, the sources will dry up. The taxpayer couldn't afford all the workers we would require if we had to find all these mechanical difficulties ourselves. These airline people have the information, and they volunteer it to us, and we make sure everybody else who needs gets it." It was the "our-sources-will-dry-up" fear, combined with the protect-our-regulated-industry desire—just like the nursing home case. But, just as there, this agency had the statutory authority to force compliance; it did not need to rely on "volunteered" information. And surely a person's right to know if a plane she intends to fly on has potential safety problems is at least equal to the corporate concern about competitive disadvantage and profits.

Robertson pursued an appeal within the agency throughout 1971 and then filed suit in district court. The FAA was claiming that FOIA Exemption 3 applied because another statute (section 1140 of the Aviation Act) specifically allowed the FAA to withhold MRRs and SWAP reports, if it chose. On November 8, 1972, the district court granted Robertson's motion concerning the MRRs and ordered those to be produced but upheld the exemption claim for SWAP reports (the two-sentence order gives no reasoning for why one was not exempt and the other was). The case was half won. Morrison and Plesser quickly filed an appeal for the SWAP reports. The case now became *Robertson v. Butterfield* (Shaffer had been replaced by Butterfield as head of the FAA—the very same Alexander P. Butterfield who testified before the Senate Watergate Committee in July 1973 that Nixon's offices were equipped with a special voice-activated system that secretly recorded all conversations and thereby set in motion events that would lead ultimately to the resignation of a president).

It was not until May 9, 1974, that the appeals court ruled. But the decision was worth the wait. "This court has continued to adhere to the position that exemptions of the Information Act are to be narrowly construed," wrote Judge Fahy for the 2-1 majority. Noting that the "ordinary meaning of the language of Exemption 3" is that the "other statute" relied on must itself specify the documents or categories of documents it authorizes to be withheld from public scrutiny, he concluded that the Aviation Act fails to do this. All the Aviation Act provision does is to allow the FAA director "to weigh whether a person [in this case an airline] objecting to disclosure would be adversely affected by it, and whether, even if so affected, disclosure nevertheless 'is not required in the interest of the public.' It would be unacceptable," the judge continued, to hold that Exemption 3 applies here. "[I]t would also be at odds with the history of the Information Act." Though there was a dissent in the case, the strong endorsement of their position by the majority made this a big win.

The appeals decision, however, had left open the possibility that the administration could attempt to prove that another exemption might apply and allowed for a remand to the district court should the executive wish to pursue this alternative. Given the timing of the win (spring of 1974)—with the Watergate scandal cresting and the House having voted overwhelmingly for amendments strengthening FOIA and with Senate passage only weeks away—there was considerable hope at the Litigation Group that the administration would throw in the towel and release the reports. Instead, when the Ford administration took over, it appealed the Exemption 3 denial to the Supreme Court. By the time the case was argued, Plesser had left the Litigation Group to become general counsel of the Privacy Protection Study Commission established by Congress in 1974, and the Supreme Court oral argument fell to Morrison. On June 24, 1975, the decision was announced: a 7-2 loss for the Litigation Group.

Chief Justice Burger's decision makes much of reading history "in light of the legislation in existence" when the FOIA act passed, and since the Aviation Act existed and no provision in FOIA clarified that it was to be overruled, the court could not overrule it. Only Congress could do so. If statutes are "capable of co-existence, it is the duty of the courts, absent a clearly expressed congressional intention to the contrary to regard each as effective." By that logic all supposedly one hundred statutes (the number was in considerable dispute) that provided for power to exclude from disclosure (even with so little guidance as "not required in the public interest") would fit Exemption 3's "specifically exempted from disclosure by statute" language.

It was back to Congress for the Nader forces. And once again they were successful, with passage of an amendment as part of the Sunshine Act of 1976. The committee report accompanying the law stated: "A statute that merely permits withholding, rather than affirmatively requiring it, would not come within this paragraph, nor would a statute that fails to define with particularity the type of information it requires to be withheld. Thus for example section 1104 of the Federal Aviation Act. . .would not qualify under this exemption." With this "clearly expressed congressional intention," the *FAA v. Robertson* decision was undone. It took seven years from Robertson's first efforts in 1969 to subject FAA safety data to public view, but finally the law, at least, was clear.

8

Policing the Professions

Morrison first became aware of the New York Bar's residency requirement when he was preparing for the bar exam before his first job in New York City. "The idea of residence seemed absurd to me," Morrison observes, "since I knew that as soon as many lawyers made partner and could afford it, they moved to Short Hills, New Jersey, or Greenwich, Connecticut, and commuted to Wall Street. It seemed to me then, as it seems to me today, to be a requirement principally aimed at protecting the bar's monopoly." Morrison had another experience early on that raised concerns in his mind about his chosen profession. He had considered at one point leaving his government job to set up his own firm and thought that he could gather a clientele by advertising. He did not know the legal rules enough at that point to understand "that solicitation of that kind was not a proper thing for a lawyer to do." He never did set up his own private practice, but when he did discover that advertising was forbidden, it seemed to him that such a prohibition might "well have some problems from a First Amendment perspective." These two issues—advertising and residency requirements—were the top items on that little scrap of yellow paper listing the issues he wanted to tackle at the Litigation Group.

Then, just prior to his interview with Nader, he happened to see a series in *The Washington Post* written by Ron Kessler about the real estate business and the various ways buyers were being taken. Two items of interest involved lawyers: the tie-ins between the real estate lawyers who did the closing and the banks who did the lending, and the minimum fee schedules used by lawyers to keep the price of real estate closings as high as possible. He added both items to his list. The Litigation Group's involvement in what is called their "policing the professions" cases is largely the result of Morrison's strong commitment to this goal from the start.

Serendipitously, Morrison was presented almost immediately with an opportunity to tackle one of these issues: minimum fees schedules. Soon thereafter another opportunity arose that enabled him to go after professional advertising prohibitions, though in this case the profession was pharmacy, not law (though

115

before long his success in this case managed to rope in lawyers as well). Both of these cases, which began within months of his coming to Washington, would turn out to be major Supreme Court victories—quite a *coup* for any law firm, let alone one operating on a shoestring and with such a green staff.

Two weeks after Morrison arrived in Washington, Lewis H. Goldfarb, an attorney employed by the Federal Trade Commission's Bureau of Consumer Protection, filed a class action suit in the U.S. District Court for the Eastern District of Virginia against the Fairfax County Bar Association, the Alexandria Bar Association, the Arlington County Bar Association and the Virginia State Bar. His complaint charged the four bar associations with illegal price-fixing under the Sherman Antitrust Act and sought treble damages for the excessive fees the Goldfarbs and other Reston, Virginia, homeowners had been forced to pay attorneys to represent them in house closings.

On October 26, 1971, the Goldfarbs signed a contract to purchase a home from a developer in Reston, Virginia. The contract included a provision that required them to use the services of a specific attorney for the closing. Goldfarb contacted the attorney designated in the contract, A. Burke Hertz, to inquire about his charges. Hertz advised him that the cost would be the fee listed on the minimum fee schedule promulgated by the local bar—1 percent of the first $50,000 of the loan amount or purchase price, whichever was greater, with a minimum of $100, and 0.5 percent from $50,000 to $100,000. In his case, the charge figured out to $522.50. [To put this fee in perspective, it amounted to nearly double the weekly salary ($15,000 a year, or $288 a week) that Morrison was getting at the Litigation Group in 1972.] The fee seemed quite excessive to Goldfarb.

"The house we selected," Goldfarb explains, "was one of twenty-one houses still under construction in a cluster built by a single developer. The sales contract specified the name of an attorney designated by the developer to handle the settlement. ... Under this arrangement the attorney would agree to provide the developer with a variety of legal services incident to the developer's acquisition of a suitable site and adequate construction financing. These services would include a complete examination of title for the entire parcel of land which was necessary to secure the construction loan. In return for these services the developer would agree to require all home-buyers to use this attorney to handle their settlements. In a typical development of thirty townhouses costing $40,000 each, the attorney would charge these purchasers according to the minimum fee schedule, a total of $12,000—just for updating his earlier title examination, a service that could not require more than a few hours of a clerk's time."

Goldfarb sent letters to thirty-six attorneys to inquire whether they would charge less for his simple closing (which he could not do himself since he was licensed to practice only in the District of Columbia). Nineteen attorneys replied by letter. None of them offered to charge below the minimum fee schedule or knew of lawyers who would. Sample replies included:

116

My office naturally follows the minimum fee schedule as endorsed by the Bar Association. ... I have no knowledge of any attorneys who do not follow the set schedule.

Enclosed is a copy of the minimum fee schedule for the Northern Virginia Bar. The cannon [sic] of ethics for our bar association prohibits an attorney from charging below the minimum.

[A]ny attorney who would reduce his fee for title examination in order to obtain your business would, in my opinion, run afoul of the 'no solicitation' rule.

Goldfarb was incensed, but trapped. He hired Hertz and paid the required fee. He had his home, but he continued to stew. Goldfarb's sense of injustice was heightened by his investigations into closing costs in other areas around D.C. In both D.C. and Maryland, title insurance companies were permitted to use non-lawyers to perform the title search, which lowered the cost to about $160 for a comparable closing. Why should he have to pay more? Why should Virginia lawyers be allowed to engage in price-fixing? What public purpose was served by allowing attorneys to gouge the public? As a consumer protection attorney, how could he let this go on?

Shortly after his closing, Goldfarb read about an opinion issued by the Virginia State Bar in response to a formal opinion issued by the American Bar Association (ABA) about fee schedules. The ABA opinion had been issued in response to pressures from Attorney General Ramsey Clark in 1965 about the seemingly anti-competitive and mandatory nature of fee schedules. The Virginia Bar stated that it disagreed "with part of the ABA Formal Opinion 323 and that it was the opinion of this Committee that evidence that an attorney habitually charges less than the suggested minimum fee schedule adopted by his local bar association raises a presumption that such lawyer is guilty of misconduct and requires the lawyer to produce evidence that such charges are not made for the purpose of soliciting business."

This clear indication that the Virginia State Bar considered the minimum fee schedule binding and enforceable by disciplinary action, combined with the nineteen admissions by individual attorneys that the fee schedule was in essence a fixed-fee agreement, provided Goldfarb with sufficient evidence to file a class action suit for damages under antitrust law on behalf of himself and others who had been forced to pay the minimum closing costs in Reston. His case on its face might seem simple and obvious. All he wanted was for the court to apply the antitrust laws to lawyers in the same way they were applied to other businesses, but this was something no court had yet done and something the bar associations had long fought. Moreover, to pursue his case he would be up against some powerful forces.

To reduce the advantage of his competition a bit, he wrote to the state attorney general requesting help. "This is a public interest lawsuit," Goldfarb noted in his letter, "which, if successful, will work to the benefit of all consumers throughout the State of Virginia. ... We are, in a very real sense, acting as private attorneys general in protecting the interests of Virginia citizens. ... We would expect the State of Virginia to support our cause and, at the very least, file an amicus brief for our position." He hoped that his plea would at least prevent the attorney general from providing a "free" defense for the state bar—a defense that, as a Virginia resident, would be paid for in part with Goldfarb's own tax dollars. Goldfarb noted that the minimum fee schedule was an action of the bar intended to benefit its members, not the public, and had not been authorized by state statute or the courts. "The funds available to support this case," Goldfarb continued, "are very limited; I am personally handling the largest portion of the legal work in my spare time. ... Conversely, the Virginia Bar is one of the wealthiest, most powerful institutions in the State with a limitless supply of legal talent. The Arlington County Bar Association alone has already hired the firm of Williams, Connolly and Califano, one of the most talented and expensive firms in the country. Surely the entire State Bar can raise the funds to pay for its own defense. It would be infinitely unfair for the State to add its resources to the already unbounded resources of the State's legal profession." His entreaty was to no avail. The attorney general stepped in and provided representation for the bar.

Within a month Goldfarb ran into a stone wall. In response to his complaint, attorneys from Williams, Connolly and Califano on behalf of the Arlington Bar raised an objection to Goldfarb's role as counsel: "Since the plaintiff, Lewis Goldfarb, will be a witness in this litigation he may not ethically act as counsel for the plaintiffs, and may not in his individual capacity represent a class of persons." Now, challenging the $522 fee would cost big bucks.

But Goldfarb had already met with Alan Morrison. When the case was filed, Morrison read about it in the local papers. It was "precisely the case that I was looking for," Morrison recalls. Mark Silbergeld (who had recently left the FTC to join one of Nader's organizations) brought Morrison and Goldfarb together. Throughout March and April, Morrison helped Goldfarb on a few matters in developing the case. When Goldfarb discovered he could not do the job himself, he turned to Morrison for help.

The bar's high-powered attorneys may have thought that their motion to dismiss Goldfarb as counsel was a stroke of genius—that eliminating him would kill the case—but the result was to bring in a full-time crusader, one whose abilities and reputation this case would help to establish. "In *Goldfarb* the facts were wonderful," Morrison recalls. "There was no doubt about the adherence by the local attorneys to the minimum fee schedule since nineteen of them admitted it in letters to the Goldfarbs. The fee charged was plainly exorbitant in light of the work required simply to review a title insurance policy, especially since there were other significant charges for every other little item. [Goldfarb's total bill from the attorney was $637.50—$522.50 for examination of title, $25 for preparation of title insurance papers, $30 for preparation of a trust mortgage and a note, $30 for preparation of the deed and $30 for a closing fee.] There was no question that the motive behind the fee schedule was greed, since the state bar's report that launched the program had bemoaned the fact that lawyers were 'committing economic suicide' and recommended fee schedules as the cure. Thus, there was plenty of 'olfactory evidence,' which did not obscure the clean legal issue of the applicability of the antitrust laws to lawyers in the most favorable context imaginable—a classic case of price-fixing that might well bring criminal charges if anyone else had done it."

It was a good case for other reasons as well. It was a perfect opening step in the long journey toward his goal of reforming the legal profession to better serve the public and the ends of justice. Like the NAACP before him, Morrison understood the importance of starting with a case that allowed the court to nibble at the bait before asking it to swallow the hook. Minimum fees were such an obvious pocketbook issue for lawyers, but their "public interest" component was so thin a veil. If he could get the court to rule against the bar on this, then the proverbial camel's nose would be under the tent. The bar associations' absolute claim to self-regulation on other matters, like advertising, would be on shakier grounds.

The practice of law, it is said, is a learned profession, not a trade. Lawyers provide personal services. They do not sell commodities or make products. The learned professions, it is argued, require self-regulation to achieve high standards of education and ethics. Professional organizations (like bar associations, medical associations or engineering associations) have the responsibility for policing their membership; only someone who was trained in the profession would be capable of determining what the standards should be and whether someone was following them (and how to punish them if they were not). We do not need antitrust laws to discipline professionals and keep them from taking advantage of us; we can trust them to be fair because, after all, they are professionals. So the logic goes. Goldfarb and Morrison did not buy the logic, but of all the professions, the law profession was likely to be the hardest to attack.

The legal community is unique as a learned profession because of its connection to the courts. Each state bar is in part a creature of the highest court in the state. Each member of the bar is an officer of the court. State law gives power to the state courts to regulate the practice of law and prescribe codes of ethics and disciplinary procedures. The state court issues rules for some aspects of the practice of law, for ethical standards and disciplinary procedures, and often delegates the rest of the power of regulation to the state bar. The bar then issues further rules for specifics the court has not acted upon. Sometimes the court officially adopts the bar's rules, sometimes not (the procedure varies from state to state). Because of this court-delegated rulemaking and enforcement power, state bars argue that they are state agencies and thus protected from federal antitrust laws that are directed at business and industrial actors. Usually they simultaneously argue that they are private entities and thus not subject to the laws that apply to public entities, such as the First Amendment, freedom of information or open meeting requirements. State bar associations do have many private functions, both social and business-related, outside their regulatory and enforcement powers. The question is, which functions are private, and which are state? Does the fact that the bar has some connection to state power protect it from laws aimed at policing businesses in the market? Does the fact that some of what the bar does is private protect it from all laws directed at holding the public sector accountable?

The question is critical to *Goldfarb v. Virginia State Bar*. Is the bar protected from charges of price-fixing when it sets minimum fees that are neither mandated nor adopted by the court? Are we expected to assume that the bar, like government agencies in general (and of course Nader's Raiders had exposed the myth there as well), is acting in the public interest when it regulates, or is it just acting like any guild by fencing out competition to maintain high prices and high profits? The answer seemed to be all too obvious: the profit motive was trumping public interest. Minimum fee schedules prevented young attorneys from charging less to get started (and denied the public a choice of less-expensive inexperience over unaffordable experience). Limits on advertising prevented young attorneys from using lower prices to attract a start-up clientele and prevented group clinic-style practices from letting potential clients know of their existence (clients that could not be gathered in the country club locker rooms or golf courses that were the venues of the big firms to rope in the big clients). Rules against prepaid legal services prevented groups of lower-income earners from paying a little regularly to ensure service when they needed it. Why were similar group insurance plans acceptable for medical services and not for legal ones? Disciplinary procedures that were secret and toothless prevented the public from knowing which lawyers were bad risks. Self-definition by the bar associations of what constitutes the practice of law, combined with the power to limit the practice of law to attorneys only, meant that many simple procedures that might easily be done by the legal equivalent of paramedics or nurse-practitioners had to be done, or approved, by expensive lawyers. Residency requirements for taking state bars exams and for practice in the state limited the ability of attorneys to practice in several states. Full-time practice requirements eliminated part-time practitioners who might be willing to charge less. And, finally, limits on the practice of public interest law firms meant that the funding for those representing the "little guys" remained marginal, discouraging more lawyers from pursuing this form of practice.

The regulation of lawyers, it turned out, was similar to what Reuben Robertson found with the regulation of airlines. It was anti-competitive and not in the public's best interest. In the case of lawyers, however, there was not a "captured" government agency that was the regulating culprit; rather it was the lawyers themselves, and cooperating (or at least not objecting) courts, who were to blame. More competition and a free flow of information for the consumer—a free and open marketplace—were the Naderites' goals, in stark contrast to their public image as the "overzealous regulation nuts."

To challenge the legal community practices that Morrison believed were destructive of the public interest, he had three options: (1) press for change within the bar organizations as a member attorney; (2) press for change in the state courts that supervise the bars; or, (3) challenge the practices in federal and sometimes state court. Morrison and other Litigation Group attorneys have tried, and continue to try, all three. None are easy. Within the bar they are up against the economic self-interest of most other current members. Though many Litigation Group attorneys are now seasoned long-termers, in the 1970s their age and lack of experience worked against them in the bar associations. Young lawyers, especially those who are challenging the status quo, are not likely to be powerful inside players within the bar association hierarchies. In the state court they faced fierce lobbying opposition from the powerful bar associations that opposed changes in self-regulation. And when they sued, they faced judges, all former lawyers, most former bigwigs in the bar associations of their states. In addition, judges have their own territorial interest in holding onto the power to regulate the bar. Fighting against these odds would be difficult at best. But it was a fight that Morrison saw as critical.

Logic might lead one to assume that all lawyers would understand the value of maintaining a public belief in the fairness of the legal process. If only the rich can afford justice, the middle class and the poor will lose faith in the civil justice system—and the middle class and poor, after all, are the majority in a system of government where an aroused and determined majority still can rule. It is never easy, though, to convince people, especially lawyers, that their short-term pocketbook interests should yield to the long-term interests of the public, or even, for that matter, to the long-term interest of their own future earning capacity. And that, of course, was what Morrison really was asking in *Goldfarb*—for the bars to let go of the protective and lucrative minimum fee schedules and let competition and the market set prices to satisfy a variety of demands.

In a gutsy move before turning the case over to the Litigation Group, Goldfarb filed a motion asking the judge who had been assigned to the case, Judge Oren R. Lewis Sr., to recuse himself on the grounds that he was "biased and prejudiced in favor of the defendants Virginia State Bar and the Arlington County Bar." The reasons for the judge's potential bias, Goldfarb's motion argued, were that he was a past president of the Arlington County Bar and an active member before becoming a judge and an honorary member since; that his son Oren Lewis Jr. was the current president of the same bar; that the son played a prominent role in the formulation of the minimum fee schedules issued in 1962 and 1969; that a second son was also a member of the same county bar; that both sons were members of the Virginia Bar; and that his two sons were members of the firm whose senior partner was current president of the Virginia Bar (the same firm in which the judge had formerly been a partner). In high dudgeon, the defendant bar associations objected. Surprising all, Judge Lewis announced from the bench that there was no cause for recusal but then stepped down anyway because he did not want to give the plaintiffs "any cause for later complaint." Though Goldfarb had to turn the case over to Morrison, he could savor one win, at least, before he let go.

Commenting later, Morrison notes that Judge Lewis' stepping down after stating there was no cause for recusal was "absolutely wrong under Court rules—rules set up to prevent judge-shopping through recusal motion threats." But then, the notion that there was "no cause for recusal was preposterous" and indicative of the problem they faced fighting the bar in court.

By mid-May 1972, three months into his new job heading up the Litigation Group, Morrison was the official counsel in *Goldfarb*. He first needed to find a Virginia lawyer to join them—to sit at the table as the official bar-sanctioned attorney because the Virginia Bar required that a Virginia Bar member be retained for all cases argued in courts (including the U.S. district and appellate courts) located within the state—another of the territorial, income-protecting rules Morrison found wanting of public-interest justification. Obviously, most Virginia Bar members were hesitant to join this particular cause, but Morrison and Goldfarb were able to find one brave soul, Leslie V. Dix, to lend his name (and his Virginia Bar membership) to their cause.

It was about this point (early September 1972) that Morrison hired Tommy Jacks, the tall Texan who worked on the Nixon impoundment cases. "I put Jacks to work immediately helping me with various aspects of the Goldfarb case," Morrison notes. One problem he felt they had to address was the question of interstate commerce. As a federal law, the Sherman Antitrust Act required that there be an effect on interstate commerce for its provisions to control. Since Goldfarb was living in Virginia when he bought the Reston house, used a Virginia bank and a Virginia title insurance company, Morrison thought they best be prepared to substantiate some interstate effect of the minimum-pricing rule. To this end, he directed Jacks to work up some "statistical evidence." Working together they devised a solution. They sent a volunteer attorney, James Owen McKenna, who was fresh out of law school (though no young whippersnapper, as he was a retired colonel who had served from 1942 to 1970 in the Army), to the office of the Recorder of Deeds for Fairfax County. Using a sampling technique invented by them on the spot, Morrison instructed the volunteer to consult every tenth deed book starting in January 1970 and continuing up to December 31, 1971. Every deed of trust within the sample was to be recorded on a preprinted worksheet noting the name of the mortgagee and its address and/or state of incorporation. Red Xs were placed by all out-of-state mortgagees; blue Xs by all in-state mortgagees; Green Xs by mortgagees whose location was unknown. The amount of money in out-of-state mortgages was then tallied for all mortgages under $100,000 (presumably a small enough figure to catch only home mortgages in the sample). The exercise came up with a figure of $38 million in mortgages provided by financial institutions outside of Virginia—a lot of interstate money.

Before the trial date, two of the local bar associations offered to settle the case. They would withdraw their minimum fee schedules and agree not to re-institute them, if Morrison would withdraw all of the damage and other claims. It seemed like a good idea to Morrison for two reasons: "First, two more law firms and two more defendants could only complicate the case. Second, the fact that two bars had settled ... seemed to me to be a psychological strong point for our case." The fact that these two bars eliminated the fee schedules, and, as Morrison puts it, "the earth continued to rotate," proved that minimum fee schedules couldn't be as critical to the future of the practice of law as the other bars were maintaining.

At trial in the district court on December 13, 1972, the parties had stipulat-ed to the basic facts, and the only witness Morrison called was his volunteer sampler. Immediately, the defendant bar association counsel objected: "[T]here is no showing that [the statistical exhibits] were prepared by use of proper sam-pling techniques, and no foundation has been laid for them." Over defendants' objections, the judge allowed the information provided by McKenna to remain in the record. The importance of this statistical evidence, whatever its statistical validity might be, was soon apparent.

After cross-examination of McKenna, defendants' counsel paraded forth a number of prominent senior Virginia attorneys obviously intended to impress the court with their wisdom or power or both. Morrison voiced repeated objec-tions, most of which the judge overruled. One strategy of the opposition was apparently to prove that the minimum fees meant that some folks got a closing for a lower cost than what the time spent would demand, thereby building a case for the "modesty" of the minimum fees. It was a strategy Morrison zeroed in on in his cross-examination of the defendants' witness, F. Sheild McCandlish, a real estate attorney who had been in practice in Virginia for twenty-five years:

Morrison: Did you say earlier in your testimony, sir, that you in some cases were charging less than the cost?

McCandlish: Yes, very definitely.

Morrison: And do you say that is true in all of your cases, sir?

McCandlish: No, I would say not.

Morrison: I would hope not, sir.

McCandlish: I certainly hope not, too. I will say this, though. I have been told at a partnership meeting on several occasions back in, I would say, 1968, 1967-68, along in there, that the real estate department was actually losing money.

Morrison: And when the new schedule went into effect in 1969, you stopped receiving complaints from your partners about the real estate, didn't you?

Morrison's cross-examination led McCandlish right into a corner. First, Morrison got the court to focus on McCandlish's earlier testimony that a set price forced some clients to pay more than warranted for the service given in order to subsidize the costs of more expensive closings. This amounted to a definite no-no under fair-pricing requirements. Second, Morrison focused on the 1969 minimum fee price increase, prompting McCandlish to highlight the pocketbook interest that drove the increase, thereby exposing the absence of any public interest motive or result. The witness did some fast talking to try to escape from his corner, but it obviously did not work with the judge.

A few weeks later, on January 5, 1973, Judge Albert V. Bryan Jr. announced his decision. It was a big win for the Litigation Group on all counts except the question of the liability of the Virginia State Bar. "Minimum fee schedules are a form of price fixing and therefore inconsistent with antitrust statutes prohibiting anti-competitive activities," ruled the judge. "The scope of the Sherman Act is so expansive that courts have been reluctant to find exceptions." The utility of the fee schedule was no defense, indeed, part of its utility was its downfall. As the court noted: "Such an across-the-board rate, coupled with the testimony of both Goldfarb as to his efforts to obtain legal services, and Attorney F. Shield McCandlish that a flat fee results in some overcharges which make up for undercharges, is sufficient for the Court to infer, which it does, that some damage resulted to the plaintiff." The court then went on to rely on the statistical study the Litigation Group had provided to conclude that interstate commerce was clearly affected by real estate sales in Virginia.

Next the court addressed the question of whether lawyers were exempt from the Sherman Act because they perform a personal service as a learned profession. A 1950 Supreme Court decision concerning real estate boards stated that the fact "that the business involves the sale of personal services rather than commodities does not take it out of the category of 'trade' within the meaning of §3 of the Act." With this guidance and no square decision on the lawyer exemption by the Supreme Court, Judge Byron declined to apply such an exemption. His comments almost show disgust with the whole issue:

> The Court has some question whether the adoption of a minimum fee schedule is itself "professional." It seems to the Court that there is a basic inconsistency between the lofty position that professional services, not commodities, are here involved and the position that a minimum fee schedule is proper. The former properly contemplates differences in abilities, worth and energies expended of those rendering the services. Such differences are made as meaningless by a minimum fee schedule as they would be by a maximum fee

schedule. Although there is as yet no evidence of this here, the minimum fee schedule does permit the charging, by an attorney, of more than the services are worth. Certainly fee setting is the least "learned" part of the profession.

It was about as pointed as judges get: if you're so learned why are you incompetent to set your own fees based on services rendered? Finishing his analysis, the judge concluded that the county bars were too far removed from the state to be shielded by the state action doctrine, but the close relationship of the state bar to the state Supreme Court was sufficient to protect it from liability for damages.

Of course, this was not the end of the matter. The bar associations quickly appealed to the U.S. Court of Appeals for the Fourth Circuit (the circuit that services Virginia—not an auspicious court from the Litigation Group's perspective as it had a very conservative reputation at that time). Morrison responded by filing a cross appeal on the question of the liability of the state bar, the question he had lost on in the trial court's ruling. Now the whole issue was set for a second performance.

As Morrison worked on the Goldfarb appellate brief, the Watergate scandal was rapidly escalating. Senator Sam Ervin's Select Committee hearings began that spring with nightly news broadcasts focused on the unfolding story of corruption in the highest office of the land. Then on June 25, 1973, Dean opened the floodgates with accusations that Nixon himself was part of the cover-up. In early October, Vice President Agnew, facing corruption and bribery charges, was forced to resign, and ten days later, on October 20, 1973, the president made what would prove to be a monumental error. He ordered the attorney general to fire the special prosecutor he had appointed just five months earlier. The Saturday Night Massacre added more fuel to the fire of the growing scandal and further tarnished the public image of politicians and lawyers; indeed, both were regularly attacked and lampooned by the press around the nation. One might think it an auspicious time to be trying to rein in the excesses of these objects of public disdain as Morrison was trying to do in *Goldfarb*.

With the potentially unreceptive Fourth Circuit ahead, Morrison sought help. In true Washington network fashion, he had developed professional friendships with a number of attorneys at the Justice Department. He knew from his contacts that Justice was contemplating entering the case and indeed that a draft brief had been prepared. Perhaps the unfolding Watergate mess consumed the department's attention or perhaps Justice simply desired to follow the matter with its own case (indeed, it soon moved on the issue by filing a court challenge to a similar minimum fee schedule in Oregon), but for whatever reason, Justice stayed out. Morrison was all alone against the Virginia State and Fairfax County bars when they faced off on November 7, 1973. When the Fourth Circuit Court ruled on May 8, 1974, it was a complete disaster—the Litigation Group lost it all.

"I can still remember my disbelief at the rationales given by the majority judges who ruled against us on everything," Morrison recalls. "It was obvious to me that they simply were not prepared to make the organized bar subject to the antitrust laws, and indeed, even Judge Craven, who dissented on the principal issues, agreed that the state bar itself could not be held liable under these circumstances."

An appeal to the Supreme Court was the only option left open. It was by no means a sure option, however. At that time the Supreme Court accepted less than 5 percent of *certiorari* petitions not filed by the solicitor general and the Justice Department. Getting Justice aboard now seemed essential. Morrison turned up the lobbying heat at Justice. "During the course of my efforts, I became friendly with Howard Shapiro, who had worked on the matter [for Justice] at the Fourth Circuit level, and with Joe Sims, who did much of the work for the department involving bar restrictions. ... Their assistance was of great value in persuading then Solicitor General Robert Bork to enter on our side," Morrison notes. There were other pressures from the broader political environment, besides Watergate, that no doubt influenced Bork as well.

During the fall of 1973, Senator John V. Tunney (D-California) held well-publicized hearings in Washington and around the country investigating the legal profession and how it was serving, or not serving, the needs of the people. On September 23, 1973, Goldfarb related the story of his case to the committee. In an address to delegates at the May 1974 annual meeting of the American Bar Association, Senator Tunney asked whether the ABA "is more interested in protecting the pocketbooks of its members than in delivering services to those who need them the most?" A *Wall Street Journal* article covering Tunney's speech at that meeting noted, "congressional scrutiny isn't the only thing bothering lawyers. Long insulated from serious change by the influence it wields, the legal profession now finds many of its traditions are being rocked by scandal, politics, public dissatisfaction and splits within the profession." The article noted that a Harris opinion poll showed only 24 percent of Americans viewed lawyers favorably.

It was about as good a political climate as one could ask for to take on the legal profession and get the Justice Department's cooperation. Solicitor General Bork filed a brief supporting the *cert* petition. With the handwriting on the wall, the Fairfax Bar tried a last-ditch effort to prevent Supreme Court review and thereby hold onto its appeals court win. With much public fanfare, it voluntarily withdrew its fee schedule. The ploy was to no avail. The writ was granted. Bork and Morrison would be on the same side in the Supreme Court for *Goldfarb*, while just months before Morrison had led the court attack against Bork's elevation to the position of attorney general after the firing of Watergate Special Prosecutor Archibald Cox. (A decade later, the Litigation Group would play a major role in Bork's defeat for a Supreme Court appointment with publication of its book *The Judicial Record of Judge Robert H. Bork*.) Such is the way of politics and the legal profession—today's ally, tomorrow's adversary.

Morrison and the "kids" set to work to put together a tough, thorough brief. They began to reread the case files, exhibits and fee schedules, finding more evidence showing how much the schedules were based on greed instead of public service. They came up with more antitrust cases to mine in support of their position. "In some cases the research involved rereading and rethinking cases, and in others it involved exploring related areas of the law that had not previously seemed relevant to this case. Part of this was due to the fact," Morrison admits, "that my antitrust background was modest, to say the least, and part of it was due to the fact that the issues only became clear as the case moved on." When the American Bar Association filed an *amicus*, not so much to protect minimum fees but because of its concern that everything lawyers did could be swept in under the antitrust laws if it lost this one, the Litigation Group attorneys scrambled to respond in the reply brief. When the D.C. Bar weighed in on Goldfarb's side, it offered an opportunity to show that attorneys could do nicely without the fee schedules (more proof "that the earth continued to rotate"). Draft briefs and suggestions flew back and forth around the cluttered offices at 2000 P Street. So blatant was the Texas Bar's defense of minimum fee schedules for protecting the profession's high income (in its *amicus* brief) that it provided just the ammunition Morrison needed to show the bar's motive. In the end Morrison submitted an eighty-six page brief and a twenty-six page reply brief. It was, Morrison explains, "probably too long, but there was a lot to be said about the opinions below. There were a great many facts, and there were three major issues."

While the briefs could be as long as needed (this was before the fifty-page limit instituted in 1977), the oral was limited to one half hour for each side. As is Morrison's rule for everyone, himself included, he prepped for the oral in several moot courts. Everyone ganged up and fired everything they could think of at him. "I knew I needed to get the argument off on the right foot," Morrison recalls, "and put the Bar in the defensive position of having to defend its greed." He found his ammunition handily provided by the Virginia Bar itself. In the report accompanying the 1962 minimum fee schedule prepared by the Committee on Law and Economics of the Virginia Bar was this statement: "Slowly but surely lawyers are committing economic suicide as a profession." Following this was the prescription for the malady: minimum fees.

Goldfarb was argued on March 25, 1975, and indeed, Morrison began with his "economic suicide" opening. Chief Justice Burger asked whether the minimum fee schedule played a "general public interest factor, a social interest in not having a system in which every title search costs only $15—mind you, not $50, but $15—because such a low fee would necessarily result in obviously shoddy work." Morrison responded, "No, the minimum fee schedules are not needed to maintain the quality of services; fee schedules are disappearing." He then noted that the Arlington County Bar and Alexandria County Bar had withdrawn theirs (he didn't note to the court at oral that both bars had withdrawn them as a result of a settlement agreement in this lawsuit, however). Justice Stewart asked:

> What about self-regulation as practiced by Ph.D.s, or doctors of divinity? If a conspiracy among them is confined to graduate schools, or to divinity schools, then the public interest is not adversely affected, and only when the public interest is hurt by the impact of any restraint only then does the Sherman Act become applicable?

Morrison agreed. Then came the big question for Morrison's long-term agenda—the question of lawyer advertising—this time from Justice White: "What about agreements not to solicit?" Morrison took it head on, replying that the antitrust law on its face included all businesses and that if there were to be an exemption, it was up to elected legislators—state or national—to let the lawyers out from under its provisions, not up to the lawyers or the courts to give them a special dispensation.

Solicitor General Bork followed Morrison, supporting the argument that there was no exemption in the law for the learned professions, bar included. "The circulation of price lists would be a Sherman Act violation if these attorneys were anyone else," Bork argued. "[O]ne searches in vain for the principle that price-fixing is ethical," he continued. "If attorneys combine, and pit their collective strength against and not in behalf of their clients, in order to win out in a commercial fee battle, why must that be viewed as ethical? The setting of a fee in fact raises a conflict of interest between the attorney and the client he is both representing and charging."

On June 16, 1975, the Public Citizen Litigation Group was treated to a grand slam—a unanimous decision (8-0), with Justice Powell not participating because of his prior partnership in the law firm representing the Fairfax County Bar). In a footnote to Chief Justice Burger's opinion was the quote Morrison had used to begin his oral argument: "Slowly but surely lawyers are committing economic suicide."

Victory was sweet, but it was just a way station on the road. The Litigation Group spent three more years sorting out the damages for the home-purchasers (members of the class in *Goldfarb*) and prodding the court to approve a fee settlement for the Litigation Group's work. "At the hearing on the settlement," as Morrison recalls, "the judge made a point of saying that he was awarding only $50,000 because that was all that had been requested, and that had we asked for more, he would have given it to us. At that point I rose and said to the court that, 'Of all the cases, this one seems singularly inappropriate for the lawyers to request a generous fee.'" The award covered seven hundred and nineteen hours of the Litigation Group attorneys' work over almost five years. A few months after the Goldfarb decision, *U.S. News & World Report* ran a report titled "Lower Fees, Better Service—Changes Coming in Law Practice." Its subtitle was:

"What lawyers are doing—and planning—amounts to a revolution in a profession that has long been a target of criticism." The article quoted an ABA expert, Philip J. Murphy, as predicting that group legal service plans were the wave of the future. Murphy estimated that "about 25 percent of all Americans will be under some form of group legal service plan by 1980." The vehicle for this expanded coverage was to be union fringe benefits, but the author in 1975 could not have foreseen the full import of the problems unions would soon be facing. Viewing the "revolution" from the vantage point of more than twenty-five years later, most would say that either it is moving at a snail's pace or the revolution was stamped out—at least if the headlined promise of lower fees and better service is the gauge. New fringe benefits were not to be in the cards; holding onto existing ones like health insurance would be hard enough.

* * * * *

While *Goldfarb* was chugging along through the courts, a companion case moved along a parallel track. When the Litigation Group moved to 2000 P Street off Dupont Circle, its new offices were across from those of an organization headed by Sandy Dement. Dement's group was working with the Virginia Citizens Consumer Council on a drug pricing survey aimed at showing that prescription drugs were more expensive in states such as Virginia that did not allow pharmacists to advertise their drug prices. Dement's studies showed vast differences in prices for the same drug in Virginia cities. For example, tetracycline prices ranged from $1.20 to $9 for forty tablets in Newport News—a 650 percent difference. Consumers were left with no way other than for each person to call around to drugstores asking for prices (and some stores would not quote prices over the phone) to find the least expensive source. It seemed obvious that the law harmed consumers. When Morrison heard about this, he quickly saw the potential for a lawsuit.

"It was such a perfect case as the first step in tackling the issue of attorney advertising," Morrison recalls. Here there was no question about how to weigh the truthfulness of an advertisement, so none of the murky issues of what advertising would or would not do to aid consumers were present. It was not a question of the quality of a service or whether something worked as promised. If the pharmacy advertised the price of tetracycline at $6 for forty tablets, the test of truthfulness was simply whether you could buy forty tablets for $6 there. "It was quite simply the best 'fact' situation we ever had," Morrison says. The law was plainly designed to protect the economic interests of pharmacists. There was simply no consumer interest in preventing price advertising—though the state tried mightily to find one. Moreover, the issue of rising drug prices was the subject of growing public concern and considerable attention, which of course meant that the compelling public interest of their litigation was easily evident.

Morrison and his lawyers began fashioning a legal challenge. Initially they decided to argue both on Fourteenth and First Amendment grounds. Shortly before the case was to be argued at the district level, however, the Supreme Court issued a ruling in a case quite similar to theirs that closed the door to a Fourteenth Amendment substantive due process claim. In other words, they could not claim a "harm" in the form of higher economic costs to consumers under the Fourteenth Amendment's due process clause because the harm was a substantive one, not a procedural one. The court would look at such a claim as not protected by the Constitution. Instead the question of regulating for the health and safety of citizens would be considered a state matter not reviewable by a federal court. Thus the only legal hook left was a First Amendment claim. Since the First Amendment by 1974 had been interpreted by the Supreme Court to apply to states, no state could deny citizens free speech or freedom of the press or any other First Amendment protection. The problem, of course, was that the people "speaking" (or more aptly not being allowed to speak) under the Virginia law were pharmacists. Morrison's clients were consumers—the listeners. He needed to show injury to listeners under a constitutional protection that on its face (as literally written) protects speakers only. While it might appear obvious that the flip side of free speech is the right to freely hear, the court had not previously interpreted it that way. Thus the challenge ahead was to package the argument to allow consumers' free speech rights to be injured by the prohibition on someone else's speech.

Morrison put Ray Bonner to work investigating the legal issues and developing a strategy. Bonner had come to the Litigation Group in May. The son of a traveling salesman from the Midwest, Bonner notes, "I was the first in my family to get out of high school, let alone college." From college in Illinois he headed to Stanford Law School and then a tour of duty in Vietnam as an attorney in the Marines. "Then I bummed around Europe backpacking for a while and turned liberal," he confesses. Bonner, as Morrison notes, "could talk and run farther and faster without breaking into a sweat than anyone else." This perpetual motion machine stayed just two years before moving on to run the Consumers Union office in California and then to become a journalist for the *New York Times*. But, in his short time at the Litigation Group, he helped Morrison launch one of the landmark cases in the Litigation Group's history.

Throughout the fall and winter of 1973, Bonner focused on drug prices and packaging the case. The main arguments were:

- But for the prohibition, pharmacists would advertise.

- Advertising would permit consumers (plaintiffs) to save money by alerting them to stores where they could purchase drugs more cheaply.

- Advertising would result in an overall lowering of prices for prescription drugs.

For the first point, Bonner needed pharmacists to testify that they would advertise if allowed. In the end, he found just one—the vice president of Revco, a chain drugstore. For the second point, he needed studies showing price variations among stores. Dement had these for four states, but as Bonner wrote in his memo: "Must confess to not being certain how to get those surveys into evidence—can they be admitted as are and in toto?—or must the person who prepared them be available to testify?—and would he/she be limited to testifying about what is contained in them, thus not permitting the survey itself to come into the record?" For the third point, he needed some drug company officers "perhaps from the marketing division" or a study by an academic. Fortuitously, on December 5, 1973, just days before the court argument in the case, the Department of Justice issued a research and policy paper called "Regarding State Restrictions on the Advertising of Retail Prescription Drugs." The report had been done in response to complaints about state restrictions on advertising drugs. Its conclusion was perfect: "[I]t is the Department's view that existing state legislation or regulations which prohibit or restrict price advertising of prescription drugs may well be adverse to the public interest." Bonner was able to get this supporting evidence entered as "Exhibit B," and he was equally successful in getting the rest of the supporting evidence he needed into the "stipulation of facts" (statements about the case to which both parties agreed ahead of time and provided to the court in written form).

In addition to what they had to prove, Bonner focused on what they would need to attack, that is, what he saw as the main arguments the state of Virginia would advance:

- Price advertising will encourage customers to shop around, thus making it impossible for pharmacists to monitor the drugs a customer is taking.

- Patients would pressure doctors to prescribe larger quantities of drugs so they could get a quantity discount.

- Ads would increase demand and thereby create a drug culture.

- Small retailers would buy large quantities and would end up selling stale drugs.

- Advertising would demean the profession.

Bonner pulled most of these arguments from an earlier case in which a drugstore that wished to advertise in Virginia had sued and lost. His responses were to find surveys, doctors and pharmacists to testify against these points or to argue that far less restrictive means were available to address them. Beyond developing the critical facts for the case, his bigger task was to fashion a successful First Amendment argument. Bonner worked with Morrison on the briefs and was grilled by his colleagues in moot court.

In late December 1973, Bonner argued the case before a three-judge court. At that point, if a plaintiff was challenging the constitutionality of a state law under the U.S. Constitution (here, the First Amendment), the case was assigned to a court made up of two district judges and one appeals court judge, not the usual single judge of a district court. The theory was that, if a state law was going to be found unconstitutional by a federal court, it ought to be more than one judge who said so. Moreover, if a case was appealed from a three-judge court decision, the appeal would go directly to the Supreme Court. (Since then, three-judge district courts have been eliminated for all but a handful of cases.)

In March 1974, the unanimous decision came down with an opinion by Judge Albert Bryan (the father of the district judge who had overturned the minimum-pricing scheme in *Goldfarb*), finding that the Virginia statute prohibiting drug advertising violated the First Amendment. "It wasn't quite the way we would have written it ourselves," Morrison said. "But it was there, it was in our favor, it was unanimous, and it was written by a relatively conservative judge."

"The right-to-know," Judge Byron wrote, "is the foundation of the First Amendment; it is the theme of this suit. Consumers are denied this right by the Virginia statute. It is on this premise that we grant the plaintiffs the injunction and the declaration they ask." The state immediately filed a motion for rehearing, but for some time the case sat in limbo awaiting further court action.

* * * * *

At this point Morrison found another means for advancing his argument that the First Amendment afforded protection for commercial speech. One thing Litigation Group attorneys regularly do is review Supreme Court opinions as they are printed in *Law Week*. (Before the Internet and instant access, *Law Week* was usually the fastest to keep up with court opinions. Some major decisions received next-day coverage in newspapers, though very few articles included the full decision.) Morrison also regularly reviewed the section that summarized cases recently granted *certiorari*. It was in this list that he came across a case that piqued his interest: *Bigelow v. Virginia*. A Virginia newspaper editor had been convicted under a Virginia statute for printing an advertisement for a New York clinic that performed abortions at a time when abortions were illegal in Virginia. It seemed clear that the appeal was to be based on a First Amendment claim of freedom of the press. That, Morrison thought, offered a potential boost to the pharmacy case, for what this was really about was the right of the listener to hear. He decided to seek permission to file an *amicus* brief in the case focusing on the consumer perspective with, as he admits, "a large focus on what it would do for us in the *Virginia Pharmacy* case." No doubt, the Virginia attorney general at times must have wished the Litigation Group would pick on someone else. But it was primarily geography that put Virginia in their sights.

The state had the bad fortune of being in their backyard, making litigation there a lot easier than say in Texas, California or New York.

* * * * *

Another case touching on the issue of professional advertising involved an effort by Sidney Wolfe of Public Citizen's Health Research Group to publish a directory of doctors practicing in Prince Georges County, Maryland. Using a group of volunteers, Wolfe surveyed doctors across the country by phone. The questionnaire sought basic information such as their specialty, medical school, languages spoken, hours of operation, whether they accepted Medicaid, fees, etc. The reaction of the medical officials in Maryland was swift and negative. They did everything in their power to persuade doctors not to respond, including a not-so-veiled threat that answering the questionnaire might subject a doctor to disciplinary action under the state regulation prohibiting doctors from advertising. It seemed an ideal situation for another case raising the right of consumers to know. Morrison also saw it as a useful step toward his goal of prompting the courts to address the issue of attorney advertising. They filed suit in federal court in Maryland. But this case was not a success story. "It was," Morrison declares, "a sad story of delay, which was so bad that at one point we actually filed a *mandamus* petition with the court of appeals against the district judge who had refused to convene a three-judge court to hear our case." After more delay the case was "shuttled off into the state court system for wholly indefensible reasons." Ultimately they lost the case in state court, but, by the time that happened, the law on professional advertising had moved ahead, forcing the state to change its rules on doctor advertising (though it took until late 1980 for this to happen).

* * * * *

Meanwhile, the three-judge district court in *Virginia State Board of Pharmacy v. Virginia Citizens Consumers Council* (hereafter known as *Virginia Pharmacy*) denied the motion to reconsider. In January 1975, the state appealed to the Supreme Court, and on March 17, the case was accepted. At about this point, Ray Bonner left the Litigation Group to head up the Consumers Union office in San Francisco. So Morrison took over the case as it headed for the Supreme Court.

June 16, 1975, turned out to be quite a day for Morrison. Not only did he win a unanimous *Goldfarb* decision, but a decision in the *Bigelow* newspaper advertising case came down, with the court adopting most of Morrison's consumer "right to know" argument. Indeed, the opinion barely addressed freedom of the press or editorial license. "It was," Morrison notes, "one of the high points of my professional career, and at the time, I told the press, who did not print it, and my friends, most of whom probably forgot it, that *Bigelow* was a far more important case for lawyer advertising than was *Goldfarb*." His reasoning was that it seemed a long shot that the antitrust laws would be interpreted to bar the rules restricting attorney advertising. But "if they escaped the antitrust laws, they were sure to run into the First Amendment, as interpreted broadly in *Bigelow*." A month and a half later, his brief was filed in *Virginia Pharmacy*. There, in the first paragraph of his argument, is *Bigelow*:

> Appellants have urged this Court to reverse the decision of the three-judge district court ... arguing that the First Amendment does not protect appellees' right to receive drug price information because that information is "commercial speech" to which the First Amendment does not apply. However ... in Bigelow v. Virginia ... this Court ruled that this is not law. ... It is now clear, as a result of Bigelow, that a State cannot abridge First Amendment rights simply by placing a "commercial" label on the type of speech that it desires to suppress.

The state had filed its brief several weeks before *Bigelow* was decided. "I sometimes wonder," Morrison speculates, "whether, if I had been in its position, I would have sought an extension of time to await the outcome of *Bigelow*." There was plenty of reason for doing so since Anthony F. Troy, the Virginia chief deputy attorney general, argued *Bigelow* and was to argue *Virginia Pharmacy*. He surely had read the argument put forth in Morrison's *amicus* brief in *Bigelow* and should have seen its potential impact if the court were to apply it in the drug price advertising case. More peculiar is the fact that the state's reply brief made no mention of *Bigelow*, despite Morrison's clear reliance on it in his brief. More peculiar still was the state attorney's comments at oral argument before the Supreme Court in response to a question from Justice Harry A. Blackmun, the author of the *Bigelow* opinion:

> Blackmun: Mr. Troy, I wanted to be sure you would touch upon *Bigelow* because you didn't. Your brief, of course, was filed before *Bigelow* came down.
>
> Troy: Yes, your Honor.
>
> Blackmun: And you haven't seen fit to file a supplemental, so I am particularly interested in your comment.
>
> Mr. Troy: Simply because *Bigelow* is simply not applicable.

Attorney Troy may not have thought it applied, and perhaps believed that he could make it disappear by just ignoring it, but that was not to be. Morrison's opening remarks were peppered with *Bigelow* references: "*Bigelow* clearly and unmistakably forecloses. ... *Bigelow* said you have got to look ... *Bigelow* said you have to find a clear relationship." *Bigelow* was woven throughout Morrison's argument as he carefully built his case that consumers have "an independent First Amendment right to receive drug price information."

"The First Amendment protects communications," Morrison argued, "and a communication is not complete until there has been both dissemination and receipt of information. Therefore, it is necessary to examine the entire context in which information is exchanged to determine the scope of First Amendment protection." If he was right on this, the state could regulate the speech only if it had a compelling state interest to protect the public in doing so. The veil of public interest here that the state could advance was skimpy indeed. While at the podium, Morrison found himself in the odd position of being asked to explain that "veil." The major public interest protection the state was claiming in preventing advertisement of prescription drugs was that it aided a druggist in monitoring the drugs a person was taking to ensure that one drug would not react dangerously with another. The reasoning behind this claim was difficult to explain, primarily because it was preposterous. But one justice clearly wanted Morrison to try anyway:

Question: And what do you perceive as the reasons for preventing the dissemination?

Morrison: In this case?

Question: Yes.

Morrison: Well, the only ones that have been suggested is the fact that pharmacy is a profession and I think the *NAACP against Button* case eliminates that. ... And the second is the monitoring argument. That is the only other one that has been put forward here.

Question: Well what about the monitoring? How do you tie that in? I mean, why does that fit in as a reason?
Morrison: Well, I don't think it fits in at all, obviously.

Question: Well, yes, but I gather that unless the pharmacy makes an adequate profit they won't be able to engage in this kind of activity. Is that their argument?

Morrison: No, that is not the monitoring argument.

Question: Well, what is it?

Morrison: Let me give you the monitoring argument, as I understand it.

Question: That is what I want to know.

Question: (from another justice): That is the other side.

Morrison: Monitoring is a practice ...

Question: You are being asked, in other words, to argue your opponent's case now. Is that it?

Morrison: No, I am stating their case. I am not going to argue it, I can assure you of that.

[Laughter]

The state was claiming, Morrison explained, that if consumers were informed about the prices of drugs at different drugstores around town, they might run around to different drug stores to fill different prescriptions in order to get the best price for each, thereby making it difficult for pharmacists to track the drugs an individual was taking. Thus the monitoring role of pharmacists would be undercut; they would be less able to warn about a potential antagonistic reaction of one drug with another. If the state law prohibiting advertising were upheld, the state seemed to be arguing, consumers would not shop around and would out of habit take all their business to the same pharmacy and thus the monitoring purpose would be easier to meet.

Morrison identified three problems with this logic. First, there was no evidence that the state law prohibiting drug price advertising had ever intended to aid the monitoring of patients; there was not even a word in the statute or its history about it. Moreover, there was no evidence that the state pharmacists' own code of ethics required druggists to perform a monitoring role. Second, it was the doctor who had the professional obligation to be sure drugs prescribed to a patient would not react negatively with other drugs. Third, if the state wanted some monitoring role for pharmacists, there were any number of less restrictive means of accomplishing this than the no-advertising rule. In addition, there was no evidence monitoring was working, since only a small minority of pharmacists monitored. The exchange between Morrison and the justices on these points covers pages and pages in the written transcript—nearly half of his oral argument. The back-and-forth repartee between counsel and the justices shows quite clearly why Morrison has a reputation as one of the best oral advocates around. At one point one of the justices asked him "how come the pharmacists are not involved?" Morrison replied, "Well, the pharmacists had a try at this in 1969. ... They didn't win that case. ... These are consumers and we thought that we could do a little better." To this the justice responded, "So far you have." It was reassuring, no doubt, to hear those words two-thirds of the way into the oral argument.

"In preparing for the oral argument in the *Pharmacy* case," Morrison notes, "we all knew that one of the questions I would be asked would be about the effect of a ruling here on lawyer advertising, especially since the state had put considerable emphasis on it in its brief." When the question came, it was in a "somewhat unexpected way. All of a sudden Justice White asked me, 'I suppose your next case is going to involve advertising for lawyers.'" Morrison paused for the laughter to die down, and was just about to say, "No sir, we have a case involving a doctors' directory on deck next." Before he could reply, though, Justice White said, "That's all right, you don't have to answer that one." It was a rare case, as Morrison notes, to have this justice let counsel off the hook. Probably just as well for Morrison, since the doctors' directory case never advanced anyway.

When the decision was announced on May 24, 1976, it was another big win—7-1 in Morrison's favor (with Justice John Paul Stevens, who joined the court after the case was argued, not participating and Justice William H. Rehnquist dissenting). Justice Blackmun, author of the majority opinion, wrote that a citizen's "interest in the free flow of commercial information ... may be as keen, if not keener by far, than his interest in the day's most urgent political debate." He went on to note that it is "the poor, the sick and particularly the aged" who are most harmed." A disproportionate amount of their income tends to be spent on prescription drugs; yet they are the least able to learn ... where their scarce dollars are best spent." A *New York Times* editorial called it "a significant victory for consumers." Around the nation, news commentary was similarly supportive.

It was a great win, with a lot of public visibility as an additional payoff, but there was one small glitch that might limit its usefulness for Morrison's aim to go after similar state rules prohibiting attorney advertising. Blackmun, who once served as counsel to the renowned Mayo clinic, observed in a footnote that different rules might apply when the courts considered advertising by doctors and lawyers. Members of these professions "do not dispense standardized products," he noted. Rather they "render professional services of almost infinite variety and nature." Thus price advertising could be deceptive and confusing for consumers. Commenting on this logic, a *Wall Street Journal* editorial said:

> [I]t is difficult to see what relationship exists between price advertising and professional integrity. Certainly there are a good many industries that affect human life that impose no special risks on consumers merely because they advertise the prices of their products and services. More likely the converse is true. The more information the public has the more likely it is to accurately judge who is the quack and who the honest and expert practitioner. The Supreme Court has opened the door to the supply of fuller infor-

mation. It can be hoped that it will not draw back from its affirmation that free and open exchange of market information ultimately is the best bet for protecting the consumer's interest.

Shortly after *Virginia Pharmacy* came down, Morrison was invited to speak
at the dedication of a new building at the University of Oklahoma Law School.
His role was to debate the issue of lawyer advertising with LeRoy Jeffers,
author of the Texas Bar's brief in *Goldfarb*. "He spoke very much in the fashion of an old Southern preacher," Morrison said. "I soon put him very much on
the defensive by reminding him of the story about George Allen, the Redskins
football coach, who when being consoled about a loss in which his team out-
gained and out-defensed the other side, quipped: 'Statistics are for losers.' And
so I said to Mr. Jeffers, 'Footnotes are for losers.'" From that point on, Jeffers
spent most of his time explaining why footnotes are vital, but in this case time
would prove him wrong. Within a year prohibitions against lawyer advertising
bit the dust under the First Amendment as well. However, it was not the
Litigation Group that got to the Supreme Court first on this one. "We had hoped
to be able to argue the lawyer advertising case ourselves," Morrison admits.
They were able to file an *amicus* brief, but that was all. The court's 5-4 ruling,
issued in June 1977, struck down the absolute prohibition on lawyer advertising on First Amendment grounds. As Morrison proudly notes, the Litigation
Group's brief was mentioned by Justice Blackmun in a footnote observing that
consumers appeared to be on the side of the advertising lawyers, even though
it was they whom the state was supposed to be protecting. Footnotes may be
for losers, but they are worth something for those who file *amicus* briefs.

9

Amplifying the Consumer's Voice

In July 1971, the International Telephone and Telegraph Corporation (ITT) pledged $400,000 to help fund the Republican National Convention, which was to be held in San Diego the following summer. Besides the size of the donation (which was the biggest sum ever promised by a corporation to a convention and twenty times as much as anyone else had pledged for that convention), what was particularly troubling was the timing. On July 30, 1971, just nine days after the pledge had been given, the Justice Department announced that its civil antitrust action, which sought to stop the merger of ITT with the Hartford Insurance Company, had been settled by consent decree. The potential of cause and effect did not escape Ralph Nader's attention.

ITT had been gobbling up small, medium and large companies in the United States and abroad throughout the 1960s. By 1970, its portfolio included a number of life insurance companies, Avis car rental, Grinnell sprinkler systems, Canteen vending and food service, Levitt, and a host of others. ITT was not alone in this expansion and diversification quest. Many other international conglomerates were being created then as well. But ITT was one of the biggest and fastest-growing among the giants. In later Senate hearings on the merger and its connection to the $400,000 donation, Senator Philip Hart asked, "Have we reached a point in our society where there has been permitted to develop a private concentration of power which, because of the enormity of their reach, makes impossible the application of public policy to them? We had better get an answer or the day will come when there will be private power—and there needn't be anybody with a black hat involved with its creation—beyond reach." This, of course, is precisely what Nader fears: when power gets too big, when no one can control it, the little guy gets hurt. When ITT Chairman Howard Geneen set his sights on Hartford Insurance, Nader set his sights on ITT and Geneen.

With Reuben Robertson leading the charge, Nader's Raiders began fighting the ITT/Hartford merger in 1970, first before the Connecticut insurance commissioner and then, working with local counsel to challenge the merger in state court. At the same time, the Justice Department had an antitrust action under way to challenge this and two other ITT mergers. However, because

Connecticut law provided that no insurance company could be sold without a finding first by the state insurance commissioner that it would be in the public interest, the state legal system offered another promising avenue for attack in the event that the Justice Department failed. Robertson filed dozens of motions, secured piles of documents and took hours of depositions, but it was all to no avail. First, the Connecticut insurance commissioner ruled that the merger *would* be in the public interest, and the state courts upheld his ruling. Then, the Justice Department and ITT settled the antitrust case by a consent decree, which allowed the Hartford/ITT merger to stand. Even after the merger was approved, Robertson continued sifting through mounds of documents he had secured through discovery and depositions taken in the state court challenge. He just knew there was something lurking among the pages, the missing piece of the puzzle that would explain why Justice dropped the case.

Two months after the consent decree was announced, Robertson wrote to Deputy Attorney General Richard G. Kleindienst objecting to the agreement and to the secrecy under which it had been reached. He also asked about the relationship between the $400,000 donation and the settlement. Kleindienst wrote back, unequivocally stating that he had no knowledge of an ITT donation and that the settlement between the Justice Department and ITT was negotiated entirely by someone else in the department. He also made a similar statement in writing to the Democratic Party's national chairman. Both denials would soon come back to haunt him.

Months passed. Nader and Robertson, as well as a number of journalists and politicians, continued to question the coincidence of the settlement following so closely on the heels of the $400,000 donation. Nader asked investigative journalist Jack Anderson if he could find out anything more about the Hartford merger. Author Anthony Sampson describes what happened next in his 1973 book, *The Sovereign State of ITT*:

> Anderson was naturally interested in the "carnivorous corporate monster," as he calls it, and he had his contacts within ITT. He "sowed some seeds, and cast some bread upon the waters," and his assistant, Brit Hume, was in touch with Reuben Robertson. Eventually the seeds came to fruition, and there came mysteriously into his hands the extraordinary document that came to be known as the Dita Beard Memorandum.

On February 28, 1972, soon after Alan Morrison arrived in D.C., Anderson's column exposing this memorandum appeared in *The Washington Post* and seven hundred other papers around the nation. And what an expose it was. "We now have evidence," Anderson began, "that the settlement of the Nixon administration's biggest antitrust case was privately arranged between Attorney General John Mitchell and the top lobbyist for the company involved." The memorandum that provided this evidence came from ITT's only registered lobbyist, Dita Beard. Her memo explicitly linked the $400,000 contribution to the consent decree and named individuals at the highest level as being involved— Mitchell, White House aide Bob Haldeman and even President Nixon, as well as a number of other top players in both ITT and the administration. The memo ended with, "Please destroy this, huh?" Its recipient, the head of the ITT Washington office, obviously did not do what ITT would move quickly to do after Anderson's column was published: turn on the shredders.

In the days following publication of that column, Hume and Robertson dug up even more. Hume managed to catch investment banker Felix Rohatyn at Kennedy Airport. When Hume asked about the Beard memo, Rohatyn exploded: "That's absolute bullshit." He knew Mitchell was not involved, and he knew this for certain because the head of ITT had assigned him to make the economic case to the administration, and to do this he had met about six times with Kleindienst. Hume shared this statement with Robertson, who reminded him of Kleindienst's denial. With this fact, the followup column's lead was even worse: "We have now established that Attorney General designate Richard Kleindienst told an outright lie about the Justice Department's sudden out-of-court settlement of the Nixon administration's biggest antitrust case."

The timing of all this could not have been worse for Kleindienst. The next day, he was to take over the Justice Department as acting attorney general for Mitchell, who was leaving to run Nixon's re-election campaign. Just days before, the Senate Judiciary Committee had closed its hearing on his nomination with a favorable recommendation to the full Senate. Almost immediately, everyone denied everything. Within days, the Senate Judiciary confirmation hearings were reopened, and the players involved were subjected to weeks of questioning. A lot came out, but in the end no clear answers emerged, and Kleindienst's nomination was approved (he did not last long, though, as the Watergate scandal would force his resignation less than a year later).

At the Litigation Group, Morrison and Robertson's legal noses were twitching. There was still a case for them to pursue in all this. They could just smell it. Morrison did some research and concluded that an argument could be made that the settlement had been procured by misrepresentation since the Justice Department had not told the judge about the meetings between Kleindienst and Rohatyn. After the consent decree was announced but before the Dita Beard memo came to light, Nader and Robertson had filed an *amicus curiae* brief in opposition in the district court, but the court had quickly approved the decree, ignoring the points raised in the brief. At that time consent decrees in antitrust cases had to be approved by a U.S. district court, and interested outside parties could seek to file *amicus* briefs or intervene. Largely as a result of the ITT case and its aftermath, the consent decree process is now more open and harder to manipulate.

60(b)(3) of the Federal Rules of Civil Procedure allows the court to revisit a final consent decree and declare it void if there is new evidence that "mistakes, inadvertence, excusable neglect, newly discovered evidence, or fraud" have occurred, provided the motion is made within a reasonable time (not more than one year after the final judgment). But only a legitimate party can ask the court to revisit the matter. As *amicus*, Nader and Robertson were not parties to the case. What they needed to do was to formally intervene, and to do that they had to show how they were or would be harmed by the existing consent decree. They also had to show that neither of the formal parties to it (the Justice Department and ITT) would adequately represent their interests. Morrison thought he could prove the harm his client could suffer since Robertson was covered by a Hartford Insurance policy and as a consumer his premiums might be affected by the merger. Moreover, both Robertson and Nader had been involved at every court and administrative stage to challenge the merger, so their sustained interest was a given. Since Justice and ITT were both a party to the secret meetings withheld from the court, it was highly unlikely that either of them would raise the issue on their own.

As to the merits of their challenge, Morrison was equally certain that he had a strong case. The argument that Rohatyn had made on ITT's behalf to Kleindienst during those six meetings (information about this came out in the Senate hearings) was that if ITT had to divest itself of Hartford Insurance, there would be economic chaos in both domestic and international markets because ITT needed the cash flow from the cash-rich insurance company to carry the cash-poor side of its portfolio. Denied the ability to balance its other debts with Hartford's riches, ITT would fail, stockholders would suffer and economic ruin would ensue. Morrison believed that the claim of "hardship to defendants and their stockholders and a possible ripple effect on the stock market" was the "single most important reason for [the Justice Department's] agreeing to the compromise." Moreover, failure to disclose this fact to the court prevented the court from accurately weighing the public interest protection afforded by the negotiated settlement. Morrison's reasoning was carefully structured to illuminate the court's vested interest in protecting its own source of information, and a court ought to be receptive to that, or so he thought. "If an affirmative duty of disclosure is not imposed on the Government," Morrison argued in his brief, "a court will never know whether it has been given sufficient information to perform its function." His motion to intervene and argument on the merits was filed on May 4, 1972, shortly after the conclusion of the Senate hearings on Kleindienst's nomination. There was no problem with the timeliness of his filing, as the final judgment had been entered just seven months earlier.

The district court judge, Joseph Blumenfeld, was not receptive to Morrison's arguments. First he denied the motion to intervene, which in effect meant there was no case, and court doctrine would require that this be the end of the matter. But, having said there was no case, this judge went on to decide the merits of the challenge Morrison made. But the judge changed Morrison's challenge from one made as "a misrepresentation" to an accusation of "fraud on the court." The latter charge required a much higher level of proof, and the judge found that it was unfounded.

At that time, all appeals from government antitrust cases went directly to the Supreme Court. As Morrison wrote in his appeal to the Supreme Court just a few weeks later: "Had appellants relied upon a claim of fraud upon the court, the District Court's determination would have been correct. However, appellants at no time alleged fraud on the court, but claimed only that the Government's failure to disclose to the Court the single most important factor that impelled it to settle the case constituted a 'misrepresentation.'" Admitting that only the "most egregious conduct will support a claim of fraud on the court," Morrison noted that, "[t]o support a claim of misrepresentation, it is not even necessary to show an intent to deceive." Having analyzed the wrong claim, the district court came up with the wrong answer. "The District Court also failed," Morrison continued, "to take cognizance of the fact that this action is not simply a controversy between private parties but is a civil antitrust suit ... requiring a determination that the agreement is equitable and in the public interest." Since the court was not given the full information, it "could not have fully determined whether the decree was in the public interest." If the Justice Department did not have to disclose, and if the court did not mandate this, then how could the court do its job? If a district judge is "simply to perform a ministerial function in signing a consent decree," Morrison argued, then the Supreme Court should "clearly and unequivocally so state in order to save considerable time and effort by all concerned." It seemed obvious to Morrison that this was not what either the law or the Supreme Court's own precedent had in mind. And since about 70 percent of all antitrust actions brought by the government ended with consent decrees, Morrison continued, it was obviously a matter of great importance.

A short time after he filed the appeal, the high court summarily affirmed the lower court decision and that was the end of the case. It was not the last word on the matter, however. In 1973, Senator John Tunney held hearings on the Justice Department's role in antitrust consent decrees, leading to passage of the Tunney Act. The new law set out elaborate procedures the Justice Department would have to follow in negotiating future antitrust consent decrees, including a requirement for making public all the reasons the department had for settling. Failure to disclose meetings such as the secret meetings between Kleindienst and Rohatyn thus would now be against the law and thereby a basis for overturning a court approval of a consent decree.

While working on the "misrepresentation" approach, Morrison and Robertson also pursued other avenues of attacking the ITT consent decree. One took them to the Securities and Exchange Commission (SEC); the other to the Internal Revenue Service (IRS).

Robertson had received a tip from someone inside the SEC about an obscure provision in the Investment Advisor Act of 1940 that provided that, if a company were subject to an injunction and performed the role of an investment adviser that sold annuities or mutual funds (as one of the ITT subsidiaries did), the company would have to get a waiver from the SEC to continue operating the annuity or mutual fund. "Just a day or two before the time in which a stockholder could object to a waiver was to elapse, Reuben found an ITT stockholder who agreed to let us represent him in an objection," Morrison recalls. So Morrison and Robertson filed an objection to the waiver with the SEC. Irving Pollack, then chief of enforcement at SEC, called a hearing on the matter, the major issue of which would be an investigation into the "character" of ITT. After all, if a company was subject to an investigation by the Justice Department that resulted in some form of corrective action (injunction or consent decree), there may be legitimate questions as to whether it was sufficiently trustworthy to be handling other people's investments. Based on his exhaustive review of thousands of pages of ITT documents, Robertson was certain that ITT's corporate character was highly questionable.

Representing ITT was Joe Flom, "a big wheeler and dealer at the law firm of Skadden, Arps, Meagher & Flom, who began his testimony by berating Robertson and me," says Morrison. "Pollack cut him off almost immediately, saying something like, 'Mr. Flom, we know Mr. Morrison and Mr. Robertson and we know their work. They are here with a client and we will have no more of this berating business. We will get to the merits.'" After the hearing, pleadings went back and forth and Morrison began initial discovery. "We had them tied in knots," Morrison said. "At one point we subpoenaed their general counsel, and the administrative law judge let us do that. The process went on for months. Reuben and I used to joke that two boys and a typewriter put them to a grinding halt." Three years later Morrison sent a "third anniversary card to one of the ITT attorneys working with Flom." In the end, ITT abandoned the application and sold the subsidiary, and thus SEC closed the hearing. Not a big win really, but rather satisfying nonetheless.

The IRS avenue was far more successful; indeed it proved quite lucrative, though it was a long time before they saw the money. While "mucking around" in the ITT documents, Robertson discovered something quite odd. ITT's initial move in its takeover effort was a purchase of a 6 percent block of Hartford Insurance stock. This purchase was for cash, but the rest of the takeover offer, when it came, was to be financed by an exchange of ITT stock for the Hartford stock. But, for the Hartford stockholders to avoid paying capital gains tax in a takeover, the entire exchange would have to be in stock. Any cash payments would spoil the deal. To avoid this problem, which was critical to obtaining stockholder acceptance of the merger, ITT got a ruling from the IRS that, if ITT would sell its 1.7 million Hartford shares (the 6 percent it had bought for cash) as quickly as possible, and if the sale were to be unconditional, then the Hartford stockholders would not have to pay about $200 million in capital gains taxes. None of this information was made public. Even more important, Robertson discovered among all those mounds of documents that the sale of the 1.7 million shares had been to an Italian bank, Mediobanca. When he and Morrison analyzed the contract for the sale, it became clear that the sale was a sham since Mediobanca bore no risk and ITT bought the stock back when the merger went through. So they prepared a memo laying out how the Italian bank had no economic risk or stake in the purchase and sent this along with a letter to the IRS asking that the tax ruling be revoked. (This information was also most useful in the SEC hearing into the character of ITT and used to good advantage by Morrison and Robertson.) On the basis of this letter and its own investigations, and the passage of several years, the IRS revoked its tax ruling allowing the sale to avoid capital gains taxes. ITT challenged this, but eventually agreed to settle and pay the tax.

A provision in the tax law allows a finder's fee for any person who gives information to IRS about a tax fraud if the IRS successfully collects the tax. Robertson and Morrison filed a request for the reward. The request languished for a long time, but the Litigation Group finally received a check for $120,000, which was split fifty-fifty with the Center for Study of Responsive Law, which is where Robertson worked when the effort against ITT began. It remained one of the largest legal fees the Litigation Group earned for many years to come.

As a result of the tax ruling in the ITT affair becoming public, another public interest attorney, Bill Dobrovir, successfully brought a suit against the IRS on behalf of Tom Field of Tax Analysts and Advocates to have private rulings like the ITT one made public. With the case largely won, but fearing adverse congressional reaction based on IRS pressure, Field, Morrison and Larry Ellsworth tried another tack. "Working with staff to the Joint Committee on Taxation," Morrison notes, "we helped hammer out a revision to a section of the tax code to require that such rulings be made public in the future."

The combination of a litigation and legislative strategy proved essential to success in this early fight against excessive accumulation of power. And though this goal would become more difficult to pursue in the years ahead, as globalization increased and more multinationals emerged, their efforts brought about change that would make the antitrust process and IRS tax rulings more visible in the future. That it brought some funds to pursue their public law practice was an added bonus.

* * * * *

Robertson's activities prior to Morrison's arrival sparked another case, this one dealing with the airlines (though Nader would be the one to ignite the really famous airline case). In May 1971, a group of seven law student volunteers arrived at Washington National Airport. Their purpose was to distribute materials concerning problems faced by the flying public—problems like lost baggage, canceled flights, being "bumped" when flights were oversold, excessive rate increases granted by the Civil Aeronautics Board, and the like. The handout was headed, "Tired of being taken for a ride?" with a cartoon character asking, "When is a contract not a contract?" A cartoon pilot replies: "When it's an airline ticket!" The back side of the sheet contained a membership form for joining Robertson's newly formed Aviation Consumer Action Project (ACAP) with a brief description of its board members and its current projects. Four of the students went inside to distribute the leaflets. The rest did so at the entrance.

The affidavit of one of the students, Barry Wilner, described what happened next. "I proceeded for about 30 minutes to quietly distribute the consumer information inside the airport. At no time did I force the leaflets upon anyone nor was there even the slightest commotion or disturbance caused by my activities. ... However, I found myself being followed by a uniformed individual wearing a badge indicating that he was an airport security guard." Shortly thereafter, a man who identified himself as the acting chief of airport operations approached, asked for a copy of the leaflet, and stated that the students would have to go outside. The students complied, but soon the airport chief returned and told them they could not distribute their leaflets outside either and threatened to have them arrested if they refused to leave. Over the next few weeks, student volunteers attempting to hand out literature at other airports had similar experiences.

In response, Robertson investigated bringing suit against the airports for denying the students their First Amendment right of free speech. Precedent was favorable to such an action. It was firmly established, by that point, that picketing and leafleting were protected activities under the First Amendment and that the nature of a facility, rather than the fact of public or private ownership, controlled whether it would be considered a public space. "The more an owner opens up his property for use by the public in general, the more do his rights become circumscribed by the constitutional and statutory rights of those who use it," the Supreme Court had noted in 1946. It seemed a great case. Being too busy himself with other ACAP issues, Robertson searched for a volunteer from the local bar who would take the case. The one volunteer who came forward ultimately withdrew. That was 1971. The case never got filed, but the issue would be back in 1973, and this time the Litigation Group would carry it forward to court. First, though, came the infamous bumping of Ralph Nader.

* * * * *

On Friday morning, April 28, 1972, Ralph Nader left his office in D.C. and headed to National Airport to catch a 10:15 a.m. Allegheny flight (on which he had a confirmed reservation) to Hartford, Connecticut. He was traveling to Hartford to give an address at a noon rally in support of Connecticut Citizen Action Group, one of the first state-level citizen groups he had helped to organize in 1971. He was also scheduled to appear at the University of Connecticut in Storrs later that afternoon. When he arrived at Gate 17 to board, people were milling around in front of the counter, and the agent was explaining that the plane was full and they could not board. Among the other bumped passengers, Nader noticed John Koskinen, administrative assistant to Senator Abraham Ribicoff (D-Connecticut). As Nader arrived, Koskinen was explaining that he had an important meeting he had to get to in Hartford. Walking up behind him,

Nader quipped, "You think you've got a problem?" Then he explained that he was the keynote speaker at a big rally at noon and asked if the agent would check to see if there were any standbys who had been boarded. He also asked if the agent would go to the plane and ask whether anybody would volunteer to take a later plane. The agent would not say whether standbys had been boarded and refused to ask for volunteers.

Nader, Koskinen and two other men were left behind as the Hartford flight took off. Allegheny offered alternative means to get to Hartford with connections through Philadelphia. All but Nader took the offer. The alternative flights would not get him to Hartford in time for the noon rally, and if he were to miss the connection, he might not make the Storrs talk either. Nader opted to fly to Boston and be driven to Storrs. There was obviously no way he could make the Hartford rally.

Toby Moffett, the director of Connecticut Citizen Action Group (who would be elected to Congress in 1974), informed the crowd at the rally that Nader would not be coming. Very quickly the crowd of about a thousand dwindled to about two hundred who remained to hear the mayor, the council president and Moffett speak. The Citizen Action Group lost the contributions expected to be generated from the larger crowd, and as U.S. District Judge Charles R. Richey would later note, "suffered extreme and very real embarrassment, loss of professional esteem and prestige" as a result of Nader's failed appearance.

Airline personnel very quickly recognized their goof in bumping Nader, as was made clear by an interoffice memo (later introduced into court) from Allegheny's regional director for ground services. "Today," the memo states, "[flight] 864 was booked to 108 passengers. 103 passengers showed up for the flight. Among the 3 [later proved to be 4] who were oversold were Ralph Nader and an aid to Senator Rubicoff [sic]." The memo pointed out that flights from D.C. were "especially critical because of the amount [sic] of high state officials traveling. It is also important for reservations to get names correct. In Mr. Nader's case today, his first initial was shown as A. Nader." Had the airline agent known that he was dealing with *the* Nader, would he have been allowed to board? In Nader's mind, this would have been even worse. Special treatment was not his goal. Fair treatment for all was. A few months later, in October 1972, Allegheny delayed a flight to wait for Nader, who was held up in traffic "by the monstrous traffic jam following the collapse of part of Connecticut Avenue." A letter to Allegheny from Nader's book publisher thanking in part and admonishing in part the airline's courtesy states: "Mr. Nader had no knowledge of the efforts made by another firm [the one making his reservation] on his behalf, namely to ask you to greet him at the door and escort him to the plane. Furthermore, it is his policy, as you might expect, to reject special treatment or privilege, for which reason he was unhappy to learn that the plane had been delayed."

The Hartford flight was not the first time Nader had been bumped. Just a few days before the Allegheny flight, an American Airlines flight had bumped him, and six months before that, he and five other people had been bumped from an Eastern Airlines flight to Miami. For more than a year, Robertson and the ACAP staff had been asking the Civil Aeronautics Board (CAB) to do something about the bumping issue (one document introduced in court during the case that followed stated that more than five hundred thousand people a year were bumped, though the exact number was the subject of considerable controversy). The CAB still refused to act. Nader had had enough. The time had come to go to court. On July 2, 1972, a case was filed in U.S. district court. A year and two months later, on September 4, 1973, after dozens of motions and counter-motions, depositions, requests for documents and extensions of time, Reuben Robertson (who was by then working half time for the Litigation Group and half time with ACAP) appeared before Judge Richey to represent Nader at trial. Squaring off against him on behalf of Allegheny Airlines was Frank Roberson. It did not take long in the trial to see that Robertson was faring better than Roberson with this judge.

The discovery process revealed the extent of the deception used by Allegheny and other airlines. Many passengers who were bumped asked the airlines whether they deliberately overbooked, to which the inevitable answer was "No." That answer was true only because in airline parlance, "overbooking" meant selling more seats than you expected there would be passengers who would show up. What everyone else called "overbooking," the airlines called "overselling," which they regularly did. But since no one asked the right question, no one got right answers. Now the cat was out of the bag, thanks to the lawsuit, and even the CAB could not ignore it.

Roberson must have had an unhappy premonition of what was to come when about halfway through the trial, Judge Richey said, "If I have learned anything from this case, I have learned that if you have to be at a meeting or have to be at any one point or place in the country or the world, where the airline is under the jurisdiction of the CAB, you had better jolly well take a week in advance to get there, to make sure you are going to make it." Roberson's effort to focus on the small percentage of the flying public that was bumped was to no avail, as the trial transcript makes clear. "Suppose I have to give a speech," Judge Richey said, "as I do, in Ohio at the end of this week and I do not get there because of overbooking. The fact that the tariff [which sets out the airline's rules and responsibilities for things like lost baggage and overbooking] provides me with a remedy of $25 plus 100 percent of the face value of my ticket, or whatever it is, is not going to compensate me for my lack of presence at this meeting."

In his October 18, 1973, decision, Judge Richey noted how substantial the bumping problem was: "In April, 1972, according to the record herein the company bumped 945 persons, and during the period from January 1969 through August 1972 some 15,969 persons were not accommodated on Allegheny flights for which they had confirmed reservations." He then ruled that the court had jurisdiction, that Nader was entitled to compensatory damages, that Allegheny had intentionally misrepresented a material fact—that Nader had a guaranteed reservation for a seat—and that, therefore, he was entitled to punitive damages, as well. Judge Richey awarded Nader $10 in compensatory damages and $25,000 in punitive damages. Headlines the next day heralded his triumph. A week later Allegheny's attorney Roberson wrote: "Dear Reuben: Congratulations on your latest contribution to the revolution. Until reading his Findings of Fact and Conclusions of Law I had not realized that Judge Richey had been designated by anyone to determine what airline practices are in the public interest." In Roberson's mind this was judicial activism pure and simple—a judge trying to make law and policy. He noted that he intended "to give a few more judges a chance to look at the problem." The case was on its way to the appeals court. But first, the question of leafleting at airports would have its day in court.

* * * * *

Emboldened by the win against Allegheny, and intent on keeping the bumping issue in the public eye, Robertson and Morrison hatched a plan of action. In just a month, the busiest air travel weekend of the year for National Airport would arrive—Thanksgiving. They arranged for volunteers to agree to hand out ACAP literature about the bumping problem (with their recent court win in *Nader v. Allegheny Airlines* prominently displayed). From past leafleting attempts, they had learned that the administrator of the Federal Aviation Administration (FAA), who was then responsible for operations at National and Dulles airports, had issued a regulation that prohibited any person from distributing any printed matter without the prior permission of the appropriate airport manager.

On November 13, Morrison called Ray W. McNall at National to arrange for permission for ACAP volunteers to distribute consumer information sheets on November 21 (the day before Thanksgiving) dealing with passengers' baggage rights and overbooking. McNall indicated that he did not think there would be a problem but that he would like to look at the leaflets first. On November 19, Litigation Group attorney Ray Bonner and two ACAP staff members sat down with McNall and the chief of safety operations at National. They requested permission to distribute the leaflets outside the entrances to the various terminals, near the baggage areas and at a table in the main concourse of the main terminal or some other central location. "Throughout the discussions," Bonner notes, "we emphasized our willingness to assure that no litter would be created in the airport and that no unusual congestion would result." At the end of the meeting, McNall promised to call the next day with an answer. At 1 p.m., McNall called to say that he was denying permission to distribute the information inside the terminal. He said he would let them know later in the day about outside distribution. When no call had come by 3:50 p.m., Morrison and Bonner left the Litigation Group headquarters and hurried over to the U.S. district court to file their complaint and a motion seeking a temporary restraining order. The necessary court papers for filing were all typed and ready. The "no" answer was no surprise; indeed, it was most gleefully anticipated.

The charge in *ACAP v. Butterfield, Administrator of FAA* was that FAA Administrator Alexander Butterfield and his agents at National Airport were imposing a prior restraint on the plaintiffs' constitutional rights to free speech. "The First Amendment precludes government control or censorship—by the FAA or any other agency—of the contents of consumer information brochures," Robertson noted in a press release about their case the next day. "The First Amendment also prohibits unreasonable government restrictions upon the manner or places in which those brochures can be passed out, and the FAA's policy has far overstepped these basic constitutional limitations." They were confident that their argument would fly with a district judge—a confidence that quickly proved well-founded.

Within an hour of their appearance before him, U.S. District Judge Joseph Waddy "[o]rdered that, for a period of ten days ... defendant [Butterfield], his agents, and employees are enjoined from interfering with plaintiff [ACAP], its agents, employees, or representatives who are distributing at Washington National Airport, consumer information leaflets relating to the rights of airline passengers." Judge Waddy limited the number of people distributing at one time to four outside the terminals and two inside. Court rules mandate that a plaintiff seeking a temporary restraining order must post a bond. The judge ordered $5 posted. Over the Thanksgiving weekend, the volunteers distributed several thousand leaflets.

Ten days later, Morrison, Bonner and Robertson were back in court seeking a permanent injunction that would prevent the airport from enforcing the FAA regulation about leafleting unless it was specifically proven that distribution impeded the operation of the terminals. Judge Waddy again extended the temporary injunction and instructed the parties to attempt to negotiate a satisfactory settlement of the issue. To that end, Morrison wrote to the assistant attorney general handling the case for the FAA, stating that ACAP would be willing to settle the case on the following conditions: (1) the FAA must rescind its regulation on distribution of literature at Dulles and National; (2) the FAA must agree to promulgate new regulations on distribution of literature only if such regulations are published in the *Federal Register* with opportunity for public comment for at least thirty days [the minimum requirement set out in the Administrative Procedure Act for issuing new rules] and only if any proposed regulation is provided directly to ACAP at the time of publication; and (3) that until a new rule was finalized, the FAA must agree to allow ACAP to continue to distribute its literature at Dulles and National except where such distribution "substantially interferes with the actual operation of such airports." When the FAA had not agreed by the expiration of Judge Waddy's second temporary restraining order, the judge extended it again and, over the next several months, again and again.

By June 10, 1974, with still no action to rescind the rule and no agreement to their terms, Morrison decided it was time to turn up the pressure by filing a motion for summary judgment, noting that "the regulation has not been amended or repealed, and defendant [FAA] continues to contend that prior permission is required for any distribution of printed matter at either National or Dulles." Morrison set out the considerable precedent supporting his case in his brief and pressed the court to rule rather than try to act as a forcing agent (as it seemed to be doing with its temporary restraining order extensions) in getting the FAA to change its regulations. Relying on a 1968 case, *Wolin v. Port of New York Authority*, in which overly broad regulations restricting distribution of materials in terminals were struck down by a federal appeals court, he wrote: "[C]ourts do not write regulations, but simply pass upon their validity in the context of the cases before them. ... Thus, given the constitutionally overbroad reach of defendant's regulations ... this Court should enjoin the enforcement" of the FAA's regulations permanently.

The FAA's counter brief argued that what ACAP was attempting to distribute amounted to "commercial advertising" because there was a solicitation for donations at the end of the leaflets, and since the FAA was working on revised regulations, the court should refrain from acting until the agency action was completed. Morrison's reply brief (filed July 2, 1974) noted that "in the seven months since this case was filed" the FAA had done nothing but make plans to act. No proposed rule had even been published for comment as yet. Though the FAA stated that it anticipated publishing one by July 15, Morrison wrote, "[it] has taken defendant seven months to be in a position to propose a modification; there is no telling how long it will take him to put one in effect." Lest the court miss the potential for delay, in a footnote, Morrison cited evidence from Exhibit 4 in the case: thirteen FAA rulemaking proceedings had been pending for more than five years, one for more than ten. Then, with particular satisfaction, he was able to rely on one of the Litigation Group's own very recent wins, the ruling in *Virginia Pharmacy*. Citing *Virginia Pharmacy*, Morrison struck a lancing blow to the FAA's other defense: "[D]efendant's legal premise—that commercial advertising is entitled to no protection under the First Amendment—is also in error."

It did not take Judge Waddy long to act. On July 9, 1974, he granted the motion for summary judgment, declared the FAA's rule unconstitutional as a prior restraint and enjoined the FAA and its agents from applying the rule to ACAP in the future. To top that off, he ordered the $5 bond returned to ACAP.

The judge's ruling did not seem to have any effect on the FAA, which went ahead and published a proposed modified rule on July 17. Robertson immediately objected to the proposal as being "misleading, incomplete and legally insufficient." Not only had the FAA failed to note that a similar rule had just been declared unconstitutional by a court, but its new rule was nearly as constitutionally suspect as the old one. Three weeks later, having had no response to his letter, Robertson wrote again. Finally, in late August, the FAA administrator wrote back, stating that he had no intention of amending the notice to include the ruling in *ACAP v. Butterfield* and no intention of withdrawing the rule. So Robertson filed a formal comment in the public rulemaking record, spelling out Judge Waddy's ruling and pointing out that the proposed regulations "are patently unconstitutional as a prior restraint ... are unreasonably vague and capable of discriminatory application ... overbroad in the extreme, arbitrary and capricious, and in excess of the FAA's authority." The ACLU (which had been in contact with Robertson while *ACAP v. Butterfield* was under way since it was involved in a similar issue defending the rights of Hare Krishnas to pass out literature at airports) filed comments echoing Robertson's points in the rulemaking process.

Years went by. No action was taken on the proposed rule, and the old rule (declared unconstitutional by Waddy) remained on the books though Robertson repeatedly wrote objecting to this. On December 8, 1977 (by then in President Jimmy Carter's administration), Robertson wrote again to the FAA: "Continued republication of the invalid FAA regulation ... is contrary to the Federal Register Act ... as well as to the order of the District Court. Accordingly, unless we hear from you by December 22, 1977, of affirmative measures to remove [the rule] forthwith from the published FAA regulations, including the CFR codification for 1978, we intend to apply to Judge Waddy for such further relief or sanctions as may be appropriate." On December 20, Robertson received a letter from the FAA: "While I do not necessarily agree that Judge Waddy's Order requires a revocation ... I have nevertheless recommended that action to revoke be initiated promptly." On February 1, 1978, Robertson received a copy of the amendment revoking the rule. It was with some relief that the long battle was finally won, a battle that had begun in May 1971 when the volunteer law students first attempted to pass out leaflets at National. The importance of long-term, full-time players who can follow the action and press for results as an issue moves from branch to branch is surely illustrated by this effort.

* * * * *

While the leafleting case was progressing, Allegheny Airlines' appeal in the Nader case was continuing as well. By late January 1974, Allegheny had filed its brief with the court. By early March, Robertson and Morrison filed their brief, and two weeks later the airline's reply brief was in. In January, Robertson and Morrison had consented to the filing of an *amicus* brief by the Air Transport Association of America (the airline trade group), which was filed promptly as well. The case seemed to be moving on a fast track. Then in June, the Civil Aeronautics Board formally petitioned the court to file an *amicus* brief. It is clear, from letters in court documents, that the CAB had come in at the request of Allegheny's attorney and that the Litigation Group attorneys had not been informed that the CAB was considering filing an *amicus* brief until after the decision was made. They objected vehemently. Not only was the federal agency coming in with arguments to help the target of its regulatory power, not a member of the public it supposedly existed to protect, but it was asking the court to let it in nearly six months after court rules allowed. One problem noted by the Litigation Group brief opposing admission of the CAB *amicus* brief was that, though "largely repetitive of the arguments advanced by Allegheny and the Air Transport Association, the Board's proposed brief is 67 pages long, including three appendices and massive factual material which is not in the record and has not been subjected to cross-examination." An example of the problem was the "draft statistical report, which the agency has not yet released to the public, on the numbers of passengers denied confirmed space during 1973 according to the airlines' own records." The Litigation Group's memorandum in opposition argued that the validity of those statistics should be "subject to question concerning the methodology employed in compiling them." The court of appeals ignored the entreaties. In late July the CAB filed its *amicus* brief. Now Morrison and Robertson were up against not two but three teams of high-powered lawyers. The win in the leafleting case came down about this point, providing at least some good news.

Oral argument in *Nader v. Allegheny Airlines* was held on December 10, 1974, before Judges Carl McGowan and Edward A. Tamm. The third judge assigned to the appeals court panel, Senior Circuit Judge Charles Fahy, was unable to be present, but the court announced that the briefs and a tape recording of the oral argument would be submitted to him. When the decision was announced in May 1975, the Litigation Group lost it all. Judge Fahy dissented, but only on part of the opinion.

The appeals court ruled that: (1) District Court Judge Richey's findings of fact concerning the bumping action "appeared to be tainted by erroneous legal conclusions" and remanded the case for retrial; (2) the finding that Allegheny committed "fraudulent misrepresentation by reason of nondisclosure of overbooking policies" was reversed and the remand stayed pending determination by the CAB of whether the airline's practices on overbooking were deceptive; and (3) while punitive damages might ultimately be assessed against Allegheny, the trial judge on remand must consider whether the carrier had relied upon the belief that its actions carried the approval of the CAB and therefore was acting in good faith.

Judge Fahy's dissent was aimed at the majority's stay of the remand pending CAB action. One of the central purposes of the law at issue here (Section 411 of the Federal Aviation Act) was the elimination of deceptive practices in the airline industry. As Fahy saw it, a past Supreme Court decision had made clear that an individual's right to seek common law remedies for fraudulent misrepresentation remained intact—and that, in giving the power to the CAB to regulate to prevent deceptive practices in Section 411, Congress had not extinguished private actions to seek damages. In this case, Judge Richey had determined that Allegheny had engaged in fraudulent misrepresentation when it sold Nader a "confirmed reservation" that the airline knew ahead of time it might not be able to honor.

Though Judge Fahy agreed that the trial court should reconsider its findings in line with the concerns raised by the majority in (1) and (3) above, he would have remanded the case and allowed it to go forward immediately—not forced it to await action by the CAB first. As Fahy noted in his dissent, the CAB may have the power to "add to common law remedies, and require a carrier to cease and desist unfair and deceptive practices [as the Supreme Court had allowed in an earlier case] ... [but] I find no support in that case for a view that the Board has power to eliminate a common law private action for fraudulent misrepresentation by deciding that past conduct of that character by an airline in a particular case was not a deceptive practice." If Allegheny's attorney, Roberson, thought the district court decision had amounted to judicial activism, Robertson had at least as strong a claim to such a charge against the appeals court. Not only did the majority decision run counter to what seemed to be clear Supreme Court precedent, but the court came up with its reasoning entirely on its own. As Robertson observed:

> This sweeping decision [by the majority], which embraces princi-
> ples of law that were never briefed or argued, not only disrupts tra-
> ditional relationships between state and federal courts and agencies
> and interferes with common law remedies, but it imposes addi-
> tional, potentially enormous burdens on the agency (or agencies)
> which will be affected by it. And neither Allegheny nor the CAB—
> the agency on which this mandatory funneling of every federal and
> state case arguably within its sphere of authority would be
> imposed—ever suggested or endorsed the result reached by the
> court of appeals.

Robertson sought to raise these objections in a motion to have the case reheard by the full D.C. Circuit. In mid-June the appeals court denied the motion and assessed costs in favor of Allegheny for $2,726. Robertson object-ed but lost, at least for the moment. No money had to be paid at this point since this ruling was stayed until the CAB had acted.

The only alternative left (save waiting around for the CAB to act, an unat-tractive prospect given that agency's normal glacial speed) was an appeal to the Supreme Court. Robertson filed this on September 22, 1975; Allegheny filed its objection to the petition in October. On November 11, the court notified him that the writ was granted—swift action, particularly since Robertson had not even filed his reply to Allegheny's objection. Morrison recalls that just before the oral argument of *Virginia Pharmacy* on November 11, someone asked Robertson when his reply brief for the writ petition in *Allegheny* was due. Morrison interrupted: "Doesn't matter, the court granted *cert.* today." Quite a day for them—one case argued, another accepted. They hoped it was a good sign.

The briefing process for the merits in *Allegheny* moved quickly too. Less than five months later, Robertson would be arguing before the high court. Fortunately, there was a new hire to help him prepare the briefs. Linda Donaldson, who arrived on September 2, 1975, was the first woman to be hired by the Litigation Group. "We very much wanted to hire a woman," Morrison says, "and her credentials were strong and right for our needs."

Donaldson's legal education at New York University Law School (class of 1974) coincided with the antiwar activism of the early 1970s. "Many of my classmates," she recalls, "were activists and the professors were very progressive both on issues and the role of the law." It was a time when women were still very much in the minority in law school, and the fact that Donaldson had obtained a prestigious clerkship with Judge Murray Gurfein on the U.S. Court of Appeals for the Second Circuit (the circuit that covers Vermont, Connecticut and New York) was impressive. After her clerkship, Donaldson had hoped to work with the Women's Rights Project at the ACLU, but there were no openings, so she wrote to Morrison, who invited her down for an interview. "I really liked the feeling of the group," Donaldson said. "In fact, the only thing I didn't like was how small the salary was—less than I was getting as a law clerk and about half what law firms were paying." Despite the salary, she accepted the job. Arriving early on her first day turned out to be a good move, as on September 2 another new hire, John Cary Sims, came aboard as well. There was only one office for them both, "and I got there first so I got the window seat, much to John's chagrin," Donaldson recalls.

Her first case involved representing Nader's father in a challenge to Connecticut's closed primary rules. The senior Nader was an independent—not registered in either party. He wanted to vote in a primary, but Connecticut party rules restricted primaries to party members. He believed that this denied him his constitutional right to vote. After a voluminous research effort ("Alan always kidded me about my tendency to research down to the last period"), Donaldson argued her case before a three-judge U.S. district court (required at the time when a state law was being challenged as violative of the U.S. Constitution) in Hartford, Connecticut. It was a tough case, as two powerful constitutional rights were involved—the right to association versus the right to vote. She remembers well that the court "was not receptive to my argument. I learned that if a judge does not want to rule with you, he will search for a plausible—any plausible— way around you." She lost. The more important lesson she took away from that experience, though, was "when you talk to a reporter they will get one half of what you say wrong!" After spending nearly an hour with a local reporter following the oral argument—trying to explain what they were arguing and why— the news article the next day "so totally misstated what I had said and misperceived what we were trying to do in the lawsuit that I was simply horrified," Donaldson believed that the reporter came in with a bias against "some outsider coming into her town and trying to force change in her political system." Donaldson quickly learned the difficulty of educating the public through the news media.

At the same time, she was helping Robertson research and write the Allegheny case brief. "Working with Reuben was quite an experience," Donaldson recalls. "He was this round and jolly character, sort of hefty and barrel-chested, whose style was tongue-in-cheek most of the time. He just loved tweaking authority and loved to play jokes on his peers." As "sort of a serious type," she admits, "it took me quite a while to tell whether he was joking or not."

Robertson's performance at the Supreme Court oral argument on March 24, 1976, gives evidence of his tweaking ability. "What this case really boils down to," Robertson explained, "is the concept that's in the Court of Appeals' decision that the CAB might have the power to approve a common law fraud. This is a new doctrine of administrative law, *deception in the public interest*. And the whole point of section 411 is that deception is not good for you. 411 was designed to protect people from deception and not protect the deceivers." [emphasis added] Later, one of the justices asked, "Mr. Robertson, do you know why the CAB isn't here?" After fighting to get in as an *amicus* in the appeals court, the CAB had strangely stayed out of the case at the Supreme Court. Robertson responded, "I have wondered about that a great deal, your Honor. I can't draw any conclusion one way or the other." This followed:

> Question: Did the court ask them to participate in the Court of Appeals or did they come in by themselves?

> Mr. Robertson: They said at the Court of Appeals level that the case was so important that they should be permitted to file a brief five months after all the briefs were due, I must say, over my objection. But then they apparently lost interest in the case. I assume they feel that I can adequately represent their interests.

General laughter broke out in the august courtroom. Chief Justice Warren Burger chimed in as it died down, "Well, then, we will let the record show that." Which was followed by a fresh burst of laughter and at just that point the oral argument ended. A week later, Robertson wrote a letter to the clerk of the court offering an answer to the question about the CAB. "[W]e are submitting ten copies of an excerpt from the official minutes of a meeting of the CAB on January 21, 1976, which reflects the agency's unanimous determination not to file an *amicus* brief." The excerpt also included a statement for the record by two of the board members noting that they had opposed the brief filed in the appeals court and that they did "not in any way feel bound by the statements made and positions taken in that brief." Having heard that the CAB's *amicus* brief before the court of appeals was being provided to the Supreme Court after the oral argument, Robertson also noted that he had filed a response to that brief in the lower court and would be "glad to provide as many copies of it as may be needed." Robertson wrote to a friend about the same time, "The argument before the Supreme Court went fairly well, and I am mildly optimistic at this point."

On June 7, 1976, the Supreme Court reversed the appeals court's ruling, treating the Litigation Group and Nader to a unanimous win by ruling that a passenger who has been bumped from a flight on which he holds a confirmed reservation has a right to bring a common-law tort action based upon a theory of fraudulent misrepresentation. As one *Chicago Daily News* editorial writer said: "The Supreme Court just wrote another chapter in the still unfinished story of Ralph Nader's bumping case. I think the case involves one of the most flagrant examples of corporate irresponsibility in America today and just thinking about it makes my blood boil. ... I look upon a confirmed reservation as a promise by the airline (or hotel, for that matter) to accommodate me, and I think I have a right to rely on that promise."

Reaction by the airlines was immediate and "dangerously close to violating the prohibition against any Airport Transportation Association (ATA) mechanism being used to influence a carrier's tariff filing decisions," as a later CAB enforcement letter to the association noted. The "dangerously close" action was a secret meeting of all airlines at the D.C. headquarters of the ATA. A sworn affidavit to the CAB from one of the participants in this meeting states: "On the morning of June 17, 1976 a call came in to one of our secretaries from a woman at ATA advising that a meeting would be held at ATA at 2:00 P.M. to discuss the Supreme Court's decision in Nader v. Allegheny. ... Mr. James Landry chaired the meeting and stated that its purpose was to analyze the Supreme court's decision in Nader v. Allegheny and possible industry response to the holding that overbooking practices could give rise to tort liability. ... The possibility of avoiding tort liability for overbooking by filing some sort of tariff rule disclosing the existence of overbooking practices as suggested by Justice Powell's opinion (see p.15, n.14) was discussed."

This admission suggests that the airlines were meeting to orchestrate a coordinated response to avoid potential lawsuits over overbooking. Efforts by the ATA to coordinate airlines in a way that might have the effect of a "restraint on trade" were very clearly against the CAB's rules. They were also against federal law under the Sherman Antitrust Act. The strategy of "filing a tariff" explaining that a confirmed reservation was not really a confirmed reservation was an attractive response to the problem in part because consumers typically didn't read tariff filings. Indeed, Chief Justice Burger had said, "I have been traveling on airlines since they began. I have never read a ticket yet." If the nation's highest jurist didn't even read the ticket, who could expect that anyone would bother to read a tariff statement filed with the CAB. It seemed a pretty safe bet that citizens would mostly remain in the dark about overbooking. It was also an attractive approach because Justice Powell had opined in footnote 14 that "if respondent's overbooking practices were detailed in its tariff and therefore available to the public ... the court could ... determine that the tariff provided sufficient notice to the party who brought suit." Powell said only that a court could find this sufficient notice, but it was reasonable to assume that a lower court judge would be likely to latch onto this guidance from one of the justices. It was a perfect solution. The airlines could protect themselves from future lawsuits without arousing public sentiment against overbooking, but it would work only so long as all of them agreed to do it. If some airlines held out, hoping for a competitive advantage in being able to say something like "come fly us, we don't overbook like those other bad guys do," then the overbooking genie would be out of the bottle. Information about the secret meeting soon leaked to Robertson. He immediately filed a complaint in district court charging that the ATA and the nineteen airlines attending the meeting were "engaging in a contract, combination and conspiracy concerning airline reservations practices and procedures, in restraint of trade in interstate and foreign commerce" and in violation of section 1 of the Sherman Act. In an unusual move, the court allowed for the immediate deposition by Robertson of those attending the meeting. At the same time, the CAB moved on its own to discover what had happened, requesting that all attendees at the June 17 meeting respond under oath to a list of questions. In the end the court dismissed the case on the ground that the CAB should be given a chance to rule first. (This case was heard by Judge Richey, the same district judge the appeals court had overruled, saying he should have let the CAB act first in *Allegheny*; perhaps the rebuke from the higher court there influenced his action here.) All that ultimately happened was a "slap on the hand" letter from the CAB to the ATA and participants in the meeting. But the bumping issue was not going away. Undoubtedly the case (and the many court cases around the nation of others seeking damages after Nader's Supreme Court victory) aroused public attention and motivated the CAB to move its rulemaking efforts forward.

On April 19, 1976, two months before the Supreme Court decision in *Allegheny*, the CAB published a notice of proposed rulemaking on the overbooking and bumping issues. On March 1, 1977, it issued a final rule requiring airlines to post the following notice at ticket counters and include a copy with each ticket they or travel agents sold: "Airline flights may be overbooked, and there is a slight chance that a seat will not be available on a flight for which a person has a confirmed reservation. A person denied boarding on a flight may be entitled to a compensatory payment. The rules for denied boarding compensation are available at all airport ticket counters." With this action the issue moved to the question of what constituted "fair compensation" and what means should be used to decide who would get bumped.

Anyone who has traveled by air over the past twenty years knows the ultimate result of that next rulemaking issue (one in which ACAP and Robertson pressed for better compensation and a requirement for seeking volunteers before anyone is involuntarily bumped). During spring break of 1999, on an oversold American Airlines flight from San Juan to Miami, the offer to volunteers began at $200 plus overnight accommodations and meals and a flight the next day. No volunteers were forthcoming. When the offer reached $500 plus the other goodies, a family of five leaped up: "That's next year's spring trip," the father exclaimed. No one was angry that the plane was oversold. The balance between allowing the airlines to try to fill all planes and protecting consumers seemed perfect. But this end was in the future, and first Robertson would have a repeat of the last round—a win before Judge Richey (1978) and a loss at the appeals court (1980).

10

The Battle Against Secrecy Continues

Getting the government to live up to the letter and spirit of the Freedom of Information Act was more than a full-time job. But to open up the government's decisionmaking processes, it would require attention to more than just that one law. Another area of concern involved the public's right to know what was going on in advisory committee meetings. As the federal government's responsibilities grew throughout the mid-twentieth century and the issues it was responsible for became more technologically complex, it became evident that the executive branch was simply not big enough or expert enough to do all it was supposed to do on its own. One alternative was to set up outside advisory committees to provide the necessary expert advice. These committees were "official" in that they were sanctioned by law, but were not to be part of the official government. That is, those serving on them would not be government employees, and they would not have any official power to exercise. They were simply to give advice. By the early 1970s, it became evident to many in Congress that the advice many of these committees gave was heavily relied upon by the executive branch and that, often, the advice was biased. In fact, the membership of advisory committees tended to be drawn from a narrow spectrum of opinion (typically carefully selected to bolster and legitimize the administration's preferred views) and/or was dominated by the industry players who were to be the subject of the regulations they were advising upon.

With Nixon's election in 1968, the national government was split between a Republican executive and Democratic Congress. Not surprisingly, this exacerbated the bias problem of advisory committees and led the Democratic Congress to enact the Federal Advisory Committee Act of 1972 (FACA) to make accountable the vast network of advisory committees—estimated at the time to number more than three thousand. The new law required that advisory committees be "fairly balanced in terms of the points of view represented" and that advisory committee meetings and committee records be open to the public.

Because of the technical and scientific complexity of its agenda, the Food and Drug Administration (FDA) used many advisory committees. Sidney Wolfe, the doctor who set up the Health Research Group (HRG) for Nader in 1971, paid special attention to the FDA's use of advisory committees. One of the early litigation battles under the FACA legislation's new openness mandate involved regulation of over-the-counter drugs.

In 1962 Congress had amended the drug laws to require proof of effectiveness for new prescription drugs before they could be sold. In addition, the FDA was supposed to examine the scientific and legal status of all drugs already on the market, including those sold over the counter. For each class of drugs to be examined—cold medications, sleeping pills, tranquilizers, antacids, etc.—an advisory committee was established to survey scientific data and prepare advice on which were safe and effective, which made claims that could not be substantiated, and which were unsafe and should be withdrawn from the market.

The Antacid Advisory Panel, a group of mostly academic doctors but including a representative of the drug industry and a citizen participant, held meetings in the fall of 1973 and early winter of 1974. All but "approximately three hours" out of fifteen days (totaling sixty-six and a half hours) of its meetings were closed to the public. The main focus of its deliberations was concern about the potential dangers of combining aspirin and antacids as a single medication. Aspirin may cause stomach bleeding and is most hazardous to people with stomach symptoms—the very people most likely to take antacids. The major manufacturer of such a medicine was Miles Laboratories, maker of Alka-Seltzer.

Wolfe learned that representatives of Miles Lab made a presentation at one of the closed meetings. Based on comments from his source, Wolfe believed that the panel had been unduly influenced by this presentation and by comments of government lawyers who were also in attendance. Wolfe attempted to gain access to the full transcripts of the meetings. All his requests were denied. Ellsworth (at the time still occupying the Freedom of Information Clearinghouse position at the Litigation Group) filed a case in district court, *Wolfe v. Caspar Weinberger* (then secretary of Health, Education and Welfare, in which the FDA was lodged).

Counsel for the FDA and Weinberger claimed that the Antacid Advisory Panel was a "government agency" and that transcripts of its meetings were "intra-agency" memoranda that qualified for withholding under Exemption 5 of FOIA. The government's defense of this position is fascinating. On the one hand, the government argued, the Antacid Advisory Panel had no power and the transcripts of its meeting were "not relied upon by the Commissioner of Food and Drugs" in his decision to approve medications combining aspirin and antacid (thereby allowing Alka-Seltzer to remain on the market). According to the FDA, since the deliberations of the Antacid Advisory Panel did not figure in the final rule, they did not need to be made public as part of the FDA's rule-making record (under the Administrative Procedure Act all documents and testimony that are relied upon in making an agency rule must be a part of the public record). On the other hand, the government counsel claimed that the Antacid Advisory Committee was a critical part of the internal agency deliberations on the rule and that, thus, it should be considered a "government agency." As a government agency, "exchanges of opinions between individual members, their motions, discussions and statements" should be exempt from disclosure as intra-agency "memoranda and discussions" under Exemption 5. This sleight-of-hand did not slip by District Judge Charles R. Richey.

"An advisory committee cannot have a 'double identity,'" Judge Richey noted in his October 3, 1975, decision. That the FDA commissioner had "adopted the OTC Antacid Panels' report as his own," was admitted by the government, he went on, and thus "it can not be doubted that OTC panels perform a crucial role in the decision-making process." But, the judge continued, the measure of the amount of influence an advisory panel has in the final decision of an agency is "beside the point." What matters "is whether it has any authority in law to make a decision. ... It is clear to this Court that the Antacid Panel does not have that 'substantial independent authority in the exercise of specific functions which would qualify it as an 'agency' within the meaning of the [FOIA] Act and, specifically, the (b) (5) exemption." The Antacid Panel, the judge concluded, is "not an agency," and Exemption 5 is "inherently inapplicable to advisory committees."

The judge could hardly have been more precise. As Reuben Robertson noted in testimony before a Senate Government Operations committee the next spring, "the courts have repeatedly rejected the argument that exemption five may be used in the advisory committee context. Still the agencies continue to invoke it on a wholesale basis." The Litigation Group was being forced to fight for open advisory committee meetings and disclosure requirements over and over again (*Nader v. Dunlop, Aviation Consumer Action Project v. Washburn, Center for Auto Safety v. Tiemann, Nader v. Baroody*). A congressional "fix" that would clearly state this point in law seemed a wiser alternative.

Congress Watch lobbyists and Litigation Group attorneys returned to the Hill, where the four-year-long effort by Public Citizen, Common Cause and others to get a "Government in the Sunshine" act passed was finally making headway. It provided the perfect opportunity for promoting their issue as well. In the end, a House provision extending the Sunshine Act's elimination of Exemption 5 (as applied to open meetings) to cover federal advisory committees was successfully added in conference. The Sunshine Act passed the House 384-0 and Senate by voice vote on August 31, 1976. Ford signed this one, perhaps because of the looming 1976 presidential elections and the strong endorsement of a sunshine law by his Democratic opponent, Jimmy Carter. Or maybe his veto of the Freedom of Information Act in 1974 had been a lesson. Regardless, the law now directed what the Litigation Group had been fighting case-by-case to secure. But, as with FOIA (even with its 1974 clarifying and strengthening amendments), getting the executive branch to follow this law was an ongoing battle.

There was one last issue hanging in *Wolfe v. Weinberger*—getting paid. In 1970, the Internal Revenue Service (IRS) had issued a ruling that prevented

501(c)(4) social welfare organizations from accepting fees for legal services—not from clients, not by court-ordered fees, not by statutory provisions for fee awards when citizens prevail against government agencies—if they wanted to hold onto the exemption from income tax that such organizations enjoyed. The IRS ruling was another piece in the Nixon administration's campaign against Legal Services and other "liberal" public interest litigators. It was no small matter for the Litigation Group attorneys. Finding ways to financially support their efforts was a continual battle, and tax-exempt status was as critical a financial component in protecting their meager funds as fee-awards would be in securing more funding.

On June 22, 1973, Alan Morrison had filed a request with the IRS to permit his Litigation Group to accept fees if those fees were approved by a court or an administration agency, either in a litigated or settled case. Five other public interest firms filed similar requests as well. The IRS did not act on these requests until November 15, 1974.

The new IRS ruling allowed the Litigation Group to accept fees in three circumstances: (1) Where attorneys' fees are awarded by a court or administrative agency based on a statute that expressly provides for such fees; (2) Where a court or administrative agency is empowered to award fees even if the statute under which a challenge is brought does not so provide; and (3) Where attorneys' fees are provided for in a settlement agreement that is approved by a court or administrative agency in a case of the type described in 1 and 2. Fees could not be accepted from clients, however, without losing the tax-exempt status.

On December 29, 1975, Ellsworth wrote to the government attorney seeking $3,496 for fees in *Wolfe v. Weinberger* (for two and a half hours of Morrison's time at $75 an hour; for seventeen hours of Ellsworth's time at $60 an hour; and for fifty hours of other assistants' time at various fees ranging from $40 an hour for an HRG attorney to $15 an hour for law student researchers; and for copying and court filing costs—all fees at the bottom end of the private bar's fees for similar work). Perhaps concerned that there might be some comment about the fee for his time, considering his short tenure in practice, Ellsworth (he had one year working with Victor Kramer at Georgetown and only two years so far at the Litigation Group), noted that he had litigated "more Freedom of Information Act and Federal Advisory Committee Act cases than any other attorney presently in private practice" (more than twenty-five by that time). It was to be one of the Litigation Group's first fee awards. They waited expectantly.

It was not a check that came. Instead, the government challenged the award, arguing that the FOIA fee-award provision should not apply retroactively, and since much of the work done on *Wolfe* was done in 1973 and 1974 prior to the effective date of the amendments (even though the decision came down in late 1975), no fee should be awarded. Finally, after a ruling from the appeals court in another case that clarified the application of the FOIA amendments in such circumstances, the administration relented and agreed to pay the amount requested. It took two years to get a decision allowing Wolfe to see the FDA's antacid panel transcripts and two more years to get paid (with no late fees or interest accruing in the meanwhile).

* * * * *

Other cases dragged on as well. *Vaughn v. Rosen* was remanded to the district court after Judge Wilkey's decision forcing agencies to make a sufficiently detailed list of all documents withheld so that plaintiffs would know what documents the agency had, with the reasons for withholding keyed to each document. The documents Vaughn sought numbered approximately two thousand, four hundred and forty-eight and filled seventeen, five-drawer file cabinets. The estimated cost of a full index was astronomical. Instead of forcing this, the Litigation Group agreed to the indexing of a representative sampling. Based on a review of the sample, the court found some to be exempt and some not to be exempt. All documents from the full files falling within the "not-exempt" category were ordered to be delivered to Vaughn. Each side had won a bit. Not satisfied, the government appealed to try to win it all. By that time, Mark Lynch had been recruited from his lobbying duties at Congress Watch to be the new FOIA attorney at the Litigation Group. *Vaughn II* (as the district court remand and subsequent appeal is known) was to be Lynch's first court argument. It was scheduled for June 18, 1975.

"I was absolutely terrified," Lynch admits. "All I could think was, suppose I just get up there and can't say anything or just forget it all. I had never done this before and, even though I had suffered through two moot courts, it seemed to me that this was a distinct possibility." For some reason, Morrison was not in court for the oral argument; instead Larry Ellsworth sat with Lynch at the counsel table. "Since we were the appellees on the appeal of the remand, I had to sit for twenty minutes while the government attorney presented his argument. In my nervousness, I was compulsively drinking water. Larry leaned over and whispered, 'If you don't stop drinking you'll never get through without having to pee.' I did make it, but I do recall wishing I had not had all that water!"

In November, the appeals court upheld the district court's decision, which meant that Vaughn got copies of all the documents the court had ordered released. Even nicer was the attorney award in the case—$33,705—though it took until December 1975 to get it. Patience, or as Morrison puts it, "passion contained," is very much a necessary attribute of a public interest litigator.

* * * * *

Soon two more FOIA attorneys arrived the scene. Both were recruited from Kramer's "nursery school for public interest lawyers" at Georgetown Law

Center, both were tall, and both were very much products of the times—but there the similarity ends. Slender, sophisticated and strikingly beautiful, Diane Cohn came in September 1976. Long, lanky and full of life, with a delightful gangling awkwardness to his presence, David Vladeck arrived a year later.

Cohn had graduated from the State University of New York at Buffalo in 1972. "My undergraduate days I remember as a time of demonstrations about Cambodia and Kent State and troops on campus," Cohn says. Her father, a Community Legal Services attorney on Long Island, provided the model for a career in law and in public interest law in particular. After college she headed to Harvard Law School—where only 14 percent of her class was female and where she participated in the Legal Services program. She graduated in 1975 and went on to become a graduate fellow in Kramer's program. The next year Morrison recruited her to come to the Litigation Group.

Cohn arrived for her first day at the $11,000 job driving a Mercedes convertible (being married, she was not so confined by the puny salary the Group was paying her). She was quite a contrast to the dungaree crowd of eight (seven men and one other woman) who by then made up the Litigation Group staff. Her style and brains were complemented by an affinity for softball—of considerable importance to this group, which took its softball league very seriously. The Litigation Group was "like a family," Cohn notes. "We all went out together en masse to long lunches at a nearby Indian or Greek restaurant where a meal was $3.25. We worked long hours together and counted on each other in a special way that is not found in most jobs." She stayed for six years (until 1982). One of her first cases involved an effort to get access to the records pertaining to the investigation of Vice President Spiro Agnew for tax evasion. It was a case that would take her entire six years at the Litigation Group to resolve. The case was started by two George Washington Law School students, Roy Baldwin and Bruce Feder, who turned it over to the Litigation Group as their graduation loomed.

In 1972, the Department of Justice and the U.S. Attorney's Office in Baltimore had begun an investigation into allegations of bribery and political corruption in Baltimore County. Their investigation revealed that Agnew, while governor of Maryland, had accepted $87,000 in bribes as part of a political kickback scheme involving government contractors. Faced with the prospect of criminal trial in the district court in Maryland, Agnew pleaded *nolo contendere* to one count of tax evasion and resigned from office on October 10, 1973.

In the spring of 1975, Baldwin and Feder tried to gain access to all documents in the by-then closed case from the Department of Justice and U.S. Attorney's Office. The FOIA was clear that, while the investigation was open, documents that were part of the investigation were exempt (under Exemption 7) from disclosure; after an investigation was closed, however, the documents could be released unless exempt under another exemption—national security, for example. Their FOIA requests were met with delay after delay, and so in the summer of 1975 they filed suit. Soon after that they submitted a motion seeking a Vaughn Index of all documents in the Agnew investigation file with the required justification for the exemptions claimed. Since the Litigation Group's win in *Vaughn v. Rosen*, agencies that did not comply with a request were supposed to itemize, index and justify each document withheld prior to the briefing and oral argument over whether the documents were exempt or not. This, after all, is what Judge Wilkey had maintained was critical so that the plaintiff could make a reasoned argument to the court.

The first action of the district judge in the case looked promising. Judge June L. Green in October 1995 ordered some documents released and then noted, "the government may not rest on conclusory allegations to support its claimed exemptions. This is particularly true where the case was closed immediately after the plea. Without some form of indexing, itemization or detailed justification, the Court is unable to intelligently assess the appropriateness of withholding requested documents." The judge concluded her order by directing the Department of Justice to provide the Vaughn Index within forty-five days.

What was released that fall were specific documents that had been divulged to Agnew and the court in order for the plea of *nolo contendere* to be warranted and accepted. Those documents revealed that Agnew had filed "a false and fraudulent joint income tax return" that stated his income for 1967 was $26,099 when as "he then and there well knew" his income for that year was $55,599. This amounted to an underpayment of taxes for the year of more than $10,000. The rest of the government's summary was a "recitation of the facts and evidence developed by the investigation to date," which included details of "cash payments in return for engineering contracts" that Agnew extracted during his term as governor of Maryland. These kickbacks or bribes were presumably the source of the unreported income. The government's summary for the court in the Agnew case was just that, a summary, and it had already been released more than two years previously and widely disseminated by the news media. Baldwin and Feder wanted access to the documents behind it. Surely, the court could not have meant simply to deliver to them something they could already get. Stubbornly, the Justice Department maintained that what it had provided fully satisfied the court order. The two law students then filed a motion with the court seeking sanctions against the recalcitrant bureaucrats for contempt of court. In addition, they maintained, the department, under the court order, still owed them a detailed justification for the remaining documents that continued to be withheld.

They waited throughout the fall of 1975. No Vaughn Index ever came. Instead a number of affidavits from the Justice Department and the U.S. Attorney's staff were served up that did little more than assert that disclosure of the documents would "interfere with law enforcement proceedings." At a December 15, 1975, hearing on the pending motions, the judge concluded that she could not accept the government's "blanket refusal" to provide any further information "because of some ongoing investigation." In response, the Justice Department filed yet another affidavit, but in this one the existence of the testimony of four specific witnesses was revealed. With this small bit of specific information about some of the documents at last known to them, the students sought specific justification for why these particular four documents qualified for Exemption 7. The judge then ordered the department to produce a meaningful response within one week. On January 13, 1976, the judge issued a one-paragraph ruling, without explanation, which enjoined the government from withholding portions of two documents, while affirming the withholding of others. The Justice Department immediately appealed the order, and the district court stayed compliance pending appeal. In other words, no documents had to be released.

The law students at this point turned to the Litigation Group for help. It was not until much later that Cohn and her clients learned what had actually transpired in this apparently sudden about-face in which the court moved from an order to produce a justification to a final order on what would be released and what not.

In a later appellate brief summarizing the events that followed, Cohn noted:

> Without notice to the plaintiffs, Judge Green conducted her *in camera* inspection of the documents at the offices of the United States Attorney in Baltimore, Maryland. In the absence of a court reporter, the Court conferred with defendant Finney and his attorneys regarding the status of investigations allegedly related to the documents at issue. On the basis of these unrecorded, *ex parte* conversations, the court concluded that two of four witnesses' statements could be withheld in their entirety, and that certain information could be deleted from two statements ordered released. This ruling was reflected in the court's Opinion of February 2, 1976 which, again without notice to plaintiffs, was filed under seal. Finally in an Order issued December 20, 1976, the court concluded that all the remaining documents were "inextricably part of the ongoing criminal investigations and prosecutions relating to political corruption in the State of Maryland" and therefore exempt from disclosure.

When the students had come to her, Diane Cohn filed an appeal in the circuit court asking for the opposite of what the government attorneys wanted in their appeal: for the order to release the two documents to be upheld and the order to allow the withholding of the others to be overturned. But instead of addressing the legality of the exemption of the four documents, the appeals court put the appeals of both sides on hold, waiting until there was a lower court decision about the rest of the documents involved in the case. Throughout 1976 they waited with no idea of what had transpired in the *in camera* inspection.

When the judge issued her December 20, 1976, ruling (now nearly a full year after her order they had appealed), Cohn immediately filed a motion for reconsideration and clarification, noting that Judge Green's opinion "fails to provide the 'detailed analysis' required by the Court of Appeals for this Circuit in Freedom of Information cases." Cohn went on: "[the Court's opinion] has not provided plaintiffs, or a reviewing court, with sufficient information concerning the number, nature or content of the documents requested." Indeed, they were in precisely the pickle that Plesser had found himself in in the *Vaughn* appeal. How could Cohn make a reasoned argument on appeal against the government's exemption claim and the district court's acceptance of it when she had no information upon which to base her argument.

In her motion for reconsideration, Cohn quoted an excerpt from Senator Hart's statement on the Senate floor (the mumbled one resulting from Plesser's messy penmanship) to prove that the 1974 amendments were intended to put the burden on the government to prove some tangible harm to a particular enforcement proceeding. No such proof had been provided here. In order for a plaintiff and a reviewing court to determine whether the tests established under Exemption 7 were applied properly in this case, Cohn concluded that since the department had not done so, "the Court must describe in greater detail the nature and content of the documents at issue as well as the Court's justification for concluding that all of the records are exempt." Her motion was denied without opinion on February 8, 1977.

"In preparing plaintiffs' appellate brief [following the judge's denial of her reconsideration motion on Feb. 8] counsel discovered the existence of the sealed Memorandum Opinion," Cohn explained to the appeals court. Concerned that something must have transpired that they had not been made aware of—which, if so, would be quite outside the requirements of fair play, let alone the court's own rules—Cohn immediately filed a motion asking that plaintiffs be allowed to see the sealed opinion. On June 1, 1977, Judge Green allowed Cohn and Larry Ellsworth to "inspect the Supplemental Memorandum Opinion but not the attachments thereto in chambers, subject to the understanding that they will not reveal to any person including the plaintiffs, the contents of the Supplemental Memorandum." Later, after the case was concluded, the seal was lifted and the contents made known. Reading the full statement of the judge, one is left to wonder (as did Judge Aubrey E. Robinson Jr., about Book D in *Ditlow*) why the Supplemental Memorandum was sealed in the first place? Covering three pages, what it basically does is describe Judge Green's trip to Baltimore with her law clerk to inspect the record and her reasoning for releasing two of the statements (the cases against Agnew were completed) and for not releasing the other two (maybe there might be further proceedings against some of his co-conspirators).

Commenting in the media on all this after the release of all the papers, Cohn notes:

> [T]hroughout the almost three-year-old legal process, Justice officials specifically cited the investigation of suspended Maryland

Governor Mandel as a case that might be harmed if the Agnew documents were released. The one thing that is quite significant now that the documents are disclosed is what's missing—any real documents relating to the Mandel case.

Indeed, when all the papers were finally released on March 12, 1978, they were of so little interest that a news article described the documents as "a collection of familiar stories of conversations between lawyers and federal investigators and tiresome minutiae from the investigation." The documents included a note that "John Allen (barber) is allowed entry to the White House on Wednesdays only." Another sheet lists the participants of a "Washington Seminar," not one of whom had any involvement in the criminal case against Agnew. There was little of importance to the Agnew case or any other. So why would a judge seal an order that on its face seems innocuous? Considering the documents' contents, why would the Justice Department fight so hard not to release them? Perhaps the supplemental document was an effort to cover the fact that opposing counsel was not informed of the *in camera* inspection, so that the judge would be protected against any charge of bias or impropriety. Why the government fought so hard to protect thousands of pages of paper (which might have contained at the very most a few dozen pages of any importance to anything, let alone ongoing criminal cases) is anyone's guess. The most obvious explanation was bureaucratic boneheadedness. Perhaps "give 'em an inch and they'll take a mile" was the guiding principle of the executive in its approach to FOIA in general. When the case against Governor Mandel was closed, the government finally agreed to release the Agnew documents in early 1978. Despite all the evidence to the contrary, the department steadfastly maintained that somehow, somewhere, in all that "tiresome" minutiae there was something of importance to their prosecution of Mandel.

* * * * *

David Vladeck came to the Litigation Group the day after Labor Day in 1977 to take over the FOIA position. "Life," he notes "is a series of accidents and this was an accident." Growing up in New York City as the son of two labor lawyers, the nightly dinner conversation swirled around the legal problems of the little guy. Since his father was an adjunct law professor at New York University, he went there for free, heading on after that to Columbia Law School. He planned to accept a clerkship with a judge. But on a whim, he went to Washington, D.C., to interview for a fellowship in Kramer's program at Georgetown—a trip that dramatically changed the course of his life. Vladeck recalls:

> Vic Kramer is this unbelievably wonderful lawyer. He is this tiny little guy who is tough as nails. My interview with him is something

I will never forget. The first question he asked me very gruffly, "How come you didn't send a certified copy of your resume?" At Arnold and Porter he had this reputation of taking a stack of resumes a foot high and saying, "Here is a pile of resumes as good as yours; you have ten minutes to tell me why I should hire you rather than one of them." I said to his certified resume question— "Well, my grades are pretty good, but they are not that good. If I were going to send a falsified transcript, I would have given myself some higher grades." My answer cracked him up and he hired me.

Vladeck intended to stay in Washington just a year. He wanted to return to New York City and work as an assistant U.S. attorney. He never made it.

"Anyway, Vic had lunch with Alan," Vladeck continues, "and came back and told me there was a position there (at the Litigation Group) for me and that Alan was the best public interest litigation attorney in the universe and if I wanted to learn about public interest law I should go.

"When I went over to be interviewed, what I saw was an extremely diverse group of incredibly bright young lawyers, hardly more than neophytes, about my age with their own cases—arguing them in court, handling their own depositions. There was an ideological drive behind everything—it was doing law for socially good purposes. A fervency and excitement was in the air. Everyone was so wrapped up in what they were doing but more than willing to take time to talk to me."

Needless to say, he joined up (though with an $11,000 salary it surely was not for the money). Proving how accurate his observations had been about the opportunities there, by the time he was twenty-eight, just four years out of law school, he would argue his own case before the Supreme Court. Keeping with family background, it involved an issue of workers' rights.

"Diane is this absolutely elegant woman, who had assembled a series of real dogs in her year as FOIA attorney," Vladeck continues. "After culling out all the good juicy cases, she left me with the complex, murky leftovers—one of which was *Murphy v. Tenn. Valley Authority and the Department of the Army*." [Cohn would hardly agree that the Agnew case was "a good juicy one," at least not by the time she finally got through with it in 1982.]

Timothy R. Murphy was an environmental activist from Kentucky who had been trying to get some information out of the Department of the Army concerning the Corps of Engineers' actions on a contract for the Kehoe Lake dam project. When his requests were repeatedly stonewalled by the Army, Murphy contacted staffers at Public Citizen's Critical Mass Energy Project, who suggested he talk with Cohn. For several months Cohn had attempted to secure the documents through FOIA requests and appeals within the agency. This effort resulted in the release of twenty documents. The Army continued to refuse to release five documents, relying on an attorney-client privilege and the deliberative process privilege under the inter-intra-agency memorandum of Exemption

5. One thing Cohn did find from the twenty released documents was that one of the five remaining had been given to Representative Carl D. Perkins (D-Kentucky). This tidbit was key, or at least they thought so.

A couple of weeks after Vladeck arrived and Cohn had handed the case over to him, they filed a complaint in district court that was assigned to Judge Gesell. "Gesell looks like a Kris Kringle character but without a beard—sort of a smiling, grandfatherly type," Vladeck says. "But looks are deceiving!" The reality: "Hard as nails, intensely pragmatic, absolutely brilliant, crusty and one who does not suffer fools."

This was to be Vladeck's first court argument. "I was so wet behind the ears, I was dripping," he says. His colleagues subjected him to the usual prologue—moot court. "For two hours I was grilled by Alan, Diane and Bill Schultz. They asked a million questions. I had answers for maybe two. I came out feeling completely plastered." Then it was on to the real thing:

> I was first to argue. My time in front of Gesell lasted about a half hour. I had maybe eight minutes to make my case, based on what the trio had done rebuilding me in the two hours of moot court. Then the rest was a dialogue with Judge Gesell. He is kind but persistent and tends to grimace or hold his head in agony, looking like he was stuck with a hot poker, when he didn't like your argument. It was an absolutely exhilarating experience for a young lawyer to joust with someone of this caliber. At the end, he said, "I have to think about this, OK?"

"OK" was, of course, the only answer. Following the oral argument, the Litigation Group crew (Morrison, Cohn, Schultz and several others who had come to watch the initiation of their new recruit) filed out of court and adjourned to a nearby dive for lunch. "Everyone was patting me on the back and saying I was great and that we were going to win," Vladeck recalls. "Alan called it 'a falling off a log case.'"

How could they lose? If an agency was willing to put a document into an envelope and send it to any individual member of Congress, it simply could not claim an expectation of confidentiality. As a matter of legal interpretation, this issue was settled. When an agency disclosed a privileged communication to a third party, it constituted a waiver of the privilege. To argue that releasing a document to an individual member of Congress was the equivalent of giving it to Congress went against legislative history. The House Report accompanying the FOIA stressed that the rights of individual members of Congress under the FOIA are no greater than those accorded to "any person." For the "to Congress" argument to win, the document would need to be released to an official body of Congress (such as a committee or subcommittee of jurisdiction on the issue or to the House or Senate). "After all," Vladeck notes, "members of Congress are notorious for holding press conferences to expose whatever

171

they get!" Moreover, if the agency thought confidentiality was important, at a minimum it would have to make that clear to the member, and that surely could not have been the case here. Vladeck had introduced a letter from Representative Perkins stating that he could not find the letter in the office files, but if he could, he would have no problem sending them a copy. Tankards of beer were raised in toast of Vladeck's fine beginning and to their impending win.

Judge Gesell had a reputation for fast turn-around, so after lunch they sent someone over to see if a decision had been announced. The opinion was ready. It was not good news. Short and to the point, it basically said that Congress is different—a special case; thus when the executive shares information with a member of Congress, it does not destroy a claim of confidentiality even if that is not made clear in the document shared. You lose.

They went from elated to crushed. "It was tough to lose my first case," Vladeck admits, "but on this case the fate of the Western World did not hang in the balance." Still they decided to appeal. Gesell's reasoning seemed to be addressed to a concern that, if he were to rule otherwise, the executive might resist keeping Congress informed out of fear of the loss of FOIA protection for documents. There was an obvious way around this fear. If the executive included an expectation of confidentiality in sharing a document, the executive could claim an exemption from disclosure and win in court—assuming of course that the executive could persuade a court that one of the FOIA exemptions was met. (Even this would not protect against a member of Congress releasing the data any more than a stamp of "top secret" was sufficient to prevent Senator Mike Gravel's reading the full Pentagon Papers into the *Congressional Record* to get them into the public domain.)

At the circuit court in the fall of 1978, with by then a full year of experience at the Litigation Group and several other court arguments under his belt, Vladeck argued before "a panel of giants," as he terms it—Judges Harold Leventhal, Harold Greene and Carl McGowan. The argument took more than two hours. The judges asked a lot of the same questions, and it was clear to Vladeck that they were worried about the same thing that Gesell had been. "Most of the time," Vladeck recalls, "the circuit judges talked by me to each other, wrestling with the problem of following congressional instructions that made it clear that the FOIA exemptions should be narrowly construed versus the need to be cautious when executive/legislative relations were at stake." In this particular case the implication for the actual policy issue involved (the question of whether to build or not build a dam) in denying the documents was unclear. There was just no compelling case they could make for what, if anything, would happen to the dam if Murphy did not get the documents. "The judges," Vladeck admits, "roughed up both sides in the argument and then took over a year and a half (the decision came in December 1979) to come to the same decision as it had taken an hour for Gesell to reach: to wit—It's a tough case, but Congress is different, so here you lose."

At that point they decided "to lick their wounds" and forgo further efforts at appeal, though they still believed that they were right. Sometimes you lose even when the facts and law seemed to say you should win. Nonetheless, a year after the circuit court ruled, Murphy got the documents he had sought in an unmarked envelope in his mailbox.

* * * * *

One of Vladeck's most challenging FOIA cases, and surely the one that consumed the most time that first year, was another case in Judge Gesell's court. This time he was far more successful in convincing the judge that his side was right, but not without "getting beaten up pretty thoroughly" first. The case was one that Wolfe had been itching to take for sometime: getting consumer access to information concerning the performance (quality of care and costs of services) for doctors and hospitals. "Most people can find out more about a car they plan to buy than they can about a doctor who may hold their life in his or her hands," Wolfe noted. Medicare, the federally funded health care program for the elderly, provided the legal hook they needed.

By the end of the twentieth century Medicare had become such a vast program that it is sometimes easy to forget that it came into existence only in 1965 when Congress added it as an amendment to the Social Security Act. In that legislation, Congress recognized the need to contain its costs and curb the delivery of unnecessary or needlessly expensive medical care by specifically prohibiting federal payment for medical services that are "medically unnecessary." Congress also recognized the need to ensure that quality care was delivered in return for federal payments. To provide for quality and cost control, Congress directed each hospital to form its own committee of physicians to oversee services provided to Medicare patients. Very quickly it became evident that these "in-house" review panels were little more than rubber stamps.

The costs of in-patient care under the Medicare program grew at an alarming rate, prompting Congress to amend the law in 1972 by directing the secretary of HEW to designate Professional Standards Review Organizations (PSROs) as external monitors of hospital-based care funded under Medicare. The law also set out the conditions that must be met for an organization to be designated a PSRO: it must be non-profit, composed of a substantial number of area physicians, be open to membership by all area physicians, and demonstrate the professional competence necessary to conduct the required reviews. Once designated as a PSRO, the organization would operate under contract with, and be subject to direct regulatory control of, the HEW.

PSROs are state organizations with a great deal of power. They are basically quasi-publics, that is private organizations imbued with public regulatory power. They have the power to reject medical treatment proposed by a doctor and to suspend doctors from practice in the state. There is one for each state and the District of Columbia.

"We wanted to test the proposition of whether these PSROs were subject to FOIA," Vladeck notes. "Sid was positively salivating to do this." The data these organizations collected could provide critical information about which hospitals were most successful at which procedures, and conversely which had the greatest failure rates as well as which doctors did the most of certain procedures and how well they performed. This was precisely the sort of data Wolfe believed was critical for consumers to know when making decisions about their own medical care. It seemed obvious to him that, since a PSRO was paid by the federal treasury to perform a federally mandated task in the public interest it should be considered "a federal agency" for the purposes of the FOIA law. The closest and easiest PSRO for them to target was the one for the District of Columbia, the National Capital Medical Foundation (a non-profit D.C. corporation).

On September 30, 1977, Wolfe filed a FOIA request with both the HEW and the National Capital Medical Foundation for access to records relating to the quality of hospital care rendered to Medicare patients in Washington, D.C. The FOIA request very carefully clarified that, "while none of the information requested requires patient identification or listing," any patient identifiers should be deleted from the data. They intended to avoid the obvious stumbling block of Exemption 6, which allowed for the withholding of personal information, such as medical files. The FOIA request was denied. The National Capital Medical Foundation took the position that it was not a federal agency and thus not subject to FOIA; the HEW claimed it had neither possession nor control of the requested records. Vladeck, Wolfe and Ted Bogue (a lawyer working with the Health Research Group) prepared to go to court. "We knew this would be controversial," Vladeck says, "so we took a lot of time drafting the complaint. It was an immensely slow slog, nearly two months just on the complaint."

"Well," Vladeck continues, "we drew Judge Gesell, whose doctor father is the guy the Gesell Institute at Yale is named after and here we were taking on the medical establishment at its heart. He grew up on the notion that doctors are special, that the medical community is special and that to question their ethics or commitment is, if not blasphemy, close to it. At the first status conference Gesell asked why we were doing this. Before we could reply, he said, 'I know why you want to do this. Isn't it true you want to tear down the medical institution?' His antagonism toward us was evident and his approach virtually hostile. It did not feel like an auspicious beginning."

There were two legal issues they had to address. First, does a PSRO count as an agency subject to FOIA? Second, if it does, do the exemptions the National Capital Medical Foundation was claiming apply (and basically they were claiming them all)? Gesell notified the parties that he intended to cut the case in two and that first they should address the question of whether a PSRO is an agency. If the answer to that question were no, there would be no need to reach the second question.

Vladeck's brief, when it was finally filed in early January 1978, was forty pages long. "It was a bear to do," Vladeck recalls. "We had just one support staffer who was not up to typing anything so long with any speed and definitely not up to the expected level of perfection (a brilliant law student but as a secretary simply awful)." The briefs prepared by the twelve government lawyers and the big law firm that represented the PSRO looked great. "Theirs were all nice and neat and perfect, while ours was a mess of white-out and smudges. I thought our argument was much better, indeed, that theirs was crummy. What I was really concerned about, though, was whether our messy brief would detract from its argument." Indeed, he was so concerned that he called Jim Brudney (now a professor of law at Ohio State), who was then clerking for Gesell, to ask if he thought that the messy brief would hurt them. The assurance that it would not did not really assuage his worry, but there was little he could do about it anyway.

The oral argument on the first question on April 11, 1978, was "a nightmare," Vladeck says. Gesell made it abundantly clear that he was troubled by the potential damage that this could do to the medical community. "[Y]ou know how the doctors are going to react if I decide for the Plaintiff. They are going to see all the spectres of socialized medicine rampant on horses and witches and everything else," the judge railed to the government attorney just prior to Vladeck's turn to argue. "Some of them are going to resign in anger and the program is all going to go into a state of absolute confusion."

Another exchange during Vladeck's argument gives some flavor of the antagonism he met. Here was a neophyte lawyer, just twenty-seven, who had been practicing law for only a year, and he was challenging the mighty medical establishment.

The Court: You want the names of the physicians?

Mr. Vladeck: We believe there is a difference between physicians and patients, Your Honor, especially physicians who are engaged in service under Government funding.

The Court: Do you agree that the program will end if you prevail?

Mr. Vladeck: We do not agree with that, Your Honor.

The Court: Do you mean you think that doctors will continue to give their frank opinions about colleagues if it is in the *Washington Post*?

"Dripping with antagonism" is how Vladeck describes the judge's attitude that day. "I was peppered with questions from the judge. It seemed to go on interminably." As the oral progressed, though, he had an opportunity to clarify what it was he and Wolfe really wanted. They were not after a "profile" of individual doctors that would include any specific statements of one doctor as to another. Presented with this clarification, the judge seemed to become slightly less worried about the medical profession's impending Armageddon. Two weeks later (living up to his reputation for fast turn-arounds), Gesell decided in the Litigation Group's favor, ruling that the PSRO was indeed an agency and subject to FOIA. His opinion was not delivered with joy, though as Vladeck notes, "It sent the message that he thought the world would come to an end because of this, mark his words." Gesell had noted that the PSRO peer review process would likely suffer "a severe setback, if not fatal blow" if the documents were made available under FOIA. Not a very auspicious message from the judge who would now rule on that second question. What Vladeck most needed was some evidence to prove to the judge that, truly, the world would not end if the data they wanted were released. Medical experts were the only ones who could provide what he needed, and getting them was one of the biggest problems Vladeck faced.

Ordinarily, doctors receive fees for their expert testimony. "The opposition had lots of wampum," Vladeck says. "We had only colored clay beads and could not pay anything." There also was no money to pay for their own travel either. "We had to rely on phone interviews to get info and find support—not the best way when the issue is controversial and you have to win hearts and minds." Moreover, they feared that few doctors would want to challenge the medical establishment.

Vladeck spent ten hours on the phone in a single day with Dr. Quintin Young of Chicago. "My question was basically, 'Tell me your thoughts about whether there is any physician/patient privacy problem with making data available that has no specific patient reference?'" That was hardly the only call, but surely the longest. It was a high visibility case, and it was tough, but Vladeck found a lot of prominent doctors willing to sign affidavits stating why they thought disclosure was important and why it would not harm the medical community. Some turned them down because "they disagreed with our position, but most who turned us down did so because they did not want to stick their necks out." Doctors had little reason to help Vladeck.

The second oral argument on whether any of the FOIA exemptions would apply did not come until the summer of 1979. By then the judge had viewed representative documents *in camera* and been provided with the pile of affidavits Vladeck had collected. On September 25, 1979, Gesell ruled. It was a slam dunk. He ruled against every FOIA claim raised by the defendants. On Exemption 3 (the other statute exemption), the judge noted that none of the statutes relied on provided the specific expectation of secrecy required. "If Congress wishes all such materials to remain secret, it must speak with a clearer voice," the judge admonished. On Exemption 5 (inter- and intra-agency memorandum that includes privileged communications such as patient-doctor or lawyer-client documents in an agency's control), the judge said: "Critical to defendants' physician-patient argument is the premise that disclosure of the records sought by Public Citizen will lead to patient identification. This premise is without adequate factual support. ... [A]ggregated data organized under statistical or topical headings that bear no relation to individual patient identities" simply did not hold out the potential of revealing patient identity. Furthermore, since the studies are accepted as final by HEW, they are final reports and thus the inter-agency exemption is "inapplicable." Of Exemption 4 (trade secrets) and Exemption 7 (law enforcement), the judge did not mince words: "The argument ... is frivolous."

Perhaps the most heartening portion of the judge's opinion for Vladeck, though, was the reasoning given for dismissing Exemption 6 (personal medical files). "Against these qualified values of patient and physician privacy," Gesell wrote, "plaintiff presents an impressive array of affiants, experienced in the health care field, articulating important public interests that attach to disclosure of the four categories of records."

"It was like this opinion was written by an entirely different judge," says Vladeck. "The experience taught me a lot about lawyering and judging. I had assumed that he had his mind made up. But he was far more open to hearing our argument than I would have thought. One thing we are in jeopardy of losing sight of as lawyers is how the facts and the factual context influence what the court does. I think we won, not by my brilliant argument, but by the affidavits we put before the court that told why the release of this data was important, why a window into the quality of medical care was important for the public to have, and why it would strengthen, not weaken, the medical profession. We had been diligent about developing a detailed factual record that supported our position, much more so than the other side. They had almost ignored doing this. I don't know why, but I assume that they became lulled into complacency by the judge's apparent support for their side and antagonism toward us. But in the end, their argument was lousy and Gesell was a smart judge who couldn't and wouldn't have the wool pulled over his eyes. Theirs was basically a slippery slope argument (if you let this out there will be no stopping point, no way to draw a line) and a paternalistic argument (the people are too dumb to be able to understand and interpret this sort of data) and a too-much-harm argument (the release of this data will drastically hurt hospitals that have lower success rates). The combination did not fly. Gesell was obviously more persuaded by our argument."

The medical community was not about to take the ruling lying down. In addition to appealing the decision, their lobbyists headed for Capitol Hill. With Congress Watch keeping an eye on that center of power, Vladeck and Wolfe soon got wind of what was going on. They were able to persuade Representative Henry Waxman (D-California), an oft-supporter of Public Citizen issues and conveniently then chair of a subcommittee with jurisdiction over health matters, to move to short-circuit the fast-track effort that the medical community was mounting to get the law amended to deny access to PSRO data.

Waxman got the Institute of Medicine to set up a special commission to study the question of doctor and hospital disclosure. He was then able to persuade his colleagues that action on the issue should await the outcome of the expert's study—a classic delay tactic that is often employed by the powerful but which occasionally works for the less powerful, as well. The affidavits Vladeck had gathered for his court case were used to set the framework for the study.

In the end, the special commission decided to "split the baby," as Vladeck puts it, agreeing that institution-specific data should be divulged but that doctor-specific should not. Congress ultimately embraced its position in amending the law. The rationale the commission presented in opposing the release of doctor-specific data was that there was just no way to adjust on a gross level for differences in patient mix on a doctor-by-doctor basis and thus it was not fair to compare one physician to another. "I think," Vladeck says, "that they were wrong but at the time we more wanted institution-specific data anyway. When we finally got it, we published literally dozens of reports comparing success rates in various procedures like C-sections, or bypass surgery."

But there was a loss first. When the appeals panel for the circuit court was announced, Vladeck got "an awful panel—two really conservative judges, Robb and Tamm, and one of the liberals, Mikva." Interestingly, at the time the government appealed Judge Gesell's decision, it had asked for a stay pending the appeal. The three judges signing the stay were Tamm, Wald and Mikva. Had Patricia Wald, another of the liberal judges, remained on the case, how different the outcome might have been. Anyway, they lost 2-1 with all three judges writing separate opinions (Tamm and Robb could not agree why PSRO was not an agency, though each was quite sure it was not). Judge Abner Mikva wrote a passionate, almost angry, dissent.

There is little doubt that it was the court case that got the issue onto the congressional agenda. And surely, the careful collection of expert opinions supporting disclosure was critical in persuading Congress, just as it was in persuading Judge Gesell. It is one of the lessons Vladeck always speaks of when he addresses audiences about the practice of public interest law. "When you win a case it is just the beginning. It is then that the forces of darkness and evil are awakened and address their efforts to undo what you have won." The practice of public interest law requires a broad strategy and ongoing attention. As proof of that, it would take until the 1990s to obtain information about doctors who had been disciplined by their own medical review boards, and to get that information out to the public, Sidney Wolfe and Public Citizen had to publish the information themselves.

* * * * *

"Another openness case that began in the 1970s, known within the Litigation Group as "Boys in the Band," was not about getting information from the executive but was very much a case about privacy and freedom, freedom from excessive government pressure. It is an example of how public interest litiga-tors can help the "little guy" when no one else is likely to do so. More impor-tantly, it is an example of how helping a few can lead to changing things for all.

In the 1970s, it was common practice in government and many large cor-porations to put pressure on employees to give to the United Way. Often the percentage of the workforce contributing and the amount raised would be used as one measure to evaluate management performance. In the federal govern-ment, the program is called the Combined Federal Campaign (CFC), and the pressure to contribute on federal workers was considerable. Few doubt the good that the United Way does, or its need for funds, but many people (then and now) find some of the charities supported by the United Way objection-able, or believe that too much of the money they give will be used to support the staff of the agency rather than needy charities. One such person was a young man named Benjamin Riddles, a sergeant assigned to the Army Band Chorus as a soloist.

During the fall of 1977, Riddles found his name, along with sixty-five oth-ers, posted on his unit's bulletin board under the heading "Non Contributors to the Combined Federal Campaign," with the word "NOTICE" in large red letters at the top. It was the last straw in a series of pressure tactics that, according to Riddles, went "back far before this egregious example of coercion." The Army had repeatedly let it be known to him that those deciding not to contribute to the CFC were "jeopardizing their privileges and ultimately, their Army careers." In 1973, his first year in the Army, Riddles did not contribute and "was sum-moned to appear before a group leader, who gave me some 'friendly advice': 'If you intend to make the Army your career, you'd better give,'" he says.

In his affidavit filed in the case, Riddles stated that he was not opposed to charity; indeed he had "deeply felt religious beliefs" that taught him that "char-ity is a private matter between God and the individual." The CFC "mocks the very spirit of charity by publicly establishing the amount which one is expect-ed to give and then designating that amount as an individual's fair share. In contrast, my religion teaches that one's ultimate share is not to be established solely in terms of amount or by reference to the gifts of others." Riddles cited "personal reasons" against the CFC as well. He describes his experience in 1972 as an assistant director of a halfway house for juvenile delinquents in Florida. When policy changes in federal funding left them without funds for three months pending renewal of their grant, they applied for temporary help from the United Way for food expenses. "We did not ask for our salaries," he noted. The United Way refused, citing its rule requiring that a group prove itself finan-cially stable for at least two years to get funding. The halfway house was "too young (1 3/4 years) to qualify." Riddles and the other staff "worked for three months without salaries and the boys ate peanut butter and jelly sandwiches three times a day until federal funding resumed." It was not an experience that endeared the United Way to this young man.

When Riddles refused to budge, he was "badgered daily" and then summoned to appear before a non-commissioned officer in charge of the band. Friends advised him to "give a buck to get them off your back," but he resisted. His situation was not unique. A unit of the Third Infantry, he was informed that a four-day holiday would be shortened unless every unit member donated. Four of Riddles' friends while in basic training were handed a contribution card by the drill sergeant and told, "This is CFC. Your fair share is $17, Sign the card." Riddles had had enough. He happened at the time to be taking a class in legal writing at American University. As luck would have it, his professor was a friend of Diane Cohn, and she sent him over to the Litigation Group for help.

Cohn listened to Riddles' complaint and decided to investigate the matter further, concluding that the Army's actions were violations of both the Privacy Act and the First Amendment. "Fashioning a lawsuit from this was not an easy thing," Cohn recalls. "It was almost like a law school problem." [Later proving how difficult this really was, the government would argue that "the Court lacks subject matter jurisdiction over the plaintiff's claim and that the complaint fails to state a claim upon which relief can be granted."] The Privacy Act included an attractive provision: the awarding of damages to plaintiffs where the government was found to have transgressed the law. The statute provided for a minimum payment of $1,000. The First Amendment, with its separation of church and state, and freedom of speech and assembly, offered an alternative legal hook. Cohn decided to file suit on behalf of all sixty-five men who had been listed on the notice and also to seek more general relief so that this would not happen again in the Army. The complaint was filed on June 8, 1978. Riddles and two others, Michael R. Dudley (a vocalist with the Army Band Chorus) and Raymond N. Miller (a clarinet player with the Army Band) agreed to become the named plaintiffs in the suit.

A *Washington Post* beat reporter came across the complaint during his regular review of court filings and wrote an article that appeared on the front page. "It made the Army look bad," Cohn recalls, "and all hell broke lose." Although the attention riled the Army, it made it a lot more difficult for the government to avoid confronting the problem.

Over the summer of 1978, Cohn worked with Alan Morrison and John Sims to prepare the documents for certification of the suit as a class action. They worried about protecting the men who had indicated to them that they wished to become part of the suit. They decided to attempt to file everything under seal, arguing that if the names of those willing to join the suit were revealed to the Army, there was the potential of retribution. At the end of the summer Morrison headed off to Harvard Law School to teach for the year. Cohn and Sims filed the motion for class certification on September 11, 1978, along with signed, sworn affidavits by Riddles, Dudley and Miller, filed under seal, chronicling the abuses each had experienced.

In the hearing before the judge on the class certification and request for sealing, "the government attorney was making her argument, trying to claim that

Photo by John G. Zimmerman/Time Life Pictures/Getty Images

Ralph Nader and his Nader's Raiders on the Capitol steps in 1969. Reuben Robertson, who later joined the Litigation Group, stands to the left of Nader. Behind Robertson is Harrison Wellford of Nader's Center for Study of Responsive Law.

(Above) Alan Morrison with Litigation Group lawyer Kathy Meyer in April 1986 after the U.S. Supreme Court argument in *Bowsher v. Synar*. Behind them are Litigation Group lawyers Bill Schultz, John Sims, David Vladeck, Con Hitchcock and Paul Levy. (Below, left to right) Con Hitchcock, Paul Levy and Eric Glitzenstein in 1988. Each argued a case in the Supreme Court that year.

Alan Morrison in his office at
Public Citizen headquarters on
P Street near Dupont Circle in
Washington in 1995.

Litigation Group lawyer Bill Schultz at
a social function in the early 1980s.

Dr. Sidney Wolfe, director and co-founder of Public Citizen's Health Research
Group, worked with the Litigation Group on worker safety and other health issues.

Litigation Group lawyers John Sims (above) and Diane Cohn (right) at a social gathering in 1985. (Below) Alan Morrison holds a press conference to announce a settlement in the Nixon tapes case in 1996.

Celebrating Public Citizen's fifteenth anniversary in 1986 are: (Front row, left to right) Nancy Drabble, Elliott Negin, Jeff Drumtra, Ken Bossong, Alan Morrison, Ralph Nader, Sidney Wolfe and Joan Claybrook; (second row) Jason Adkins, Craig McDonald, Ron Williams, Carol Daugherty, Margaret Lawton and Ian Gilbert; (back row) Eric Glitzenstein, David Vladeck, Paul Levy, Bill Schultz, Kathy Meyer, Franci Livingston, Pam Homer and Tom Tobin.

Illustration by Ray Driver. Reprinted from the October 1986 issue of *Public Citizen* magazine.

(Above) Alan Morrison in the late 1970s. (Right) Morrison scribbled his ideas for public interest litigation on a piece of yellow paper that he kept in his wallet for years. (Below) Jagdish Chadha with Morrison in 1982 after a U.S. Supreme Court argument in *INS v. Chadha*.

(Top left) Joan Claybrook in the late 1970s during her tenure as administrator of the National Highway Traffic Safety Administration. (Top right) Litigation Group lawyer Arthur Fox with his daughter Courtney in 1985. (Below) Litigation Group's David Vladeck in 1989.

David Vladeck greets U.S. Attorney General Janet Reno in 1995. Vladeck, a lawyer in the Litigation Group for twenty-five years, served as its director from 1993 to 2002.

Former and current Litigation Group lawyers at a reunion in 2003. (Front row, left to right) Marka Peterson, Allison Zieve, Brian Wolfman and Alan Morrison; (back row) John Sims, Bill Schultz, Paul Wolfson, Kerry Scanlon, Arthur Fox, Kathy Meyer, David Vladeck, Con Hitchcock, Eric Glitzenstein, Larry Ellsworth, Paul Levy, Michael Tankersley, Scott Nelson and Gerry Spann.

the need for sealing was unnecessary," Cohn recalls, "when Judge Oberdorfer leaned over and said, 'I was in the Army and I know this happened all the time.'" On October 10, the judge certified the class and took the affidavits and other documents under seal. They continued negotiating with the Justice Department over a settlement. As the discussions progressed, Cohn was careful to keep the issue focused on what changes would be made in the Army's CFC program and how they would be implemented and monitored so that individuals would not feel forced to give. "We held the money damages issue aside, holding out for agreement on the bigger issue first," Cohn notes. Shortly after the class action papers were filed in September 1978, Riddles was denied a slot as soloist with the chorus, a slot he had held regularly before. When Cohn complained to the lawyer in the civil division of the Justice Department who was responsible for privacy law issues, the Army responded:

> While it is true that prior to the institution of this lawsuit Sergeant First Class Riddles performed solos with the Army chorus on a regular basis, the Command became uncertain as to the propriety of permitting him to continue in this capacity after initiation of this suit against the Department of the Army. Further, the solo performances were an extra duty which required additional preparation on Sergeant Riddle's part. The extra preparation could be equated as an extra duty for Sergeant Riddles. The Commander, mindful of the extra effort required in performing solos, determined that the U.S. Army might be accused of placing additional requirements on Sergeant First Class Riddles in retaliation for his exercise of First Amendment rights in filing this lawsuit. Based upon the foregoing reasons, the Commander reduced Sergeant Riddles' workload to participation in the Army chorus. We have asked the Commander to give SFC Riddles the same consideration extended all other members of the chorus who desire solo slots.

A dissembling explanation if ever there were one. As Riddles noted in his affidavit: "Since filing of this action, my assignments as soloist with the Army Band Chorus have terminated; I am therefore no longer performing the double duty which promotion requires. I was just recently informed by Colonel Allen that I may be considered to be too overweight to permit me to re-enlist, even if I met the standards for height and weight established and published by the Department of the Army."

After filing suit, Cohn had attempted to discuss a settlement proposal with the government attorney. They were after a means to enforce the existing Army regulation that explicitly prohibited most of the coercive practices that had been identified in their litigation. In response, the government offered to send around a memorandum that would basically restate the existing language of the regulation. Cohn noted in her reply that this regulation "has been flagrantly ignored during the course of the Army's CFC activities." She continues, "You can therefore understand our position that a simple memorandum to installation commanders will not be enough to bring about any real change." Instead she insisted that any resolution be embodied in a court order as a protection against future abuse and that there be a program agreed to as part of the settlement that would spell out how the Army would notify all its enlisted personnel and officers about the changes. Then, since the government was not moving forward, she sought to depose a number of officers identified as those who coerced her clients. She also sent notice to the judge that there had been coercion after the class had been certified.

In the early winter, the Justice Department indicated that it was finally ready to really compromise and reach a settlement but that before doing so it would like to at least read the sealed affidavits. "Basically," Sims says, "they just wanted to make sure we really had a case." Sims and Cohn were not really worried that Justice would show the documents to the Army and knew that what they had would be persuasive in moving the case to settlement. So they agreed to send the papers over to the Justice Department attorney in charge of the case. The next day, as Sims recalls, "we got a desperate call from Justice admitting that they had lost the papers. They wanted to tell us before they told the judge. They were very upset. It was not going to be fun to tell the judge that they had handled papers under seal in so careless a way." After reading the documents, someone at the Justice Department had turned them over to a messenger to deliver them to the Litigation Group. Traveling from the Justice Department to Dupont Circle requires changing trains at Metro Center. Apparently the messenger, in a rush to catch the connecting train, had left the papers behind.

Sims told them "to hold tight for a bit and perhaps the papers would turn up." He knew that this incident had given them a big advantage but "we just didn't want to push our luck or be too heavy handed. Our true reaction," Sims admits with glee, "was that we thought it was hilarious. We knew there was no way the document was going to make its way back to the commander of the Army band, so there really wasn't a problem. We also knew, though, that since they had been so inept with their handling of this document that they were going to have a very difficult time explaining this to the judge if it didn't turn up." Well, it did turn up. Apparently some honest soul found it on the train and, since it had "Department of Justice" conspicuously displayed all over, must have dumped it in a mail box. "There wasn't any need then to tell the judge," Sims says, "and we figured if we treated them decently at a very difficult moment for them, it might be better for us."

It was time to come to agreement from both side's perspective. On February 15, 1979, Cohn wrote to Riddles, Dudley and Miller: "[T]he Army has agreed to allow individuals to either submit their pledge form or contribution to some central accounting office, which would not be part of the soldier's direct unit. This is a significant (if not the most significant) part of what we wanted." With only a couple of minor details left to negotiate on the process issues, the question of damages was next. The government had offered $200 per person in the class. She would try for more.

On February 26, 1979, Cohn wrote again to her clients, "[H]old on to your hat because we have just reached a settlement in our case." The Army had not only agreed to virtually all the safeguards they had been insisting upon but had agreed to pay a sum of $27,500, which would amount to $423 each if all sixty-five men on the list opted back into the class (many had opted out because of fear of retaliation, but the judge had allowed for an opt-back provision when the class was certified). In the end, fifty-three men each got a check for $518 and change.

More satisfying even than the settlement, though, was that within a year, new federal rules were finalized that prohibited all government agencies from coercing employees to give to charities. "Last spring, a group of military employees won a court case against the Army for using coercive fund-raising techniques," a *Washington Post* article reported in December 1980. "The court decision, plus heavy criticism from a congressional subcommittee [which Riddles, Dudley, Miller and Sims all testified before] led to a new set of rules against coercion, which could serve as a model for state and local governments and private companies." Three young men had the courage to stand up, and there was someone to turn to for help—making a difference for many. "I really think you can be proud that you cared enough to see this thing through and to undertake certain risks in order to stand up for your principles," Cohn wrote to Riddles after he had left the Army and returned to Florida.

There was to be one more feather in Cohn's and Sims' hats on this one. When the final check to all fifty-three class members was cashed, the two turned to the question of attorneys' fees. Not surprisingly, the Justice Department signed off without much haggling, agreeing to pay $8,768.78.

"I have thought a lot about this case over the years," said Sims, who is now a law professor in Sacramento, California. "When that huge scandal blew up in 1995 where the chief executive of the United Way of America [William Aramony, who was convicted and sentenced to seven years in prison for embezzling $1.2 million] was raking off money and using it for improper purposes [for a romance with a teenage girl, vacations abroad and chauffeur services], I couldn't help but be satisfied that at least the government had not been forcing its employees to contribute." One of Riddles' points was that he ought to be able to know where his money was going. "These were not skinflints trying to save nickels, they were people who believed that charity ought to be more than a corporate process and they also had a high sense of individual freedom," says Sims. "They resented being ordered by anybody to be charitable. I'm sure it was a shock to those commanders that these individual soldiers were willing to stand up. They found it offensive. I thought it was wonderful."

* * * *

When Nixon agreed to open up his vice presidential papers on March 22, 1978, *Brandon v. Sampson* became moot. "While it is true that ultimately the documents were released at this time through the decision of former President Nixon to amend his chattel deed," Morrison admits, "there is no question that he was impelled to do that by reason of this lawsuit and a concern about being subjected to further discovery concerning the original and modified deeds." The Litigation Group believed that it was their effort that forced the opening of the papers and that therefore they were entitled to attorneys' fees. The stipulation dismissing the case that the government and Cohn, as attorney for Brandon, signed on March 29 specifically reserved the right for the Litigation Group to seek attorneys' fees and for the government to object. Less than a month later, Morrison sent a letter to the Justice Department asking for $11,693.75 in fees and court costs. His letter pointed out that the Litigation Group was still using the same hourly rate that the Department had accepted in *Vaughn*, though much of the work in this one had been done more recently, and thus "a higher rate would be justifiable." The letter also noted that he was willing to settle and asked for a response within thirty days. More than triple that time passed before the department finally denied the request on July 18. If the Litigation Group wanted to get paid, it now had to go back to court.

Two weeks after the Justice Department's final denial of the fee request, the district judge who had handled *Brandon* (Judge Waddy) died, and the case was subsequently reassigned to Judge Charles R. Richey. At the Litigation Group there was change as well. Larry Ellsworth, who had handled *Brandon*, left that spring to join his former mentor, Vic Kramer, at the Senate Select Committee on Ethics investigating attempts by Korea to influence members of the Senate. And Alan Morrison left that summer to spend a year teaching at Harvard. It was, as Vladeck notes, "the year of the children's crusade." Cohn had taken over *Brandon* just before the stipulation was signed in March, so the fee issue landed on her desk. With all the other things on her agenda, the fee issue (which had no deadline set in the stipulation order) slipped in the queue.

On February 9, 1979, Cohn filed a motion with the court seeking a fee award. Over nine months later, on December 17, 1979, the district court entered a one-paragraph order denying her motion. Although Judge Richey agreed that the Litigation Group had substantially prevailed, he found it not entitled to attorneys' fees "because there was a colorable basis for the government's refusal to release the documents" and because the motion was "untimely." There were two options at this point—throw in the towel or appeal.

Cohn advised against appeal because, in her opinion, the reviewing court would most likely give deference to the lower court on both points. Since a determination of "timeliness" is really one of "reasonableness" and that test requires by its very nature "a factual determination based on all the circumstances involved, I would assume the reviewing court would give deference to the trial court," Cohn pointed out. "While we could argue on appeal that a finding of colorable basis does not end the court's inquiry, and that Judge Richey's order does not specifically reflect a weighing and balancing of all the Senate criteria [for awarding attorneys' fees in FOIA cases], this issue is again one in which the district court is given broad discretion. There have to be cases where the facts are more favorable to us for trying to limit the application of this reasonableness basis standard." In conclusion, Cohn wrote: "I think it is hard to ignore the fact that Judge Richey is generally favorable to us, and that he must have felt pretty strongly in ruling against us the way he did, another factor which argues against an appeal or a motion for reconsideration."

Morrison was not convinced. In his mind their effort had resulted in a significant public service. It defied reality to suggest that Nixon would have lifted the restrictions on the papers without their five-year court battle. There had been no sign of his doing so along the way, no sign until the threat of deposition loomed. Both reasons the judge used for refusing to grant a fee award seemed plain wrong. On December 28, 1979, he wrote a long letter to the assistant attorney general. His letter focused on *Brandon*, suggesting a resolution of the fees rather than an appeal. But only thinly veiled was his counter to the preposterousness of the timeliness charge the department had put forth against them in *Brandon*. "While we have made repeated efforts to settle attorneys' fees questions in other FOIA cases, the greatest problem we have encountered is the Department's delay in responding, and in some cases failure to respond at all." Morrison raised the problems in three other cases, most pointedly in *Weisman v. CIA*. There they had "obtained a significant ruling from the Court of Appeals concerning the scope of Exemption 7 and the CIA's authority to conduct domestic surveillance and the subsequent release of virtually all of the documents at issue in the case." Their request for fees was submitted to the department in April 1978. Eighteen months later they still had no answer. Later, when the department finally responded to Morrison's letter, the explanation for the *Weisman* delay: "[T]he delay in responding to your settlement proposal in *Weisman* was partly the result of the departure from the department of the attorney assigned." Pretty frustrating to be accused of delay by the very hands getting away with it against you (especially when the FOIA law made clear that such requests were to have expedited treatment by the government).

The department would not budge, so Morrison and Cohn appealed. A brief excerpt from their reply brief of September 19, 1980, gives some taste of their determination to do battle on this injustice.

> Contrary to the government's contention, an award of fees would not "leave the government with no choice but to release documents deposited with it under the Libraries Act and requested under FOIA." It would simply reflect the right of the public to demand that GSA properly comply with the provisions of the Libraries Act, particularly in accepting restrictions on public access to material of extreme historical significance. We are unaware of any public pur-

pose to be served by encouraging the making of false statements and the back-dating of deeds, and the private restricting of access to government records, which is what was at issue in this case.

At oral argument before the appeals court, Cohn tried a different tack:

We think that under the guidelines established by this Court, we are plainly entitled to fees. The government's position is that we are not, because if we had continued to litigate the merits of this case, the government claims it would have won. The first problem with this argument is that [if accepted] in every case that has been resolved prior to final judgment, the parties would nevertheless be required to litigate the merits in the context of an application for attorneys' fees. The burden such a ruling would place on the courts is clear from the facts of the case.

It was an heroic effort, but in the end they lost. Cohn's warning was undoubtedly on the mark. On May 15, 1981, the appeals court affirmed Judge Richey's denial of fees. The full opinion reads: "Plaintiff filed his motion for a declaratory order more than six months after the final administrative denial of his fee request: the District Court acted well within its discretion in declaring that motion untimely." The court did not rely on the reasonable basis for withholding issue, and it did not explain why six months was the magic cut-off for filing a fee motion. It was aggravating considering the incredible delay they had faced at the department's hands. One small win: the district court had awarded their court costs in the *Brandon* FOIA case. A check for the grand sum of $441 had arrived on March 17, 1978.

One big potential problem was avoided: Cohn had been worried that if they appealed, the government's claim that the records involved here were "not agency records" (a question Judge Richey "found unnecessary to reach") might be addressed by the appeals court. "We surely don't want the Court of Appeals to address this very complex issue in the context of an attorneys' fees request," Cohn had argued. Just what constitutes "an agency record" when it originates in the Executive Office of the President was an issue that would be on their agenda in the years ahead, and it would give rise to one of the longest series of court battles and ultimately one of the most rewarding wins (including on the attorneys' fees issue) in the Litigation Group's history.

* * * * *

Perhaps there was something about vice presidents that jinxed fee awards to the Litigation Group, because the Justice Department mounted the same sort of delay and resistance to its request for the documents and then for the attorneys' fees in *Baldwin v. Baker* (the case seeking access to the investigation of

Agnew papers). As Morrison noted in the same letter raising his concerns about *Brandon*, "We asked for only $2450 in attorneys' fees for preparing our appellate brief." That was in February of 1979, and eleven months later, "we are still awaiting a response." When it was denied they went to court. It is interesting that the resistance to paying attorneys' fees for their effort to bring to public view the documents regarding two Republicans forced to resign the highest offices in the land in disgrace was resisted by the Democratic Justice Department of the Carter administration. Therein lies a lesson: the attorneys at Justice most often perceive their role to be defender of the executive branch and to protect the prerogatives of the presidency, no matter which party or which individual controls the White House. It is a reality that those who litigate against the government need to keep uppermost in their minds.

One of the special features of the Freedom of Information Act is its attorneys' fee awards provision. It does not always bring funds into the coffers, but it has accounted for some significant funds to aid the Litigation Group's cause. Many of the other areas in which the Group litigates do not have the financial reward at the end of a winning case.

11

Policing Government and Big Business

In 1977, the Litigation Group turned five. The staff spent an evening at the Tabard Inn on February 5 to, as the party "summons" said, "eat, drink, dance and make merry." The offices were closed—a very unusual Saturday for the nine overworked, underpaid young lawyers of the Litigation Group. On most Saturdays, many lights could be seen aglow on the seventh floor of 2000 P street. Morrison and Robertson, the gray eminences of this public interest law firm, were both in their late thirties. Arthur Fox, who was focused on union cases, was just a couple of years younger. The rest of the team at that point was composed mostly of twenty-somethings. Larry Ellsworth, the most senior in tenure among the youngsters and the most experienced (but still not quite thirty), joined the Litigation Group in September 1973. Gerry Spann, arrived in mid-1974 straight out of Harvard Law. John Sims and Linda Donaldson arrived the same day in September 1975, both right after one-year clerkships with federal judges. Bill Schultz came just a few months later, in January 1976, also after a clerkship with a federal judge. Diane Cohn, who, like Ellsworth, was snapped up by Morrison after her one-year fellowship in Vic Kramer's "nursery school for public interest lawyers" at Georgetown University Law Center, arrived in the early fall of 1976. David Vladeck, also recruited from Kramer's program, was not there for the party as he did not join them until seven months after the Litigation Group's five-year anniversary.

By the tender age of five, the Litigation Group already had argued six cases before the Supreme Court: two losses—*Alexander v. Americans United* (1974) and *Administrator, FAA v. Robertson* (1975); and four wins—*Campaign Clean Water v. Train* (1975), *Goldfarb v. Virginia State Bar* (1975), *Nader v. Allegheny Airlines* (1976), and *Virginia State Board of Pharmacy v. Virginia Consumer Council* (1976). Dozens of their cases had been decided by federal district and appeals courts, with some losses, but an impressive number won or settled favorably. This would be quite a record for any law firm. For such a new firm with such a young and inexperienced crew, it was extraordinary.

The year also brought a new political administration to the nation. After eight years of Republican control of the White House, the Democrats were back with Jimmy Carter in office. For Public Citizen and allied organizations, a

Democratic administration held the promise, or at least the hope, of more vigorous enforcement of health, safety and consumer standards. It also provided an opportunity that several lawyers in the Litigation Group and others from Public Citizen would find irresistible—to become part of the government team responsible for enforcing the law. Joan Claybrook, then head of Congress Watch, Public Citizen's lobbying arm, accepted the position of administrator of the National Highway Traffic Safety Administration (NHTSA). Ultimately, Ellsworth (who went first to work with Kramer on a special commission investigating Koreagate for the Senate and then to the Department of Energy) and then Robertson (who went first to the Interstate Commerce Commission and then was director of the Bureau of Consumer Protection at the Civil Aeronautics Board) and finally Donaldson (who went to the Office of Legal Counsel in the Department of Health, Education and Welfare) were hooked as well. Friends on the inside might make the Litigation Group's job easier, but only time would tell.

* * * * *

After he graduated from Yale University in 1970 and was married, Bill Schultz went to law school at the University of Virginia and then completed a clerkship for Judge William B. Bryant of the U.S. District Court for the District of Columbia. "I thought about working for Nader," Schultz recalls, "but I didn't think I could possibly afford to do so. I had heard about the puny salaries of $6,000 or less he paid." Then he heard through a friend that the salary at the Litigation Group was better. He sent an application. In early December 1974, Morrison called him to set up an interview. "He said he was really busy but thought he could see me at 6 p.m. on December 31," says Schultz. So on New Year's Eve, as most people were heading off to celebrate, Schultz headed over to 2000 P Street for an audience with Morrison. When he arrived, Morrison was fielding calls from journalists about the 3M stockholder derivative suit he had just settled. The suit was one of the group's more creative undertakings, and most financially rewarding.

The 3M company had pleaded guilty to one small illegal payment to Nixon's re-election campaign and had been fined, but no corporate officers had been indicted. All of this, of course, made the newspapers, and the Litigation Group believed there was more to the story. Acting on behalf of a cooperative shareholder, the group wrote to 3M to demand full disclosure and repayment to the corporation of all damages. "We had no idea what the amount actually was but doubted that it was 'one small payment' of something like $25,000, as the corporate officers had claimed," Morrison said. Their request was ignored. Then "a little birdie told us there was real gold there." They filed suit, naming a couple of 3M people they knew were involved.

Through the discovery process, Morrison obtained an internal report showing the "company was out about $700-800,000, not counting legal fees." With this proof, Morrison was able to force a settlement that called for various individuals in 3M who had been involved to pay $475,000 back to the company and fully disclose the extent of the illegal contributions and who had made them. The Litigation Group received 10 percent of the settlement, enough to pay the salaries of four of its lawyers for a year. But more important was the policy result. First, the case brought to light that the Watergate investigators who discovered these illegal donations in their examination of Nixon re-election campaign records were allowing companies to conceal the extent of their losses from stockholders, even when the government forced them to pay back illegal contributions. Second, it created new personal penalties for executives who authorized illegal contributions. Third, it energized the Securities and Exchange Commission's enforcement against such illegal payments, and the agency began to go after companies on its own. It was quite a coup, and Schultz was fascinated by Morrison's discussions with the press as he sat waiting. At one point, between calls, Morrison handed him a docket of the cases they had done and were doing. "Every one was a case I would have wanted to do," Schultz says. Of Schultz, Morrison has this to say: "I was immediately struck by his good sense and judgment, someone whose advice I would want to seek in a tough situation."

Schultz's next interview was with Nader. "One of the first questions Ralph asked me was what I knew about the Freedom of Information Act," Schultz recalls. "I had worked on a number of FOIA cases for the judge, so I was able to make a few intelligent-sounding remarks before he interrupted, asking, 'Is the post office covered by FOIA?'" When Schultz admitted that he did not know, Nader told him to write a memo on the subject. Nader explained that he suspected the post office was tampering with his mail. Here was someone he could put to work right away to find out if a FOIA request would work. It was "typical Ralph," Schultz says. "He never let an opportunity pass, so I went home with homework from an interview." When Morrison called soon after with an offer and an $11,000 salary, Schultz signed on. Several Litigation Group attorneys asked Schultz to join them for lunch on his first day. "We went to this cafeteria down the street and I ordered a hot dog." Sims, who was standing next in line, leaned over, "Don't think you are going to be eating hot dogs after you have been working for us for a while." Schultz, who would soon become the Litigation Group's food and drug expert, says that Sims' prediction proved accurate.

Morrison assigned Schultz to fashion a case to challenge the constitutionality of the Price-Anderson Act, which limited the liability of nuclear power plant owners in the event of a meltdown or other catastrophe. The resulting case would wind up in the Supreme Court.

* * * * *

"When clerking," Schultz recalls, "I reviewed an opinion in a case on the

Price-Anderson Act in which a court had found that it could not be challenged until a nuclear accident actually happened, so my first reaction was that we would surely have a ripeness problem." But Morrison said they would find a way. Two days later, a North Carolina lawyer called Morrison asking for help, and Schultz had his case.

In his book *Insuring Against Disaster: The Nuclear Industry on Trial*, professor John Johnson describes how the North Carolina attorney happened to call Morrison. Since 1970, a group of property owners had been fighting a proposed nuclear power plant to be built by Duke Power Company in North Carolina. The first efforts of this group, called the Carolina Environmental Study Group (CESG), were focused on persuading the Atomic Energy Commission (AEC) to deny a construction permit. When this failed and a permit was issued to build the McGuire Nuclear Station on Lake Norman, three attorneys associated with the North Carolina Civil Liberties Union Legal Foundation filed a case on behalf of the CESG in the U.S. District Court for the Western District of North Carolina. The case against both the AEC (soon to be replaced by the Nuclear Regulatory Commission) and Duke Power raised numerous challenges: (1) that the permit had been granted without an adequate environmental impact statement as mandated by the National Environmental Policy Act of 1970; (2) that the construction of McGuire would have a "disastrous effect" on the human environment by creating significant health and safety risks; (3) that AEC's decision to grant the permit represented a decision by a body with a built-in conflict of interest because the AEC was responsible for both promotion of nuclear power and its regulation; and (4) that the Price-Anderson Act was unconstitutional. On January 6, 1976, District Judge James B. McMillan ordered a four-day evidentiary hearing. The date the judge set, September 27, was just nine months away. This news was both gratifying and troublesome to the three volunteer civil liberties lawyers. Though the opportunity to fully present evidence in open court was attractive, none of the three thought they could devote the time necessary to prepare for such a hearing. They were exhausted after three years of effort in a case that had already produced mounds of paper. Moreover, neither they nor the state civil liberties union had sufficient funds to pay for the expert witnesses they figured would be necessary to prove their case.

One attorney, who was familiar with Nader's stand against nuclear power, suggested that they contact him to see if he would be interested. Morrison responded enthusiastically to the inquiry. A week later he and Schultz flew to Charlotte, North Carolina, to meet with one of the attorneys, George Daly. Daly admits to relief when he turned over his files. "At that point I hated the damn files," he said. Schultz was much better positioned to take on the project. "At that point, I had no cases on my docket, so I could devote full-time to the effort," he recalls. He also worked with a team of lawyers who could offer and provide help. And, of course, he had Morrison. "It was incredible," Schultz said. "What a first case to have all your own." Schultz traveled several times to North Carolina, usually staying with Daly, who remained as local counsel. Daly was this "great character, very connected around town, wealthy and much the Southern gentlemen," Schultz recalled. "He used to take me around to local restaurants and introduce me to all his friends as, 'This is a Nader's Raider.'" Schultz knew that sooner or later Daly would ask him how long he had been with Nader. "I lived in fear of his reaction since my answer would have to be given in days." It was soon clear that what he lacked in experience was very much compensated by brains and determination.

To prove the points raised by the CESG complaint, Schultz needed experts to testify about a variety of things: the risk of nuclear accidents and the high and low estimates of economic damage; the problem of nuclear plant not having to carry enough insurance to pay for the potential damage and homeowners not being able to buy their own insurance to cover such damage; the environmental damage that would occur in the event of even a minor accident; the environmental damage that would occur just from the normal operating of the plant; and the health and safety risks to people living nearby. It was an enormous task for a young attorney with limited contacts. He spent hundreds of hours on the phone, running down leads and learning. He finally found all the experts he needed. "We didn't have to pay any of them," Schultz noted. "In the kinds of cases we bring we rarely have to pay for expert witness. There are usually willing volunteers who support our goal and they know we aren't making any money out of it."

All too soon it was time to go to court. From Monday, September 27, to Friday, October 1, 1976, Schultz (accompanied by Morrison and Daly) argued the case before Judge James B. McMillan in the U.S. district court in Charlotte. Counsel for the opposite side numbered six—four for Duke Power (all well-experienced, prominent members of the North Carolina bar) and two for the Nuclear Regulatory Commission (one from the Department of Justice, the other a staff attorney for the NRC). The power in the courtroom seemed tipped against them, but Daly knew the judge to be sensitive to human welfare and environmental interests and "absolutely unswayed by the power and influence of governmental agencies and private utilities." Just a year after being appointed to the federal bench, Judge McMillan had ordered Charlotte's public schools desegregated and soon thereafter issued the first court-ordered busing plan in the nation. His environmental rulings were equally dramatic, including halting several public works projects in Charlotte for environmental reasons. Judge McMillan was definitely not the stereotypical Southern judge.

The bulk of Schultz' case was examining expert witnesses. He had to not only get his witnesses accepted as experts but also get the evidence into the record in a way that would convince the judge. He also aimed to question the credibility of experts on the other side. One of Schultz's goals was to prove that private citizens could not buy their own insurance policies to cover losses caused by a nuclear plant accident. The point being that, if a homeowner could not cover herself for the loss, the only insurance to cover it would be the plant's insurance, which Schultz was able to show was woefully inadequate. Schultz had contacted Lloyd's of London, the insurance company famous for insuring all manner of assets, asking if it would write an insurance policy for nuclear accident damage for a private homeowner. Lloyd's had said no. Schultz had that entered into evidence. A witness for the other side claimed that it would be irrational for a homeowner to buy nuclear accident insurance. Schultz recalls his strategy for cross-examination. "I asked him, 'Is it irrational at any price?' He responded, 'Yes, no matter what it costs.' So I asked, 'What if it cost a hundred dollars?' He said, 'No, the risk is so small it would be irrational.' So I went on asking him, 'What if it cost ten dollars?' And then, 'What if it costs one dollar?' He kept saying, 'No, the risk is too small.' Then I said, 'What if it cost one cent?' Unbelievably, the answer was still no. It really destroyed his credibility." When Schultz finished with the witness and sat down, Daly leaned over and whispered, "You know, I would have stopped after one dollar."

On the final day of the weeklong trial, Duke Power conducted a tour of the partly finished McGuire nuclear plant for the judge, the attorneys, the journalists and witnesses present that day in the hearing room. Duke had offered a tour on the first day and planned carefully to guard against the transmission of any inadmissible testimony or evidence to the judge when there was no court reporter. In the drive to the plant, one attorney for each of the three parties accompanied the judge—a witness and potential objector for each in the event that an inappropriate word passed the lips of any other. No objection ever came, but Schultz recalls one amusing and, to him, telling incident from the tour. Just prior to the Duke trial there had been an accident at the Browns Ferry nuclear plant in Alabama that had begun when a match used to test for leaks caused a fire. As the group entered one room particularly festooned by pipes and wires, the judge turned around and whispered to Schultz and a couple of others nearby, "Don't anybody light a match!" The comment gave Schultz his "first inkling that we had a shot at winning the case."

Six months later, on March 31, 1977, Judge McMillan announced his decision, which begins with a description of the plaintiffs as "a group of people with a common interest in protecting themselves, and other present day citizens and their children, against what they see as the deterioration and destruction of their property. ... Some of them have fought against nuclear power at numerous administrative and legal levels. They have opposed licensing ... to construct nuclear plants, and they oppose ultimate issuance of a license to operate those plants. They have not slept on their rights. They are vigorously represented by able and experienced counsel. Their claims are seriously advanced." To Schultz, the words of praise were flattering, but what came next was even better. "It was a home run," Schultz recalls with satisfaction. "We won on everything—standing and merits."

After covering all the evidence that plaintiffs had advanced as to the harm they would suffer in excruciating statistical and scientific detail, the judge concluded that "the construction and operation of the power plants would have immediate adverse consequences for plaintiffs, including exposure to a small amount of radiation, heating of nearby recreational lakes, and engendering of present fear of a future nuclear accident ... [and that] the operation of plants also posed the risk of future adverse consequences, in the form of personal injury or property loss arising from a nuclear incident." Having thus found that the CESG had standing, Judge McMillan went on through another exhaustive discussion of the evidence presented on the constitutional issues, concluding that the Price-Anderson Act "violates the equal protection provision that is included within the Due Process Clause of the Fifth Amendment because it provides for what Congress deemed to be a benefit to the whole society [the encouragement of the generation of nuclear power], but places the cost of that benefit on an arbitrarily chosen segment of society, those injured by nuclear catastrophe." These folks, the judge went on to note, are "by definition least able to stand such losses." and further, "the limitation was unnecessary to serve any legitimate public purpose" as "other arrangements" more "rationally related to the interests asserted could easily be devised." In conclusion, the judge wrote:

> Some of the witnesses so minimized the risks of nuclear power plants that the court is tempted to forget the evidence to the contrary and to conclude that there are no major dangers, and to say like Pollyanna, that "everything will turn out all right." That temptation subsides in the light of the strong evidence that the dangers are real, and when it is remembered that the Price-Anderson Act was sold to Congress in 1956 and re-sold in 1975 by government and industry spokesmen as being necessary to induce power companies and investors to build atomic power plants. In those days, they sought the Price-Anderson's limitation on liability upon a practical premise more consistent with Robert Burns' classic thought that:
>
> > The best laid schemes o'mice an'men
> > Gang aft agley
> > An' leave us nought but grief an' pain
> > For promised joy."

The "grief an' pain" in the offices of Duke Power was seen as decidedly different from that which the judge was attempting to reference. To the company, the decision was potential economic ruin. In less than two weeks, Duke Power's attorneys filed a notice of appeal to the Supreme Court. Since the district court judge had ruled a U.S. statute unconstitutional, the avenue of direct appeal to the high court was available as an alternative to appealing first to the appellate court. "On the same day," as Johnson reports in *Insuring Against Disaster*, the attorney for Duke Power "wrote to two of the Carolinas' U.S. senators ... asking for cooperation in assuring that the Duke appeal would be granted 'probable jurisdiction' by the Supreme Court." Senator Ernest "Fritz" Hollings (D-South Carolina) wrote immediately to the solicitor general of the United States, Wade Hampton McCree: "The uncertainties created by ... [Judge McMillan's] decision could adversely affect the efforts of electric utilities to construct and operate nuclear power plants. This would be a move in the wrong direction. ... We in Congress believe that the Price-Anderson Act is very much in the public interest and that it is constitutional." Hollings mentioned the "tight energy situation" in 1977 and urged the court to take the case to rid us of "the cloud of uncertainty regarding the validity" of Price-Anderson. Soon thereafter, the Justice Department filed its own notice of appeal on behalf of the Nuclear Regulatory Commission. It too raised the specter of economic disaster should the Supreme Court not step in and overturn the district court's ruling: "unless revised, the decision below could stand as a major impediment to further private development of nuclear energy in this nation." The Supreme Court announced that it would take the case, and oral argument was scheduled for March 20, 1978.

Duke Power's attorneys gathered *amici* to support their position. In the end, eleven organizations or corporations submitted briefs in support of the company's position. Every one was represented by prestigious Washington or New York law firms. Literally billions of dollars were at stake.

Schultz knew he had an enormous task ahead and he also sought help. He wrote to several law professors who had written about the Price-Anderson Act or on issues connected to the standing, ripeness and constitutional issues he and his opponents were raising. He wrote to Jeffrey O'Connell at the University of Illinois, who had been quoted in an article in *Business Week* responding to a suggestion that if the Supreme Court upheld the lower court decision it might affect liability limitations in state no-fault laws, asking if the professor would have time to talk with him and if he would be interested in filing an *amicus* brief. Another letter was sent to a student at the University of Virginia, setting out a long list of "research topics" that students at the law school could help with, such as finding and listing all law review and other academic articles that discussed the constitutionality of the Price-Anderson Act; checking newspaper indexes to articles on referendums in several states about requiring nuclear plant owners to fully insure their plants; and researching the common law in England and the rest of Europe and assessing the consistency between the admiralty statutory limitations and the common law. Schultz also sent his brief around to a number of law professors asking for help (from the letters in the file, most seem to be former professors of other Litigation Group attorneys). He was leaving no stone unturned, but this thirty-year-old lawyer (who admits he had trouble then passing for twenty-five) with barely two years of litigation experience under his belt, had only volunteers and his colleagues at the Litigation Group to rely upon as he prepared to go to the highest court in the land to argue against some of the most experienced and top-level talent in the legal field.

Each side was allotted forty-five minutes to argue. The solicitor general and Duke Power's attorney would split the appellants' allotted time. Schultz would get all forty-five minutes to himself. Schultz put his all into preparing for every question he and the rest of the Litigation Group attorneys could imagine the justices might ask and to trying to develop the strongest argument possible—suffering through two long moot courts in the process.

The argument in *Duke Power Company v. Carolina Environmental Study Group* was scheduled to begin at 11:30 a.m. Schultz, Daly and Morrison sat at the appellees' counsel table. As appellant, Steve Griffith, senior counsel for Duke Power, went first. Schultz was surprised that the questioning from the bench seemed both overly gentle and quite sparse. The Duke Power attorney had been given more than ample time around the questioning to make his case. Following his argument the court broke for lunch and a nervous Schultz sat through a meal with not much appetite. When the court reconvened at 1 p.m., it was Solicitor General McCree's turn. Again, Schultz was surprised by the soft-glove questioning from the bench directed at the solicitor general. It was all "most deferential" with the justices repeatedly referring to him as "general." Nothing in what he witnessed prepared him for the forty-five minutes of grilling he received at the hands of the nine justices. As George Daly observed, "Bill got up and talked for about ... one-half minute and then got a question and got beaten from pillar to post" for the rest of his forty-five minutes. The questions were non-stop and "came so thick and fast" that he was "intercepted in mid-answer by another question." When an exhausted Schultz finally sat done, Morrison passed him a note commending him for "combat duty." Looking back more than twenty years later, Schultz says, "It was without any doubt the toughest argument I ever did. It made everything after seem like an easy sail."

On June 26, 1978, the Supreme Court granted standing but overruled the district court, thereby upholding the Price-Anderson Act as constitutional. "The liberal standing ruling helped us for years as a precedent enabling us to get other cases into court," Schultz says. With the Price-Anderson Act upheld and an oil shortage (still existing as a result of OPEC's first oil embargo in 1973 and subsequent price increases) that would soon worsen with OPEC's second oil embargo in 1979, prospects looked bright at that moment for nuclear power. Then, on March 28, 1979, the Three Mile Island Unit 2 nuclear reactor near Harrisburg, Pennsylvania, experienced the worst civilian nuclear accident in U.S. history. A series of staff mistakes following a stuck valve incident resulted in escaping radiation, a relatively small hydrogen explosion and radioactive contamination of a nearby river. But it was still a fairly minor accident compared to the potential of full-scale nuclear plant disaster (the 1986 catastrophe at Chernobyl, Russia, would come a lot closer to a worst-case scenario). Then, two months later a federal district court in Oklahoma found the Kerr-McGee Corporation liable under the Price-Anderson Act to the estate of union activist Karen Silkwood, who had been contaminated by plutonium while working in the company's plant in Crescent, Oklahoma, and subsequently died in a suspicious car crash while driving to deliver documents to a *New York Times* reporter. Silkwood's estate was awarded punitive damages of $10.5 million, an award that was upheld in 1984 by the Supreme Court. Next, the movie *The China Syndrome*, depicting the terror of a nuclear meltdown, played to packed audiences around the country. The rosy future of nuclear power was clouding up fast. Indeed, from the Three Mile Island accident forward, no new nuclear plant projects have been started in the United States, and many that were then under construction were abandoned.

The Three Mile Island accident took nearly twelve years and cost approximately $973 million to clean up, making Schultz's estimated costs of tens of billions for a major disaster seem quite realistic. In fact, shortly after Three Mile Island, the NRC and much of the scientific community repudiated the Rasmussen report, which had pegged the probability of a major nuclear accident occurring at an American reactor at less than one in a billion. The Supreme Court had relied upon the report repeatedly in its *Duke Power* decision. "If the Supreme Court case had come just a year later, after Three Mile Island," Schultz wonders, "would the decision have been different?" Did the fear of American reliance on foreign oil, and its potential impact on American independence, motivate the decision? Was this a court making a constitutional ruling for national security and economic policy reasons? There is no way to know for certain, but it is surely a reasonable speculation. And, though the brakes were put on nuclear power plant construction by other events, had the Litigation Group prevailed in *Duke Power*, the number of operating nuclear plants might have decreased more rapidly. Instead, the safety problems of these remaining plants and the NRC's continued reluctance to exercise its regulatory power would remain a major focus of the Litigation Group and of Public Citizen's Critical Mass Energy Project for decades to come. By 2004, there were still 103 nuclear plants operating in the United States.

* * * * *

Soon after Schultz argued the Price-Anderson case before the district court, a case landed on his desk that resulted in another lengthy, technologically complex and challenging trial. The litigation would stretch on for six years and fill a tall cabinet with depositions, scientific and legal research, and court papers. *Mink v. University of Chicago* began in 1976 when U.S. Representative Patsy Mink (D-Hawaii) received a troubling letter from Dr. Marluce Bibbo. "During the years 1951 and 1952 when you were an obstetrical patient at the Chicago Lying-In Hospital," the letter began, "some obstetrical patients received an estrogenic hormone known as Diethylstilbestrol, during pregnancy." Mink was one of the patients who had been given this drug, known as DES, and recent studies suggested that women taking the drug during pregnancy might give birth to children with abnormalities of the reproductive organs. The letter asked Mink to have her daughter contact the hospital as soon as possible so she could be included in a federal study to determine whether abnormalities occur and at what rate in children of women who took the drug. The tests would be free and the results would be shared with the child's physician upon request. The letter included this unsettling statement: "while recent reports ... have shown that the abnormal conditions, when found, were generally benign, in a few cases there was a finding of malignancy." Mink's only child, Gwendolyn, was turning twenty-four the next day. It was not much of a birthday present.

While studying law at the University of Chicago, Mink had become pregnant and, as a student with limited funds, she chose to seek medical care for her pregnancy at the university's clinic. Unbeknownst to her and more than two thousand other pregnant women receiving medical care there in 1951 and 1952, she was part of a double-blind medical study. Under the direction of a Dr. William Dieckmann, who had died by the time Mink received the letter, the women were divided into two groups. One group was given a daily dosage of DES, a synthetic estrogen then believed to be useful in preventing spontaneous abortions in at-risk pregnancies. The other group was given a placebo. None of the participants was informed that they were part of a medical experiment; indeed, most were told that they were being given vitamin pills, while a few were told that the pills could help prevent complications late in pregnancy. All of the women were used as human guinea pigs without their knowledge. Mink was furious. Even more infuriating was the fact that the university had taken years after discovering the dangers of DES to inform her that she had been given the drug. "If the hazard were to me," says Mink, "I could deal with it. I could develop my own defenses. But the hazard is to my child."

Concern about DES began surfacing in the late 1960s. Then in 1971, three doctors at Massachusetts General Hospital found seven cases of clear cell adenocarcinoma of the vagina in young girls aged fifteen to twenty-two. This was a life-threatening cancer normally found only in much older women. Indeed, seven cases were more than had been reported previously in such young women in all the world's medical literature. Soon after the doctors reported their findings in the *New England Journal of Medicine* (April 22, 1971), the FDA issued a warning about using the drug during pregnancy. Yet it had taken from 1971 until 1976 for the University of Chicago to contact Mink. "Morally, there is no excuse for their failure to do everything humanly possible to reach the mothers who were victimized this way," she noted at the time. "Their failure to do so is utterly unbelievable." When they did contact her, it was not out of concern for her daughter, but to get her to be part of another experiment

After seeing that her daughter had a thorough medical checkup, Mink sought legal advice. Though she talked to several different attorneys about suing the university clinic, none was interested in the case. She called Sidney Wolfe, head of Public Citizen's Health Research Group, who was fast gaining a national reputation as a health crusader. Mink's story was not the first Wolfe had heard about the University of Chicago program. In January that year, while giving a lecture, he had met Gladys Lang, a professor of sociology at the State

University of New York at Stony Brook, who had received a letter similar to Mink's in August 1975. She was as furious as Mink about the experiment and the delay. "I was at one of the best medical hospitals in the country," Lang notes. "Who would have ever thought that they would administer a harmful drug to us under the pretense that it was something good." And, like Mink, she wanted to do something about it. Mostly, they wanted the university to accept responsibility. Wolfe suggested that they consider a lawsuit. Morrison put Schultz to work investigating how this could be done. Mink and Lang agreed to be plaintiffs. A third DES subject, Phyllis S. Wetherill, who ran a family counseling clinic in Washington D.C., soon joined the suit. "One of the greatest things about the Litigation Group is time," Schultz says. "I could go spend two weeks in the library researching without worrying about a client's bill. We could be careful to research every issue, every theory, all the legal requirements before we jumped in, which meant that, when we jumped in, our case would be well developed and catch the other side off guard." Schultz first considered a malpractice case, but Illinois law required he show physical injury. None of the clients had an injury, and none of their daughters had yet developed cancer. They had, however, developed cervical adenosis, an abnormal but benign tissue change in the vagina or cervix that some doctors considered a possible precursor to cancer. "So we researched further and came up with the idea of using the theory of battery, which had the beauty of not needing a physical injury. When the doctor gave the women the pills, we reasoned that it constituted a 'touching' without permission. So we developed our challenge as a battery action. We also tried to design the case as a class action with our three clients representing the more than one thousand women who had unwittingly been part of the study and given DES."

On April 25, 1977 (just ten days after the district court had given him his home run in *Duke Power*), Schultz filed his case in U.S. district court in Chicago, naming as defendants both the University of Chicago and Eli Lilly, the drug company that had provided the DES for Dr. Dieckmann's study. The next day, *The Washington Post* carried a front page article about the case. The fact that the lead plaintiff, Mink, was at that point assistant secretary of state (having lost her 1976 senatorial race) made the case even more newsworthy. Later that year, the famous *Washington Post* editorial cartoonist Herb Block drew a cartoon of two witches—one labeled "Multibuck Drug Co.," the other "University Hospital Research"—stirring an evil-looking stew pot of "DES Cancer-Causing Drug For Warding Off Evil Spirits from Pregnant Women," around which were strewn skulls, fish bones and a dead cat.

With the government's appeal in *Duke Power* now back on Schultz's desk, John Sims volunteered to share responsibility for the DES case. They would work together on it for the next five years. Sims had come to the Litigation Group just four months before Schultz. "My mother graduated from Fordham law school in the early 1940s and worked as an enforcement attorney at the Office of Price Administration during the war—a time when women attorneys were unheard of," says Sims. Though she stopped practicing when she married and moved to Cleveland to raise five kids, she taught him "at an early age to view the law as an important way to serve and accomplish good things for people. I always knew that I wanted to be a lawyer." When Sims arrived at Georgetown University in 1967 to begin his undergraduate education, he soon began volunteering for Nader. He worked with Reuben Robertson some and helped with the Raiders' study of the Food and Drug Administration at the Center for Study of Responsive Law. After getting his bachelor's degree in 1971, Sims attended Harvard and graduated with a law degree in 1974. He spent a year clerking for a judge on the U.S. Appeals Court for the First Circuit in Portland, Maine. But from the start, Sims wanted a job at the Litigation Group. So he called Morrison soon after his clerkship began and traveled to Washington that December to be interviewed. "From the start I was impressed by John," Morrison says. "He had this special off-beat way of looking at a problem." He was among the more laid back characters in the Litigation Group, Morrison also notes.

The next stage in the Mink case involved filing motions for discovery and responding to the various delaying motions filed by the other side. "We were suing one of the major institutions in Chicago," Schultz notes, "and the judge clearly was not very receptive to us or our case." On March 17, 1978, the judge upheld their battery cause of action against the university clinic and allowed them to proceed with discovery and depositions, but it took until June 1979 for him to deny certification of the class and until January 1980 for him to dismiss the case against Eli Lilly. While the judge procrastinated, Sims and Schultz traveled all over the country deposing witnesses—women who had been given DES in the study, doctors and nurses who had worked at the clinic during the study, current and former employees of the university and Eli Lilly, and scientific experts on DES. As usual, they traveled cheaply, so each typically went alone. "I really feel I learned how to do a deposition well in this case, and another thing I soon learned is that the styles of attorneys varies enormously around the country and the differences come out most starkly in depositions," Schultz says. "In some parts of the country lawyers behave themselves; in other areas they can be obnoxious, aggressive, and downright rude." And in his experience, "Chicago attorneys are at the extreme end of the aggressive scale." Whenever Schultz or Sims deposed a witness, the Chicago lawyers would be there. "They seemed not to have prepared their witnesses adequately or be prepared to question ours, so their method was to obstruct the process, making every deposition a long, drawn-out ordeal." They also did not follow the rules of discovery, holding back information and failing to tell the Litigation Group attorneys of some of the witnesses they intended to use at trial.

The jury trial, with Judge John F. Grady presiding, finally took place in February 1982. Though the case was ultimately settled before the trial was completed, Sims and Schultz spent nearly three weeks presenting their side and sat through the beginning of the defendant's case. For the duration of the trial, they stayed (along with their clients and Nan Simpson, a Litigation Group secretary who came along to help organize the mounds of material in the case) at the Union League Club, a men's club right across the street from the courthouse. "We were going to bed at 2 a.m. and getting up at 6 a.m. for three weeks," Schultz recalls. "It was exhausting but at the same time exhilarating. Opposing counsel kept adding witnesses to their list that we had not been told about and introducing documents that they had denied to us existed during discovery." When this happened, the judge let Schultz and Sims depose the surprise witnesses during the trial. It made it fairer but surely not easier. After a day in court, they not only had to prepare their questions for the next day and prepare their witnesses and spend time with their clients making decisions, they also had to depose the opposition's surprise witnesses. They also had to participate in settlement negotiations with the opposing attorneys. (The opposition wanted to delay the trial and concentrate on settlement negotiations, but the judge, perhaps hoping that the trial's progress would encourage more serious negotiations, insisted that the trial proceed at the same time.)

Two women who had been in the DES study were witnesses for the university and were prepared to say that a doctor had told them about the drug and the experiment. "So we had to show that this was an exception, not what most had been told," Schultz says. Their strategy was played out on what they jokingly referred to as "Mother's Day." They put mother after mother (twenty in a single day) from the DES study on the stand. Each of them swore that she had not been told. "It was pretty powerful," says Schultz. After all, the jury would have to believe that all twenty were liars to believe that informed consent had been obtained, and that was hard to accept about this parade of highly educated women.

On February 26, 1982, a highly satisfying settlement was reached. It was only a couple of days into the presentation of the university's side of the case. Mink, Lang and Wetherill would each receive about $50,000, and all of the Litigation Group's expenses would be paid as well. Far more significant, though, was that the university agreed to continue free clinical exams for all adult children of the mothers who were part of the DES study and to provide free medical treatment to any daughter who was exposed to DES during the experiment and who developed clear cell adenocarcinoma prior to age seventy. These last two provisions, providing at least some relief for others who had been unwilling subjects of the study, could not have come out of a jury verdict, as the judge had not certified the case to be a class action. Most of all, as Schultz would note in letters to his clients and witnesses, "It is our hope that the case will have an effect on university research in general since it established that universities can be held liable for the injuries caused by their research." The practice of using unsuspecting patients as guinea pigs in medical experiments would ultimately be shown to be far more pervasive than most could imagine and in some cases involved the federal government.

Courting Change

* * * * *

For reasons that seem almost incomprehensible from the vantage point of the twenty-first century, no car safety development was fought by the automobile industry more vehemently, or for so long, as air bags.

Though seat belts had been mandated for all passenger cars in 1967 as one of NHTSA's first regulatory actions, and though they were proving to be enormously successful in reducing death and the severity of injuries, the level of usage (estimated in 1977 to be only 20 percent) remained far too low. In early 1952, a U.S. patent was granted for a safety cushion that would automatically inflate on impact. The device would not require any action by driver or passenger, even so minimal as "buckling up," to effectuate its protective potential—hence its handle as a "passive restraint" mechanism. As the discouraging statistics about seat belt usage became evident, the question of whether cars should be required to have passive restraints was added to NHTSA's agenda. In 1969, NHTSA announced a proposed rule that would require front-seat air bags that would deploy automatically during crashes to be installed in all automobiles beginning with the 1972 model year. Soon thereafter, the effective date was postponed until 1973. Not satisfied with the postponement, the automobile companies in 1971 sued the agency, challenging the requirement as beyond its power. While the court challenge was under way, the auto industry brought its case to the White House during the re-election campaign of President Nixon, who was receptive to corporate complaints. To no surprise, the powerful automotive industry was successful in this strategy, and the Department of Transportation (DOT) postponed the required date for air bags again, to the 1975 model year. Though the air bag rule was eventually upheld as within the power of the agency, the court found other problems (lack of objectivity in the provision for testing the air bags by a crash with a dummy) and remanded the standard to the agency to address this problem. This action effectively suspended the 1975 start date, as no standard could be mandated until the dummy problem was addressed. Despite the Department of Transportation's own figures estimating that air bags could save between eight and nine thousand lives per year and prevent more than five hundred thousand serious injuries, no action to fix the dummy problem was taken. Instead, in December 1976 (after President Ford's defeat to Carter) lame-duck DOT Secretary William Coleman announced that he would not require air bags. Instead, he requested that at least two automobile manufacturers enter into a voluntary agreement with the DOT to equip about two hundred and fifty thousand cars with passive restraints in each of the model years 1980 and 1981.

The delay and then the withdrawal of a federal standard mandating air bags was almost incomprehensible to Nader and Clarence Ditlow. Without a mandate, the number of cars with air bags would likely remain low and thus not be sufficient to allow for the economies of scale that would bring the unit price down. If the cost remained high, fewer consumers would buy them. Secretary

Coleman admitted that air bags could save thousands of lives and prevent hundreds of thousands of serious injuries. If ever there were a situation in which the power of government should be used, this seemed it.

With just a month left before Ford and his administration would turn the reins of power over to Carter, Coleman tried to solidify the voluntary agreements. Ditlow tried to persuade Coleman to include a public representative in the negotiations between the DOT and any automobile manufacturing companies that volunteered. Nader filed an objection to Coleman's program with the Department of Justice, suggesting that such agreements might violate antitrust laws. On the last day of the Ford administration, Justice ruled that the voluntary agreements would not run afoul of antitrust laws. Before the administration left office, it was announced that General Motors, Ford and Daimler-Benz had agreed to offer some optional air bags in their 1980 and 1981 models, though the total number was down to just sixty thousand.

Soon after the Carter administration took over, new Transportation Secretary Brock Adams announced that he intended to re-examine the air bag issue. A week later, on February 15, 1977, Joan Claybrook, director of Public Citizen's Congress Watch division, was appointed to head NHTSA (the agency within the DOT with prime responsibility for auto safety issues). Nader and Ditlow had every reason to believe that the air bag rule would soon be restored. Then in June, Secretary Adams announced his decision. This new regulation required automakers to equip all cars with air bags or passive seat belts by 1984. They would be phased in over a three-year period, beginning in 1982. Nader viewed this timetable as unconscionable and nothing less than a capitulation to the automobile companies' claims that they needed so much time to comply. Thousands would needlessly die in the meantime. The proposed date would also mean that no air bags would be mandated during Carter's first term in office. It was not prescience that motivated their concern; the Nader folks simply realized that another administration could change the rule yet again, which happened when President Ronald Reagan took over in 1981.

In response to the DOT's revised standard, in 1977 Nader wrote a scathing letter to his friend Joan Claybrook. He accused her of failing in her duty to the consumer and going back on her promise in accepting the position at NHTSA "to fulfill the neglected potential of the 1966 auto safety law and reduce the human casualties that comprise the nations' daily highway epidemic." Having one of his own on the inside was not playing as well as hoped, and Nader was no less hesitant to attack her, both privately and publicly, than any other administrator he saw as not doing her job.

But the greater problem came from another direction entirely. On September 1, 1977, the Pacific Legal Foundation (PLF), a conservative public interest litigation firm that had been formed by a number of then-Gov. Reagan's supporters, filed suit in the U.S. appeals court in Washington, D.C., challenging Adams' air bag rule as an invasion of individual privacy rights—the right to choose the safety device the individual deems best in his or her own judgment. The claim was similar to those who oppose mandatory helmet laws for motorcyclists: the government cannot force citizens to protect their own lives. The lawsuit also raised a number of other claims, including that air bags were not effective and that they would cause more harm than good.

Nader and the Litigation Group wanted the court to consider their position. Though Nader clearly supported air bags, he believed: (1) that the agency had acted arbitrarily and capriciously in delaying the air bag requirements by failing to follow its own technological evidence and the vast majority of evidence submitted during the rulemaking process; (2) that since the standard allowed the auto companies a choice between air bags and automatic seat belts (belts that would automatically buckle when an occupant closed the car door) there were virtually no defensible reasons for the long lead time permitted; and (3) that because of the provision allowing the choice between air bags and automatic seat belts, there was no need to submit the standard to Congress for review and possible veto, as a 1974 law required for air bags. This last point was of considerable importance since Nader says he heard Claybrook say at a press briefing on November 30, 1977, that the rule was close to the mark in terms of political acceptance and that Adams' handling of the issue was important because of the congressional veto factor. Claybrook denies that the threat of a congressional veto guided the substantive decision. But Nader told Morrison (who was at the same time challenging the constitutionality of the congressional veto in another case) that the rule was not based on evidence and facts but rather was fashioned in response to political pressure and fear of a congressional veto. Moreover, since Standard 208 did not mandate air bags, but rather allowed auto companies to choose between automatic seat belts or air bags, there was no need (at least under Morrison's reading of the law) for the DOT to send the rule to Congress for potential veto, and thus no reason for it to fashion a politically safe rule. Thus, the rationales advanced by the DOT "for refusing to promptly implement Revised Standard 208 cannot be sustained," Morrison argued in his brief filed in the spring of 1978.

Under the Constitution, all legislative power belongs to Congress, thus only Congress can make laws. But since Congress does not possess sufficient expertise on the vast variety of issues upon which it must legislate, it must rely on others. The Supreme Court weighs whether a delegation of power to the executive branch to flesh out congressional law is permissible under its "non-delegation doctrine." Though the court has always allowed significant delegation of power to the executive branch, the requirement that administrative rulemaking be based on a rational reliance on a soundly developed public record remains. Thus, it is the expectation that if a decision involves politics, the legislative branch should make it; but, if a decision requires expertise, then it is acceptable for the executive branch to exercise the power, with the caveat that any rule or regulation it issues must be reasonably related to the evidence the agency is relying upon. Claybrook's comments gave credence to precisely what Nader and Morrison suspected—that the department had succumbed to political pressure on the air bag issue.

To understand the importance the DOT placed on the congressional veto here, it is necessary to look at something else that happened a few years before concerning passive restraints. In the early 1970s, Ford Motor Company had developed a system whereby if seat belts were not fastened, a buzzer stayed on until they were. Ford promoted its so-called seat belt interlock system to DOT as a better alternative to the proposed air bag standard. Responding to this pressure, the Republican administration at DOT issued a rule requiring the interlock system, beginning with all 1974 models. Public reaction was swift, negative and intense. Congress was deluged with complaints blaming the scheme on excessive bureaucratic zeal. Lawmakers reacted by passing a law that overturned the interlock standard and subjected any future passive restraint law that subjected air bags or anything other than a passive belt system to review by Congress before it could become final. The review process required the department to send any rule on air bags to Congress for a sixty-day period, during which both houses of Congress could vote to overturn it. This is called a two-house veto and, before it was declared unconstitutional in 1983, did not allow for a presidential signature or veto. If sixty days passed without an overturn or vote, the rule could go into effect.

Morrison knew they needed proof in a form acceptable to a court that the DOT had altered the timetable for the new air bag standard in response to political considerations and fear of a congressional veto. Courts do not just accept hunches, inferences, or guesses about such matters. Unfortunately, there was no public transcript of the press conference at which Nader claimed to have heard Claybrook's statement. Morrison was certain that, if he could depose Claybrook and Adams under oath, he would get the proof he needed. Case precedent indicated that the court was not likely to accept such depositions. Court challenges to agency regulations are handled by U.S. courts of appeals, where there is no further fact-finding. Indeed, absent a strong preliminary showing of bad faith or misconduct, or formal findings upon which the agency decision was based, the courts do not allow oral testimony to be taken from agency decisionmakers. Morrison did not have much support in the case law for either of these requirements, but there was one precedent that offered some hope. So he petitioned the judges: "The depositions sought are for extremely limited purposes, and this Court plainly has the power to permit them," Morrison wrote. "Petitioners recognize that this power is rarely exercised, but believe that this is an appropriate case for the Court to permit these depositions." Justice Department attorneys opposed the motion, and the court quickly denied it. Morrison then tried another tack. He had Nader execute a sworn statement describing the press conference he had attended, during which Claybrook had mentioned the "congressional veto factor" and a number of other conversations he had with DOT personnel that showed fear of a congressional veto played a role in the decision. Morrison attempted to file this with the court along with his brief on March 6, 1978. Justice Department attorneys objected, and the court denied permission to file the affidavit. So Morrison's argument that the final standard was based on political considerations outside the responsibility and power of the DOT to consider went forward with little to back it up. This would prove to be a fatal flaw in this part of the case. "Petitioner's assertion [that the legislative veto distorted the Secretary's decision on the implementation schedule] is supported only by an arguable inference from one event in the record," wrote Judge J. Skelly Wright in his February 1, 1979, decision. "In the absence of concrete evidence we must accept the substantial reasons offered by the Secretary for his decision."

"Like Scylla and Charybdis, the petitioners in these two cases challenge from opposite sides," Judge Wright notes in his decision upholding the DOT standard against the challenges from both right and left. Then the Pacific Legal Foundation's petition for Supreme Court review was denied. Perhaps Nader's presence as the Scylla countering the PLF's Charybdis created a situation that enabled at least some rule to remain in place. Still, the long lead time the new rule allowed permitted thousands of needless deaths in crashes.

* * * * *

Ditlow and his Center for Auto Safety (CAS) have called on the Litigation Group to represent them on many occasions, but perhaps on none so bizarre as the Firestone 500 tire fiasco. John Sims calls what happened in this situation "about as disturbing as anything I encountered in my years at Public Citizen. It represented such a gross abuse of power by a corporation." Toward the end of the 1970s, a NHTSA survey suggested that Firestone 500 tires were unsafe. Fearing publication of the survey, Firestone "ran into its 'hometown' court filing for a temporary restraining order (TRO) to prevent NHTSA from releasing the findings, claiming they were not accurate and that the documents NHTSA had secured from the company in its investigation were protected as 'trade secrets,'" Sims notes. The hometown U.S. district court granted the TRO. Meanwhile, Ditlow had filed a FOIA request with NHTSA for everything relating to the Firestone tire issue. In response, NHTSA sent over a large file of documents. Ditlow came across four pages or so of the results of the survey—the very information the company had sought to keep from being released. Though he had no idea how the pages got into the released documents, Ditlow knew just what to do when they arrived. He called a press conference. The next day, Firestone 500 problems were front page news. Needless to say, Firestone was not happy; nor was the district judge who had issued the TRO. "But," Sims points out, "Clarence was not a party to the lawsuit, nor was he subject to the court order. So the only possible impropriety was if someone who was subject to it [meaning some policy level official at NHTSA] had cooperated with him by sending the information." Of course, the obvious subject in the minds of the folks at Firestone was Joan Claybrook, head of NHTSA, and former Naderite. "That just goes to show," Sims says, "how little they understood Joan. There is no doubt that she is completely in support of auto safety and I'm sure wanted to release the Firestone 500 facts straightforwardly, but she is scrupulous about complying with her responsibilities and also she knew she would be the obvious suspect. It is absolutely inconceivable that she would have had anything to do with the release of this material." Sims might have been positive about Claybrook, but Firestone and its attorneys were equally positive that their suspicions were correct, so they proceeded to subpoena documents and force depositions of people at the DOT and the CAS in an attempt to track down the source of the leak. Sims was called to represent the CAS during those depositions.

"One day during the depositions, I had this huge stack of documents in response to their subpoenas," Sims said. "As I was walking out of my apartment, I accidentally dropped them down the stairs." He was running a bit late so he "scooped them up trying to get them into some kind of neat pile" and dashed to the meeting. Handing them over to Firestone attorney John Strauch, Sims with some glee anticipated the meaning that would be put to these oddly mis-ordered documents. "With anyone else in the world, I would have been helpful, but having sat through days of his endless, repetitive, harassing questions I had no such inclination here." He was "the least civil attorney" Sims had ever dealt with, and as the days continued, the attack mode became increasingly irritating. "We had absolutely nothing to hide," Sims says, "and cooperated fully, providing them with every conceivable document." The depositions went on for weeks, with Firestone seemingly willing to spend endless amounts of money on this "pointless witch hunt." There was no way Firestone could erase the public's awareness of the problems with its steel-belted tires and no way it could refute the evidence. "It was pure vindictiveness on their part," Sims says. "It's like what we have seen with the cigarette companies going after anyone who crosses them. There is so much money at stake that no cost is too excessive in their effort to grind down anyone who stands in their way and thereby hope to scare anyone else from crossing them in the future."

Sims was up against a horde of high-priced lawyers, some days as many as eight, but he did have some help on his side: one young attorney, Kathy Meyer, who was then serving on the CAS' staff and who would soon be hired at the Litigation Group. Kathy Meyer has passionate beliefs, enormous energy and a vibrant sense of humor. As a college student she had gone to hear Nader speak and was inspired by his call to public service. "I knew right then that I wanted to be a public interest lawyer and work for him," Meyer explains. After college she attended law school at Catholic University in Washington, D.C., spending a good deal of her years there working for the Legal Services Program and volunteering for Nader. After graduating in 1976, she tried to get a job at the Litigation Group. When this did not work, she signed up to work with Ditlow at CAS. But all along she wanted to get on Morrison's team. "It was very frustrating at CAS because every time we'd get an interesting case that needed litigating it would get shipped over to the Litigation Group," Meyer says. "I finally persuaded Clarence to insist that I be allowed to help with the next shipped-out case." That case turned out to be the Firestone 500 litigation. Meyer joined Sims, assisting with the depositions.

Once, Sims had an important deposition in another case scheduled for three in the afternoon. A deposition with the Firestone crew that should have taken about an hour was taking all day, so Sims had to leave Meyer alone. "I never mentioned that I had never done a deposition on my own before," Meyer admits. "I was between terrified and delighted to have the chance." Soon after Sims left, the CAS engineer who was being deposed by Firestone's attorneys was asked which reporters he had talked to. "He asked to confer with me in private [a deponent is allowed to talk in private with his attorney for advice] and he then said to me that he did not want to answer that question." It was late and she was tired, but in typical Meyer fashion she pulled an answer out of thin air. Turning to Firestone's team of attorneys she said, "My client will not answer that under the public interest privilege." She had no idea if such a thing existed, but it sounded like something that ought to fit under the First Amendment. Perhaps because they were equally tired, the opposition did not challenge this, and soon the session was adjourned for the day. "When I told Alan about this the next day," Meyer says, "he said, 'What? What?' in an incredulous tone." But it had worked, and though, as Sims says, "she definitely described it in a way that it had not previously been described, at base her point was valid." It was just such creative brain power that Morrison was after, and soon after the depositions, Meyer got a job interview.

"Why should I hire you?" Morrison asked Meyer. "Because it would be a real boon to my public interest career," she playfully responded. Then Morrison asked her: "What's pissed you off lately?" Three hours later, as Meyer tells it, she was still talking and Morrison had found his next Litigation Group attorney and a question to ask many of his subsequent job candidates.

The Firestone depositions ended with no evidence emerging that Ditlow or the CAS or anyone at NHTSA had done anything wrong. NHTSA continued to investigate, and then sued Firestone. The lawsuit produced damning internal documents and eventually forced Firestone to recall twenty million tires—but not all that Claybrook wanted. Soon thereafter a number of top executives at Firestone were fired and the new head honcho came to meet with Nader and Ditlow. "He told us they were going to recall the rest of the 500s just as we and NHTSA wanted them to do," Ditlow says. It was a very satisfying, if hard won, result.

* * * * *

In 1973, Reuben Robertson had been treated to the big district court win in *Nader v. Allegheny Airlines*. Following a trip to the court of appeals and the Supreme Court, the case was remanded to the district court with the charge that the judge would need to find evidence of "fraudulent misrepresentation" in order to award damages. After some additional discovery and exhibits were added to the record, Judge Richey reviewed the entire record, and on January 10,1978, once again found for Nader, awarding him $10 in compensatory damages and $15,000 in punitive damages (significantly less than the original award of $50,000, but still a win). Allegheny once again appealed, and once again it won.

On September 8, 1980, John Sims, who had taken over the case after Robertson left to join the Carter administration, wrote to Nader:

> I am afraid the sad day is upon us when we must turn our attention to *Nader v. Allegheny Airlines*. If we want to file a petition for *certiorari*, it's due on September 16. ... The *Allegheny* case was decided against us on May 16, with all three judges joining in the opinion. As you remember, the panel consisted of Judges MacKinnon, Robb, and Wilkey, who are about as hostile to consumer causes as any panel which could be formed in this Circuit. We asked for rehearing and rehearing *en banc*, and these were denied on June 18, 1980. None of the judges on the Court requested that the *en banc* petition be put to a vote.

Sims described the grounds on which the appeals court had overturned Judge Richey's second decision: (1) since Nader must have known about the overbooking practice, he could not rely on being deceived; (2) the agency had approved the practice of overbooking; and (3) overbooking was an open practice. "It is plain to me," Sims wrote, "that the Court's decision is wrong." But he then pointed out that to win they would have to win on all three issues. Though he believed the Supreme Court might have had some interest in reviewing the notion that the agency had approved the overbooking practice, as that seemed to go against the high court's own 1976 ruling in the case, the other issues "are tort law questions of such narrow scope that the Supreme Court ordinarily wouldn't touch them." Since the Supreme Court pays almost no attention to whether a lower court has merely decided a case wrongly—as opposed to deciding an issue which is potentially one of general application, it is extremely unlikely that the Supreme Court will wish to consider these issues."

Sims recommended against filing a petition. He had one more point to make. The case "has pretty much dropped from sight ... [and] as far as 99.9% of the public is concerned, you won ... I think we should try to keep things that way." A handwritten note from Morrison is appended to the top of the Sims' memo: "I concur regrettably, but fully. Alan." It was an unsatisfactory end to the case, but not to the practice of overbooking.

In May 1981, *The Washington Post* ran an article describing a case that had just been filed by a group of twenty Texas state judges who were bumped from a Houston-bound plane when returning from a judicial conference in Amarillo. The judges claimed they wanted "to show that passengers are not cattle" and to counter the airline industry's "deity complex." "Consumer activist Ralph Nader was the first person to successfully argue the point after being bumped from an Allegheny Airlines Washington-to-Connecticut flight in 1972," the *Post* article states. Then it goes on to note that "Nader won $25,000 for himself and an equal amount for the group that sponsored his visit; it remains the largest award granted by a court in a bumping case." No mention was made in the article of the 1980 appeals court decision overturning the award, nor of the reduction of the award to $15,000 by Judge Richey in his second hearing after the Supreme Court remand. Sims was correct in his estimation of public perception about the case, and perhaps that is all the win they needed.

12

Union Democracy —
Protecting the Rank and File

Ralph Nader's concerns about defects in automobiles landed him in the national limelight and sparked the political movement that led to creation of a new federal agency to regulate automobile safety. But cars were only part of the problem on the highways. Big trucks were the other. Though an existing federal agency, the Interstate Commerce Commission, was responsible for enforcing truck safety, Nader questioned whether it was adequately doing its job. In 1970 he assigned Robert Fellmeth, one of his young Raider volunteers, to investigate the ICC. *The Interstate Commerce Omission*, published as a result of Fellmeth's investigation, exposed a near total lack of regulatory enforcement. Highways were clogged with unsafe trucks, or "accidents waiting to happen," the report found.

As part of his study, Fellmeth bought ad space in an industry magazine called *Overdrive* to distribute a questionnaire to truck drivers. As the questionnaires poured in to Nader's headquarters at the Public Interest Research Group (PIRG), the full extent of the problem was driven home. Truckers were being forced to drive for long hours without rest, and many used amphetamines to stay awake. Trucks were being put on the road with faulty brakes, worn tires and engine problems. Truck drivers feared for their lives, as well as the lives of others on the highways. And the drivers' own protector—the Teamsters Union—seemed to be doing nothing at all about safety. Nader decided that something had to be done. He convened a conference in Washington, D.C., for truck drivers to discuss safety problems with the hope that the publicity surrounding the event would motivate Congress to act or force the union bosses to press for action. Joan Claybrook was tapped as organizer and promoter. Surprisingly, more than three hundred truckers, most of them middle-aged family men, paid their own way to the capital to vent their complaints. Media coverage led to congressional hearings but not much else. Nader decided the truckers needed something more than talk—an organization that would be a safety watchdog. He set out to find himself a pit bull to turn his vision into reality. He found Arthur Fox.

Like Morrison, Fox had grown up in a prosperous suburb of New York City—Rumson, New Jersey. The son of one of the original Bell Telephone laboratory physicists, his was a life of comfort quite removed from the blue-collar world of the truckers. His parents were liberal Democrats in a town dominated by Republicans, who, Fox says, helped him "to learn at an early age to stand up for what I believed." After completing his undergraduate education at the University of Virginia in 1965, he continued there to law school. "I just couldn't get interested in contracts and torts and all that," Fox says. "What I most wanted was to do something to make the world a better place, and somehow this Madison Avenue practice approach just did not cut it." For his first two years he spent more time hunting and oil painting than studying. But in his final year he took a class with a visiting professor, Bernie Dunau, a labor attorney who was "a live wire" and who "inspired me ... most of all by persuading me that labor law was exciting—exciting because it was still being shaped and was one that focused on the needs of people." Fox was hooked, and though he was barely in the middle of his class, based on his first two years of non-engagement, Dunau spotted his talent and dedication and opened a door for him at the National Labor Relations Board (NLRB), the federal agency responsible for enforcing federal labor law.

"The NLRB was a great place to work at first," Fox recalls. "We did all our own cases all the way to the Supreme Court, unlike most other agencies that had to turn the best cases over to the Justice Department just as the litigation was getting interesting." He traveled around the country, appearing in appeals courts in enforcement actions, making companies reinstate people they had illegally fired for union activities, forcing payment of back pay, ensuring that companies followed the rules. By 1972, though, Nixon had appointed new leaders who were no longer interested in vigorous enforcement of the laws to protect union activity and union workers. "I was not so happy anymore," Fox said. A wife of one of his colleagues who was working with Nader at the Pension Rights Center told him about Nader's interest in the truckers' problems. Fox called Nader. "I remember most of all Nader talking about speeding buses that day," says Fox. "He had this bug biting him about those Greyhound monsters speeding on the Baltimore-Washington Parkway and wanted me to do something." The something Nader had in mind was for Fox to clock the buses and get the results into *The Washington Post*. Nader's endless stream of ideas ranged from the brilliant to the nutty, and Fox thought this one was definitely at the nutty end of the spectrum and could be safely ignored (though he would soon find that Nader would not so easily forget it).

In September 1972, Fox joined the Nader forces. At his own insistence, he took on two positions. The first, which was Nader's priority, was to become director of a new organization to be called the Professional Drivers Council for Safety and Health, or PROD. The second position was to be a lawyer working with the Litigation Group. "I wanted to be certain that I would be able to continue litigating, not just be a money-raiser and organizer," says Fox. "But I was also convinced that PROD would be a temporary necessity, which would not be needed once we got the safety issues the visibility and attention they needed. Little did I realize just how hard and long the job would be."

When Fox arrived for his first day, PROD was little more than an idea on paper. Most of his time over the next few years was devoted to designing the organization, articulating its goals, planning how to accomplish them and building a dues-paying membership (at $20 a year per member) to finance the effort. Kenneth C. Crowe, author of *Collision: How the Rank and File Took Back the Teamsters*, describes Fox as a young man with "an appreciation of opera and a knowledge of gourmet cooking and eating. Yet he had this remarkable ability to look tattooed truckers in the eye and win their trust." For quite some time, Fox was a one-man show traveling around the country to recruit members, talking at spaghetti dinners in church basements, speaking at truck stop rallies and meeting people in truckers' homes. In between his recruiting trips, he wrote articles about truck safety and did all of the things necessary to establish an organization. He designed a logo with a steering wheel and scales of justice, and printed bumper stickers. He found a volunteer graduate student at George Washington University who set up a computer membership-maintenance program. He started a member newsletter. All the while, he researched the issues with an eye toward reform and inserted information about truck hazards into the congressional record. One of his early "action items" resulted from a weeks-long search of the literature on driver fatigue, which lead to his submission of a rulemaking petition to the Department of Transportation (DOT), which by now had assumed jurisdiction over truck safety from the ICC. The petition sought to increase the frequency and timing of driver rest breaks during a twenty-four hour period. He drafted other rulemaking petitions seeking stronger punishments for violations of the agency's rules and more vigorous enforcement. Few of his petitions got beyond the discussion stage, at least not for a long time.

The biggest boon for Fox's recruiting efforts came when he donned his litigation hat. In his travels, he met many drivers who shared their complaints about the grievance process spelled out in the National Master Freight Agreement and state-level supplemental agreements—contracts that are periodically renegotiated and accepted by both management and unions. They establish pay and benefit levels as well as the rules governing the trucking industry's relationship to its employees and the procedural steps to be followed whenever there is a disagreement or challenge to how the rules are being implemented. The grievance resolution process, for the most part, is an effort to force most disagreements to be resolved out of court. This prevents the courts from being swamped by cases, much like the conflict resolution procedures in unemployment and disability compensation law aim to do. The procedure provides for a grievance to be heard by a joint grievance committee made up of equal numbers of representatives from the union leadership and company management. Truck drivers told Fox that they always lost grievances involving claims that an employer refused to follow the safety rules set forth in national and state law and covered by the national and state agreements. Indeed, the very structure of the joint grievance committee practically ensured this result. Unless the union people on the joint committee could persuade one of the management representatives to vote with them on a grievance brought by the union, there was a deadlock, which meant the union lost. If the complaint was brought on behalf of all union members and the union's determination was strong, the threat of some union retaliation offered at least some hope of persuasion. But when the grievance was brought on behalf of a single member (especially a dissident) and the union decided it was not sufficiently important to fight for, a loss was almost a certainty. Fox thought that this deficiency needed to be addressed and soon came across two cases with considerable promise.

* * * * *

Clay Ferguson, a driver for Roadway Express in South Carolina, was fired on March 24, 1972, for refusing to drive a tractor that he believed to be unsafe from Nashville to Columbia, South Carolina. The truck was shimmying in a way that made it difficult to hold the road, as Ferguson described it. He hailed another Roadway driver who happened by and asked him to give the truck a test drive. That driver later stated at trial: "Well, it scared me. I thought maybe it was going to break in two. ... I didn't see how that I could drive the truck because I thought it was unsafe." With his concern confirmed, Ferguson drove slowly to a nearby truck stop and called his company to report the problem. He was told to have the truck stop mechanic look at it. "I told him," the mechanic later stated, "that I wouldn't drive it, and that in my opinion the tractor was not safe to be on the road and [could] get somebody else killed." Again Ferguson called in. He was told to wait there for a company representative. Two arrived and both stated that the truck was safe. Ferguson was not satisfied and requested that a DOT safety inspector be called. Shortly thereafter, the DOT inspector arrived and inspected the truck (but did not road-test it). He would not say whether it was safe, merely that he could not find anything wrong with it. Ferguson had been behind the wheel, and assurance from someone who had not driven the truck was not sufficient in his mind. "Unless someone from Roadway Express signs a statement that they will be responsible for the unit," Ferguson stated, he would not drive it. No one would sign such a statement, so he went home. He was fired when he reported for duty a couple of days later. Two weeks later, the state grievance committee denied his appeal. He tried appealing to the NLRB, claiming that the grievance committee had not applied the national trucking safety law correctly. Again he lost.

The second promising case Fox found involved James Banyard, who had worked for twenty-two years as a truck driver for McLean Trucking Company in Ohio, where he served as the union's shop steward. On October 6, 1969, he was sent to Cleveland, where he discovered that the load would be considerably over the legal weight limit (forty-four thousand pounds, when the limit was thirty-two thousand pounds). He called his company to have the load reduced but was told to bring the whole load anyway. He refused and was discharged the following day. He too filed a grievance with the joint grievance committee and then the NLRB, and he too lost in both places.

National law as well as the National Master Freight Agreement promised truck drivers that they would be protected against having to drive unsafe rigs. But to Ferguson and Banyard and many other drivers, the promise was hollow. If they stood up for their legal rights, they were fired. Most drivers had families to support and bills to pay. The choice was between risking an accident and risking financial ruin. Fox believed that it was time to get the courts to force the reluctant NLRB to do its job. Ferguson and Banyard both agreed to have Fox represent them and appeal their cases. Since the law allows any petition for review to be filed in Washington, D.C., Fox was able to file both the Ohio and the South Carolina cases in the U.S. Court of Appeals for the District of Columbia Circuit.

It seemed to Fox that both cases were perfect for obtaining a favorable appeals court decision. In Banyard's case, the NLRB had upheld a joint grievance committee decision that had allowed a company to blatantly violate state law by putting overloaded trucks on the road—a practice that the transcript before the NLRB showed the company regularly followed. One driver even testified that he was told "to pull an overload and not get caught." The NLRB had brushed aside this problem, claiming that it had to defer to the "expert" decision of the joint grievance committee. But, as the appeals court would later note, this was not deference, it was "abdication." On June 10, 1974, Fox argued the case before Judges J. Skelly Wright, George Edward MacKinnon and Malcolm R. Wilkey. Two months later he was treated to a unanimous decision authored by Judge Wilkey. Both Wilkey and MacKinnon were Nixon appointees and among the more conservative judges on the court at the time, while Wright, a Kennedy appointee, was one of the most liberal. Both cases were remanded to the NLRB with "instructions that deferral not being appropriate, the Board should proceed to consideration of the unfair labor practice issues in a manner not inconsistent with this opinion."

It was a great victory and Fox savored it. When the NLRB ordered reinstatement and back pay for both drivers, Fox flew down to South Carolina to hand-deliver the money to Ferguson, meeting him in a local steak house for the ceremony. A picture of the event appeared on the front page of PROD's next newsletter. Memberships poured in as a result of these two wins. At its height, PROD had more than seven thousand members. "We had won a legal battle for two guys, but there were literally hundreds of others with claims they thought just as valid who too had lost and hoped for help," Fox says. "For years I would get cardboard boxes full of documents and long cassette tape explanations from truckers wanting me to represent them." Expectations had been aroused that simply could not be filled. The Litigation Group was not a legal aid society; it simply did not have the resources to pursue dozens of individual cases. What it looked for in union cases was no different than what it looked for in its other areas of expertise—cases that could influence the development of law and policy in a way that would help many others. *Ferguson* and *Banyard* ended a practice of NLRB deference to state joint grievance committee findings. In future cases the agency would have to thoroughly review these decisions to ensure that they complied with both national and state law and regulations. It became a tricky balancing act to present PROD to its members in a way that would not raise expectations too high but that would hold onto membership—a balancing act that eventually would fail. In 1979, PROD merged with Teamsters for a Democratic Union (TDU). TDU was a grassroots organization agitating for greater representation within the Teamsters union. Fox and the Litigation Group continued to represent this new group, though PROD ceased to be a separate member-based organization.

* * * * *

With the growth in membership dues in the mid-1970s after *Banyard* and *Ferguson*, Fox was able to add staff to PROD. One of his early hires was a young New York University law student named John Sikorski, who initially came as a 1975 summer intern but ended up staying for nearly two years. Sikorski had been a member of a Teamster local while working in two summer jobs in his hometown of Cleveland and had carried his union connection with pride. During his undergraduate years at Harvard, he recalls, he had "worn his Teamster jacket, got the Teamster magazine and hung out with labor economists." He had developed a deep-seated distaste for exploitive union bosses. He was a natural for PROD, and Fox put him to work on a project to investigate potential proposals for the 1976 National Master Freight Agreement, which was up for renewal that year. Sikorski's research produced a report that punctured the myth that the Teamsters were the highest-paid blue-collar workers in the nation. Steelworkers, coal miners and autoworkers not only earned higher wages, but received better fringe benefits. This news was not happily received at Teamster headquarters. The next project Sikorski and Fox undertook, though, landed like a bombshell.

On July 30, the same summer that Sikorski was investigating salary and benefit levels of different unions, Jimmy Hoffa was abducted from the front of the Machus Red Fox Restaurant in a suburb of Detroit. The abduction, which was assumed to have been orchestrated by the mob, occurred just a week after *Wall Street Journal* investigative reporter Jonathan Kwitny published a three-part article on the Teamsters' Central States Pension Fund. The series exposed how organized crime figures and Teamster insiders were ripping off the pension fund by loaning large sums to themselves. Not only were union bosses raiding the pension funds for their own and their mob friends' benefit, they were also paying themselves handsome salaries from union dues and pension fund treasuries for non-jobs. It was an auspicious time to be targeting the transgressions of union bosses.

To Fox's delight, Sikorski decided to stay on after the summer and investigate further. The next seven months he spent buried in the catacombs of the Labor Department sifting through financial reports of Teamster locals around the nation, especially homing in on the activities of big union bosses (using Bobby Kennedy's book *The Enemy Within* as a source for some of the most crooked bosses). It is worth recalling that Sikorski's effort was undertaken before the days of computerized files, where tapping a few keys enables one to search through and order mounds of data in moments. The union financial reports, like many federally mandated reports, accumulated in huge file rooms, gathering dust as government officials simply did not have the time to do much more than make sure required reports were filed. Few researchers were willing to spend the months required to dig through such piles. It was one of the Nader's Raiders' greatest strengths—time and willingness to undertake and stick to such onerous and overwhelming tasks.

Sikorski's careful analysis of the financial data documented the excessive salaries and perks of dozens of individual Teamster leaders as well as the criminal records of many individual union bosses. Fox combined Sikorski's data with his own analysis of the Teamster constitution and the host of anecdotes about union transgressions that PROD had accumulated from its own membership. The result was a stinging indictment of the Teamster leadership. With a grant from the Field Foundation, Fox and Sikorski published a book, *Teamster Democracy and Financial Responsibility*. Then, with just three weeks to go before the 1976 National Teamsters Convention, they mailed three copies to every Teamster local in the nation. Along with the report they appended a list of suggested amendments to the Teamster constitution, including ending multiple salaries, capping compensation paid to Teamster officials and providing for direct election of all officers. Copies of the report, of course, were mailed to the press as well, resulting in banner headlines for a book that "exposed the Teamsters union for what it had become," as Fox describes it.

Their bombshell prompted a vehement reaction from Teamster President Frank Fitzsimmons. In his "state of the union" address at the national convention in Las Vegas, on June 14, 1976, Fitzsimmons attacked PROD and Arthur Fox, thereby putting them on center stage in the minds of journalists and the delegates. "I ask the question of Arthur Fox and his organization of PROD," Fitzsimmons thundered from the podium. "Who in the hell appointed them to act as the Teamster conscience?" He went on: "This self-styled savior of the Teamsters, Arthur Fox, esquire, he is a lawyer, you know, really never worked at a craft which entitled him to a Teamster or any other trade union membership. ... For those who say it is time to clean up this organization, I say, 'Go to Hell!'"

The chance for reform of the Teamsters at the national level looked dim after those remarks. Still, their book had focused public attention on the corruption with the Teamsters. Within a year, the Internal Revenue Service would force Fitzsimmons to resign from the Central States Pension Fund Board. Soon thereafter, a court would order that the pension fund be overseen by professional money managers to prevent further looting of its assets by the union bosses and their mobster friends.

Fox and Sikorski's exposé prompted at least one union member to act. One of their books had landed in the hands of Donald E. Brink, a long-hauler who was a member of Teamster Local 311 in Baltimore. A vocal, tough-minded character who stood six-foot-four and weighed more than three hundred pounds, who called himself "Meatmouth" because "I sink my teeth into things," Brink was angered by the revelations about Leo DaLesio, the chief officer of his Local 311. Not only was DaLesio's salary excessive, he had set up an incredibly generous special retirement fund just for himself. He drove around in a brand new, luxuriously equipped Cadillac. He had memberships in local clubs and an unlimited expense account that picked up the tab for at least one meal per day at Baltimore's finest restaurants. All of these perks were provided by money from the rank-and-file's dues and contributions to their pension and welfare funds. Brink and a small group of other activists in his local had created a PROD chapter to which he was elected president. He knew just where to turn for help and, more importantly, was willing to go out on a limb himself to challenge the actions of his union leaders.

"When I first brought up the charges, I took a lot of mouth from some of the members," Brink said. "I got argued down at union meetings. They said I didn't know what I was talking about. But I took a stand and proved what was going on was not right." He was a brave man, no doubt. Without the free legal help of Fox and the Litigation Group, though, it is doubtful that his bravery would have gotten him very far. It would take thousands of hours of legal time and talent and nearly four years to win Brink's case at the district and appeals court levels and then another five to retrieve the money that had been stolen from the union. Brink was there to relish the first court victory, though by then he was already in retirement and very ill after a brain tumor operation. Sadly, he died before the final battle was won and the money returned. Brink's case would lead to one of Fox's most satisfying litigation triumphs. It would return nearly $1.5 million to the local's pension and benefit funds and provide the Litigation Group with one of its most lucrative court-ordered fee awards. It also established an important precedent that would aid other rank-and-file union members in holding union bosses accountable to their fiduciary responsibility.

* * * * *

When Brink contacted PROD headquarters, Fox was excited about the prospect of the case. It offered an opportunity "to put a handle on the abuses exposed in the PROD book." Although the Justice Department had prosecuted a fair number of union officers for corruption, it could prevail only when it could prove *mens rea*, the criminal state of mind, and neither the Labor Department nor the NLRB had shown much interest in litigating the rights of union members against union officials under the laws they were responsible for enforcing. By pursuing a case against a union leader by a union member, Fox hoped to establish that union members could, in a civil action, shift the burden to their officers, forcing them to prove that their conduct did not amount to an abuse of power and fiduciary responsibility. The difference in burden of proof was critical. In a criminal action, criminal intent was the measuring rod and the burden was on the prosecutor to prove his case against the accused. In a civil action, when the charge was brought as a breach of a fiduciary duty (a common law and statutory requirement), the burden was on the defendant to prove his innocence. If Fox could persuade the court to accept Brink's civil action against DaLesio, then the level of proof necessary to win would be much lower than what the government faced. Critical in persuading Morrison and Nader to fund the case was the fact that the laws under which Fox planned to file the action (Landrum-Griffin and the Employee Retirement Income Security Act, or ERISA) included payment of attorneys' fees in the event of success. They all understood that *Brink* would be an expensive case to mount, with discovery and deposition costs that would strain the Litigation Group's limited budget.

Before Fox could file his case, a federal grand jury convened to investigate DaLesio. Much of the evidence Fox would later use was brought out by news coverage of the facts unearthed during the grand jury investigation. "East Baltimore was crawling with FBI agents," said one man who was questioned by federal investigators," according to one news account. "They asked about real estate, about cars and condos and gambling and about Leo's family. They were relentless. But one day I look in the paper and see where they found nothing." Apparently there was just not enough evidence to prove criminal intent, though the investigation continued for more than a year. There was lots of juicy stuff, though, showing blatant disregard for a fiduciary's responsibility to protect the union members' pension and welfare funds.

When Brink contacted Fox, he was told that the first step would have to be an effort to get the local union to file a case against DaLesio since the Landrum-Griffin Act (which creates a scheme of fiduciary duties required of union officers) requires this before a private individual action can be filed. So Brink attempted to get his union officers to go after DaLesio. But, as Fox would later write in his court brief: "When some members of DaLesio's own executive board took action ... DaLesio promptly fired the individual who 'instigated' the 'plot.'" The Board then voted not to take any action.

Meanwhile, a Baltimore newspaper reported that DaLesio's beach condominium and hotel suite had been provided by Alfred Bell, whom DaLesio had personally chosen as the administrator and insurance consultant for the four employee pension and welfare trust funds. The plot got thicker as the facts about Bell surfaced in the media. Bell was skimming significant money from the union members' retirement and benefit funds through a web of business entities he operated. Apparently unbeknownst to anyone, Bell had been double-dipping—charging the union a percentage of the employer contributions to the pension and welfare benefit funds for his services as a consultant, administrator and procurer of insurance coverage, while at the same time collecting a hefty fee from the insurance companies he hand-picked to provide the coverage for health and other benefits for doing the same thing. Of course, all the costs ultimately came out of the union funds' coffers, making their health and benefits coverage among the most expensive of any Maryland union. It was also reported that a fancy beach condo in Ocean City used solely by the DaLesio family had been purchased by Bell for $60,000 at DaLesio's suggestion. After the purchase, Bell had handed the key to DaLesio and paid the taxes, condominium fees, insurance, utilities, repair bills and even the monthly cable TV fee. At nearly the same time, DaLesio had moved the local union headquarters from a building where the rent was $2.50 per square foot to a building Bell had just purchased where the rent was $7.31 per square foot. News documenting the transgressions of DaLesio and Bell was regularly splashed on the front page of local papers as the grand jury continued its investigation. Fox decided to expand his suit to add Bell as a defendant as well.

Things were looking especially bleak for DaLesio by late 1977. A provision in his special retirement plan would cause him to lose the benefits if he were convicted while in office. DaLesio decided to retire rather than seek re-election. At the same time, Bell moved to get as many of his assets into his wife's name as possible and sell his insurance administration business before the courts could move to stop him. Bell's actions, however, did not come out until much later in the discovery process.

Hearing of DaLesio's impending retirement, Fox raced to file the lawsuit before DaLesio could get his hands on the first payment from his retirement fund, which was reported to be worth more than a quarter of a million dollars. Fox was swamped, and so another new Litigation Group lawyer, Paul Levy, was pressed into service to draft the complaint and stop the $50,000 payment to DaLesio.

* * * * *

Tall and lanky with long sideburns, clad in blue jeans and a T-shirt festooned with a suitably liberal message, Levy arrived at the Litigation Group headquarters in December 1977. He was not then, nor is he now, a Litigation Group uniform type. Khaki pants and button-down collars are not for him. Levy's persona is one that dates back to his youth. He grew up on the south shore of Long Island in Freeport. As a high school student, he participated in weekly vigils on the steps of the local post office to protest the war in Vietnam. One day Levy wore a black armband to high school. School officials demanded he remove the band, or he would be expelled. A call to the Nassau County

American Civil Liberties Union (ACLU) resulted in this group representing him in a legal challenge to the school's refusal to let him wear the popular antiwar symbol. Meanwhile, Levy returned to school wearing a black tie, which became his signature statement—one the "powers" could not stop.

"The ACLU attorney had to exhaust the appeal up through the school system to the state education department before filing in court, or it might have been *Levy v. Renkin*," Levy notes. "But *Tinker* [referring to *Tinker v. Des Moines Independent Community School District* (1969), the Supreme Court ruling that wearing black armbands to school as an expression of opposition to the hostilities in Vietnam is protected under the First Amendment] beat me to it."

Levy's interests from a young age were both political and strongly liberal. Throughout high school and college he had worked on a number of election campaigns for candidates running for the U.S. Congress, the New York state legislature and other state and local offices. He contemplated running for office himself someday. After taking off his senior year at Reed College to work on the McGovern presidential campaign (and recovering from that lopsided loss), Levy decided to go on to law school at the University of Chicago because he thought law would provide the most useful training for a career in politics. "I soon became persuaded that I was too left, too uncompromising, too cerebral for a career in politics," Levy explains. "but I soon became interested in another career path." While at law school his interest in public interest law was piqued in part because of a close friendship with Staughton Lynd, who sat next to him in one of his first classes. While he was a history professor at Yale University, Lynd had directed the Freedom Schools of the Mississippi Summer Project in 1964 and the next year chaired the first mass march on Washington, D.C., to protest the Vietnam War. After that he traveled, against the government's wishes, to Hanoi on a peace mission. Denied tenure at Yale (some claim because of his political activities), Lynd decided to go to law school. Although separated by many years, the two activists quickly became friends. When Lynd turned down an offer for a summer job with a local public interest group, he recommended Levy, who grabbed the opportunity. It was the first step in what would become a career for Levy, though it was not so clear then that this would be the result.

Following graduation, Levy won a clerkship with Judge Wade McCree, who was then serving on the U. S. Court of Appeals for the Sixth Circuit. Levy traveled to Detroit to begin his two-year clerkship in the summer of 1976. President Kennedy had appointed McCree as a federal district judge in 1961 (the second African-American to be appointed to that bench) and President Johnson had elevated him to the Sixth Circuit (the first African-American appointed to that court) in 1966. Another presidential appointment for McCree ended Levy's clerkship almost before it began. After the November 1976 election, President-elect Jimmy Carter selected Judge McCree to be solicitor general. When the judge offered to take Levy to the Justice Department with him, "I was overjoyed," Levy recalls, "but the bigwigs in the solicitor general's office were not so thrilled. I just did not fit their profile of the right sort of lawyer. I was not law review, had not worked for a big firm, had only clerked for a short time and then only for an appeals judge—not the preferred Supreme Court clerkship." And on top of all that, even when "suited up," his hippie-like looks came through. Still, the new boss had made a promise, so a compromise was ultimately reached that gave Levy a job, but not as a part of the litigating team. Sidelined, after a time Levy became frustrated with his assignments, so he contacted the Public Citizen Litigation Group. When Morrison offered him a job to help Fox with his overload of labor law cases, "I agonized and agonized over the salary, which at $11,000 represented a forty-plus percent cut in pay." In the end, the opportunity to have his own cases in an area of the law that whetted his progressive political appetites won out.

Levy was only a year and a half out of law school and had been at the Litigation Group for less than two months when he and Fox filed the Brink case on January 30, 1978, in federal court in Baltimore. Representing Brink and the other beneficiaries of four employee benefits plans sponsored by Local 311, the suit against both DaLesio and Bell sought redress for a "pattern of violations of fiduciary duties imposed on union officers and fiduciaries of employee benefit plans." The complaint made it clear that all money recovered would go back into the plans.

However, DaLesio was on the verge of drawing his first payment of $50,000 from his special retirement fund. The galloping growth of DaLesio's personal fund, which was worth more than double the total assets of Local 311, had been carefully hidden from the union members until it was exposed by the Sikorski and Fox book and subsequent news coverage. DaLesio could take his first payment of one-fifth of the value upon retirement, with the next payments coming in equal portions over the next four years. The lawsuit would take time to prosecute, so Levy asked U.S. District Judge R. Dorsey Watkins to issue a temporary restraining order (TRO) to prevent the withdrawal.

To obtain a TRO, Levy had to show that there was a likelihood that he and Fox would prevail on the merits; that there would be irreparable damage to the plaintiffs if the TRO were not granted; that there would be little damage to DaLesio if it were granted; and that granting it was in the public interest. "Our argument was pretty simple: The bank has this money. It will continue to have the money if the TRO is granted, and interest will continue to accrue. If DaLesio wins he can have it all, plus interest. If it is given to him he will spend it and it will be gone if we win." All the basic facts were there in news articles that had been spread across the front pages of the Baltimore newspaper, *The Sun*, so it did not take much to persuade the judge that there was ample evidence to give the plaintiffs a good chance of winning. The public interest in preventing the looting of union funds was obvious. "We were told that this judge never gave TROs, but the same day he granted us a temporary one, scheduling a full hearing." Levy returned to court on February 9 and again the judge sided with Brink. "We were nowhere near ready to go to trial, so we decided to offer a trade. We'd agree to let the first $50,000 payment be made if the other side would agree to accelerated discovery, that is to agree to provide all the documents and depositions we wanted without delay and on a timetable faster than the court normally allows," Levy said. They agreed, and the first installment was paid out. But then DaLesio reneged. That left only $200,000, which "the bank decided to retain, so that we could not claim they had wrongly paid it out."

Indeed, discovery was anything but expedited, taking more than two years. DaLesio immediately refused to submit to depositions on the grounds that he might incriminate himself. While the grand jury continued, the judge allowed this and told Levy and Fox to take discovery from everyone else instead. They took hundreds of hours of depositions and spent hours poring over the financial documents of DaLesio and Bell—at least any they could get their hands on. They managed to get some documents from the grand jury investigation through a cooperative prosecutor. "We assumed they were willing to share the information because they had already decided that DaLesio was too small potatoes to bother with or maybe that they could not tie him close enough to the mob," Levy speculates. "Whatever their reason, they ultimately dropped their criminal investigation and left it to us to get him through our civil case." As the time and costs escalated, Fox and Levy tried to get the Labor Department to take over their civil case since enforcement of both the ERISA law and the Landrum-Griffin Act was within its jurisdiction. But the government left it to the Litigation Group.

It was a long undertaking with no money coming in to cover any of the considerable costs—a problem Fox and Levy had to vigorously defend on a number of occasions. "At that point, Ralph was still head of Public Citizen and he personally signed all checks," Fox recalls. "We'd do the depositions and send him the court reporter's bill and he'd not pay them. He'd complain that they were 'too long,' that we should learn how to ask 'shorter questions.' Then we'd go in and yell and scream about it and finally he'd relent." Nader hated paying the money. There were so many things competing for the limited funds, but the chance of winning a cutting-edge case that would provide important new protection for rank-and-file workers ultimately won the day.

They were suing DaLesio to get back the value of the beach condo, the Cadillac and the expense account meals as well as the value of his $250,000 special severance fund. Since they were suspicious that there might be more evidence of money he took without justification, they combed through all of his expense account documents. They became bleary-eyed in the process but added a long list of other special goodies that DaLesio had gotten the union to pay for, including more than $2,000 in repair bills for the Cadillac. They also did a thorough analysis of the wages and benefits of other union officials in the Baltimore area, using this data to show how far out of line the generous salary and benefits DaLesio got really were. Then came a surprise helping hand.

"Leo's right-hand man had long been a man named Ralph Watson," Levy recalls. "Watson thought of himself as the rightful successor to assume the throne when Leo stepped down. But that did not happen. We learned Watson was ready to talk about how the severance fund was really set up and what the financial shenanigans behind it were. We never knew just why he talked. Perhaps it was anger at not being tagged to take Leo's place, but, whatever the reason, it was an exciting prospect." The testimony of a critical insider could make their case ironclad. They eagerly talked to him, first by phone, and then he agreed to meet in person. "I was to meet him in a bar. I was to come in my car to such and such a parking garage. Come out the back door of the parking garage and go down the alley into the back door of such and such a bar and he would be there," Levy said. It sounded like some clandestine spy meeting and sent chills down Levy's spine. "It was the only occasion I was ever nervous about my personal safety." He arranged to call the Litigation Group at a certain time—or lawyers there were to call the police—and then he left to follow his instructions. His caution proved unnecessary, as everything turned out fine. No one was lurking in those back alleys to bump him off. Levy and Fox met with Watson several more times, and ultimately was to testify as their star witness to help prove that the membership had no idea about the amount of the severance fund or the big annual increases in donations to it; that even the executive board was confused as to the amount; and, further, that that was precisely how DaLesio had planned it.

By this point, Fox and Levy had spent nearly two years gathering evidence for the trial. They still needed to get DaLesio to answer the long list of questions (interrogatories) they repeatedly had sent to his attorney and to depose DaLesio in person. Both requests were refused. On January 8, 1980, with the court-ordered date for the completion of the discovery phase set for January 15, Fox and Levy wrote to the U.S. district judge assigned to their case, Joseph H. Young. In a three-page letter, they listed the various ways DaLesio and Bell were obstructing their effort to complete discovery. DaLesio had refused to comply with the court's order of October 5, 1979, to provide financial data. Both Bell and DaLesio continued to claim the protection against self-incrimination, even though the federal grand jury investigation had been closed without indictment and thus no criminal matter threatened DaLesio and no criminal action was pending against Bell. Bell continued to refuse to deny or admit a long list of questions they had submitted repeatedly, claiming he "could not remember" or was "unfamiliar with" the issues, which were all related to checks listed in his own and his businesses' checkbooks. The letter concluded with a request to the judge to compel the defendants to respond and a request to extend the discovery process until they did so. Describing the meeting with the judge on January 10, Fox wrote to Brink:

> [W]e had another conference with the Judge today. He gave DaLesio's and Bell's lawyers a real tongue-lashing for obstructing our discovery of information and documents by hiding behind the

Fifth Amendment; he ordered them under threat of contempt to drop their claim of privilege and to tell ALL by February 10th. And, we have been given until March 1st to conclude our discovery, depositions, etc.

Fox described how they had finally gained access to "a mountain of financial records in the possession of Alfred Bell and his accountant ... and now we have to digest them before the trial but it is a heavy chore and we are bringing in various experts to help." He also noted that "Bell's lawyer moaned and groaned today about how just one single, discontented union member had driven his client out of business and into the poor house (a laugh a minute) ... and claimed that we were on a witch hunt and proceeded to tell the court about all the sophisticated studies we had conducted using bank records and Department of Labor computers." These final words must have brought some satisfaction to Brink, who was by that time undergoing chemotherapy and radiation treatment. His lone effort to stand up and stop the looting of his fellow drivers' benefit funds was having some result, at least, if one of the biggest looters was feeling the heat.

Finally the trial date arrived. For three weeks in May 1980, Fox and Levy sat in U.S. district court in Baltimore. There were long days of endless detailed questioning, but one moment stands out in Levy's memory. DaLesio repeatedly claimed that he had no record of things he bought because he always used cash. DaLesio said he had bought a number of items worth $15,000 for the beach condo and therefore had "contributed" significant worth to the condo in exchange for its use. There was no record that DaLesio had purchased any of the items. Some of the items, like central air conditioning, would have cost over a thousand dollars. Levy just did not believe the claim. "I had this brilliant idea for questioning him that I was sure would trip him up and make his claim that he bought such items for cash appear ridiculous," Levy said. Levy led DaLesio through a long train of questioning about what he bought and what it would have cost. When he got to the air conditioner Levy asked: "How much would it cost to buy a central air conditioner?" DaLesio replied: "I don't remember the price. I think I paid $1,200 for it. I am not sure. I may have paid less." The exchange went on:

Levy: Do you often pay such large amounts of cash?

DaLesio: In cash?

Levy: Yes

DaLesio: Sure, I carry large amounts of cash with me. Why not?

Levy thought he had him and pounced: "How much cash are you carrying with you today?" He was sure that, like most people, DaLesio would have a nominal amount of cash, but to his horror DaLesio pulled out a large wad of cash and began to count it—$400 in all. "It was not my best moment," Levy admits. "I was so sure it would work." Instead Levy was the one skewered. As he recovered and moved on, DaLesio's attorney managed to get in a little jab: "Would you like to check me? I have fifteen cents." Levy and Fox took turns over the days ahead examining and cross-examining Bell and DaLesio and other union officials and union members. On May 20, the trial concluded. They now had only to wait for the judge to act, or so they thought. A week later a letter from Judge Young arrived with a long list of issues that the judge "suggested" they "might consider" in preparing post-trial briefs that were to be due in three weeks. Fox and Levy went back into high gear preparing a brief addressing in detail every one of the judge's nine detailed questions of law and submitted their product on June 18.

On August 20, Judge Young announced his decision. It was a big win—not all they wanted, but nice anyway. DaLesio was ordered to pay back more than $164,000—including half his special retirement fund as well as the cost of using Bell's condominium and a number of the other perks the union had paid for, such as season tickets to Baltimore Colts football games. DaLesio and Bell together were ordered to pay $209,186 in penalties to cover the fees the union had paid to Bell for administering the pension and benefit funds. Only $1 was awarded the union for the excessive rent cost for the move to the building Bell owned because, the judge said, the plaintiffs had not proven that the charge was excessive. The judge denied the application of interest to the money owed and also ruled on an issue that none of the parties had raised at trial; he denied the standing of Brink and John Eline (a member of the union who agreed to be added as a plaintiff just weeks before the case was heard) to act as legitimate parties for two of the benefit funds by which they were not covered. *The Washington Post* called the ruling "one of the most sweeping applications of recent legislation designed to reform the way union leaders and pension fund administrators handle members' funds." But the win and all its headlines did not bring any money into the union funds or into the Litigation Group's meager coffers either. DaLesio and Bell quickly appealed, and Fox and Levy just as quickly filed a cross-appeal over the interest, rent recovery and standing issues.

On November 9, 1981, Fox wrote to Brink and Eline: "Enclosed you will find evidence of our 'smashing victory' dealt by the Fourth Circuit. Enjoy." And smashing it was. On November 5, the appeals court ordered DaLesio to pay another $30,000, plus interest, and he and Bell were ordered collectively to pay another $810,000, plus interest, to the pension and welfare funds. The amount included reimbursement for the excessive rent cost in Bell's building. The interest would pump up the amount another couple hundred thousand dollars. The bottom line was more than $1.5 million. The appeals court had not granted standing to Brink and Eline to represent the interests of the second pension fund that did not cover them but ordered the lower court to allow the intervention of the officials of the fund for the purpose of including them in the case. Intervention motions had been filed by the officials of all four union trust funds after Judge Young had announced his decision, but not one of the four funds had attempted to intervene while the case was under way. No one really thought they would win but, when they did, union officials with dollar signs spinning in their eyes scrambled to jump aboard (the two funds the judge had ruled that Brink and Eline could not represent were awarded no recovery by the district court decision and so their intervention was critical or they would get nothing).

"Cheers!" Fox concluded his letter to Brink and Eline, "You are to be congratulated as well for your perseverance. The union and its welfare funds owe you a huge debt of gratitude, particularly in light of all the grief they have directed your way." Once again, though, no money came. DaLesio and Bell filed endless motions and appeals to avoid payment and even though DaLesio died before the appeals were concluded, his estate and heirs fought on. It would take nearly four more years for the court-awarded funds to reach the pension and welfare benefit accounts. Ensuring that the Litigation Group's fees would be paid from the proceeds was not easy either. The appeals court order had made the collection of the judgment amount the responsibility of the trustees of the four union pension and welfare funds that DaLesio and Bell had raided. It was not the Litigation Group's responsibility to collect the money, but it had a vested interest in seeing that it was collected. And Fox and Levy had a strong case for being at the front of the line to collect money as it came in. Thus Fox sought to get the fees paid on an accelerated basis. After all, it was the Litigation Group that had incurred all the costs. As Fox wrote to the attorney for the funds in 1981 shortly after the appeals court ruling:

> First and foremost, had it not been for plaintiffs' vigorous—and yet uncompensated—prosecution of this action, the Funds would not be in a position to recover one cent from Bell and DaLesio for their many fiduciary derelictions. Second, under the common law of trusts embodied in ERISA, it is the trustees' duty not only to protect trust assets, but also to pursue claims on behalf of the trust. ... Technically speaking, the trustees should, therefore, have realigned the Funds as plaintiffs in this action and taken over the prosecution of the claims against Bell and DaLesio at Fund expense. Had they done so, the Funds would today have been out-of-pocket a substantial sum of money, with a large judgment awaiting collection. Instead, the trustees let plaintiffs and their counsel advance all the costs and shoulder the entire risk not only that the action might not be successful, but that the costs might be assessed against them. Fortunately, plaintiffs and their counsel were both willing and able to do so; indeed, they were willing to accede to the Funds' request to be dismissed from the action, thus sparing them even the

expense of having to pay their own counsel to sit through the trial.

Fox listed the provisions of ERISA that provide for attorneys' fees and noted that both trust and bankruptcy law provide for attorneys' fees to have priority. Finally, he suggested that he could ask the court to take the legal fees and expenses directly from existing assets in the funds. He then held out an olive branch: if the trustees were willing to re-consider payment of the Litigation Group's fees on an accelerated basis as the money came in, the Litigation Group would be willing to avoid this route. It was a generous offer that the trustees grudgingly accepted. It was one that the Litigation Group would come to regret, though, as it waited along with the pension funds for four more years before any money was collected from Bell or DaLesio.

On April 10, 1985, true to their agreement, the pension funds officials sent a check to 2000 P Street attorneys in the amount of $150,000. The second check, for $3,923, arrived four months later. It represented interest earned between the time the trustees got $400,000 from the DaLesio estate in December 1984 and the time the trustees sent the check to the Litigation Group. It was a most welcome financial bonanza at that particular moment, as the Litigation Group, like the rest of Public Citizen, was in a tight financial situation by 1985. As the Reagan administration's stranglehold over health and safety regulatory agencies (OSHA, NHTSA, FDA and the like) grew ever tighter, as the conservative economic and social agenda became ever more ascendant, and as Reagan's court appointees became more numerous on the federal bench, winning in court and fund raising for liberal groups became harder and harder. The usefulness of the money at the moment did not excuse the delay, but it was at least a silver lining of sorts.

* * * * *

While the Brink case was under way, Fox and Levy pursued several other union cases. One, *Smith v. Wilson Freight Company and the National Labor Relations Board*, also sought to protect Teamster workers when their own union and the NLRB failed to do so. This time, they were not so successful, though they won eventually on the issue involved by going to Congress.

On October 5, 1979, Paul A. Smith, a former full-time employee of the Chelmsford, Massachusetts, terminal of Wilson Freight Company and the elected union steward of that terminal, penned a letter to Nader seeking help. His purpose in writing was to share with Nader a recent circuit court of appeals decision.

I thought you might be interested since you have been involved so much with public safety. The case involved could go to the Supreme Court but in talking to the N.L.R.B. the odds are strongly against it. Although the government lawyers admit that the judge's decision is based on factual mistakes, they claim that nothing can be done.

The government spends millions of dollars to advertise that an employee cannot be discharged for filing safety complaints with O.S.H.A. or the D.O.T. The N.L.R.B. advertises that an employee cannot be fired for union activities. My employer took the opposite position. He said a shop steward has not the right to file charges with these various government agencies. My employer even put his feelings in writing. He proved his point. Laws were not meant for big business that are above them and the circuit court has upheld his feeling. ... The reality that stuns me the most is the statement from the government lawyers that no matter how many factual mistakes a judge makes in making a decision like this, nothing can be done.

The letter included a copy of the appeals court decision and Smith's long list of challenges to factual errors he claimed were made in the opinion. Smith's story was troubling, to say the least. He described how many of his fellow employees at Wilson Freight believed that the company was seriously deficient in living up to the health and safety requirements of both state and federal law and to provisions of their collective bargaining agreement. For example, "Wilson frequently sent out trucks in snowy conditions without tire chains required by law, thereby endangering both the drivers and the public. The loading areas of the terminal were not adequately heated, and dockworkers were not given protective clothing when handling dangerous materials." The company also ignored a provision of the National Master Freight Agreement and the state supplement that required that starting times for workers performing specific duties be set in advance and included in the terminal-wide process of selecting jobs according to seniority, known as 'bidding.'

The problem Smith and his fellow employees faced was that the local union business agent assigned to them, Patrick Lee, was unresponsive to their complaints. On issue after issue, they found that he would not answer their calls for help. Only by the most persistent prodding could Smith, as the union steward, force Lee to stand up for their rights by filing grievances. Under the National Master Trucking Agreement and the state supplement, only the business agent officially appointed by the union could file a grievance to the joint grievance committee for resolution. But there was nothing in the agreement that prevented a shop steward or individual member from reporting a violation of national safety law to the appropriate federal agency. Indeed, Smith believed that he had a right, just as any citizen does, to go to his government to seek enforcement of the law. (The First Amendment of the Constitution provides the right to all citizens "to petition the Government for a redress of grievances" against federal, state and local governments but it does not protect against the actions of private employers such as Wilson Freight Company.)

Thus, when the official union agent refused to act, Smith wrote to the responsible federal and state agencies. For example, he contacted the DOT about the failure to issue tire chains, OSHA about the failure to issue protective clothing, and the Massachusetts Department of Labor and Industries about the inadequate heating on the docks. In the last case, not only had Smith acted, but when the state agency failed to respond to his request to enforce the state law requiring adequate heating in work areas, he sent a petition signed by thirty-five of his fellow workers. The petition concluded with this: "To some our cause may seem meaningless, but to us it represents another act of repression by big business against the little guy. ... No longer is ours a democracy for the people and by the people, but a government against the people." On September 3, 1976, the company fired Smith. He then lost his grievance before the joint committee, which provided no explanation. In a terse two sentences, the joint committee merely said that Smith had exceeded his authority as steward and that the discharge was therefore valid. Following this loss, Smith appealed to the NLRB, filing an unfair labor practice charge. After a hearing, the NLRB ruled that because Smith wrote to the agencies on behalf of his fellow employees in his unit, he was engaged in concerted activity protected by statute. It also overruled several other claims made by Wilson Freight, found the discharge to be illegal and ordered him rehired with back pay. Smith went back to work on February 10, 1978. But the case continued when Wilson Freight appealed and the awarding of Smith's back pay was put on hold.

When the case came before the U.S. Court of Appeals for the First Circuit (which covers Massachusetts), the court ruled against both the NLRB and Smith. Though the NLRB and most circuits had ruled by this point that a discharge is unlawful if the employee's participation in protected activities was a substantial motivating factor in the decision to discharge, in 1979 the First Circuit had ruled that a discharged employee would have to prove that his participation in a protected activity, like complaining to federal agencies about violations, was the *sole* reason for the discharge. This was a heavy burden of proof. In *Smith*, the circuit court "announced the novel rule," as Levy would later write, "that the Board [NLRB] must defer to factual findings of the arbitrators" even though the joint committee had not provided any factual findings in its two-sentence ruling. The circuit court had decided that various factual findings were implicit; lurking there in those two sentences were all sorts of facts about why Wilson fired Smith. Accordingly, the NLRB had to defer.

It all seemed most bizarre. How could the NLRB defer to something that was not there? The circuit court solved that problem by laying out what it saw as those implicit facts, relying almost entirely on claims made in the brief submitted by Wilson Freight's attorney. These were the "facts" Smith was objecting to as false in his letter to Nader. Not only did the court adopt the claims of one side in the case without findings on them by the trial-level actor (the arbitrator in this case), but it also decided that Smith's communications with the agencies were not protected activities because the Master Freight Agreement and its state supplement prevented Smith from acting alone in complaining to federal agencies and thus no remand to NLRB was necessary. Just as the court had found "facts" where none existed in the record, it found in the Master Freight Agreement (where Smith and others did not) proof that the union had bargained away a union stewards' right to complain to his own government. "The decision of the Court of Appeals opens a critical loophole in the right to resort to government agencies," Levy noted in his petition seeking Supreme Court review. "The singling out of union stewards, generally the more aggressive and articulate employees who are most willing to stand up for workers' rights, is particularly egregious because they are the most likely source of complaints against violations of health and safety laws."

At issue in Smith's case was protection for whistleblowers—a subject of considerable concern to Nader, Fox and Levy. After all, if the safety laws they so vigorously supported were to be effective, there had to be protection for workers who reported violations by employers to the federal agencies. There simply are not enough federal employees to regularly inspect workplaces, nor is there much evidence that employers will voluntarily follow the rules. Complicating the case, however, were the factual issues. The high court rarely reviews lower court decisions in civil cases when the issue is a question of the truth of or correct interpretation of facts. That sort of case tends to be so specific to the litigant involved that a decision on review is not much use as precedent for other cases and courts in the future. A petition for a *writ of certiorari* in such a case is nearly always doomed. But Levy believed that if the court's attention could be focused solely on a question involving a legal interpretation, then they might stand a chance. The appeals court decision did include an interpretation of law—the question of whether any worker who complained to a federal agency about his employer's failure to follow federal law was protected from retribution. Nader, Fox and Levy would really have liked clear protection in national law to provide protection for all whistleblowers, but, with few exceptions, such a law had not yet been passed by Congress. The case Smith described seemed a promising vehicle to raise the issue to the Supreme Court level because it held the prospect of a legal precedent that would protect workers who blew the whistle on their employers.

On January 28, 1980, Levy filed a *cert* petition with the Supreme Court. The next day he sent letters to the Justice Department, OSHA and the National Highway Traffic Safety Administration (NHTSA), asking the agencies to pressure the Justice Department to petition for *certiorari* in the case as well. To OSHA, he wrote:

> We seek review of a Court of Appeals decision that says, among
> other things, that a union and an employer may waive contractual-
> ly the right of employees under the National Labor Relations Act to
> complain to government agencies, such as OSHA, about workplace

health and safety conditions.

Although the particular agency whose order was overturned was the NLRB, the court's decision strikes a severe blow against OSHA. Some of the complaints for which petitioner was discharged had been made to OSHA. ... Moreover, although OSHA has its own retaliatory discharge statute [a whistle blower protection provision], if a union may waive the right to blow the whistle as protected by the National Labor Relations Act, the same reasoning could well apply to permit waiver of the right protected by § 11 (c) of the OSH Act.

I am sure you will agree that the Department of Labor's interests are threatened by the decision below. ... I hope you will urge [the Justice Department] to request the Supreme Court to take the case for review.

Levy believed he had made a strong case in his brief and had been able to pinpoint a difference in rulings on the law among the circuit courts, one of the major reasons the Supreme Court will hear an appeal, but he knew that he needed the government's support to get *cert* granted. Hundreds of cases involving federal law are appealed to the Supreme Court each year, but only a small handful are accepted without the Justice Department's support. Levy was leaving no stone unturned. To Claybrook, who was then still head of NHTSA, he had Fox write a personal note: "Joan—Any influence you could exert on Justice &/or the NLRB to abandon a neutral position and support this petition would be appreciated. It strikes very close to home."

On March 26, Levy wrote to Smith, reporting that although Justice did not oppose the *cert* petition, "neither did they support it. ... I'm afraid that hurts our chances of getting review." His concern soon proved accurate. The court denied the petition in May. Shortly thereafter, a thank-you note from Smith arrived:

Even though we were unsuccessful in our attempt, in no way does this lessen the gratitude that my family and myself will always have for you. I do wish I were saying this in person because I feel it is my loss not to be able to shake your hand.

I often sit and wonder how different events would have been if I had met some people of your caliber in government agencies, instead of the incompetent sell outs I did meet. The contrast could never be overstated. Government agencies and courts whose job it is to enforce laws look for reasons why they should not have to. Your group, on the other hand who didn't know me or have any obligation to me looked for ways to try and correct a wrong.

Although I am bitter at the outcome, my life will always be a little brighter just knowing there are still some people like you out there that care.

In June 1980, when Smith's letter arrived, Levy was in the midst of drafting the lengthy post-trial brief in *Brink*. "On the hard days when nothing seems to be going right, a letter like yours helps one keep going," Levy wrote back. "I appreciate your feeling. I suppose it's easy to say from my ivory tower vantage point, but I certainly hope that your justified bitterness will not keep you from returning to the fray. Fighters like you are sorely needed." Even when the cause is lost, the knowledge that one has tried to help is satisfying, especially after a letter like Smith's. Perhaps it explains more than anything why Litigation Group attorneys like Levy keep at it for so long. And though it would not help Smith, Levy and Fox continued their efforts to have whistleblower protections written into law to protect employees like Smith, regularly promoting the issue to anyone on Capitol Hill who would listen.

During a lame-duck session after the 1982 elections, while Congress was madly trying to pass its final appropriation bills for a number of big agencies like the DOT and Labor, circumstances were finally favorable for action on whistleblower protection. The agencies whose appropriation bills had not passed by October 1, the beginning of the federal government's fiscal year, had been existing on "temporary continuing appropriations." After the November elections, Congress was forced to reconvene to pass the final appropriations laws or the government would be forced to shut down. Members were anxious to move quickly so they could get back home for the holidays. In mid-December, Congress simply Scotch taped all the remaining appropriations bills into one mammoth omnibus bill that grew even bigger as members stampeded to attach amendments to service powerful special interests and home districts. *The New York Times* called the giant money bill "a Christmas tree" bedecked with "baubles" and plums."

"This is not a carefully planned bill," one member admitted. In fact, dozens of floor amendments were not even printed—some were even handwritten, with no copies available for other members to look at before the vote. The final omnibus bill was accepted by voice vote in less than two minutes by the Senate and with similar speed by the House. Thanks to Fox and Levy, whistleblower protection for the trucking industry was one of those "baubles," though its inclusion had little to do with congressional concern for safety or workers.

Pressure had been mounting on members of Congress to mandate that states allow heavier and bigger trucks (especially the tandem trailer ones) on interstate highways. Gas prices remained high after the second oil shock of 1979, and the country faced high inflation, high unemployment and high interest rates. It was clear that a provision for bigger trucks would pass as an orna-

233

ment attached to the omnibus appropriations bill. Still, some members were "having trouble justifying their support for this provision," Fox recalls. "I did not in fact support the larger size limit, but all of us at Public Citizen knew there was just no way of stopping it. So I held my nose and grabbed the opportunity" by finding a number of members to co-sponsor a whistleblower amendment and introduce it on the floor. "I knew full well that the main interest of most of those supporting the amendment was providing themselves a bit of cover for embracing the size and weight increase. This was at least some 'goody' for the little folks to balance the unpopular 'goody' for the trucking industry." The amendment would have raised significant opposition from the trucking industry had it been introduced under normal legislative procedures, but it simply got lost among the many other amendments riding this legislative train.

On December 21, an amendment to Title IV of the Highway Improvement Act of 1982 that set forth provisions for protection of employees who file complaints or institute proceedings relating to violations of commercial motor vehicle safety rules passed into law as an attachment to the omnibus bill. It also directed the secretary of DOT to "institute civil action for injunctive relief to assure compliance with this title." It was too late for Smith, and not exactly a victory that would cover all workers, but it was at least a step in that direction.

* * * * *

Among the dozens of union cases begun by the Litigation Group in the 1970s was one that did make it to the Supreme Court. The case, *Barrentine v. Arkansas-Best Freight System*, came to the Litigation Group in the summer of 1979 when Levy and Fox were swamped with depositions in *Brink* and thus it landed in David Vladeck's lap. Vladeck, who came to the Litigation Group in the summer of 1977 to take over the FOIA litigation from Diane Cohn, had little experience with labor law. He did have strong family connections to the issue. His father, Stephen Vladeck, had founded a law firm in New York City that represented labor unions, and both his mother and sister had also joined the firm. "As a kid, my family would sit around the dinner table and my mom—a superwoman long before working professional moms were given that appellation—would use us all as a sounding board for her cases," said Vladeck. "We always 'ruled' the right way, of course, but what I learned most was a great appreciation of why what she did mattered." So it was with some excitement and personal satisfaction that Vladeck took the case, though in the form that it landed on his desk it did not look very promising. He surely never guessed that it would lead to his first opportunity to argue before the Supreme Court.

The issue in *Barrentine*, at least the issue Vladeck would focus on, was quite simple: does a company have to pay at least minimum wage to an employee during the time that employee is performing a federally mandated task? In this case the task was the inspection of trucks by the driver for safety problems, a requirement mandated by DOT regulations. When a driver, like Lloyd Barrentine, arrived at Arkansas-Best Freight System to take a scheduled trip, he first had to punch in and do some office paperwork. Then he would punch out and inspect his assigned truck for safety defects. If he found none, he would embark on his trip and his pay would cover the full time from punch-in to the end of his trip. In other words, the punch-out was ignored. If the driver identified a problem with the rig, though, he would have to drive the truck to the company's on-site repair facility and punch in at the repair facility. When a defect was found, the driver was not compensated for the time he spent inspecting the rig and driving it to the repair shop. And though this did not amount to a lot of time for each instance (court documents claim the average time was 15 to 30 minutes for each inspection), over time it added up to a lot of uncompensated time for anyone who found safety problems. The company claimed that since this time was spent doing the government's work, not the company's, it should not have to pay. Obviously, this interpretation might impose a certain amount of pressure on drivers to overlook safety problems.

The union, on behalf of Barrentine and several other drivers, challenged the company's failure to pay for this inspection time in a grievance before a joint grievance committee. But their official union representative apparently struck a bargain that, in effect, would allow the company not to pay for the time. Barrentine and the others believed that the union representative had failed to adequately represent them and had entered into an illegal agreement, so they sought local counsel to mount an appeal in court. The complaint filed on their behalf raised two challenges: first, a claim that Arkansas-Best Freight had failed to pay them at least minimum wage for the inspection time as mandated by the Fair Labor Standards Act; and second, a challenge based on the union's inadequate representation. At trial, their counsel focused mainly on the latter point. When the district court ruled against Barrentine and the other drivers, the judge addressed only the issue of adequate representation, concluding that on such a claim he must defer to the joint committee's decision. After they lost, the PROD network led Barrentine to Public Citizen's door.

Vladeck knew that persuading a court to involve itself in a labor dispute would be a lot easier if the issue were framed as an interpretation of federal law rather than an interpretation of the responsibilities of union or management under a labor-management contract (which here was a question of the provisions of the National Master Freight Agreement). Even after the *Banyard* and *Ferguson* rulings that deference cannot be automatic, courts tended to defer unless there was a clear issue of federal statutory interpretation involved. Why the lower court simply ignored the Fair Labor Standards Act's minimum wage issue is unclear. On December 5, 1979, Vladeck flew to St. Louis to argue the case before a panel of the U.S. Court of Appeals for the Eighth Circuit. "It was clear that one of the judges thought I was nuts and that one thought I was absolutely right. What the third thought I couldn't tell as he never said a word," Vladeck said.

Upon returning he wrote to Barrentine, "I just wanted to let you know that oral argument in your case was held in St. Louis last Thursday, December 6th and went much better than either Arthur [Fox] or I had anticipated. The Presiding Judge, Judge [Gerald] Heaney, understood our arguments and seemed relatively sympathetic. The other two judges—Judge [J. Smith] Henley and Judge [Albert] Schatz—were harder to read." Vladeck warned that it might take a year or more to get a decision. When the decision arrived on February 20, 1980, it was clear where the silent judge came down. It was a 2-1 loss, though Judge Heaney wrote a strong dissent. Three days later Fox wrote to Barrentine, "It goes to show that the time and place to win a legal proceeding is at the trial level. ... There would be no point in pursuing the case further in my opinion." Vladeck was not so sure about that conclusion, and after talking with Morrison, they decided to try to carry on. They did have one important factor in their favor: there were now two different appeals court rulings (one in another case) on the same matter. A difference in interpretation of a law among the circuits is one of the major reasons used by the high court in granting *cert*. Getting in the courthouse door, though, would not be enough to win. "Having Heaney's dissent was critical," Vladeck notes, "especially in persuading the folks at the AFL-CIO and the Justice Department to support our petition for *cert*." Both the Department of Labor and the AFL-CIO submitted *amicus* briefs in support of their position and, interestingly, the Justice Department never asked for time at oral argument. "I guess it was a compliment to me that they did not do so," Vladeck said.

On January 13, 1981, Vladeck was scheduled to argue *Barrentine* before the Supreme Court. For most litigators, an argument before the Supreme Court is a dream never realized. Vladeck was not yet thirty years old and had only a little more than four years in practice. Although he had argued several cases in federal district and appeals courts, this was awe inspiring. "No one at the Litigation Group even suggested taking the argument away from me and giving it to someone with more experience," says Vladeck. "In hindsight, if they had any sense, they should have." *Barrentine* was a complicated case, forcing a balancing of the statutory minimum wage provision against the statutory provisions in labor law that provide a process for labor union and management contract negotiation and dispute resolution with minimal court interference. "I was subjected to three of the most grueling moot courts I have ever experienced," Vladeck remembers, "one by my colleagues at the Litigation Group, one with the folks at Justice and one with the AFL-CIO people." He was confident that he had a good legal position and that he was prepared as much as anyone could be, but he admits to being "scared to death."

Vladeck's argument was that every individual employee had a right under the Fair Labor Standards Act to be compensated for any work that is "integral or indispensable to the primary activity of the employer." The words "integral" and "indispensable" were found in the Fair Labor Standards Act and had been the subject of nearly forty years of judicial construction. Once he could show that the inspection of the trucks was indispensable to Arkansas-Best Freight's trucking business (and that was relatively easy, as failure to do it would put the company at risk of enforcement action by the federal government), he could argue that failure to pay for this time was in conflict with the overriding purpose of the Fair Labor Standards Act as construed by the Supreme Court in a number of cases.

Another problem he faced was whether the employees, having chosen arbitration and having lost, could then turn to the court. Arbitration is generally regarded as a final, unappealable process agreed to ahead of time by all parties involved. The Master Freight Agreement and state supplemental agreements (which both union and management sign off on) provide for this method of conflict resolution, and courts usually stay out of the process. Vladeck knew that the opposing side would argue that this "second bite of the apple" was unfair and would burden the court with a flood of employee-generated appeals. He would have to prove that the employee could still take his statutory right claim to court for review *de novo* (for trial anew without any requirement that the court defer to the arbitrator's findings). As precedent for this argument, Vladeck had a 1974 Supreme Court ruling in *Alexander v. Gardner-Denver* that an individual's right to be free of discrimination (under Title VII of the Civil Rights Act) allowed him to appeal to court for protection of that right even if his case had been submitted to the union-management arbitration process and he had lost. In addition, the Seventh Circuit had ruled that a prior arbitration award did not bar a subsequent suit under the Occupational Safety and Health Act, thus providing him not only with a useful precedent but with an argument that there was now a different interpretation of law among the circuit courts. His task would be to convince the court that the right to be fairly paid was a statutory one that deserved a full hearing every bit as much as did a Civil Rights Act claim or an OSHA claim. After all, under the Constitution, the power to interpret the law resides in the courts, not in an arbitration process made up of labor and management representatives. Although the issue sounds simple on the surface—an hour's pay for an hour's work—the legal complexity facing Vladeck was anything but simple.

On that cold January morning that *Barrentine* was to be heard before the Supreme Court, Vladeck donned a new suit and a suitably conservative tie and headed for the office. "Alan's view is that we should avoid having more than one or two pieces of paper in front of us when we argue, and outlines are taboo," said Vladeck. The art of oral advocacy, according to Morrison, is to use a question as a bridge to a point you would like to make. Thus the advocate has to be able to take whatever opportunity comes her way to get in the points that best help the case. Vladeck listed on one page the affirmative points he wanted to make and on another he listed the questions he thought he would most likely be asked (most of which had surfaced in the moot courts) and brief summaries of suggested answers. He had written out an outline for his remarks, in the event there were not many questions from the justices, then had distilled it down into ever-shorter outlines. With Morrison's advice as guide, he left all these behind and headed to court. Arriving a bit early, he had coffee and a muffin. Soon his mother, sister, brother and girlfriend arrived (sadly, his father had passed away before this event) to sit through the morning cases. *Barrentine* was scheduled for the first case after the lunch break, but all were anxious to take a read of the mood of the justices before Vladeck's turn. "I remember everything about that day, even what I had for lunch at La Brasserie," Vladeck reminisces. Despite his nervousness, he ate it all, recalling nearly two decades later that it was delicious.

During the moot courts, several people had chided Vladeck for using his hands too much. So when his turn came to approach the podium before the justices he grabbed either side and held tight, never letting go. "The setting at oral argument before the Supreme Court is very intimate," Vladeck notes. "You stand so that the proximity between you and the justices is almost close enough to touch. Everything else recedes into the background as you look up at them and begin to speak." As counsel for appellants, Vladeck went first. "Mr. Vladeck, you may proceed when you are ready," said the imposing Chief Justice Burger. "I got off to a kind of shaky start, scrambling to deal with the questions that rained down from the bench." Soon his hours of preparation began to show and his responses became more forceful and confident. With only five minutes remaining in his allotted half-hour to argue, Vladeck said "I'd like to reserve the rest of my time for rebuttal," pried his hands from the podium and sat down to watch as his opponent was equally "roughed up" by a barrage of questions. Vladeck's final few moments flew by and then it was over. Only one question had caught him unprepared, related to the Norris-La Guardia Act and two cases known as *Boys Market* and *Buffalo Forge*. "I knew the two cases concerned strikes, but what I did not know—and indeed still don't know—is what relevance Justice Rehnquist, my inquisitor, thought they had to my case." The first thing Vladeck did when he left the court was "to ask Mom what the hell that question was all about? She, with decades of labor law experience, had no idea, and we had this suspicion that the justice was just tweaking the young kid." Everything they could do had been done. Just three months later, the court gave Vladeck a 7-2 victory, with only Burger and Rehnquist dissenting. But just as in *Brink*, it would take forever to get the money. Not until 1986 did Barrentine finally see his overtime pay and the Litigation Group finally see its attorneys' fees.

Having found that the court below must review the statutory claim raised by *Barrentine*, the Supreme Court remanded the case to the district court. More than two years later, on June 16, 1983, based on the transcript and evidence submitted at the first trial (which Barrentine had lost) and without further court hearing, a different district court judge found in their favor. The ruling stated that the pre-trip inspections constituted "an integral and indispensable part of the plaintiffs' duties of driving trucks as employees of Arkansas-Best Freight ... [and thus] plaintiffs are entitled to minimum wage compensation for the time."

A delighted Vladeck informed his clients that at last it looked like they would soon get their money.

This hope was soon dashed, though, because the trucking company appealed—raising almost the same claims it had already lost on in the Supreme Court. On December 10, 1984, the Court of Appeals for the Eighth Circuit upheld the district judge's findings and remanded the case to the district court for enforcement of the judgment. Now, surely the back wages would be paid. Not so. The trucking company appealed again, filing a petition for a *writ of certiorari* to the Supreme Court. The petition was denied, but the trucking company still resisted. Its gambit this time was to demand a trial in the district court on the issue of damages and attorneys' fees.

On May 3, 1985, Vladeck wrote to Arkansas-Best Freight's attorney in an attempt to nudge the company into settlement negotiations. He noted that Arkansas-Best Freight was "already liable for the substantial attorney's fees that I have incurred. As I am certain you understand, I plan on pursuing the damage issue as vigorously as possible in order to secure the best relief I can for my clients." Then he pointed out that the company would be liable for his costs in the damage suit and that since the damages owed to his clients were "not overly burdensome" and probably a good deal less than his fees would be for carrying the case on (he estimated this to be in the $20,000-$30,000 range), perhaps the company might consider settling. His effort failed; the company proceeded with its case. A week later a copy of the "Proposed Findings" submitted by Arkansas-Best Freight's attorney to the court was delivered to Vladeck's office. He was incredulous. The company was not just fighting the amount of the damages, it was still claiming that it should not have to pay any damages at all! Vladeck submitted his response on May 23, 1986, noting that the defenses Arkansas-Best Freight stated it was planning to make had all been "fully litigated and that this Court, the Court of Appeals, and the United States Supreme Court have all rejected ABF's argument. In these circumstances, settled principles of *estoppel* and law of the case bar ABF from relitigating this issue."

A phone call from the company's attorney on June 4, made it very clear that settlement was out of the question and that the company really did intend to fight paying any damages at all. Vladeck was incensed. This amounted to nothing less than a misuse of the legal process. He fired back a strongly worded challenge of his own:

> As I understand it, ABF's principal defense will be that the plaintiffs are not entitled to damages because over the relevant time period their annual wages have exceeded the minimum wage. In response, I told you that we would stipulate [agree] to that fact. But far more importantly, I pointed out that ABF raised that precise issue eight years ago during the first trial in the case, and it was rejected by Judge Arnold. Moreover, the question was again raised in ABF's brief to the Court of Appeals, and ABF sought Supreme

Court review of that issue in its petition for *certiorari*. In every instance, ABF has failed to prevail on that question. As I explained to you, in my view that issue has been finally and conclusively resolved in this litigation against ABF, and ABF is now barred altogether from relitigating that issue before the district court in the forthcoming damage proceeding. Indeed, as the most recent Court of Appeals opinion makes clear, the only issue remaining to be resolved in this case is the extent of the plaintiffs' damages.

"It is for this reason," Vladeck continued, "that I regret to have to inform you that if this is the position ABF takes before the district court, I will be constrained to seek sanctions against you personally pursuant to Rule 11 of the Federal Rules of Civil Procedure, as well as damages against ABF." Rule 11 prohibits an attorney from using the litigation process solely as a means to delay a case or solely to delay paying damages and/or attorney fee awards, or simply to increase the cost of litigation for the other side. It provides sanctions against attorneys who engage in these impermissible tactics. Such a strongly worded rebuke is rare in the usual "gentlemanly" exchanges between opposing counsel, even in the most heated cases, but Vladeck had finally had enough. He went so far as to inform Arkansas-Best Freight's attorney that he would use this letter as a document in a Rule 11 proceeding if the company continued with its effort to deny its legal responsibility to pay the court-ordered damages and attorneys' fees.

The threatened Rule 11 action apparently worked, in part at least. The company gave up challenging the fact that damages were due, but it still refused to negotiate a settlement. Just before the scheduled trial date, the company gave in. A negotiated settlement was reached that the company would pay minimum wage for the time each safety inspection had taken and would do so in the future. In late 1986, Barrentine and the other truckers finally got a check to compensate them for inspection work done between 1974 and 1986. The Litigation Group got a check for $50,000. "Given the fact that the case had taken over eight years, been through the appellate process twice, required a full-scale Supreme Court proceeding, and was settled on the eve of the trial after I had done all of my trial preparation work, ABF got off pretty lightly," says Vladeck. Perhaps the cost of breaking the law would send a message to other companies that it would be cheaper for them to simply follow it. Whatever the reality of that hope, the win in *Barrentine* clarified that federal law gives employees a right to be paid for all work they do for an employer, that arbitration awards, even adverse ones, cannot interfere with the enforcement of statutory rights, and that federal courts have a responsibility for ensuring that these rights are protected. It is exactly the sort of broad policy result that has application beyond the litigants at hand and that is the central goal of the Litigation Group.

Union Democracy — Protecting the Rank and File

* * * * *

Many of the legal gains won for union members through cases the Litigation Group began during the 1970s were threatened in the decades to follow. Efforts to enhance the power of rank-and-file members within the union and to protect union workers against the excesses of corporate power would run into insurmountable roadblocks. But the problem would come not so much from the rulings of more conservative courts, as would be the case in so many other areas of individual rights and government regulation. Rather the rapid globalization of corporate giants led to a workplace where national law, even when enforced, could not protect workers against loss of jobs and decreasing union membership.

13

Reining in the Legal Monopoly —
The Rosemary Furman Case

On April 4, 1977, Rosemary Furman of Jacksonville, Florida, wrote to Morrison. Her letter began: "Re: HELP!" and went on to describe how the Florida Bar had sent undercover investigators to her business to get evidence that she was practicing law without a license. Furman, a former school teacher and a trained legal secretary with over thirty years of experience, was an active participant in the women's movement and served on the board of Hubbard House, a home for battered women. She knew that many abused women could not afford a lawyer for such critical procedures as obtaining a divorce, child support or restraining order. Since she had been responsible for filling out court forms for these sorts of procedures with little or no supervision from the lawyers in the firm where she worked, she offered to help fill out the same forms for free for women at the shelter. Seeing a desperate need, in 1975 she set up her own business, the Northside Secretarial Service, to fill it.

"From the outset of her efforts in 1975," court documents later said, "she has clearly stated that she is not a lawyer, and at no time has she represented any person in court or signed any pleadings." Florida law allowed individuals to represent themselves in divorce and several other proceedings, so Furman helped these self-filers prepare for court. She had the individual seeking her help fill out an intake form and then she would type up the necessary papers. If a person was not able to read or write, she might ask the questions on the form and fill it out. In addition, she would give "a detailed practical explanation of how to proceed, including where to file their cases, what to do with each copy of the papers, how to pay the court fees, how to set up an appointment for the final hearing, whom to bring to the hearing, and even how to address the court." For example, she helped women prove Florida residency, a requirement for divorce. "You've got to take a witness [to court] who knows you. ... You better take a female. When you take a male person, they (judges) get a little crazy, because they think you're divorcing to remarry," she says. Her reasoning was that, since Florida has a no-fault divorce law for uncontested divorces (as most self-filers are), it is none of the judge's business why one is

242

divorcing; but, "[t]he judges get their jollies interrogating frightened young women about their sex lives."

Furman charged a flat fee of $50, though if the person could not afford that much, she would accept $25 or even nothing. At the time she began helping self-filers, members of the Florida Bar were charging $350 for an uncontested divorce. Furman made no attempt to hide what she was doing. Indeed, she repeatedly attacked the attorneys, the bar and the courts for their failure to serve middle- and low-income earners in need of legal assistance, thereby denying them justice. "The law," Furman argues, "belongs to all the people. It does not belong to lawyers to sell by the pound or by the yard. ... If the people cannot use the courts, then the whole system is worthless." She aimed to pry open the courthouse door a bit.

Undoubtedly, her efforts were not aided by her own very public and noisy campaign against the whole legal system and the problems she saw. Furman's style was not that of the dispassionate legal crusader—more the pit bull. The Florida state judiciary, she charged, were "pompous political hacks, most dismally incompetent." She called the state's Supreme Court justices "The Seven Dwarfs ... the most hilarious bunch of misfits I've ever seen." The bar was "a parasitic growth on society" and lawyers "sneaky bastards ... bloodsuckers .. . [and] habitual liars, because they will never disclose something that will be harmful to their case." Such zingers got her news coverage but hardly endeared her to the groups she was trying to change; indeed, they probably sparked the vicious and vehement counterattack that would eventually push her into court.

For example, Jacksonville Circuit Judge John Santora (who filed many of the complaints used in the Florida Bar's case against Furman) was quoted in the *Jacksonville Monthly* explaining his antagonism toward her clients who appeared before him: "They should not take it personally. Rosemary and I go back a long way. I bust her every chance I get." His attack on Furman, however, mostly harmed the poor men and women who had turned to her for help. "They are," notes the author of the *Jacksonville Monthly* article, "for the most part, the carpenters, housewives, sailors and barmaids of North Florida ... trapped in a legal system that has made no place for them."

Furman counter-attacked, accusing Santora of misfeasance. The Florida Judicial Qualifications Commission investigated and, though the judge was cleared, Furman managed to publicize a series of embarrassing affidavits issued by women who had appeared in Santora's court. But Santora was hardly alone in such harassment, as the article notes. One, involving an appearance by a woman seeking a no-fault divorce before Circuit Judge Lawrence Fay, is particularly telling. She showed him her papers, introduced her residency witness and was asked to leave.

"You're not telling me what I want to hear," Fay told her.

"Judge, what should I be saying?" she asked.

"I can't tell you," he replied. "I think you should hire yourself a lawyer."

There happened that day to be a reporter in the courtroom who pressed the judge after the hearing to explain what was wrong with the woman's case. The judge claimed that he was "dissatisfied with her residency witness ... [and] there was a key document—a joint stipulation—missing." But when the reporter checked the court documents they showed that the joint stipulation had been assigned to the judge's file. Returning to the judge, the reporter asked that he check the file, and the stipulation was right on top. Judge Fay made a quick about-face, granting the divorce without further testimony. Not every Furman client was fortunate enough to have a gutsy reporter present, though. Judge Fay later said, "I get so furious when I see that woman's name. The problem is with these secretarial services."

Furman's first letter to Morrison explained how an undercover investigator for the Florida Bar had come to her office using the alias of "Anderson" and asking for help filling out divorce papers. He was informed that the stenographers in her office served only women. But he persisted and persisted, so one of them finally typed his papers as he dictated his answers. Soon thereafter Furman was served with court papers from the Florida Bar charging her with giving unauthorized legal advice, with Anderson listed as one of four cases to be used against her. She wanted to file a counter-suit against the Florida Bar. Was this entrapment? Invasion of privacy? An antitrust violation? "Something ought to work," she thought. Morrison wrote back immediately, regretting that he couldn't help. The Litigation Group is a tiny public interest law firm not equipped to act as a legal aid society for individual interests. He did suggest that she get in touch after the preliminary hearing in either state or federal court.

Letters went back and forth over the next couple of months as the case against Furman progressed. She wrote to Morrison about the harassment her clients were experiencing at the hands of some judges, and about the effort of the bar to get a referee appointed (who would be a retired judge) and her effort to get the case dismissed. "I am wondering how the citizens of Florida can gain access to their civil courts ... how we can break the iron grip of the Bar's monopoly on domestic actions ... I am in the delightful position of 'showing cause' to a tribunal of lawyers on a charge brought by what is essentially a trade union of lawyers."

Furman's case at this point seemed a potential vehicle for reforming the legal system—a goal both Morrison and she shared. By mid-summer 1977, Morrison agreed to help. He needed to find a Florida lawyer who would work with him, no easy task when the opponent was the Florida Bar and one Florida judge had publicly called Furman and other legal stenographers a "cancer on society."

"Of all the restrictions regarding the practice of law, the clearest case of protectionism has always seemed to me," Morrison notes, "to be the requirement that a person be a resident of the state in order to be admitted to the Bar there." The Florida Bar, like many states, had this residency requirement, and in order to practice in Florida, in either state or federal courts, a lawyer had to be a member of the state bar. Morrison and other Litigation Group attorneys were fighting these sorts of restrictions in a number of other cases at that time, but this did not help him here. He could not help Furman unless he could find a Florida attorney to work with him and to seek temporary admission to the bar for himself for this case only (called a motion to admit *pro hac vice*).

Morrison wrote to Chesterfield Smith, a former president of the American Bar Association (1973-74) and then a partner in a Lakeland, Florida, law firm. Smith, he knew, was an exception to the norm among the powerful in the bar on this issue. "Most unauthorized practice issues arouse emotion in the Bar, because there's an economic interest at stake," Smith had noted. "But if we let a person with no skill be his own attorney, why not let someone with some skill help them?" Morrison hoped that Smith's prestige might enable him to stand against the powerful state bar where others might be afraid to do so.

Though Smith did not volunteer to serve himself, he did put Morrison in touch with Albert J. Hadeed. Smith was on the board of directors of the Southern Legal Counsel, a nonprofit, public interest litigation firm just then being formed in Florida, at which Hadeed was about to work. On the eve of its first day in existence, the board agreed that Hadeed could serve as local counsel in the Furman case. His participation was critical. Not only did he do a great deal of the work, but he was there every day and his past practice in Jacksonville, where the case would be heard, enabled him "to provide invaluable local color. It would have been impossible to deal with the Florida Bar," Morrison says, "whose lawyers were basically uncooperative, without his help." In October, Morrison flew to Jacksonville to confer with Hadeed and Furman in preparing their defense.

In late November Hadeed wrote to Morrison: "It appears that the Florida Bar is summoning the troops in defense of its unauthorized practice of law campaign." He enclosed the November 1977 issue of *The Florida Bar Journal*, which was devoted almost completely to the unauthorized practice of law. Two weeks later Hadeed sent another piece of news: "I have been served with a pleading which indicates that the Florida Bar has secured the *pro bono* services of Lacy Mahon Jr., as its lead counsel. Lacy is an attorney of considerable political stature in the State." Not good news. Interesting too, in a state that had an abysmal record of providing *pro bono* services for those in need. In his pleading, Mahon had also filed a general denial of all Furman's defenses.

Hadeed also reported that a referee was to be appointed to handle the initial hearing on the matter and that he was working on a motion to restrict the authority of the referee. Under Florida rules, a referee was empowered to make findings of fact, conclusions of law and recommendations regarding discipline, but there was some precedent suggesting that a referee could not rule on legal issues without the consent of both parties. The condition was designed to protect the due process right to have decisions on law made by the judicial authority charged with that responsibility. Hadeed noted that "the Florida Bar, as *amicus curiae*, supported this contention in a case before the Supreme Court of Florida" which he thought ought to make his motion acceptable to the bar. Referees were normally chosen from a list of retired judges and thus were more likely to be attorneys from an older generation who tended to be more conservative on the issue. Hadeed thus believed that they would fare better by having the legal question of what unauthorized practice is decided by a court, not a referee. Sadly for them, his motion was denied.

More sadly for them, the referee who was appointed, retired Judge Revels, proved to be all they had feared. They filed a motion for discovery to gain access to the process the bar followed in gathering evidence and deciding to file suit—a process dictated by state law that the bar must follow in order to bring suit. The referee quickly denied it. They appealed, arguing that there was nothing in the law that "cloaks these records with privilege." The referee denied the appeal. They served interrogatories. The bar delayed and then refused to answer most of them. They filed a motion to depose certain members of the bar. It was denied. They asked for a delay to await a state Supreme Court rehearing in another Florida case involving a charge of unauthorized practice of law (*Florida Bar v. Brumbaugh*). Interestingly, the bar agreed to the postponement and the request was jointly made. It was denied.

When the delay to await the rehearing in *Brumbaugh* was denied, Morrison and Hadeed sought to negotiate a dismissal of the charges. The *Brumbaugh* decision had set out new guidelines as to what constitutes the unauthorized practice of law in Florida. They were fairly vague guidelines at best (which, in part, is why counsel there was seeking a rehearing) but basically required that a non-lawyer could only type what a client put on a form. As the bar interpreted this decision, no corrections at all could be made—no correcting mistakes, clarifying the ambiguous, eliminating contradictions, or assisting at all where the client was unable to read and write. Nor could information about where to properly file forms or how to present necessary evidence or answers to questions about which forms to use be given. The decision did allow for lay persons to sell blank forms for use in a divorce proceeding and to include written instructions with them. If Furman agreed in the future to abide by both what the court specifically said and the bar's interpretation of what it meant, and to admit that she had committed "at least one act which would have constituted unauthorized practice of law" as defined by *Brumbaugh*, then the bar might consent to drop this case. Furman attempted to adjust her practices to these requirements but soon discovered that she could not provide adequate services this way. So the consent decree route failed and the case went on.

On July 18, 1978, the referee heard testimony in the case. Mahon questioned eleven former clients of Furman's. He questioned each relentlessly, trying to show that Furman did more than just type what they wrote, that she gave advice and answered questions. Morrison then questioned Furman, attempting to show how carefully she limited her service to filling out of forms and providing simple advice, but that, in order to effectively do this, she sometimes had to ask a question or give oral instructions. In part, he aimed to show the court that the *Brumbaugh* decision was too confining, that servicing the sort of clients who could not afford attorneys' fees required more than just providing forms for them to fill in and typing them up. For, as Morrison, Hadeed and Furman all agreed, this was their real objective. Furman could not really do what she was trying to do unless they could get *Brumbaugh* modified.

Morrison asked Furman if she had illiterates as clients. "Oh, yes sir," she replied. "Do you have people who are able to read and write minimally but not read and write forms?" he asked. "Yes," was her reply. "And is it possible for you to service them without giving them oral instructions?" he asked. "I don't see how," she replied. "People have difficulty understanding and they need clarification." His questions went on and on, pulling out the problems of communicating with her clients.

Mahon's cross-examination seemed aimed at proving that Furman was in business for the money, plain and simple—that her $50 fee was not altruistically motivated, though she had never claimed that it was (altruism was when she did it for free). He then sought to expose her lack of formal legal training. Other than legal stenography courses, she had none. Mahon responded to this admission with a litigator's bravado: "Any person sitting in the audience, the bum on the street, the alcoholic, as far as qualifications are concerned, they would be as qualified to provide the service as you, in that you have no legal training either?" Furman had her own sharp retort: "I would say anyone who is able to type accurately, anyone who has put in twenty years as a court stenographer who understands basic procedures, anyone who has put in a number of years as a legal stenographer under the supervision of an attorney, yes, they would be qualified to do what I do."

Two days later, as they awaited the results, Furman wrote a letter of thanks to Morrison, saying that she was "only just recovering from my traumatic 'Mahon' experience." She told Morrison of a party at which she and about eighty cheering friends had hung Mahon in effigy and that "[t]he Women's Movement loves you! Hubbard House loves you! I love you! And we are all very grateful for your help and kindness, and understanding of the woman's plight here. ... By the way, the women were smitten (Jee-Suz isn't he handsome???) but I assured them that you were a happily married man)." It was nice to be so appreciated, but it would be nicer still to win. That wasn't in the cards. On August 17, 1978, Judge Revels issued the Report of the Referee. It was a disaster and went way beyond what even the bar had requested. Hadeed summarized the report for Morrison, who was by this time at Harvard Law School to teach for the year.

The referee found that Furman had been engaged in the unauthorized practice of law for three years, and he recommended that she be held in contempt and enjoined from typing legal papers, filling blanks on legal forms or giving oral or written advice. This amounted to a full-scale retreat from the Florida Supreme Court's small step forward in *Brumbaugh*, which at least allowed written advice and directions. Not a good omen for their aim of getting the court to liberalize that decision. The referee also recommended that "any self-filer who utilizes a secretarial service for assistance be charged with committing a fraud upon the Court by pretending to represent themselves, and therefore, should be subjected to disciplinary action by the Court." Hadeed told Morrison of a recent case in which Judge Revels had confiscated the pleadings and refused to grant the divorce because Furman's office had prepared the papers. There was only one small bit of good news to report. "Judge Revels chastised the bar indirectly by urging the court to increase legal aid services, to have lawyers moderate their fees to reflect the client's ability to pay and the amount of work involved and to take more cases on a *pro bono* basis for destitute wives."

Morrison wrote back a couple weeks later after reading Revels' report. He sounded a less defeated note. "I think we got out about as well as possible. He has plainly added support for our contention that the shortage of lawyers willing to serve for reasonable or no fees has created a serious problem which is a necessary predicate to our position." Morrison also remarked that the referee's "overt hostility" to Furman in both his rulings, during examination of the witnesses and in his decision to highlight in his report only the adverse comments made by any witness "undercuts much of the sting in his position." Moreover, since they had never been given an opportunity to brief the issues (like the contempt citation) that he did pass on, Morrison felt confident that they would do better after having the opportunity to brief them before the state Supreme Court.

On February 9, Morrison traveled to Tallahassee to argue the case before the Florida Supreme Court. Once again he defended against the bar's charges by seeking modification or clarification of *Brumbaugh*, and by asserting that the state's unauthorized practice rules could not constitutionally be applied to preclude her from assisting indigents seeking a divorce. He fared no better there.

On May 10, 1979, the court issued its opinion concluding that Furman had been engaged in the unauthorized practice of law. The court ignored the request for clarification or modification of *Brumbaugh*. It simply repeated what it had said there and announced, "Our directions could not have been clearer." Morrison and Hadeed had spent nearly two-thirds of their brief arguing their constitutional claim—that due process required the state to either provide a lawyer for indigent clients seeking a divorce from a state judge or allow people like Furman to provide the necessary help. The court "failed to devote even a sentence to refuting it." Even more serious from Furman's perspective was that the court found that she was in contempt of court and directed the parties to submit further briefing on how she should be punished. Immediately, Morrison and Hadeed filed a motion for rehearing, objecting to the contempt finding and any punishment against Furman on due process and fairness grounds. The case had been tried under Florida's civil injunction rules, not its criminal contempt rules, which differed considerably in the amount of self-protection afforded a witness. They also again requested a clarification of *Brumbaugh*, pointing out that the Florida Bar itself had made a similar request, and furthermore asked the court to address the constitutional claims they had raised. For six months, Furman and they waited.

Finally, in November 1979, the court issued a brief order that made no changes other than to remove the references to contempt and eliminate any punishment. At least Furman could breathe free, but her ability to carry on her work and her goal of getting the unauthorized practice rules liberalized were lost unless they carried on. The only option at that point was an appeal to the U.S. Supreme Court. For this route they had to stick to the constitutional issue, as jurisdiction on a state matter such as this could be found in federal court only if there were a federal right. The right involved here, the right to obtain a divorce, had been ruled on by the high court as being the equivalent of the right to marry, which is a fundamental right that states, under the Fourteenth Amendments' due process and equal protection clauses, cannot deny.

While working on the appeal, Morrison received a helpful tidbit from a colleague at Harvard Law School, who wrote of an October 9, 1979, decision by the Court of the European Community he had heard about at a colloquium in Florence. It was a great find that Morrison quickly incorporated into his appeal brief: "The European Court of Human Rights ... concluded that Ireland had violated fundamental human rights by requiring a person seeking a judicial separation to pay for the cost of an attorney when she was financially unable to do so. In so ruling, the Court noted that her theoretical right to represent herself was not dispositive because it does not provide 'an effective right of access' due to the practical difficulties involved in *pro se* representation. ... If international rights are violated by such a denial, appellant has surely presented a substantial question as to whether the United States Constitution forbids such a deprivation as well." Powerful persuasion, Morrison hoped.

On November 30, the appeal (in the form of a Jurisdictional Statement) was filed. "This appeal," Morrison wrote, "raises the question of whether a state may constitutionally apply its otherwise valid rules prohibiting the unauthorized practice of law to preclude indigents from utilizing lay services that are essential to exercise their fundamental right to obtain a divorce." Hadeed spoke with the Florida Bar attorney to see when the bar planned to respond to the appeal. The first problem was that none of the bar attorneys were admitted to practice before the U.S. Supreme Court, so they had to apply for admission. The bar's attorneys were unsure how to proceed. They had two options, to file a motion to dismiss the appeal or, alternately, to affirm the Florida decision. Hadeed noted that "they have not decided as a tactical matter which to do, failing to recognize that they probably should do both." So Morrison and Hadeed and Furman waited.

In February, the U.S. Supreme Court dismissed the appeal "for want of a federal question." Morrison was surprised, but there was not much they could do at that point. The case for now was over. But Furman's troubles with the Florida Bar were just beginning, and what lay ahead would be far more traumatic than what she had been through so far.

For the next two and a half years, Furman continued to try to serve her clients. Hadeed provided periodic advice concerning compliance with the injunction that limited her actions. Unbeknownst to them, however, the bar was busy investigating Furman. Later court documents show that the bar spent $2,836 on a private investigator (a retired FBI agent) trying to prove that she was violating the state Supreme Court injunction.

On September 17, 1982, the Florida Bar filed a petition with the Florida Supreme Court, requesting that it issue a ruling to show cause why Furman should not be held in indirect criminal contempt for six alleged violations of the court's 1979 order. Two months later the court issued the show cause order. Circuit Judge A.C. Soud Jr. was designated to hear the case. While the case was in the pretrial stage, the Florida Bar filed a second petition, which alleged ten additional violations. Later in his brief to the court in the case, Morrison noted that the bar had not followed the court's rules for filing petitions for indirect criminal contempt. The court rule states that "circuit committees shall conduct investigations of unauthorized practice of law" and make a "prompt written report of its investigation and findings to the Standing Committee on Unauthorized Practice of Law." Neither step was taken. The bar attorney, acting solo, filed the additional charges. The referee would "characterize these omissions as 'Bar Irregularities' and 'technical deviation[s]' which may be overlooked." Court rules were applied far more leniently to attorneys than to Furman, it would seem.

It was back to court—an unsettling prospect this time, since violation of a court order allowed for a fine of up to $2,500 and five months imprisonment, or both. Since there were sixteen separate alleged violations, for any one of which she could get the maximum sentence, potentially Furman could be jailed for more than six and a half years. She sought a jury trial, arguing that if she were to be tried before a referee (most are retired judges) given her "acrimonious relationship with the Bar, the local judiciary and the Justices of the Supreme Court of Florida, the risk of unfairness [would be] intolerably high." After all, the complaints against her were filed, "not by disgruntled clients, but by judges sitting in the same court as the Referee (and a few by lawyers who practice before those judges), and a number of judges had publicly expressed personal interest in the outcome of the proceeding" against Furman.

Furman and Hadeed felt certain due process required a jury of her peers. To this end they filed a motion for a stay with the Florida Supreme Court. It was denied without opinion. Trial before the referee, Judge Soud, lasted a day and a half. The bar questioned its witnesses (all former clients of Furman, none of whom had complained about her service). The experience of one of the witnesses (a local disc jockey who faced a child support suit by his ex-wife for a child he was sure he had not fathered) was reported in a 1984 article on the Furman case.

> "A lawyer went to court with me twice," says Johnson. "He wanted to charge me $100 a visit. But after he saw the way the case was going he said he could win it for me because he had worked (formerly) in the judge's chambers. I'm not sure what he was trying to say. He said it could cost me $750 to get the matter settled. I went to Mrs. Furman, and she gave me the courage to fight it on my own."

> He had a laboratory perform a blood test and disproved paternity charges. When the Florida Bar called him a few weeks later, he told investigators his problems were with lawyers, not Furman.

> "I told them I had no intention of filing any kind of complaint against Furman. I wasn't even going to talk to them, until they kept calling my house. They called and called and called," he says. "I finally agreed to go down and answer some questions."

> Johnson said he never got a chance during Furman's two-day hearing before Soud to tell his version of the story. "The lawyers directed their questions at me, and I never got a chance to say what I felt. I believe the lady is right. I feel that lawyers can be a ripoff."

After the bar completed its case, Morrison and Furman had to decide if she would take the stand. Failure to testify on her own behalf might seriously prejudice her case. Their intent, if the referee ruled against them, was to appeal to the Florida Supreme Court and, if necessary, to the U.S. Supreme Court again—this time under the requirement of the Sixth Amendment of the U.S. Constitution that "[i]n all criminal prosecutions, the accused shall enjoy the right to a speedy and public trial, by an impartial jury of the State and district wherein the crime shall have been committed." If their appeal were successful, a second trial, this time by jury, would be held. Morrison feared that Furman's testifying now "would give the bar a significant advantage at retrial before a jury." They decided against her taking the stand.

The referee set a schedule for briefing. Oral argument was set for August 15. At the conclusion of that argument, Morrison asked the referee if, "in the event that he made a recommendation of a finding of guilty, he would provide the parties with his written report prior to the hearing on mitigation" in order to allow them to prepare adequately. If guilt were found, Furman might need to testify on her own behalf if the recommended punishment were severe. The referee refused. On October 10, the decision was announced recommending that Furman be found guilty of indirect criminal contempt on every one of the twelve charges on which the bar had presented evidence (on four of the sixteen, it had not). In fact, Soud had even made two findings that the bar had not requested—the first, that Furman was "motivated by monetary gain," and the second, that she had violated the court's order "willfully and maliciously." Morrison asked for a short recess so that he could read the full findings and recommendations before the mitigation stage of the hearing proceeded. (Mitigation hearings provide an opportunity for the defendant found guilty to enter evidence on her own behalf that might persuade the court to lessen the punishment.)

When Morrison read the twenty-eight-page document, he discovered that it already included "detailed written findings regarding mitigation and aggravation, even though respondent had not yet been given an opportunity to present her case on this issue." This contravened the requirements of the court's own rules. Again, regulations of the court seemed not to apply to the bar or the court, only to Furman. The worst part of it all was that Judge Soud had already decided that only jail would be an appropriate punishment. The only thing not filled in was how many months she should be incarcerated. He also wrote that she should serve her time in the state prison, rather than in the county jail. It seemed clear that mounting a mitigating circumstances defense would be futile before this referee. Furman did not testify. Judge Soud then recommended four months incarceration.

Morrison appealed to the Florida Supreme Court as the only option. Though much of their argument was directed at securing a jury trial, Morrison left no stone unturned, including arguments about the bar's failure to follow court rules on the second set of charges and the referee's disregard of the court rules on mitigation. In concluding his brief to that court, Morrison wrote:

> Perhaps [Furman] is fortunate that Judge Soud's conduct removed any doubt that his mind was closed to her claim of good faith reliance on the advice of counsel on the meaning of *Brumbaugh* and *Furman I* and that he would disbelieve anything and everything that she said, no matter what supporting evidence she adduced.

> But as a result, it is now clear that his recommended punishment must be rejected entirely because of his obvious unwillingness to base it on the record before him. Indeed, his conclusion on the recommended sentence is like the thirteenth stroke of the clock, ineluctably rendering all that has gone before it unbelievable.

In April 1984, the Florida Supreme Court ruled against Furman on all counts. The only positive note was a reduction in the punishment by allowing ninety days of the four months to be suspended if she did not violate the court's 1979 order and to allow her time to be served in the Duval County jail rather than in the state penitentiary. In its decision, the court barely addressed what had been the focus of their brief, her due process claim to a trial by jury. Moreover, the court assessed costs of $7,802 against her. Furman was going to have to pay all the expenses of the bar's witch-hunt against her, including $2,836 for the investigator. The only option now was appeal to the U.S. Supreme Court. Since the state court had denied (on July 11) a motion to stay her jail sentence while they appealed, the first order of business was to keep her out of jail.

Morrison filed an emergency application for a stay with the U.S. Supreme Court. On August 8, Justice Lewis F. Powell ordered the stay. Their brief seeking review of the Florida Supreme Court decision was filed on August 6. On October 29, 1984, the U.S. Supreme Court announced that it would not take the case, citing a lack of "a substantial Federal question." An effort to get the Florida Supreme Court to eliminate the jail sentence was denied on November 13, and she was ordered to surrender to serve her sentence on November 15. The only court left now was the court of public opinion, and that is where they won the battle to keep Furman out of jail.

National press coverage of the Furman case had been considerable during its long progression through the courts. Mike Wallace did a segment on her case for CBS's *60 Minutes* just after Soud's ruling in *Furman II*. Furman also appeared on the *Phil Donahue Show*, NBC's *Today*, ABC's *Good Morning America* and many other radio and television shows. Furman's cause would not have gained such national attention without the drama of her court case. And, though she lost in court, the problem of affordable legal representation had a lot more public notice and debate than it otherwise was likely to have garnered.

Many legal publications focused on her and the problems of legal representation for poor and middle-class citizens. For example, an assessment of a number of state bars' unauthorized practice committees published in 1981 by the *Stanford Law Review*, concluded that in the seven states their study covered, these committees operated to protect the business of their bar association members—to protect lawyers' incomes, not the public. The study also noted that seven states had already abolished their unauthorized practice of law committees.

In just two days, despite the support in the press and public, this fifty-seven-year-old grandmother would have to go to jail for trying to help those who could not afford justice. The powerful Florida Bar "got her," but in doing so its own shortcomings were publicized in editorial and news pages across the country. One editorial stated:

> In the case of Miss Furman, the word to the Florida Bar is that its image has suffered far more than any pecuniary loss it might have felt as a result of her activities. It looks to be a pretty mean bunch of lawyers.

Editorial cartoons were even more pointed. One cartoon depicted a posse (one rider labeled "lawyer" and the horses' rumps of two others labeled "FLA SUPREME COURT" and "FLA BAR") as it surrounds Furman (who sits astride a horse with noose around neck). The lawyer is saying, "We declare this a legal trial and pronounce you guilty." Furman sent this one to Morrison with this note: "Both Bar and Court are horses' asses! I love it. R."

One supporter wrote that "Rosemary Furman has become a symbol in the fight to open our system of justice to all ... to the poor, the illiterate—to the man on the street." The public stood behind her throughout her fight. There were "Free Rosemary" rallies; "Citizens For Furman" fliers; a national campaign to rally support sponsored by HALT (a Washington, D.C., lawyer reform group); mounds of letters; and even a song in her honor (sung to the tune of *The Battle Hymn of the Republic* at one of the rallies).

> Oh, mine eyes have seen the twisting
> By the bastions of the law;
> Their high fees and other antics
> Stretch our nerves till they are raw.
> The courts should be for the people,
> But the lawyers are the flaw,
> And the Bar goes marching on
> Glory, glory to Rosemary!
> Stop the Bar from marching on.

Her supporters flooded Florida Governor Bob Graham's office with letters and calls urging him to act, for the only avenue left was an appeal for clemency. On November 14, the day after the Florida Supreme Court refused to reconsider the thirty-day jail sentence, Morrison wrote to the governor seeking a reprieve of her sentence for sixty days to enable her to file an application for clemency as set out in the Florida Constitution (a process that requires a majority vote of the Clemency Board, which is made up of the six elected members of the Florida Cabinet and the Governor). A thirty-day reprieve was granted. On November 27, the Cabinet and Governor voted unanimously (7-0) to grant executive clemency, thus erasing the thirty-day jail sentence.

But even with that, the case was not yet over. There was still the problem of $7,802 the court said she owed the bar for the costs of its case against her. In August, Morrison had filed a "Motion in Opposition" in the Florida Supreme Court. It was not until May 1985 that court finally ruled and, although it did reduce the amount owed to $2,805, she still had to pay. "How can they be called court costs when there's never been a trial?" Furman asked.

The loss did not deter either the pit bull or the public interest lawyer. Morrison pursued a class action lawsuit on behalf of Furman's clients against the Florida Bar and state Supreme Court on lawyer-less access to the courts (an effort to get the rules on unauthorized practice liberalized to allow for less expensive legal services for people who need them), and Furman spoke at Kiwanis, Rotary and other organizations around the state, bringing her message about problems in the legal system to any and all who would listen. The Florida Bar responded to the press coverage by launching a $25,000 public relations campaign. It also took a few small steps such as introducing easier forms for do-it-yourself, no-fault divorces and conducting some studies that showed just how bad legal services for the poor in Florida really were.

Despite the loss in *Furman*, the Litigation Group's "policing the profession" cases during the 1970s resulted in some of its most impressive victories, adding considerably to the recognition and respect the public interest law firm was rapidly gaining.

14

Fighting Reagan Deregulation

Ronald Reagan's election may have been anathema to Public Citizen, but it was seen as a blessing by the auto industry. Any doubt that the new president would live up to his oft-repeated campaign promise to cut back on government regulation was dispelled when on January 30, just ten days after being sworn in, he announced a sixty-day freeze on all pending regulations. A few days later, the association that represents the auto industry wrote to the new occupant of the White House: "On behalf of the companies that manufacture more than 99 percent of all domestically produced motor vehicles we are writing to you on a matter of grave concern." The five-page letter laid out a laundry list of requests described as critical to preventing disaster in the depressed domestic auto industry and concluded by noting "delight" with "the Administration's desire to work with us on these urgent issues." Among the requests were: (a) the elimination of "excessive and counterproductive government regulations"; (b) the continuation of "the temporary moratorium on the issuance of new regulations"; and (c) a "reexamination of antitrust policy." As part of the last item, the letter urged the administration to withdraw a consent decree that dealt with anti-competitive activities of automobile companies.

In the 1950s, domestic auto manufacturers had conspired to restrain the development and marketing of exhaust control technology. As described in a Department of Justice memorandum, "the crux of the alleged conspiracy was an industry-wide patent licensing scheme, pursuant to which these manufacturers agreed to refrain from competing in developing emission control devices by pooling present and future technological developments, and by refusing to accept licenses under third-party patents unless all manufacturers were awarded identical rights." In other words, all the car companies got together to quash any and all innovations in pollution control and ensure that if technology did advance, it could not be used by one company to achieve a competitive advantage. If they all agreed not to work on the technology and to keep promising technological developments secret, then they would not be forced by the government to install new exhaust systems. Items like stereo radios, fancy leather upholstery or annual design changes that ratcheted up car prices were acceptable because they boosted profits. But industry executives were sure that purchasers would balk at paying much for pollution-control devices that would be buried under the hood. They saw little or no additional profit from such features, and the added cost could potentially reduce sales.

A rapidly growing smog problem led the California legislature to pass a law in 1959 requiring that new cars sold in the state be equipped with exhaust controls "one year after the state certified the effectiveness of at least two workable control devices." At that point, as the Justice Department memorandum notes, the conspiracy among the auto companies "took a more ominous turn." The companies "allegedly agreed to delay installation of existing emission control devices, forestall development of improvements to such devices, and deliberately misrepresent the industry's progress to the California Air Resources Board." In 1964, four non-automotive companies developed devices that worked and California certified them. General Motors, Ford and Chrysler abruptly announced that they could install their own anti-smog devices in 1966 models. By using their own devices, the automakers ensured they would not have to pay for the devices designed by the non-industry companies. But it clearly showed that the automakers had been lying to the California board. They obviously had the capacity to develop and install the technology to meet California's mandate, even as they were claiming that they did not.

The Justice Department filed an antitrust case against the companies. But for reasons that remain unclear, the government chose to file a civil complaint rather than a criminal indictment (*United States v. Motor Vehicle Manufacturers Association*). On October 29, 1969, the case was settled by what became know as the smog consent decree. The decree required the auto companies to terminate the elaborate cross-licensing and patent pooling arrangement and to make all technological developments so licensed or patented available to everyone without any royalty payments. It also prohibited the auto companies from conspiring: (a) to prevent, limit or delay development or installation of emission control devices; (b) to restrict publicity of their research concerning such devices; (c) to condition their acquisition of patent rights upon the availability of such rights to other defendants; (d) to jointly assess the value of any third parties' patent rights; and (e) to cross-license any rights to patents for future inventions. Two other restraints were included but limited to ten years unless extended by the court. One enjoined the auto companies from agreeing to exchange confidential information relating to applied emission control research to ensure that the industry would not try to coordinate development of emission control devices efforts "to the pace of the industry laggard." The other enjoined the companies from presenting a common industry position concerning advancements in vehicle emission control or safety technology to regulatory agencies to ensure that the government would not be misled into adopting standards that were more lenient than technology would dictate.

In October 1978, the Justice Department filed a motion in the U.S. district court in California, where the original case had been filed and settled ten years earlier, for a ten-year extension of both soon-to-expire provisions. Supported by affidavits and documents supplied by the Environmental Protection Agency (EPA), the National Highway Traffic Safety Administration (NHTSA) and the California Air Resources Board, Justice argued that "there is a continuing need for competition in the development of emission control devices and that these provisions served to ensure such competition." In March 1979, the district court extended the provisions for another ten years. Four months later, the court changed its mind. The reasons given were: (1) that national interest in fuel efficiency required a reduction in competition in producing emission control devices; and (2) that a reduction in competition was now justified because circumstances had completely changed (though what had changed was not spelled out). On the Justice Department's appeal, the Ninth Circuit Court of Appeals reversed the district court's decision but directed the lower court to address the question of whether some provisions of the now-extended decree should be modified, which the district court did. That is where the case stood when the Reagan team took over.

On March 2, 1981, Lloyd Cutler, counsel for the big-four auto companies (American Motors, Chrysler, Ford and General Motors) and their industry association (Motor Vehicle Manufacturers Association), wrote to the new attorney general, William French Smith, asking him to take steps to vacate the consent decree and withdraw the government's appeal of the district court's modifications.

On April 13, Reagan said, "The American automobile industry is in serious trouble." He then listed six steps his administration promised to take "in aid of this industry." Fifth on the list was a promise that the attorney general would move quickly to "seek the lifting of certain prohibitions against cooperative ventures and joint presentations before regulatory agencies." His choice of the words "cooperative ventures" and "joint presentations" made the industry actions that had led to the decree appear innocuous. A few weeks later, Cutler sent another letter to Justice, elaborating on why the consent decree should be terminated. By June 24, Cutler had sent a draft letter for Justice to send to the judge who was considering the consent decree on remand. The letter began: "At the request of the President of the United States, the Department of Justice has undertaken a review of the continued need for the provisions of the 1969 consent decree ... [and] has concluded that extension ... is no longer necessary or appropriate." Justice memos later obtained by the Litigation Group provide evidence of regular communication and cooperation between Cutler and department attorneys in developing the strategy for getting rid of the decree. Of course, no one at the Center for Auto Safety (CAS) or the Litigation Group knew about this collaboration at the time. On August 3, 1981, the Justice Department filed a single-sentence stipulation in the California district court to withdraw the government's appeal, thereby ending the case and leaving the department free to end the consent decree as well.

At CAS, Clarence Ditlow was incensed. Though Justice and the automakers were close to a resolution, Ditlow figured that if he acted fast maybe he could derail it. A litigation strategy was the only hope, and David Vladeck was tagged to handle the matter. Since CAS and Ditlow were not parties to the original smog case that resulted in the consent decree, they could not ask the court to do anything unless they officially intervened—and the judge had control over that. Vladeck filed a motion on Ditlow's behalf to intervene. Their legal argument was that the stipulation was improper because the government had failed to comply with its obligations under the Antitrust Procedures and Penalties Act to give the public notice of its action and the opportunity to comment on the propriety of it. What was done in secret should have been open for public view and comment—basic requirements to hold a representative government accountable to the people. This sort of visibility was clearly mandated in antitrust law for the process of negotiating consent decrees in the first place, but what they were seeking was to get the court to interpret the law to require similar transparency for the process of modifying or eliminating such decrees. The automobile companies "went berserk," Vladeck recalls. "They had been promised this, and here I was—this young nobody—trying to strike daggers through the heart of America's premier industry." While the court was considering the intervention motion, the Justice Department and the automobile manufacturers submitted a joint motion to modify the entire decree, seeking to eliminate many provisions and phase out the remainder over a five-year period.

"On a number of occasions, while I was working on the case, I talked with a young associate at Wilmer, Cutler & Pickering [Lloyd Cutler's firm] who was working on their brief and as the date for argument approached I mentioned that I was looking forward to seeing her in California," Vladeck says. To his surprise she replied that she was probably not going. He asked who would be arguing the case. "When she replied that Lloyd probably would, I was amazed. This was a fairly routine case—a simple intervention motion and a narrow legal question about notice. Was the big guy really going to wade in?" It might not have seemed to be a big legal issue to Vladeck, but to the powerful companies on the other side it was very important. "God isn't available, so Lloyd will have to do," she told Vladeck.

Facing an argument against Cutler was a bit intimidating to Vladeck, because of antagonism between Nader and Cutler. "Ralph viewed Lloyd as the embodiment of everything that is wrong with the Washington legal establishment, and Cutler's view of Nader was no less negative," Vladeck says. Still, Vladeck was emboldened by his winning performance before the Supreme Court in *Barrentine* in January. In mid-October, Vladeck went to California for the argument. Following a restless night in a cheap hotel, he set out on foot early the next morning for the district court's old WPA-era building. He sat down alone at the big plaintiff's table. "We rarely have sufficient funds to send more than one attorney for out-of-town cases. But we are always confident that the level of preparation and grilling we subject each other to makes us worthy opponents," he said. Sitting at the opposing table "was a phalanx of three-piece suits from the individual auto companies, from Wilmer and Cutler, and from the

Department of Justice. A half-dozen pair of eyes looked at me like I was lunch meat soon to be devoured." The courtroom was packed.

Vladeck was scheduled to argue first. "I argued my position for about twenty minutes with no questions from the judge." Then it was Cutler's turn. "Lloyd looked perfect. He was the embodiment of central casting's senior partner—white-haired, a perfectly starched shirt, a Yale tie, a beautiful, beautiful suit. But about ten minutes into his argument, the judge leaned over and said something to the effect of, 'What sense does your position make?'" Cutler tried to answer, but, as Vladeck remembers it, the judge said, "Mr. Cutler, I think I understand your position." Such a comment, says Vladeck, "is a kiss-of-death signal from a judge. Cutler did not seem to notice, though, and plowed right on with the same line of reasoning. I got up and made a last point and then said that it seemed to me that the questions from the bench had framed the issue well."

Vladeck was flagging a cab at the curb when a long line of limos arrived to pick up the other side's lawyers. One of the opposing lawyers congratulated him on a good job and noted that the auto companies had "sent their plane" to take them home. Vladeck would be taking the red-eye. "Limos and private planes! At that point I felt a headache coming on, so I picked up my bag and walked to a nearby drug store." As he searched for a headache remedy, "this guy came in with the biggest gun I ever saw, robbed the clerk behind the counter and then ran out." A stunned Vladeck emerged with his bottle of pills, walked up to the register and offered up a five-dollar bill. "The clerk said, 'I can't make change. That fucking bastard took all my money. Just take the pills.' So I walked out and headed for the airport and home."

A week later the judge's ruling came: "The Department of Justice failed to comply with the procedures set forth in the Antitrust Procedures and Penalties Act ... and it is therefore ordered that the order and stipulation of August 3, 1981 ... are hereby vacated and set aside." To change the consent decree, the Justice Department would have to give fair notice and an opportunity for public comment. It was a win of sorts, although temporary. The government needed only to follow the correct procedure. A notice was published in the *Federal Register* describing the action the government planned to take and allowing a sixty-day period for public comment.

To comment effectively, though, Ditlow and CAS needed access to the reasoning and evidence supporting the termination of the consent decree and withdrawal of the government's appeal to extend the two expired provisions. Ditlow wrote to Justice requesting "all documents relating to the government's decision to seek modification of the consent decree." And because the comment period was only sixty days and the clock was already ticking, Ditlow asked that the request be handled expeditiously. At first the department stalled and then denied the request, claiming that all twenty-two pages of correspondence between Justice attorneys and the auto companies and their attorneys and all three hundred and fifty-two pages of draft stipulations and modified consent decrees were exempt from disclosure under Exemption 7(a), which covered investigative records "compiled for law enforcement purposes, the release of which would interfere with law enforcement proceeding." When the comment period expired, the consent decree was modified. The auto companies got what they wanted. But it was not the end of the matter.

Ditlow and Vladeck were certain that they had a right to see all the documents, so they sued under the Freedom of Information Act (FOIA). As Vladeck wrote in his brief on June 25, 1982: "the Department is arguing that documents relating to the elimination of existing sanctions are somehow equivalent to documents relating to an enforcement proceeding. This is, at best, a perverse interpretation of Exemption 7 and should not be accepted by the Court. ... To argue that a joint effort to dismantle a consent decree is tantamount to an investigation is nothing less than disingenuous." Although it would take another year to get a ruling on the matter, in the end it was a slam-dunk win. On June 16, 1983, the court ruled that "none of the documents withheld by the DOJ are entitled to the protection of Exemption 7(A)." The thirty-six page opinion adopted nearly all of the arguments Vladeck advanced in his brief. In a letter, Vladeck urged District Judge Thomas F. Hogan to publish the memorandum opinion. "As you know, this case established for the first time that certain documents submitted to, or prepared by, the Department of Justice in connection with the modification of an antitrust consent decree are subject to the mandatory disclosure provisions of the Freedom of Information Act," Vladeck wrote. This was a case with broad implications and the first time a court had ruled on the matter. If the decision were not officially published, as many decisions are not, it could not be used by other attorneys as a precedent in future cases. Courts rule on many matters not considered important enough to publish, and Vladeck wanted to be sure that this case not meet that fate. On this point, he also won. The case was published as 576 F. Supp. 739. So, though they lost on the substantive issue of the Smog Consent Decree, they made it possible for the public to find out about future government negotiations to protect industry before it was too late to have any influence on the matter at all.

* * * * *

The auto industry was not alone in asking and receiving special favors from the newly elected Reagan team. Among many others were the chemical manufacturers and dozens of industries that use hazardous materials in the workplace. One of their targets was a regulation published in the last days of the Carter administration called the "hazards communication standard." The "right-to-know rule," as it was dubbed by its supporters, had a long and tortuous path, with the Health Research Group (HRG) and its leader Sidney Wolfe there pushing it forward every step of the way. In all, it took three court cases and eleven years to get a final rule in place.

When it was passed in 1970, the Occupational Safety and Health Act included a provision mandating that the National Institute of Safety and Health

(NIOSH) conduct research on hazardous materials used in the workplace and advise the Occupational Safety and Health Administration (OSHA) on appropriate action. Over the next four years NIOSH found that "25 million workers, or one in four, were potentially exposed to one or more of the nearly 8,000 hazards" identified at the time. In more than five thousand worksites NIOSH visited as part of its survey, eighty-five thousand individual trade-name products were identified. These products accounted for 70 percent of all recorded exposures by workers. Yet in 90 percent of the cases where trade-name products containing hazardous chemicals were being used, neither the employer nor the employees knew the identity of the chemicals in those products. Not only were employees being exposed to dangerous chemicals, they did not even know what chemicals were in the workplace so they might best protect themselves. Without the knowledge of what the dangers were, workers could not decide if the job was worth the risk.

Producers of chemical products, however, claimed that the ingredients were "trade secrets" that should be protected. If ingredients had to be listed, competitors might replicate their products and their profits would vanish. In 1974, NIOSH finally completed its study and recommended that OSHA issue a standard requiring employers to inform employees of "the nature of the chemical hazards, both potential and actual, to which they may be exposed." NIOSH specifically addressed the "trade secret" issue. "It is clear that the major objectives of the OSHA Act override narrow self-interest on the part of manufacturers. No trade secret can justify exposing great numbers of American workers to cancer-causing agents or other toxic chemicals. Any trade-name product containing a substance known to be hazardous or a carcinogen must be clearly labeled so that precautions may be taken." OSHA took no action.

In 1976, a House subcommittee held oversight hearings that resulted in a "strongly worded report calling for immediate action by OSHA to ensure that employees be made aware of their exposure to potentially toxic materials." At about the same time, Wolfe and U.S. Representative Andrew Maguire petitioned OSHA to issue a standard requiring employers to inform employees of the generic names of all chemicals found in the workplace. Still, little happened until after Jimmy Carter was elected president in 1976. Then OSHA published advanced notice of rulemaking, requesting public comments on whether a standard on identification of hazardous materials should be developed. It did not necessarily mean OSHA would propose a standard, but it was a good start.

Moving at glacial speed, OSHA took four more years to gather comments and fashion a proposed rule. Wolfe tried to speed the pace by filing a complaint, but in early 1980 the court ruled that OSHA could not be compelled to act. Finally, at nearly the last possible moment—after Carter had lost the presidency and just four days before Reagan was sworn in—OSHA published a notice of proposed rulemaking in the *Federal Register*. Less than three weeks later, as the first official action of newly appointed Labor Secretary Raymond Donovan, the proposed rule was withdrawn "for further consideration of regulatory alternatives." OSHA is part of the Labor Department and therefore subject to political direction from its secretary. Later evidence revealed that the president of the Chemical Manufacturers Association had written to Donovan attacking the hazards communication standard as an "enormously expensive and unnecessarily burdensome regulation." The rule was just one of hundreds of proposed regulations targeted by a regulatory review process led by then-Vice President George Bush and pushed by Reagan's political appointees at the White House Office of Management and Budget. Many court challenges by Litigation Group attorneys and others resulted. Among these was a challenge to a rule dealing specifically with ethylene oxide. Vladeck's success in that case played a major role in elevating him to lead counsel for a large group of plaintiffs and *amici* in the hazards communication standard case.

* * * * *

Ethylene oxide is a toxic gas used as a sterilizing agent, fumigant, pesticide and intermediate in the manufacturing of products including automotive antifreeze, textiles, films, bottles and detergents. It is a critical component in the sterilization process used in hospitals. But unprotected exposure to certain levels of ethylene oxide can cause cancer. In 1971, OSHA set a maximum exposure limit of 50 parts of ethylene oxide per million parts of air (ppm) as a time-weighted measure over an eight-hour working shift. In 1979, two studies examining workers breathing ethylene oxide in their workplaces at levels well under the 50 ppm limit found unexpectedly high cancer rates. Then in January 1981, the results of what is known as the Bushy Run study were published, showing that ethylene oxide at levels well under the OSHA limit caused leukemia and other cancers in rats.

Reacting to the new data, Sidney Wolfe petitioned OSHA in August 1981, asking that the agency issue an emergency temporary standard lowering the level of allowable exposure for workers to 1 ppm. In the petition Wolfe, wrote that "according to the National Institute for Occupational Safety and Health (NIOSH), over 100,000 workers are now exposed to this deadly chemical." He also pointed out that "the danger is so apparent that a small number of chemical production companies have set their own much lower limits of exposure." Texaco Chemical Co., for example, set its own standard at 2 ppm. But the vast majority of exposed workers remained subject to the old 50 ppm standard. Wolfe knew that persuading an administration "hell-bent on getting government off the back of business" to undertake an expedited regulatory action was not going to be easy. But in this case, the evidence seemed so compelling, the danger so severe. Moreover, the OSHA law required the agency to issue an emergency standard if necessary to prevent grave danger to workers exposed to hazardous materials in the workplace. On September 26, 1981, Assistant Labor Secretary Thorne G. Auchter wrote to Wolfe: "Although there is important new health data on the carcinogenic risks of EtO [ethylene oxide], the information available to the agency as to current levels of exposure indicates that an Emergency Temporary Standard is not 'necessary' for employee protection under existing circumstances." Wolfe turned to the Litigation Group and David Vladeck.

Vladeck needed a legal hook on which to hang his case. The challenge was really one of agency delay—that is, that the agency was delaying action unreasonably. Some laws have built-in hammers to force an agency to act by a certain date or within a certain period, but the Occupational Safety and Health Act had no such provision. And without such a requirement, past case law indicated that courts would defer to agency expertise and agency discretion as to whether action was needed. Up til this time, there was simply "no species of litigation," as Vladeck puts it, "that claimed 'unreasonable delay' as a court-enforceable means to get an agency to exercise its discretion under the law." So Vladeck and the other Litigation Group attorneys brainstormed. "We literally had to make things up as we went along, not having any idea if they would fly or not. We didn't even know quite where to file such a case."

They filed in the U.S. District Court for the District of Columbia, seeking an order "directing defendants to comply with the statutory duties ... by issuing an emergency temporary standard significantly reducing the permissible levels of worker exposure to ethylene oxide." They argued that the refusal to issue the emergency standard was "arbitrary and capricious, and constitutes agency action unlawfully withheld." The "arbitrary and capricious" standard of review is found in Section 706 (2)(A) of the Administrative Procedure Act, which sets out the scope of review that a court may undertake of an agency's rulemaking activity. It empowers a court to look over the rulemaking record to determine whether there is a reasonable connection between the evidence in the record and the rule issued. Challenges under this level of review are usually brought by business interests claiming a rule is too harsh. As the number of public interest litigation firms grew in the 1960s and 1970s, however, challenges from the other side became more frequent. Deference by the courts to agency expertise was the norm, though courts did step in to overturn agency actions as arbitrary or capricious on occasion. Vladeck's tactic was new and different, though not without legal bases. He was simply asking the court to exercise its power under another part of the Administrative Procedure Act's Section 706 that allows a reviewing court to "compel agency action unlawfully withheld or unreasonably delayed."

Vladeck's complaint, filed in court in September 1981, was a scant four pages that set out the broad contours of his case. His full brief required a lot more creativity. Vladeck worked on developing a "legal theory of unreasonable delay" over the fall of 1981 and winter of 1982. Then in early spring 1982, a package wrapped in plain brown paper arrived at 2000 P Street. Inside was the smoking gun that would make his case—a copy of an internal memo from the health scientists and technical staff of OSHA to the agency's senior regulator, the director of technical support. Vladeck read the memo with a mixture of glee and disbelief. According to what he read, Auchter, the assistant Labor secretary, had directed a joint team of professionals led by John Martonik, acting director of the department's health standards board, to review Wolfe's petition and the scientific literature on ethylene oxide and recommend what the agency should do. The review team's twelve-page memo, dated September 11, 1981 (thus obviously available to the agency before it refused to issue an emergency standard) ends with this recommendation: "It is the conclusion of the health scientists and technical staff conducting this review that recent and accumulated toxicity data on EtO exposure document a serious health hazard risk for workers, and that the current Federal PEL of 50 PPM is inadequate to protect worker health. We recommend that the Agency proceed with rulemaking by Agency option (1) Issue an Emergency Temporary Standard (ETS) followed by an immediate Regular Section 6B Rulemaking or (2) Begin Regular Section 6B Rulemaking, but decline to issue an ETS. If option (2) is chosen, then we recommend that Agency efforts in the 6B rulemaking process be expedited."

The danger was that the memo might not be authentic. If they submitted it as evidence and it proved to be a fraud, it might undercut the rest of their case. Morrison and Vladeck decided that rather than submitting the copy they had been sent, they would file a discovery petition with the court asking for any and all memoranda resulting from Wolfe's petition. "The agency went nuts," Vladeck recalls. "Their reaction was all the affirmation of the memo's validity we needed, but the question was what to do next?" The problem they faced was that the agency was claiming that the document was an internal memorandum that could not be shared, and very possibly that argument could prevail.

The case was before U.S. District Judge Barrington D. Parker, "an extremely bright, crusty conservative who did not suffer fools," Vladeck says. "The memo was loaded with statements that I was sure would curdle the blood of even the most hardened." Those included statements like this: "[T]he demonstration of persistent chromosomal abnormalities in workers exposed at levels well below the current OSHA standard raise serious concern about the risk of heritable genetic damage in humans from EtO exposure." Vladeck was certain that if the judge could read it, he would be brought to their side. He filed a motion to compel disclosure of the document but held out a compromise. If the government would show it to the judge for viewing *in camera* (by his eyes only), that would be satisfactory. The government complied. At the same time, though, the government also submitted an affidavit from Martonik to be included in the case file that was open to the public. Vladeck was furious when he read the affidavit. It was dissembling, pure and simple. But since he had not admitted that he had a copy of the original memo, he could not just attack the affidavit as a lie. He had to find some other way to object. Arguing that the affidavit amounted to "a post-hoc agency rationalization," he moved to have it struck from the record. As a back-up, he also argued that if the affidavit were to remain in the record, the original memo should be released and entered in the open record because the affidavit relied on it. His motions were denied, but it soon became clear that this judge was not taken in one bit by the agency's effort to rewrite history.

In a report to his plaintiffs after oral argument before Judge Parker on October 22, Vladeck wrote: "The argument went well; the Judge is obviously quite troubled by the Department's inaction." When the judge issued his ruling on January 5, 1983, Vladeck's observation proved correct. "He really castigated the agency and took a very hard line," says Vladeck. "And there was little doubt that the internal memorandum played big in his decision." Parker ordered that OSHA "shall promulgate within 20 days from this date an appropriate emergency temporary standard addressing worker exposure to ethylene oxide ... [and] shall report their results to the Court on or before January 31, 1983." In so ruling, the judge first noted that he was unaware of any cases reviewing the denial of a petition for an emergency standard. But, the fact that this was unprecedented did not trouble this judge: "Examination of the administrative record in this proceeding compels the conclusion that the agency's decision resulted from a clear error of judgment ... [and] could not have been based upon a proper assessment of the relevant considerations." His castigation of the agency concluded that "OSHA's decision denying the plaintiffs' petition for an emergency standard cannot withstand the 'thorough, probing, in-depth' scrutiny required under the Administrative Procedure Act. ... The record before the agency presented a solid and certain foundation showing that workers are subjected to grave health dangers from exposure to ethylene oxide at levels within the currently permissible range. ... [G]iven the record, the decision of the agency to deny the petition and implement a procedure which insured the continuing existence of the challenged standard constitutes abuse of discretion."

It was all Vladeck could have hoped for, but even more satisfying was the judge's comment about the Martonik memorandum and the after-the-fact Martonik affidavit. "A review of the document itself demonstrates that Martonik's description of the contents of the memorandum is faulty in its selectivity," wrote Judge Parker. The affidavit had mentioned only the recommendation to issue a proposed rule; it did not mention the recommendation that was listed as No. 1, to issue an emergency standard. It also failed to mention that if the proposed rule alternative were chosen, that it should be undertaken under expedited procedures.

The government filed an immediate appeal and a petition for a stay of the district court's order in the U.S. Appeals Court for the D.C. Circuit. The appeals court put the case on a fast track—an incredibly fast track. Late in the afternoon of February 5, 1983, just one month to the day after the district court ruling, the court of appeals issued an order directing both sides to file final briefs on the merits no later than 3 p.m. on February 11. Vladeck wrote again to his plaintiffs, reporting the schedule and noting the composition of the appeals panel he faced. "We have drawn," he wrote, "what is at best a mixed panel." The panel was composed of Judge Malcolm Wilkey, "known to be extremely conservative in administrative procedure cases;" Judge Ruth Ginsburg, "an able and liberal jurist;" and Chief Judge Spotswood Robinson, "labeled as a liberal in most areas, but who really occupies the middle ground on administrative law questions." Vladeck wrote that "while we did not do as well as we could have hoped given the present composition of the D.C. Court of Appeals, we do have a panel of smart, thoughtful judges." Judge Parker's "strong and favorable opinion," Vladeck concluded, "would also surely help."

On Friday, February 11, 1983, the day the briefs were due in court, it snowed in D.C.—a lot. Vladeck was not able to submit printed copies of his brief to the court or to his opponents as required because his printer had closed early. He made copies on the Xerox machine and walked them through the snow to the government attorneys and the appeals court. Late in the afternoon on February 14, just two days before oral argument, he received a copy of the government's sixty-five-page brief. It was not a very cheery Valentine. Indeed, Vladeck was astounded at how vicious it was, especially in its attacks on the district court judge: "The court's error on this issue was compounded by its blatant substitution of judgment in evaluating the record before the Secretary. ... The decision below is legally erroneous and constitutes an abuse of discretion by the lower court. ... The lower court misapprehended the holding. ... The lower court should have deferred to the rational interpretation advanced by the official charged with administering the daily operation of the statute. The refusal to do so was mistaken." The focus throughout the brief was on separation of powers. The district court was trying to take on the constitutional and legal responsibilities of the executive branch; an activist judge had vastly overstepped his bounds, the brief claimed.

The appeals court was packed on the day of oral argument. "I got peppered with questions from the bench about separation of powers issues," Vladeck recalls. Clearly the government's effort to turn the focus of the case from an abuse of discretion by the agency into one of an abuse of discretion by the court was ringing the "judicial activism" bell. Vladeck's novel administrative law case was being turned into a constitutional confrontation. Vladeck repeatedly tried to return the focus to the dangers of ethylene oxide and the department's responsibility under the OSH Act, but it was an uphill fight throughout. At one point, Vladeck recalls Judge Wilkey leaning back in his chair and interrupting him. "Well counselor, how would you feel if we modified the D.C. order to say the agency has to publish a proposed rule quickly and a final rule reasonably promptly?" the judge asked. Vladeck remembers pausing for a minute to consider the wisdom of the response that was on the tip of his tongue, then diving in: "Well, you honor, I would rather just win this case." Everyone in the courtroom cracked up and so, to his credit, did Judge Wilkey. Wilkey's question telegraphed to many the direction the court would take. The unanimous, *per curiam* (unsigned) opinion was announced just a month later. The court's decision did not uphold the district court's order to issue an emergency temporary standard. The higher court found far more discretion in the statute, inhibiting the court's power to intrude. But the higher court made quite clear that the agency's failure to act expeditiously was carrying that discretion a bit too far.

"This is a difficult case," the court noted, "which we must decide under pressing circumstances." The court pointed out that OSHA had in the past "on its own initiative, issued emergency standards which were promptly brought to court for review by industry complainants." In both cases cited in the opinion, the reviewing court had vacated the emergency standards. Thus the legitimacy of court review of emergency standards was established by precedent. "We are unaware, as was the district court," the opinion continued, "of any prior case in which a court was invited to review OSHA's denial of a petition and emergency standard. ... While it is a close question, our review of the record indicates that, in ordering an emergency standard, the most drastic measure in the Agency's standard-setting arsenal, the district court impermissibly substituted its evaluation for that of OSHA. Nonetheless, we fully agree with the district court that "OSHA has embarked upon the least responsive course short of inaction. Beyond question, despite the efforts of many companies, the record shows a significant risk that some workers, and the children they will hereafter conceive, are subject to grave danger from the employees' exposure to EtO. We therefore hold that OSHA must expedite the rulemaking in which it is now engaged. ... To assure that OSHA will give due regard to the need, urgent for some workers, for a new EtO standard, and to prevent undue protraction in OSHA's conclusion of this matter, we direct the Assistant Secretary to issue a notice of proposed rulemaking within thirty days of the date of this decision and to proceed expeditiously thereafter toward issuance of a permanent standard for EtO. While we do not set a day certain for a final rule, in view of the significant risk of grave danger to which some workers and children they may conceive are exposed, and the time OSHA has already devoted to EtO, we expect the Agency to bring this matter to a close within a year."

It was not as good as the district court win, but it still held out the promise of a club to force this slowest of slow agencies to get the job done. Though a proposed rule was issued nearly on time under the court order, the timetable for the final rule soon began to slip. In March 1984, Vladeck wrote Assistant Secretary Auchter to express his "deepest concern over what appears to be the agency's unwillingness to comply with the mandate laid down by the Court of Appeals." A full year had elapsed and the agency was still far from completing the rulemaking. Of greater concern to Vladeck was leaked information suggesting that OSHA intended to send the final rule to the OMB for review before publication. By 1984, three years into the Reagan administration, it was well known that OMB review was the kiss of death (or at least dismemberment) for regulations. Dozens of environmental and safety rules from many government agencies were bottled up in OMB, and there was no way to obtain information about their status. Efforts to seek information under FOIA had been met with a wall of resistance. Vladeck objected to the ethylene oxide rule being sent to

OMB given "the dubious legality of OMB review," but his words fell on deaf ears. While the new ethylene oxide standard languished at OMB, Vladeck and other Litigation attorneys had plenty of other battles to fight against OSHA. Indeed, by the spring of 1983, at about the same time the appeals court ordered OSHA to expedite the modification to the existing ethylene oxide standard, the hazards communication standard was returning to the front burner.

* * * * *

On March 19, 1982, thirteen months after it had withdrawn the Carter administration's proposed hazards communication regulation, the Reagan administration published a revised proposal. It was a standard of sorts, but it so drastically altered the Carter-OSHA proposal that the Health Research Group viewed it as fundamentally flawed. Not only were all non-factory workers (such as hospital and construction workers) left out of the standard's coverage, the number of chemicals covered by the rule was cut back sharply and, even more troubling, the revised proposal provided a broad trade secret exemption, in contrast to the original proposal's narrowly drawn exemption. On November 25, 1983, OSHA published a final rule. It was no better than the proposed one. At the Litigation Group, the result was no surprise.

Indeed, the very same day the final hazards communication regulation was published, Vladeck filed a challenge in the Third Circuit Court of Appeals in Philadelphia on behalf of Public Citizen and eleven other named petitioners who represented workers and community groups active in occupational safety and health issues. Public Citizen had been well aware of what sort of standard would emerge and had already lined up a group of plaintiffs who would clearly pass the standing test. Vladeck's petition stated that review of the hazards communication standard was sought "on the grounds that the standard is inconsistent" with the dictates of the OSH Act of 1970, "is not supported by substantial evidence, and is arbitrary and capricious because it fails to provide workers with adequate information relating to the hazards they are exposed to in the workplace."

Within days, a veritable flood of similar cases poured into courts around the country. On behalf of the United Steelworkers, the AFL-CIO filed in the Third Circuit just a few days later. Suits soon followed by the Flavor and Extract Manufacturers Association in the Fourth Circuit; the State of New York in the Second Circuit; the Fragrance Materials Association in the District of Columbia Circuit; the State of Illinois in the Seventh Circuit; and the Commonwealth of Massachusetts in the First Circuit. The labor secretary filed a petition with the Third Circuit requesting that all the cases be consolidated and heard there. On February 9, 1984, the Third Circuit ordered the cases consolidated and set a briefing schedule for all the parties. Soon after, Larry Gold and George Cohen, lawyers for the United Steelworkers and the AFL-CIO, invited all of the plaintiffs to a meeting to be held on March 20 at the Washington, D.C., headquarters of the union to discuss how to coordinate their briefs to ensure that all issues would be adequately addressed and that arguments would not undercut each other.

Vladeck's recent experience with the ethylene oxide rule challenge made him something of an expert on the law. The files at Public Citizen are full of letters throughout the spring of 1984 between Vladeck and other plaintiff attorneys discussing strategy. There were essentially three major issues raised by the various plaintiffs: (1) a challenge to the merits of the rule (the claim that it was arbitrary and capricious); (2) a challenge to the trade secrets provisions (that the rule afforded too much protection to companies and too little to workers); and (3) an issue of particular concern to the states—whether the new federal right-to-know standard would preempt any existing state standards that were more protective of workers. Vladeck and the United Steelworkers focused primarily on the first two, leaving the preemption issue to the state attorneys general to advance. "Essentially, as I understand it," Vladeck wrote in a memo to Morrison, "Sid [Wolfe] advocates that we urge the preemption argument ... [to] take the position that OSHA's rule cannot displace <u>stronger</u> state laws." This was the "only issue on which we might take a substantially different position from that of the AFL-CIO." Vladeck continued, stating: "I should make it clear that I do not think that the argument Sid wants to advance can be sustained under a strict reading of the OSH Act, or that it can succeed in light of the fact that there are only a handful of state provisions which are even arguably more protective than OSHA's. ... I simply do not think that the argument can be squared with the provision that Congress used to spell out federal-state relations under the OSH Act." The union attorneys recommended arguing that the OSHA standard would only preempt existing or future state standards in the manufacturing sector (since it was limited to application there) and thus all state and local laws with respect to other sectors would be preserved. Vladeck agreed that Wolfe's argument was the most defensible as a policy matter, but he simply did not think it could win. Advancing a losing proposition would take up time and potentially divert attention from their stronger arguments. In the end, his reasoning won the day; their brief did not address preemption.

Though the court originally set a tight schedule for briefing and hearing the case, the dates soon began to slip. Petitioners' briefs were due in late May and all made it in on time. Faced with the briefs of five named petitioners, two intervenors and six *amici*—in total more than three hundred pages of arguments challenging the rule—the Labor Department wrote to the court in June requesting an extension for its own brief to ninety-five pages, a request that was granted. Soon the Labor Department sought another extension. (Respondents are able to write their brief with the full argument of their opponents available to them and thus, in order to ensure fairness, court rules give petitioners the chance to submit a reply brief to respond and counter arguments after seeing the brief of respondents.) Of course, the extension for the Labor Department required an extension in the original timetable for the plaintiff reply briefs as well. All briefs were finally in by mid-September and soon thereafter the court announced that it was setting oral argument for early January 1985. The date slipped to March 18.

"Overall, the argument went quite well," Vladeck wrote in a memo to his petitioners. He reported that "the states had managed to force OSHA to concede that the standard should not preempt community right to know provisions and that the standard should have no preemptive effect outside of the manufacturing sector. However," he added, "I do not think that the states will prevail on their broader preemption argument, but rather the Court will uphold OSHA's power to preempt state law at least insofar as the manufacturing sector is concerned." His prediction for the two issues he was primarily responsible for briefing and arguing was more hopeful. On the question of the standard's application to just the manufacturing sector, he noted that the "court was plainly troubled by OSHA's failure to cover workers outside of manufacturing and showed some skepticism at OSHA's justifications for so strictly limiting the coverage of the standard." On the trade secrets issue, "the court appeared to be troubled" particularly with the "broad trade secret definition" and "concerned over OSHA's restriction of alleged trade secret information to only certain types of health professionals." Vladeck also warned his clients that the "court seemed to be concerned that we were asking it to essentially second-guess OSHA's policy determination" in regards to the hazard determination process (a challenge aimed at forcing OSHA to extend its list of potentially hazardous chemicals rather than leave it up to industry to determine which additional chemicals to provide information about under the standard).

It turned out that Vladeck's reading of the court was right on target when the appeals court decision was announced two months later. First the court ruled that the "Hazard Communication Standard preempts state hazard communication rules as they apply to employees in the manufacturing sector." It directed the labor secretary "to reconsider [the Standard's] application in other sectors and to order its application in those sectors unless he can state reasons why such application would not be feasible." The secretary's rejection of a longer list of chemicals that pose a hazard was upheld by the court, just as Vladeck predicted. And also, as he had predicted, the trade secrets definition was judged to be invalid and the secretary was directed to reconsider a narrower definition that would allow chemical identity information to be made available. The restriction limiting information to health professionals was also ruled invalid and the secretary was "directed to adopt a rule permitting access by employees and their collective bargaining representatives."

The case did not end there, though. The problem of getting paid for the legal work required another set of briefs and took many more months. The Equal Access to Justice Act (EAJA) allows the awarding of attorneys' fees to groups that might otherwise not be able to afford legal representation when they prevail against the government. EAJA's fee provision is restricted to groups with less than $7 million in assets and that employ fewer than five hundred people. All of the Litigation Group petitioners fit under the EAJA limits, and they had prevailed on two out of three of their main claims. Vladeck submitted a motion for an award of attorneys' fees in the amount of $24,595, an extremely modest sum given the complexity of the case. The government's attorneys objected, arguing that the Litigation Group's petitioners had not been the exclusive prevailing party. They had been only one of two parties asserting the same position, and the other party (the Steelworkers) were the lead and thus the more important challenger. In response, Vladeck wrote that this argument "should be rejected because it inaccurately reflects the role petitioners played in this litigation and is inconsistent with the Act. ... The Secretary's claim that petitioners' work in this case was largely duplicative of that of other petitioners—apparently referring to that of petitioner United Steelworkers of America, AFL-CIO—is at best farfetched." He laid out how "counsel for petitioners worked closely with the Steelworkers' lawyers to ensure that any potential overlap or duplication in the arguments presented would be minimized if not altogether eliminated." Moreover, Vladeck continued, his brief and not that of the steelworkers had "emphasized the legal theory ultimately adopted by the Court," challenging the coverage of the standard to the manufacturing sector alone. He also noted that "the Steelworkers did not even address petitioners' chief trade secret argument-namely that the definition of trade secret fashioned by the Secretary was overbroad. ... Without question, the trade secret issue was the primary focus of petitioners' briefs—which was not true of the Steelworkers—and it was precisely for that reason that the Steelworkers' counsel agreed that counsel for petitioners should present oral argument on this key aspect of the case." To the extent that any petitioner took the lead on the trade secret issue, it was plainly Vladeck's petitioners, not the Steelworkers. In addition, while the Steelworkers had focused on the effects of the standard on organized labor, Vladeck's briefs repeatedly emphasized the rule's impact on non-union workers, a concern expressly cited by the court in its opinion. In conclusion, Vladeck focused the court's attention on the EAJA's primary purpose:

> This case raised questions of profound importance for every working man and woman in this Country. The core purpose of the EAJA is to assure that individuals, and small organizations such as petitioners no longer have to rely on government or large institutions (such as labor unions) to voice their concerns, but can make their views known in Court, and challenge agency action which affects them, without having to bear the heavy cost of litigation where they prevail and demonstrate that the government acted unreasonably. It would be difficult to imagine agency action which strikes closer to home for the American worker. To suggest ... that the small worker organizations which effectively participated in this proceeding and prevailed on two vitally important issues should be denied fees

is to stand the purpose of the EAJA on its head. We submit that when measured against the fee requests this Court has passed on previously, the petition here is modest by any measure. This is not a case where lawyers are seeking a windfall, or participated in the case because of the prospect of a fee. Rather, counsel has vigorously represented worker groups with just as direct a stake in the outcome as any petitioner in a difficult and complex case, and have done so with substantial success.

One week after Vladeck filed his reply brief on the fee award issue, the court granted the fee award. A handwritten note penned by the ruling judge states that "[t]he petitioners will be compensated for 50% of the hours spent on the merits and for time spent in preparation of the fee application for the total award of $15,064.50." It was not all they wanted but much better than nothing. But it took months for the money to appear.

Soon after the circuit court ruling in the hazards communication case, the head of OSHA resigned under pressure. "The public perception of OSHA is as low as it's ever been," one longtime OSHA official stated in a June 1985 article in *BusinessWeek*. The article also pointed out that OSHA had issued "only two standards for toxic substances in the past four years." Even industry was disgruntled with OSHA, as the vice president for safety, health and environmental affairs at DuPont noted: "This Administration needs to give an indication soon that OSHA is a functioning agency responsive to public needs." While the Reagan team sought a new OSHA head, the hazards communication standard languished. It would take another court case, which resulted in a court order to OSHA to issue a standard within sixty days, to get action. And even then, the final rule did not meet the court-ordered deadline.

In *United Steelworkers of America v. Auchter*, the appeals court had ruled that the trade secrets definition was invalid and ordered the secretary of Labor to reconsider it. On this point, OSHA complied by issuing a revised final rule in late 1985. On the question of expanding the hazards warnings to workers outside the manufacturing sector, the court had ordered the secretary to reconsider the standard's "application to employees in other sectors and to order its application in those sectors unless he can state reasons why such application would not be feasible." OSHA chose not to comply, or at least to delay indefinitely. After more than a year had passed, Vladeck filed a second action for enforcement of the judgment in *Auchter*. His brief asked the court to find the secretary in contempt.

On May 29, 1987, a clearly angry Third Circuit let OSHA know that it was not going to put up with its orders being ignored:

> Sixteen years after Congress directed the Secretary to "prescribe the use of labels or other appropriate forms of warnings as are necessary to insure that employees are appraised of all hazards to which

they are exposed," no standard has been promulgated covering approximately two thirds of all workers covered by the OSH Act. This court is empowered by the Administrative Procedure Act to "compel agency action unlawfully withheld or unreasonably delayed." Moreover we may issue "all writs necessary or appropriate in aid of" our jurisdiction. Thus, we can issue orders necessary or appropriate to the enforcement of our prior judgment. Exercising the powers conferred by both statutes, we will direct that the Secretary shall, within sixty days of the date of our order, publish in the Federal Register a hazard communication standard applicable to all workers covered by the OSH Act, including those which have not been covered in the hazard communication standard as presently written, or a statement of reasons why, on the basis of the present administrative record, a hazard communication standard is not feasible. Such reasons will be supplied separately as to each category of excluded workers. Because our prior judgment did not include a specific time limit we will deny, at this time the petitioners' motion to hold the respondents in contempt.

The court's "unreasonable delay" reasoning was precisely what Vladeck and the other Litigation Group attorneys had dreamed up back in 1981 in fashioning their challenge to the ethylene oxide regulation. But even with this crystal clear order, a revised hazards communication standard was not in place until 1988.

* * * * *

The problems were even worse for the ethylene oxide regulation. It took two more court cases to force OSHA to act. As noted above, in March 1983, the U.S. Court of Appeals for the District of Columbia Circuit had ruled that OSHA's delays in promulgating a final safety standard for ethylene oxide were unjustifiable and mandated that the agency complete its rulemaking proceedings and issue a final rule within a year. After extensive public hearings, OSHA was ready to issue a final rule on June 14, 1984 (three months later than the court's expectation), but before doing so (in compliance with Presidential Executive Order 12291) it sent the final rule to the OMB for approval. The final rule included both a Permissible Exposure Limit (PEL) of 1 ppm of ethylene oxide, based on an average concentration over eight hours, and a short-term exposure limit (STEL) of 5 ppm averaged over any fifteen-minute period during the workday. When OSHA got the rule back from OMB, however, the part about the short-term limit had been crossed out by a heavy black marker. None of this would have been known except that the agency was under such pressure to meet the deadline that it did not have time to retype a document, which produced another leak.

On the day that OSHA got the rule back from OMB, with the court and Vladeck breathing down its neck about the long delay, it sent the final rule to the *Federal Register* for publication. That very day Vladeck got a call from someone at OSHA (he never found out who) who said that Vladeck should go over to the *Federal Register* building right away and ask for a copy of the document filed by OSHA on the ethylene oxide rule. There he found the marked-up document. It was back to court, this time challenging the final rule not only for its failure to protect workers by not including a short-term exposure limit, but raising a constitutional challenge to the role OMB had clearly played in excising part of the regulation (*Public Citizen Health Research Group v. Tyson Acting Assistant Secretary, OSHA*). This "two pronged" attack, as the court would label it, charged that the failure to issue a short-term exposure standard was "unsupported based on the record" before the agency and that the "role played by OMB in these proceedings was unlawful." On the second point, Public Citizen was joined by several members of the House of Representatives as *amici*. Meanwhile, a number of industry representatives filed suit, contending that the long-term limit was unsupported by the record. Again an agency was being attacked from two quarters—the industry claiming it had exceeded its statutory authority, the unions and Public Citizens claiming that it had failed to live up to it.

The court addressed the industry challenge first, discussing the validity of the scientific studies upon which OSHA had relied to initially determine that exposure limits were necessary. "Taking the epidemiological and experimental studies together, OSHA found that EtO causes cancer in laboratory animals and poses a significant risk for humans. While each study may not be a model of textbook scientific inquiry, the cumulative evidence is compelling." The court continued:

> Contrary to the apparent suggestion of some of the [industry] petitioners, we need not seek a single dispositive study that fully supports the Administrator's determination. Science does not work that way; nor, for that matter, does adjudicatory factfinding. Rather, the Administrator's decision may be fully supportable if it is based, as it is, on the inconclusive but suggestive results of numerous studies.

After exhaustive review of the various studies, the court concluded that OSHA had complied with the legal standards in setting the 1 ppm standard for long-term exposure. Industry's challenge failed.

Then the appeals court turned to OSHA's failure to issue a final rule for short-term exposure limits (STEL). The court ruled in no uncertain terms that OSHA's refusal to issue a STEL rule was not going to fly. "As of June 14, 1983, the agency had apparently concluded," said the court, "that the record supported the issuance of a STEL." For proof of this, the court relied on the Draft Final EtO Standard, the one obtained by Vladeck after the anonymous call from

OSHA. "After receiving OMB's objections to the STEL," the court went on, "OSHA decided to have a supplemental proceeding. Throughout the supplemental proceeding, OSHA's scientific staff supported the issuance of a STEL." The court also noted that OSHA admitted that "no new experimental or epidemiological studies were submitted" and that ethylene oxide exposures at the long-term limit set out in the regulation still allowed a significant health risk. There were no rational reasons in the record that supported the agency's change of heart. The unspoken suspicion, of course, was that the agency had succumbed to political pressure from OMB. "On remand," the court ordered, "we expect the agency to ventilate the issues on this point thoroughly and either adopt a STEL or explain why empirical or expert evidence on exposure patterns makes a STEL irrelevant." Having decided the case on these grounds, the court concluded that it did not need to reach the "difficult constitutional questions presented by OMB's participation in this episode."

Once again, the Litigation Group and those exposed to the dangers of ethylene oxide were forced to wait for the painfully slow administrators at OSHA to act. A year later, Vladeck headed back to court, this time charging that OSHA had "contemptuously and unreasonably delayed promulgation of a Short Term Exposure Limit" for ethylene oxide. This time the court spoke in no uncertain terms.

"At some point," said the court, "we must lean forward from the bench to let an agency know ... that enough is enough." The question the court asked was "whether that point has been reached" in this case. "We conclude that it has." Though the court was unwilling to find the agency in contempt, at least at this point, it did make a finding of "unreasonable delay." Still, the court hedged against ordering its own resolution.

> Fortunately, OSHA has presented to us a specific timetable in this case [representing] that a final rule will issue in March 1988. Although we are disappointed with this target date, we cannot find any specific aspect of the proposed rulemaking schedule that is impermissibly slow, in light of the complexity of the health questions involved. ... The five-year history of the EtO regulatory process convinces us, however, that the proposed timetable treads at the very lip of the abyss of unreasonable delay. ... Consequently, we find that any delay whatever beyond the proposed schedule is unreasonable.

> [W]e order OSHA to adhere to the schedule set out in its response to petitioner's contempt motion. OSHA's final decision on the EtO short-term exposure limit regulation is to issue no later than March 1988. Failure to comply with this timetable may well expose OSHA to liability for contempt.

It was as direct an order to an agency from a court as one could hope for, but still it gave OSHA nearly eight more months to finish its rulemaking process. And this agency had little credibility with these judges, who went even further to ensure that OSHA would comply:

> Moreover, given OSHA's apparent reluctance to keep petitioners informed as to the progress of the STEL rulemaking, we order OSHA to submit to the court a concise progress report every 90 days from the order's date of issuance until the final rule is in place. With these two commands, we hope and expect that the court's Sisyphean efforts to force agency action on this matter will finally be at an end.

There were many other challenges in the unending battle to force OSHA to provide worker protection against other equally dangerous chemicals such as formaldehyde, ethylene dibromide, benzene and cadmium. With an ever-expanding number of new chemicals, and an OSHA still reluctant to vigorously pursue its mandate, there was no end in sight to the litigation battles for worker safety.

15

Separation of Powers and the Legislative Veto

"I like to think that I'm on the side of the Constitution. I don't have a vendetta against Congress or the executive branch. I basically believe that we have a good system and we ought not to monkey around with it. There is no substitute for hard politics, and many shortcuts like the legislative veto and the deficit reduction act are just ways to get around our system of checks and balances. They amount to a dangerous abdication of lawmaking power by the legislative branch that is potentially destructive of our form of government."

— Alan Morrison

The U.S. Constitution does not set up a direct democracy. The people do not vote on every issue but rather choose representatives to whom the Constitution gives such power and who are held accountable through the voting booth. In operation, however, the government is quite different from the constitutional blueprint, which provides for the Congress to make the laws, for the president to execute and enforce the laws, and for the courts to interpret them By the 1980s, Congress had delegated broad power to the executive branch. The reality was, and is, that unelected bureaucrats and officials appointed by the president exercise enormous decisionmaking power. But if elected representatives do not make the decisions, how is government held accountable? The only way to maintain accountability to the people is through public access to government—open records, fair and reasoned decisionmaking processes and the opportunity for enforcement of these requirements by court review. Without these procedural protections, citizens cannot even find out what their government is up to, let alone influence the results. The Litigation Group's open government and regulatory cases are based on the principle that *process matters*. Its separation of powers cases are underpinned by the principle that *constitutional design matters*.

* * * * *

Separation of Powers and the Legislative Veto

On a stormy March morning in 1976, Alan Morrison headed out of his office for a meeting across town. Persuaded by the pouring rain to forgo his normal bike ride, he hailed a cab. Scanning the pages of *The Washington Post*, his eyes stopped at the headline "House committee reports regulatory reform bill." The first paragraphs told of provisions of a bill that seemed sensible or at least innocuous, but it was with almost total disbelief that he read what came next. The final paragraphs concerned a provision that appeared to enable a majority of either house of Congress to veto any regulation promulgated by any executive branch or independent agency. Moreover, it appeared that Congress would be able to do this, as Morrison later remarked, "for any reason, for wrong reasons or for no reason at all." And this proposal had been unanimously endorsed by one of the major committees of the House.

"It was preposterous," says Morrison. "How could it possibly operate sensibly?" Congress was already so overburdened that it sometimes could not even get the annual budget and appropriations bills finished on time. There was no way Congress could review the mountains of complex regulations, with their volumes of accompanying records, in any sort of rational manner. "My first reaction to the generic veto was that it was clearly not the right way to run the government." There had to be some sort of constitutional challenge that could be raised. Though he did recall that the 1974 Budget, Impoundment and Control Act (BICA) had a similar legislative veto provision, he had not given it much thought. When he returned to his office, he called in Larry Ellsworth and put him to work investigating the matter.

"While there were many statutes under which a challenge might possibly be raised to the constitutionality of the legislative veto," Ellsworth recalls, "we chose the federal election law because it required the immediate certification of the issue to the court of appeals for prompt resolution." For a law firm on a tight budget, like the Litigation Group, a fast-track process had great appeal. It also "appeared that a candidate for office would have standing," Ellsworth notes, "and thus we would have a good chance of avoiding the Justice Department's usual efforts to evade a decision by attacking the plaintiff's right to sue." So they set out to find a plaintiff. They really hoped to find a conservative, preferably Republican, candidate. They did not want to have this appear to be a liberal attack on President Gerald Ford's administration. "We saw it as a good government, not a political, issue," says Ellsworth. But, discussions with several prospective clients went nowhere. Fortuitously, the director of Nader's Corporate Accountability Research Group, Mark Green, had just agreed to head up the campaign of Ramsey Clark for the U.S. Senate. Clark was a former assistant attorney general (1961-65), deputy attorney general (1965-67) and attorney general (1967-68). He would be familiar with the constitutional issues involved and was well known and respected by the judges.

On January 30, 1976, in *Buckley v. Valeo*, the Supreme Court had ruled unconstitutional a number of provisions in the 1974 Federal Elections Campaign Act (FECA) Amendments. Congress had significantly amended 1971

FECA in reaction to Watergate and lesser scandals involving congressional campaigns. The law created the Federal Election Commission (FEC) to establish and enforce election rules based on Congress's intent. But with the Nixon administration's abuses in mind, Congress wanted to establish a commission that would not be under the complete control of the executive branch. So lawmakers devised a six-member FEC consisting of two members appointed by the speaker of the House of Representatives, two by the president pro tempore of the Senate, and two by the president. All six were to be subject to confirmation by a majority of both houses of Congress.

This solution, however, did not fit into the Constitution, which specifies that "the president shall nominate, and by and with the consent of the Senate, shall appoint ... all other Officers of the United States, whose appointments are not herein otherwise provided for." Known as "the appointments clause" this wording expressly states that "all" not "some" other officers of the United States will be so appointed. In *Buckley*, the Supreme Court ruled Congress's mixed-appointment process unconstitutional. The 1974 FECA amendments also included a legislative veto provision that subjected all rules made by the FEC in implementing the act to review and possible veto by either house of Congress. In a footnote, the Supreme Court explained that it did not address the legislative veto issue, writing that because "of our holding that the manner of appointment of the members of the Commission precludes them from exercising the rule-making powers in question, we have no occasion to address this separate challenge."

Following *Buckley*, Congress passed a revised law providing for presidential appointment of the commission members and making several other changes necessitated by the decision. Not only was the legislative veto provision left in the law, it was strengthened by allowing either house of Congress to veto any portion of a rule the body concluded was a "single separable rule of law." When Ford signed the amendments, he said that he believed the one-house veto provision was unconstitutional and directed the attorney general "to challenge the constitutionality of this provision at the earliest possible opportunity."

The legislative veto is a curious device that effectively stands the presidential veto on its head by requiring the executive branch to submit various decisions, such as agency-developed regulations or even a presidential decision (to sell weapons to Egypt, for example) for congressional review and potential veto. The legislative veto provision came into play whenever Congress included it in a law that delegated authority to the president or agencies under his control. Legislative veto provisions usually mandated that an executive actor notify Congress of a pending decision, provide Congress with documentation on the decision, and then wait a specified time to see if Congress would act. Congress could then either: (1) do nothing and the executive regulation or presidential decision would go into effect, or (2) vote by majority of either chamber or both houses (provisions varied as to which was required) to veto the rule or decision. If the latter occurred, the rule or decision could not go into effect. It was a handy device from the congressional perspective. Congress could go on passing laws mandating all sorts of good things, such as clean air, clean water, safe products, pure foods and safe workplaces. Then, when agencies attempted to implement those goals by issuing rules to define more precisely how clean air was to be achieved and how enforcement would be carried out, members of Congress could step in and veto the rule to protect powerful interests that would face paying for the solution. The beauty of a legislative veto was that lawmakers could continue to embrace the goals of clean air while killing a specific rule as too expensive, or unwarranted, or stupid, or for no expressed reason at all—a perfect "have your cake and eat it too" design. This was not an attractive prospect to Nader, the Litigation Group or, indeed, most other public interest advocacy groups.

Between 1932 and 1980, Congress approved at least one hundred and sixty-seven laws with one or more legislative veto provisions. Of these, more than half were enacted in the 1970s, forty-two during the Carter presidency alone. Prior to the mid-1970s, most provisions for veto review were contained in acts dealing with executive branch reorganization, conduct of foreign affairs and national defense—that is, they were aimed directly at presidential-level decisionmaking in laws like the War Powers Act. In the mid-1970s, however, legislative veto provisions increasingly targeted subordinate executive branch actors to whom rulemaking power was being delegated. Presidents did not like legislative vetoes directed at them. Likewise, Public Citizen and other public interest groups did not like legislative vetoes directed at programs of concern to them.

When the Litigation Group filed its case, the reaction at the Justice Department was gleeful. As then-Assistant Attorney General Rex Lee later explained:

> The legislative veto was a perpetual thorn in the side of the executive branch. There was, however, always some reason not to fight it: either we needed the statute in question, or it was politically inopportune, or it was impossible to get a case. But *Clark* was different. We loved the posture of the case. It was nonpartisan-after all, this was a Democratic, liberal ex-attorney general who was on our side. It would put the Ford Administration on the side of "right and good"—after all, the vetoed regulations had been for disclosure and openness of elections. And no federal program would be put in jeopardy if the Court were to rule the legislative veto unconstitutional in the Act.

It did not take long for the Justice Department to file its own request to intervene as a plaintiff in the case, thereby putting the Litigation Group and the Republican Ford administration on the same side. Just as in *Buckley v. Valeo*, the named defendants in the *Clark* case were Frances Valeo, secretary of the

Senate, and Edmund Henshaw, clerk of the House. Under federal election law, Valeo and Henshaw were responsible for various duties such as submitting reports to and serving as *ex officio* members on the FEC. Just as it had done in *Buckley*, the Senate and House appointed counsel to represent them. In accordance with the expedited procedures set out in the election law, on September 3, 1976, the district court certified the case for hearing before the full Court of Appeals for the District of Columbia Circuit. And keeping with the statutory command for swift action, the court ordered that briefs from all parties be filed within five days. The day after Labor Day, September 8, was the deadline. Oral argument was scheduled for September 10.

At the Litigation Group, that Labor Day weekend was no holiday from work. "We faced writing a brief we had never written before," Morrison notes, "on a problem as complicated conceptually as any we had ever had to write." Working nearly around the clock, they turned out in one weekend a brief that presented the basic theory that would carry forward in all of their subsequent legislative veto cases. "We decided that we didn't need to get agreement about what the legislative veto was, that is, whether it was an executive, legislative or judicial activity. It didn't make any difference which it was determined to be. If it were executive or judicial and being carried out by Congress, that was a violation of separation of powers. If it were legislative, it was being carried out without following the constitutional requirements of bicameralism and the presentment clause." As their brief concluded, "Therefore, under an analysis of the functions actually performed by Congress in the operation of a Congressional veto, these provisions either allow Congress to perform non-legislative tasks which are the province of another branch, or they permit Congress to carry out legislative activities in a manner not contemplated by the Constitution. Under either assumption, they are unconstitutional."

On the due date, the Litigation Group submitted its brief; all but eight of its sixty-four pages were devoted to the constitutional issues. At the same time they were given the briefs from the Justice Department and opposing congressional and FEC counsel. Amazingly, counsel for the House and Senate defendants had not even addressed the constitutional issues. Both briefs focused entirely on trying to persuade the court to dismiss the case, to not decide the issue. "One reason we had chosen the election statute," Morrison recalls, "was to avoid problems of standing and ripeness and so forth, because we thought the statute was about as broad as it could be in that regard. Well, the statute may have been as broad as it could be, but Congress was not the least bit interested, it turned out, in having the statute challenged. From the beginning, counsel for Congress argued that the case had no business being in court and should be dismissed." Having not had the opportunity to respond in writing, as a normal briefing schedule would have allowed, Ellsworth and Morrison had to decide whether to focus their oral argument on these so-called "barrier questions" or to stick to the constitutional issues. "We were here to challenge the constitutionality of the legislative veto, so we decided it made more sense to focus on that." Meanwhile congressional counsel stuck with its avoidance strategy. "We could never even get them onto the constitutional issue."

Four days after the oral argument, which Ellsworth handled, Ramsey Clark lost the New York Democratic primary to Daniel Patrick Moynihan, placing a distant third with only 10 percent of the vote. More than four months later, January 21, 1977, the appeals court announced its decision. "We lost rather badly, but not on the merits," Morrison says. "Basically, what the court decided was that it didn't want to decide unless it had to decide, and it was willing to wait to see if the Supreme Court would say it had to, which is precisely what the same judges had done in *Buckley*." Clark's defeat in the Democratic primary had provided the court with an easy way out. "Any ripe nexus arising out of Clark's position as a senatorial candidate vanished" when he failed to win the nomination, the court said. The next question the Litigation Group faced was whether to appeal to see whether the Supreme Court would help, as it had in *Buckley*.

By the time the appeals court ruled, however, a new presidential administration was in place. The Democratic Carter administration was far less receptive to challenging the legislative veto than its Republican predecessor. In fact, Carter had begun his term by pressing Congress for a new law allowing him to undertake certain government reorganization, for which inclusion of a legislative veto was essential for congressional passage. Having tried in vain to get Carter's Justice Department to join it, and with the February 10, 1977, deadline for filing an appeal fast approaching, the Litigation Group proceeded alone. Soon after its appeal was filed, the Supreme Court entered an order requesting the views of the Justice Department. In a formal response, the solicitor general advised the court that it should wait for a better case, one that was already under way in the Ninth Circuit, *Chadha v. INS*. "When we heard about *Chadha* and the Justice Department's interest," Morrison recalls, "I told one of my colleagues to get on the phone to see what was going on in the case so we could include the information in our *Clark* reply brief, which was due in the Supreme Court soon." That telephone call provided them with their next legislative veto challenge and it came none too soon for them or Chadha. Two weeks later, the Supreme Court announced its decision affirming the appeals court's dismissal of *Clark*.

* * * * *

Jagdish Rai Chadha, a young man born in Kenya, arrived in the United States in 1966 to study at Bowling Green State University in Ohio. Chadha's father had immigrated to Kenya from South Africa; his mother had come from India. When Kenya became independent from Great Britain in 1963, all persons born in Kenya prior to that date were automatically made citizens, except for those whose parents had not been born in Kenya. People in that category had to apply for citizenship before 1965. At the time, of a total population of more than 8.6 million, only two hundred and seventy thousand were non-Africans. One hundred and seventy-six thousand of those were from India and Pakistan; most had arrived during the four decades preceding independence. Though Chadha had applied for Kenyan citizenship before coming to the United States, his application, along with thousands of others, had not been acted upon. While Chadha was in the United States, Kenya passed the Immigration and Trade Licensing acts of 1967, severely limiting the employment of non-citizens. After completing an undergraduate degree in business administration and a master's degree in political science and economics in December 1971, Chadha needed to find a job, but he knew that his student visa would expire in six months and that his employment in Kenya, and even his ability to return to his home country, was unlikely.

As a citizen of a former British colony, Chadha had a British nationality certificate and a British passport even though he had never been to Great Britain. Chadha wrote to the British Consulate in Washington, D.C., about the possibility of his finding employment in Great Britain. Responding to a flood of immigrants, mostly Indian and Pakistani, who were pouring into the country from Kenya in the mid-1960s, Britain had passed a law setting up a strict quota system for admitting Asians from East Africa after 1968. Then in January 1972, Idi Amin toppled the post-colonial regime of Milton Obote in Uganda and ordered the immediate expulsion of all Ugandan Asians. Britain was again inundated by emergency immigration requests. Chadha's request for admission to Great Britain came during this inopportune time.

His letter elicited a quick response suggesting that it could take years for his request to be acted upon and advising him "to arrange for your immigrant status here [in the United States] to be regularized so that you can obtain employment here and remain here indefinitely." So Chadha headed to California, where a school friend told him of a job possibility. But every time he had an interview, he was asked about his residency status. After a year of one dead end after another, Chadha went to the U.S. Immigration and Naturalization Service (INS) office in Los Angeles to seek help. There he was promptly arrested and fingerprinted for overstaying his visa and ordered to appear before a hearing to show cause as to why he should not be deported. Thus began the case that would end up overturning more federal laws than had been overturned in the entire prior history of the nation.

After two hearings before an administrative law judge at the INS, on June 25, 1974, Chadha was granted a suspension of deportation that would allow him to remain in the United States because of his race and the difficulties he would face if deported. There was a catch, however. Congress had delegated the power to grant suspensions of deportations for "good cause" to the INS, an agency within the Department of Justice, but had included in the law a requirement that any suspensions be submitted to Congress for review and potential veto by either chamber. Thus Chadha's suspension stipulated that it would be final only if Congress did not veto it before the statutory deadline for action.

Separation of Powers and the Legislative Veto

Under the statute, Congress had to act by the end of the session following the one it was currently in. On December 16, 1975, nearly a year and a half after the suspension and on the last day in which Congress could act, the House of Representatives voted to veto six deportation suspensions out of the three hundred and thirty-nine then before them. No reason for the veto was given or ever discovered. Chadha's name was among the six. Once again, he was subject to deportation.

"When I heard about the veto," Chadha remembers, "I just knew it was wrong." He went to the local law school library and read everything he could find about the constitutional concepts of fairness and immigration law. "It was mind-boggling. Even with an advanced U.S. education, it seemed impossible [to me]. Imagine the problem an average immigrant must face." After much effort, he found a lawyer to represent him at the immigration hearing before the same administrative law judge who had granted his suspension. There they tried to raise the issue of the constitutionality of the legislative veto provision in the immigration law but were told that the administrative law judge had no authority to rule on a constitutional matter. On March 9, 1977, having lost at the hearing, Chadha received a notice that he would be deported to Kenya in just twenty days. His attorney, John Pohlmann, immediately filed a petition for review with the U.S. Court of Appeals for the Ninth Circuit in San Francisco.

A petition for review requires only a short statement concerning the court's jurisdiction to hear a case, a brief summary of the facts proving that the petitioner has exhausted remedies at the agency level, and a precise declaration of what relief is being sought from the court. Pohlmann covered all of this in two pages. By so doing, Chadha's deportation order was postponed until the court's final ruling. That was good news for Chadha. But for Pohlmann, who had just started a solo law practice that required frequent trips out of the country, the bad news was the looming court deadline for filing a full brief. "I was at the end of my rope with the Chadha case," Pohlmann recalls. "Then out of the blue I found that an angel had come through my telephone." It was the Litigation Group on the telephone. Pohlmann contacted Chadha to ask his permission to seek help from the Litigation Group and then called right back. "If you guys know something about the constitutional issues in this case, I'm just an immigration attorney and I sure could use some help."

"It took all of an eighth of a second," says Morrison, "for us to decide to jump on board." With the brief due on July 17 and little chance of getting an extension (Pohlmann had been granted two extensions already), Ellsworth geared up for another pressure cooker brief-writing session. "What I most remember," Ellsworth says, "is that, except for the facts, the brief in *Chadha* was essentially the same argument as in *Clark*." When he filed the brief, Ellsworth left for a two-month vacation in which he toured the country visiting national parks. Upon his return he accepted a position with Victor Kramer, special counsel to the Senate Ethics Committee, to investigate the possible bribery of U.S. senators by agents of the Korean government. At that point Morrison took over the *Chadha* case.

Things had changed by the summer of 1977. The Carter administration's position on the legislative veto was beginning to not only mimic past administrations but to surpass them in word and deed. Carter had quickly found that the legislative veto hindered his agenda. He had been forced to give up on using the reorganization process for creating a Department of Education, and his administration had had to withdraw plans to sell AWACS aircraft to Iran under threat of a congressional veto. Getting rid of this presidential nemesis became a top priority in his administration, and the *Chadha* case provided a handy vehicle for doing so. When the Justice Department filed its brief on behalf of the INS on October 25, 1977, a problem quickly became evident. The brief took a position that was almost identical to the Litigation Group's brief, that the legislative veto in the immigration statute was unconstitutional, and made essentially the same legal arguments. There was, in fact, no controversy at all between the parties. Recognizing this, the Justice Department had appended a letter to its brief suggesting that, "In order that this Court be provided with full argument on this fundamental and far-reaching issue, we hereby suggest that the Court invite the Senate and the House of Representatives to submit briefs as *amici curiae* on the issue of the constitutionality of the [legislative veto]."

Following the Justice Department's advice, the clerk of the Ninth Circuit wrote to the Senate and House inviting them to enter the case as *amici*. Both chambers accepted, turning to the same counsel who had represented them in *Clark*. Once again, the briefs were disproportionately directed toward convincing the court that it should not decide the constitutional issues involved.

When the congressional briefs were finally filed in February 1978, the court allowed both the Litigation Group and the Justice Department to file reply briefs to these *amici* briefs—a variation on the normal court process where an appellant (Chadha) is given an opportunity to reply to appellee's (Justice's) brief. Obviously, with both the Litigation Group and the Justice Department making the same arguments, the normal process would be of little use. The case was set for oral argument on April 10, 1978.

Morrison flew to San Francisco and stayed with former Litigation Group lawyer Ray Bonner on Sunday night. They got up early Monday morning and jogged through Golden Gate Park. "It was a bright and sunny day and I felt pretty comfortable about the argument," Morrison remembers. They had done a couple of moot courts to practice the case, and he felt that he could handle any questions the judges might come up with. At 8:30 a.m. Morrison walked into the Ninth Circuit courthouse, a building that "for sheer grandeur easily outclasses the Supreme Court's quarters in Washington, D.C.," and on into Courtroom 1. Other than Chadha and Pohlmann, opposing counsel and court officials, there was almost no one there. Neither the public nor the press yet understood the significance of the constitutional challenges in this case of one immigrant's battle to stay in the United States. "There were not many questions from the judges," Morrison recalls, "but I do remember one point I made that seemed to cause several judges to sit up and take notice." In preparing for oral argument, he had come up with a line of reasoning that he had not thought of before:

> The framers knew quite well what a legislative veto was. Senate approval of treaties and presidential appointments were, in fact, one-house vetoes, and the framers had provided specifically for them in the Constitution. Under the doctrine of *expressio unius est exclusio alterius* (the expression of one thing is the exclusion of another), the fact that they made no allowance for legislative vetoes elsewhere in the Constitution is proof that they did not intend them to be used for any other purposes. The point had been made before but not quite in this way. It had the great advantage of being relatively easy to make, unlike most of the others in this case.

Later, Morrison would be particularly satisfied to find this reasoning relied on in part of the Supreme Court's majority decision. But that satisfaction would be a long time coming—more that five years into the future. Much of the delay would be caused by an inordinately long wait—two and a half years—for the Ninth Circuit to decide.

* * * * *

The snail's pace of action from the courts allowed congressional proponents of the legislative veto, Morrison says, "to pin legislative vetoes on virtually any bill that would hold still." Having the administration on his side was better than the alternative, but it seemed hardly to make much difference. In 1979 alone, more than one hundred bills or amendments containing legislative veto provisions were introduced, and though only eight made it into law, the potential for more was depressingly great. Morrison testified about the constitutional defects and policy dangers of the legislative veto before congressional committees, wrote articles for law journals and gave speeches when he could. But, as he notes, "No one seemed much interested except a few academicians and bar committees."

What Morrison most wanted was another case to bring to court. One reason was that the legislative veto in *Chadha* was so unlike the legislative vetoes in the regulatory programs of most concern to the Litigation Group. Even a favorable ruling, should it come, might not be of much help to Public Citizen's mission. The immigration statute's legislative veto provision was unique. It gave Congress review power over executive actions that resembled judicial activity, or what were often termed "quasi-judicial" proceedings. Almost no other legislative veto provision did this. Chadha's INS hearing had been very much like a court hearing, the major difference being that it was heard before an executive branch employee called an administrative law judge, as opposed to a federal judge. The court might very well see Congress' interference in such a situation as harming the due process rights of an individual, an issue of central concern to the courts. As Morrison notes, "*Chadha* was the best case in that it was so clearly not the way for the country to be run. Not even an alien should be treated this way. But it was the worst case because there was a real danger that the court would rule too narrowly." If, in overturning the immigration law's veto provision, a court were to restrict its reasoning to just this sort of legislative veto, Morrison would still need to find a case to challenge the legislative vetoes involving executive actions that resembled legislative activity, or quasi-legislative functions, such as rulemaking. So he kept his eyes open for such an opportunity.

In May 1980, Congress passed amendments subjecting all regulations promulgated by the Federal Trade Commission (FTC) to legislative veto review. Congress also vetoed five regulations—four issued by the Department of Education and one by the Federal Energy Regulatory Commission (FERC). The latter provided Morrison with just the opportunity he was seeking. He was intrigued by the House's 369-34 vote to veto the FERC regulation because there were quotations from the floor debate, cited in a newspaper article, indicating that Congress was using the veto to change the law. One house was legislating all by itself and admitting to it. It was a dream come true.

What Morrison was reading about was the incremental natural gas pricing rule that the FERC had been directed to issue by the Natural Gas Policy Act of 1978. The rule submitted by FERC would have made industrial natural gas users pay about sixty cents more per thousand cubic feet of gas than residential, small commercial and other small customers paid. Incremental gas pricing to protect consumers had been the *sine qua non* demanded by many Democrats for their votes in favor of natural gas deregulation because of their concern that deregulation might cause the price of natural gas to rise too high and too fast for the small user to manage. Congressional action on the law to deregulate natural gas pricing had taken eighteen months. During the conference committee's action on the bill, a one-house legislative veto had been appended to the authority delegated to FERC to issue an incremental pricing rule. There is no record of who added it or why. Given the complexity of the bill and the number of other compromises made in conference, it is unlikely that most members of Congress even noticed its addition at the time.

Much had happened, however, between passage of the bill and the issuance of the rule by FERC. Economic and market conditions had changed drastically over the intervening two years. Oil prices had more than doubled following the 1979 oil crisis, when OPEC cut back on oil production to force prices up. Demand for energy had decreased in response to presidential and congressional initiatives mandating and encouraging energy efficient appliances and other conservation measures. And the natural gas market was in a period of supply surplus, in contrast to the shortages of 1978. Many in Congress, as well as most of the FERC commissioners, thought that an incremental pricing rule now made no sense. But the law had not given FERC the discretion to decide whether a rule was needed. It had, rather, directed that such a rule be issued by May 12, 1980. If FERC thought a rule unwise at this point, its option under the Constitution was to so inform Congress and ask it to amend the law to eliminate the requirement. An amendment to drop the incremental pricing rule, however, could take months to pass, during which time the rule would stand. Moreover, many believed that the whole gas deregulation scheme would fall if the issue were to come to the floor at this point. Maintaining majority support in both houses for deregulation would be a near impossibility. Vetoing the regulation was a much easier way around the problem. Members could argue that this particular rule was wrong-headed while assuring their constituents that another more sensible one might follow. It was precisely the concern Morrison had about the legislative veto—that Congress could pass a law with protection for the little guy and then gut it in the veto process.

Morrison, who admits that he knew little about the 1978 Natural Gas Policy Act, sat down to read this lengthy and complicated piece of legislation. He needed to challenge Congress' veto, but there was no way he could sue Congress. His action had to be directed against the agency, and he needed a client to represent. He did not have to look far for the client. Public Citizen was then headquartered in a small commercial building that it rented in Washington. Heated with natural gas, the building would qualify for the lower cost under the incremental pricing rule. In addition, the Consumer Energy Council of America, a public interest organization allied with Nader's consumer groups, had participated by filing comments during FERC's consideration of the incremental pricing rule.

Soon Morrison found his hook to go after the agency as well. He could go to the agency and say, "Where is the regulation you were required to issue by May 12, 1980?" The agency would reply that the House had vetoed the rule and so it could not go into effect. Then he could file a lawsuit challenging the legislative veto's constitutionality. On June 5, 1980, Morrison filed a petition to FERC noting the May 12 deadline for a rule and asking for an order putting the rule into effect as directed by statute. As expected, the commission's response was that it could not do so because the House of Representatives had vetoed it. But the commission did not stop there. Under what appears to have been significant congressional pressure to avoid a court challenge at all costs, the commission announced the same day it denied Morrison's petition that it was revoking the incremental pricing regulation altogether. In explanation for its actions, the commission stated that if the veto provision were declared unconstitutional, and the regulation were allowed to go into effect, the result would be undesirable because "the Commission has not yet independently evaluated whether the rule meets the social and economic goals of the incremental pricing program," and because "we might well have very serious reservations as to the wisdom of making the rule effective."

"What this meant was that there was now no rule to challenge," Morrison says. It seemed a bit sneaky, but Morrison was not deterred. "In its haste to do me out of a court case, the commission had not complied with the Administrative Procedure Act's requirement for notice and comment. It had changed [by eliminating it] a final rule without notice and without opportunity for public comment." Back Morrison went to FERC with a petition for a rehearing so he could challenge the summary withdrawal of the rule. On October 2, FERC denied his petition, claiming that there had been good cause to ignore the APA in this case. Now Morrison had a case again, as the APA law allows sixty days to file a court challenge to any denial of a rehearing petition. It was not just the denial of the rehearing that he challenged. His real target, of course, remained the constitutionality of the legislative veto. It was back to brief writing for Morrison. One of his first actions was to call the Justice Department to see if its lawyers were interested in joining the case to challenge the legislative veto's constitutionality. The Justice Department waffled, so Morrison continued alone. His contacts in the Justice Department, however, were as concerned as he was about the long delay in the *Chadha* case and had written to the Ninth Circuit in April and again in August to seek information and urge action. No response, other than that the case was still under submission, was forthcoming. The Justice Department asked Morrison find out whether Jagdish Chadha was still employed. He had found a job in a stereo store after the administrative law judge had initially suspended his deportation, and he still held the job at the time of the Ninth Circuit hearing. The Justice Department apparently wanted to see whether Chadha was having any problems that could provide a hardship claim with which to pressure the court.

Morrison called Chadha only to find that he had gotten married on August 10 to a U.S. citizen. Though this was happy news for Chadha, it could be devastating for the case. Marriage gave Chadha the opportunity to apply for citizenship as an immediate relative of a citizen, though it would take three years to qualify. Morrison and attorneys in the Justice Department investigated their options. A review of the immigration laws showed that a permanent resident could apply for citizenship after a five-year waiting period and, if the INS were to interpret the law to allow the waiting period for Chadha to be retroactively adjusted to December 1975—when Congress had vetoed his deportation suspension—then Chadha's five-year waiting period would soon elapse, and he would be eligible for citizenship in just two months (December 1980). This analysis would mean that he would still benefit (citizenship eligibility in two months versus three years as a spouse of a citizen) from a favorable court decision. In other words, the case would not be moot. Morrison discovered that Chadha had not applied for citizenship as a spouse and was willing, indeed eager, for the case to proceed so that no other alien would have to face what he had. On November 26, Morrison informed the Ninth Circuit and notified counsel for the Senate and House of Chadha's marriage. On December 5, counsel for the Senate officially notified the court of its intention to submit a motion requesting the case to be dismissed as moot. But it was too late.

Rejecting the marriage issue in a footnote, on December 23, 1980, the Ninth Circuit finally announced its long-delayed ruling declaring the legislative veto in the immigration act unconstitutional. It was a win, but just as Morrison had feared, the ruling was narrowly confined to the immigration law. Indeed, the opinion written by Circuit Judge Anthony Kennedy (who was later elevated to the Supreme Court), specifically stated that the legislative vetoes over agency rulemaking "might present considerations different from those we find here, both as to the question of separation of powers and the legitimacy of the uni-cameral device." Having won, though, there was nothing further Morrison could do in *Chadha*. An appeal to the Supreme Court would depend on action by the losing side. Just who was the losing side, though, was certainly open to debate. After all, the INS had fully agreed with the winner's position—a fact that would engender considerable debate ahead.

With the deadline on filing his FERC brief rapidly approaching, Morrison pored over the Ninth Circuit's *Chadha* decision so he could incorporate it into his argument. At the Justice Department, the pressures were even greater. With Ronald Reagan's win over Carter in the November elections, Justice would soon face direction from a new president, who seemed as enamored of the legislative veto as Carter had been on first taking office. In fact, during the campaign Reagan had stated that both Congress and the president should be granted greater authority to veto regulations. The rush was on to get the administration on record in support of an appeal to the Supreme Court in *Chadha* and to join the *FERC* case. And, though notice of intent to appeal in *Chadha* and a brief in the FERC case were filed before the Carter administration expired, a new battle ensued when the Reagan administration took over.

* * * * *

It did not take long for the new Reagan appointees in the Justice Department to begin to take a negative view of the legislative veto. But others, including Vice President George Bush, whom Reagan had appointed to head his new Task Force on Regulatory Relief, continued to voice vigorous support for the veto. Describing the Justice Department's effort to win support in the White House for its campaign against the legislative veto, then-Deputy Attorney General Edward Schmults said, "It was like sailing through shoals, trimming here and there so we could reach our destination. It took a feel for White House staff and congressional concerns, a willingness to be open to concessions so we could avoid being stopped dead in the water by underestimating the depth of others' commitments or needs." While the internal battles over the legislative veto raged on, the Justice Department requested an extension in the formal filing date for the appeal in *Chadha* from March 13 to May 1, which the Supreme Court granted. Finally, at an April 20 Cabinet meeting, a decision was made to proceed with the *Chadha* case and to stay in the FERC case, but the compromise reached would allow the congressional tidal wave of veto provisions to continue with the president's acquiescence, if not support.

On May 1 the administration filed its appeal in *Chadha*. To ensure that the Supreme Court would hear the appeal, the Justice Department had to prove that the question involved was substantial and that the department had standing to appeal. The first was easy since the case presented "constitutional issues of the most fundamental nature regarding the distribution of powers among the branches of the federal government and the manner in which those powers may be exercised." The second required a decidedly more slippery defense. After all, it is the losing side in a case that has a right of appeal. The INS had argued that the legislative veto in the immigration law was unconstitutional, and the Ninth Circuit had agreed. There was a way around this barrier, or at least one that allowed for a good argument. Section 1252 of Title 28 of the United States Code provided that "any party may appeal to the Supreme Court from ... [a] final judgment, decree or order of any court of the United States ... holding an Act of Congress unconstitutional in any civil action, or any proceedings to which the United States or any of its agencies, or any officer or employee thereof ... is a party." INS was a party, and an act of Congress had been declared unconstitutional, or so they argued.

Not surprisingly, congressional counsel vigorously disputed this logic. Neither the House nor the Senate wanted an appeal. It was bad enough to have an appeals court rule that a legislative veto was unconstitutional. But at least *Chadha* had been narrowly decided and thus did not immediately call into question the constitutionality of legislative veto provisions in other laws. Why chance a broader ruling from the Supreme Court? Following the appeals court decision, counsel for the House and Senate had moved to formally intervene in the case, thus becoming a party rather than just *amici*, so that they could request a rehearing *en banc* of the full Ninth Circuit in the hopes of reversing the decision by the three-judge panel. When this was denied, congressional counsel was prepared to accept the limited defeat dealt by the appeals court. When the INS appealed to the Supreme Court, congressional counsel filed a motion to dismiss, arguing that, "INS is one of the prevailing and non-aggrieved parties below, in a proceeding in which there was no adverseness whatever between the parties. The INS therefore has no standing to invoke this Court's appeal jurisdiction." In concluding its argument against the appeal, congressional counsel noted that this was "the first time in the history of the American government, the Congress of the United States has been forced to intervene in judicial proceedings in order to protest before this Court an assault upon its legislative prerogatives by another branch of government." It was not the first time, of course, that Congress had defended its laws in court, but prior to this, when the executive and congressional branches had disagreed over the constitutionality of a law, one branch had appeared as a party and the other as *amicus curiae*. If Congress lost when appearing as *amicus*, it was the Justice Department that would, if Congress wished, appeal for the aggrieved branch.

Under this arrangement, since Congress had lost and did not want an appeal, none would have been filed. The only exception to this model had been the Clark case, in which Congress had been a party and the Justice Department had formally intervened to challenge the legislative veto in the federal election law. There, though, the question of who would appeal was not involved. Having lost, the Litigation Group was able to do so on its own.

Fearing that the Supreme Court might decide to hear *Chadha* and attempting to gain control over the questions that would be presented for review and the order of briefing, counsel for both houses of Congress also filed *certiorari* petitions. House counsel made clear Congress' displeasure at having to do so:

> Neither the House nor the Senate is a litigating body. But they have no alternative when first the Executive Branch and now the Judicial Branch have mounted a serious offensive against the exercise by Congress of its vested powers under the Necessary and Proper Clause. Both the House and the Senate are confident that this Court will take appropriate steps to preserve and protect our tripartite form of government.

A little less than a month earlier, the FERC case had had its day in the D.C. Circuit court. In that case, counsel for Congress had vigorously argued for dismissal, charging that "it is an inappropriate vehicle for resolving a great constitutional conflict that exists between the President and Congress." Counsel for FERC and a number of natural gas producers and associations defended FERC's withdrawal of the rule and also argued for dismissal. Morrison, of course, went after the constitutional issues—or at least tried to. In contrast to the Ninth Circuit, where the judges had few questions, Morrison barely got a sentence out in his FERC argument before the judges pounced. It was obvious that the judges were concerned about the standing issue. Every time he would try to move on to the constitutional issue, a question from the bench would drag him back to standing. He had only a few moments at the very end of his thirty minutes to get to his real argument. The Justice Department, now there as *amicus*, also had a turn, but again the judges focused questioning on the standing issue as well as the legitimacy of the court acting as arbitrator between the branches. The oral argument was frustrating but over very quickly, and then it was back to the waiting game.

On Oct 5, 1981, the Supreme Court granted the *certiorari* petitions of both houses of Congress in *Chadha* and postponed the question of the INS' standing under Section 1252 until its decision on the merits. Since the Supreme Court had granted *cert* to Congress, its briefs were due first—arriving at the court on November 19. On the afternoon of New Year's Eve, Morrison filed his brief on behalf of Chadha. The next brief to arrive was an *amicus* brief from the American Bar Association in which the hand of Antonin Scalia, a strong opponent of the legislative veto, was clearly evident. Though the bar association brief presented a strong indictment of the veto, it predicted that the Supreme Court would rule narrowly in the case, as had the Ninth Circuit, even as it argued strongly against this result. A few days later the brief from the Justice Department was filed. Before the final briefs (the reply briefs from the two houses of Congress) were due, the FERC decision was announced. It was a decision that surely complicated matters for congressional counsel.

* * * * *

Morrison received a call from a former student who was clerking for a judge on the D.C. Circuit. "Congratulations, the court has just announced its decision in FERC. You won!" the clerk said. Morrison held the phone out and shouted to his office mates. "We won! We won *FERC!*" It was quite a surprise that the court had ruled so quickly, because at the time the D.C. Circuit was not moving its cases very fast and this was a complex case. "Of all the cases on which I had worked," Morrison notes, "there had never been one as complicated and full of roadblocks that could trip me up and keep the court from deciding as this one." Written by one of the most conservative judges on the court, Judge Malcolm Wilkey, the decision was unanimous. But the real surprise was the breadth of the reasoning the court used in ruling the legislative veto unconstitutional. Later commenting on this, Judge Wilkey noted that he had been "determined to cover every blooming point that could be raised about the veto, in part for my own personal satisfaction, but also to do a job for the Supreme Court." Wilkey knew that since the high court had not yet ruled on the issue, it would not have case precedent to rely on but rather would have "to consider carefully the applicability of the constitutional provisions relied on by both sides to the dispute."

Wilkey's sweeping condemnation of the legislative veto was the result of nearly five months spent almost exclusively on the task. Wilkey concluded:

> What emerges from our analysis of the purposes of the lawmaking restrictions in Article I [of the Constitution] is that the Framers were determined that the legislative power should be difficult to employ. The requirements of presentation to the President and bicameral concurrence ultimately serve the same fundamental purpose: to restrict the operation of the legislative power to those policies which meet the approval of three constituencies, or a supermajority of two. If the legislative veto represents an exercise of legislative power, then, it must be exercised only in compliance with these constitutional requirements.

Wilkey went on to prove that there was no doubt about what Congress had done in vetoing FERC's incremental pricing rule. Congress had changed what the law said, thereby exercising lawmaking power. To Morrison's glee, Wilkey had used as proof of this point many of the quotations from the floor debate, which he had included in his brief, about how the veto would rectify an error in the law. Wilkey carried his reasoning well beyond the presentment clause approach, noting that,

> The contention that the separation of powers doctrine does not apply to independent agencies is manifestly groundless. ... Congressional unwillingness to use its constitutional powers cannot be deemed a sufficient reason for inventing new ways for it to act. The genius of our Constitution, its adaptability to changes in the nature of American society, depends ultimately on the steadfastness with which its basic principles and requirements are observed. Otherwise its critical protections against governmental tyranny would quickly become meaningless, as the Government in power could shape it to suit whatever purposes seem sound at the present. The Article I restrictions on the exercise of the legislative power, as well as the principle of separation of powers, are fundamental to the constitutional scheme.

For Morrison, the opinion was made to order. Virtually all of the veto provisions that had been placed over consumer, environmental and safety regulations should be deemed unconstitutional under this reasoning. It was too late for him to incorporate the decision into his Supreme Court brief in *Chadha*, but not too late for congressional counsel (whose reply briefs were due on Lincoln's birthday, February 12, 1982), though it was with much less enthusiasm that they faced the task. Oral argument in *Chadha* was scheduled for February 22, George Washington's birthday.

* * * * *

In scheduling oral argument for *Chadha*, the court had allotted an hour and a half for arguments, as opposed to the usual hour, to accommodate the fact that four parties wished to speak—Morrison, the Justice Department, the House of Representatives and the Senate. Since *cert* had been granted to the House and Senate, they would argue first. "Originally, the solicitor general wanted to do the whole argument for our side," Morrison notes. "Obviously this was unacceptable to us. My client was on the line, and besides I had argued the case before and I knew more about the record. Moreover, our interests were not entirely congruent with the Justice Department's." After considerable discussion, a compromise was reached. Justice would get twenty-five of their side's forty-five minutes and argue the constitutional issues. Morrison would get twenty minutes and would focus on the procedural issues. In practicing for the oral argument, Morrison went through several moot courts, but he could not fully outline the argument ahead of time. As the last one to argue, he would have to wait and see "how things would go and be prepared to move in to refute, expand or clarify points made by the other attorneys."

Between the Ninth Circuit argument back in 1978 and the Supreme Court argument in 1982, the importance of the case had become far more widely recognized. The Supreme Court was filled with onlookers that afternoon as the *Chadha* oral argument began. Morrison had to wait as the other three attorneys took their turns at the podium. As he listened to the arguments, it became clear to him that his client's role in the case was being lost to the bigger constitutional and jurisdictional issues. He decided to grab his opening moments to rectify this.

> Much of the debate on this case involves what Mr. Gressman [counsel for the House of Representatives] referred to as a tug of war between the executive branch and the Congress. While those concerns are important, there are other interests at stake as well, and it is important not to lose sight of the fact that legislative vetoes in general, and this one in particular, affect the lives of many people subject to the laws of this country. I want to begin by answering the question posed about the effect of Mr. Chadha's marriage ... something that was called an academic matter by counsel for Congress. If Mr. Chadha's decision here is affirmed, he will be a citizen by the 4th of July. ... That means that he will be able to vote, he will have other rights that aliens do not have, and he will have them almost immediately.

He went on to point out that the alternative—filing as a spouse of a citizen—would take years. It was about all he was allowed to get out before the questions started, but as one reporter covering the argument noted, "For a moment, it almost seemed as if Morrison would offer Chadha himself up to the court as a sort of visual aid. It was a nice touch, a way of converting jurisdictional and procedural niceties into flesh and bone." Questioning was vigorous, and Morrison was ready for everything the justices threw at him. "I thought the argument had gone quite well," Morrison remembers. "But then, I often think that even when it's not the view of others, and sometimes when I thought so, we lost anyway." In this case, others agreed with his assessment. "Morrison turned the seemingly mundane and thankless assignment [of responding to the procedural challenges] into the best performance of the day," commented one reporter.

* * * * *

The oral argument behind him, Morrison turned once again to fighting the seemingly endless battle against Congress' penchant for subjecting regulations to the legislative veto. On March 24, 1982, the Senate had voted by an overwhelming margin (69-25) to add a two-house generic veto amendment covering all executive branch and independent agency rulemaking authority to a regulatory reform bill. In the House, support for the measure was equally strong, with more than two hundred and fifty members co-sponsoring the amendment. But action was being held up by the Rules Committee's refusal to schedule the regulatory reform bill for floor debate. Then on May 18, 1982, the Senate voted 69-27 to veto an FTC regulation aimed at providing consumers with information about the condition of used cars. A week later the House followed suit, vetoing the regulation by a similar vote margin, 286-133. The used car rule had been issued after more than five years of study and numerous compromises. It was a weak rule at best, requiring only that a sticker be placed on a used car's window stating whether there was a warranty and listing any known defects. Dealers could add that there might be defects unknown to them, and there was no requirement that a dealer actually inspect a car. It was far less than what the consumer groups supporting it had wanted, but it was at least a first step. Senator Slade Gorton (R-Washington) had noted in support of the rule that allegations about deceptive practices in used car sales were some of the leading consumer complaints he had received as a state attorney general. "I am inclined to think," he said, "that this is not the type of regulation that we should seriously consider overturning if the legislative veto process is to work successfully and have credibility in the eyes of the public." But his position was a lonely one in Congress at that time.

When the FTC had announced the final rule in September 1981, lobbyists from the used car industry had descended on Capitol Hill, spreading money liberally around among members' re-election campaign chests. Staffers from Public Citizen's Congress Watch combed the Federal Election Commission files on campaign donations and discovered that car dealer political action committees had given $571,626 to about 85 percent of the sponsors of the legislative veto resolution. Congress Watch sent out press releases, but the resulting news coverage did little to deter the members from voting to kill the rule. Thus another opportunity to challenge the legislative veto arose, and Morrison worked closely with the attorney for Consumers Union, who filed suit before the same court that had decided the FERC case. While the briefs for the FTC case were under way, the end of the Supreme Court's session arrived—and still there was no decision in *Chadha*. Instead, the court announced that it was postponing a decision until the next term and was scheduling the case for re-argument.

Just ten days after the October 12 oral argument in the FTC case, the appeals court announced its decision in a two-page opinion that simply adhered to the analysis in its FERC decision. Congress and the natural gas and used car industries appealed both the FERC and FTC cases to the Supreme Court. But the court just sat on the cases, neither agreeing to hear them nor denying them.

Given the scheduled re-argument in *Chadha*, there was no reason for the Supreme Court to hear the FERC and FTC appeals. When Morrison appeared before the justices for the second time on December 7, 1982, it was an uneventful argument. "The few questions from the bench were not sharp and gave little evidence of new concerns not addressed in the first oral," he says. It was back to the waiting game for Morrison as he continued to fight against the veto where ever and whenever the opportunity presented itself.

* * * * *

Morrison jogged to work on the morning of June 23, 1983. He was just cooling off at his desk, still in his jogging shorts, when the phone rang. It was a call from the Supreme Court clerk's office telling him he had won *Chadha*. "I just about went through the ceiling," Morrison remembers. As the news spread through the offices of the Litigation Group, everyone began to jump and shout and hug one another. And then the phone started ringing. The first call was from a newspaper reporter in Dallas and typical of those that followed. "Would you explain to me what this legislative veto thing is all about?" asked the caller. After all the years of writing and talking and trying to educate the public, Morrison was to learn that the veto remained a mystery to nearly everyone.

Morrison had not even seen the opinion at this point, so he asked the reporter to read some of it to him. "Today the Court not only invalidates [the veto] of the Immigration and Nationality Act, but also sounds the death knell for nearly 200 other statutory provisions in which the Congress has reserved a 'legislative veto,'" the reporter said, reciting the opening lines of Justice Byron White's dissent. Next he read the first couple of sentences from the concurrence of Lewis F. Powell: "The Court's decision based on the Presentment Clauses ... apparently will invalidate every use of the legislative veto. The breadth of this holding gives one pause."

"My God," Morrison thought at the time, "we didn't just win, we won it all." Thinking he had better read the full decision before further comment, he sent someone to get a copy. As he began to read, he realized that it really was a grand slam. The next morning, banner front-page headlines around the nation confirmed the importance of the win. A *New York Times* editorial termed the majority opinion a "supremely simple" decision in which Chief Justice Burger, "writing like a patient schoolmaster" proceeded to explain the court's reasoning in "familiar and basic terms. Remember what we all learned in social studies about how the laws are made? Well that's just how it should still work." Burger explained that "explicit and unambiguous provisions of the Constitution prescribe and define the respective functions of the Congress and of the Executive in the legislative process." If an action was "legislative in character," which he defined as "any action that has the purpose and effect of altering the legal rights, duties, and relations of persons outside the legislative branch," it was to be taken in accord with this process. Congress, in other words, could legislate only through bicameral passage and presentment to the president for signature or by passage by two-thirds majority in both houses over a presidential veto. He relied on Morrison's *expressio unius* argument, noting that if the framers had wanted to provide for a legislative veto, "they knew very well how to do it," having provided in the Constitution for one-house action in the case of confirmation of appointments and ratification of treaties. It was an analysis entirely based on the presentment clause, containing none of the messy separation of powers arguments that involve balancing "fundamental purposes" and "core powers" of each branch with which Judge Wilkey had grappled in *FERC*. The chief justice concluded on a note similar to Wilkey, though:

> The choices we discern as having been made in the Constitutional Convention impose burdens on governmental processes that often seem clumsy, inefficient, even unworkable, but those hard choices were consciously made by men who had lived under a form of government that permitted arbitrary governmental acts to go unchecked. There is no support in the Constitution or decisions of this Court for the proposition that the cumbersomeness and delays often encountered in complying with explicit Constitutional standards may be avoided, either by the Congress or by the President. ... With all the obvious flaws of delay, untidiness, and potential for abuse, we have not yet found a better way to preserve freedom than by making the exercise of power subject to the carefully crafted restraints spelled out in the Constitution.

In his vehement dissent, Justice White defended the veto as "an important if not indispensable political invention that allows the president and Congress to resolve major constitutional policy differences, assures the accountability of independent regulatory agencies and preserves Congress' control of lawmaking. ... The apparent sweep of the Court's decision today is regrettable. ... To strike an entire class of statutes based on consideration of a somewhat atypical and more readily indictable exemplar of the class is irresponsible." But to White's support for the legislative veto's utility in enabling compromises to be reached between the executive branch and Congress, one could counter that the legislative veto's effect on citizens who are subject to the law is a far more critical focus. And, to the claim that the legislative veto ensures the accountability of independent regulatory agencies, one could ask whether the actual results in the FERC incremental gas pricing and FTC used car rules were to hold the agencies accountable to the law or merely to service powerful economic interests at the expense of average citizens.

Two weeks later, the high court announced, without argument and without further comment, that it was affirming the lower court decisions in the FERC and FTC cases on the bases of the *Chadha* opinion. Morrison remains convinced that it was the complex issues in *FERC* that prompted the court to rule as it did. "Without *FERC* in the wings, the Supreme Court would never have ruled so broadly in *Chadha*," he says.

It had taken more than seven years and four complex cases (*Clark, Chadha,*

FERC and *FTC*) to get a ruling from the Supreme Court. And though it took almost another year, until April 10, 1984, for Chadha to become a citizen, he did realize that goal. Without the Litigation Group to carry his case from 1978 on, he most likely would have been deported along with the other five people whose deportation suspensions were vetoed by Congress. For the public, it meant that Congress could not arbitrarily overrule health, safety, consumer and environmental protections that had been put in place by agencies after months and sometimes years of study and preparation. In addition, *Chadha* would remain a powerful and critical precedent for future separation of powers cases in the decades to come. Alan Morrison would be back in court time and again fighting under the constitutional separation of powers banner to maintain what he sees as its critical role in protecting citizens from a potentially overbearing government.

16

Reagan Deregulation and Reye's Syndrome

The onset of Reye's Syndrome usually occurs during a child's recovery from the flu, chicken pox, respiratory infection or other viral illness. It was first described in 1963 by Douglas Reye, an Australian pathologist. Its symptoms begin with explosive vomiting. Then the child "plunge[s] into deep confusion and delirium. The brain swells; chemicals in the blood tumble into imbalance; the kidneys lose their capacity to filter and detoxify selected poisons, particularly ammonia. Without immediate identification ... and prompt and aggressive treatment, victims proceed rapidly through convulsions and coma and then die." During the early 1970s, as many as eight of every ten victims died. By the early 1980s, with heightened awareness of the disease and its symptoms, the mortality rate fell to about 30 percent, though many survivors were left with permanent brain damage.

In December 1973, the Centers for Disease Control (CDC) undertook the first nationwide surveillance and monitoring of the disease and by 1980 estimated that Reye's Syndrome affected between six hundred and twelve hundred children a year. Scientists have never clearly identified the cause of Reye's Syndrome. But medical investigators began to suspect that there might be some contributing factor or toxic agent that triggered its onset. One suspicion was that medicine given to children might be involved. Aspirin, then the major home remedy for flu and fever, was a prime suspect. In December 1976, the U.S. Food and Drug Administration's (FDA) Neurologic Drugs Advisory Committee recommended against giving aspirin to children whose signs and symptoms indicated Reye's Syndrome. Arizona, Michigan and Ohio conducted epidemiological studies to determine if there was any measurable connection between the use of aspirin and Reye's.

Scientific studies involving human subjects are governed by ethical and moral rules. Controlled experiments, such as giving aspirin to one batch of children sick with the flu while giving another batch of flu-sick children no aspirin or a placebo, are simply unacceptable when a health risk is involved. Epidemiological research offers "a substitute for the unattainable scientific gold standard of a randomized experimental trial," according to the authors of an article in the *New England Journal of Medicine*.

The state studies attempted to assess, retrospectively, the relationship between Reye's Syndrome and the use of aspirin. To do so, researchers identified past cases of Reye's Syndrome, then found out if the child had had the flu and had been given aspirin before the onset of the symptoms. The investigators compared these subjects to a control group of children who had suffered from flu or chicken pox but did not get Reye's and asked in those cases whether aspirin had been administered or not. Obviously, there was potential for error. For instance, the memory of parents might prove inaccurate. The rigor of a traditional scientific experiment could not possibly be met.

Most scientists would agree that the findings of any one of the studies conducted by the three states, standing alone, would be inconclusive. But, when the studies all reached the same conclusion—that children who were given aspirin for the flu or chicken pox were up to twenty-five times more likely to develop Reye's than children who were not given aspirin—the results were compelling.

In 1980, scientists at the CDC reviewed the state studies and published a recommendation in the November 7, 1980, issue of *Morbidity and Mortality Weekly Report*, stating: "there is strong epidemiological evidence for, and association between, the occurrence of Reye's Syndrome and the prior ingestion of salicylate [aspirin] containing medication." It warned that "parents should be advised to use caution when administering salicylates to treat children with viral illness, particularly chickenpox and influenza-like illnesses." Not many parents read *Morbidity and Mortality*, so very few would be effectively informed by this warning.

The following March, a "consensus development conference" was held at the National Institutes of Health to discuss diagnostic criteria and treatment of Reye's Syndrome. Final results from the state studies had not been made available to the participants, but the conference nonetheless concluded that "caution in the use of salicylates (aspirin) in children with influenza is prudent."

In November 1981, the CDC gathered a group of consultants to review the state studies. They concluded, like the CDC a year earlier, that evidence showed a strong association between Reye's and aspirin. They recommended that "until the nature of the association between salicylates and Reye syndrome is clarified, the use of salicylates should be avoided, when possible for children with virus infections and during presumed influenza outbreaks." Note that the warning evolved from parents should use *caution* in using aspirin under the stated circumstances to parents *should avoid* its use. The consultants' recommendations were sent to FDA Commissioner Arthur Hayes in a December 4, 1981, letter stating that aspirin should be avoided for children with chicken pox or flu and recommending that the presence of aspirin should be clearly identified in cold remedies and other medicines. The CDC consultant's recommendations were also published in the February 12, 1982, issue of *Morbidity and Mortality*.

On March 9, 1982, less than a month after publication of the warning in

Reagan Deregulation and Reye's Syndrome

Morbidity and Mortality, Sidney Wolfe, director of Public Citizen's Health Research Group (HRG), formally petitioned the FDA to require labels on all aspirin-containing medicines to warn of the association between aspirin and Reye's Syndrome. "Every day's delay in requiring warning labels," he wrote, "will guarantee the continued death and injuries" of children from Reye's Syndrome. Wolfe's HRG and the Litigation Group already were pressing the FDA to issue regulations addressing the connection between the use of high-absorbency tampons and the onset of toxic shock syndrome, suing it to force a re-evaluation of its over-the-counter drug regulations, and trying to force it to issue rules to require testing of all infant formula to make sure that it contained the correct levels of essential nutrients. By 1982, Wolfe knew well how publicize his health and safety campaigns. The Reye's Syndrome issue, with all its attendant horror, was tailor-made for media coverage.

FDA officials knew they had to respond, so they formed an internal working group to review the available data to determine the quality and strength of the association between aspirin and Reye's. This group came to the same conclusion as the CDC and investigators in the state studies:

> [C]ases of RS [Reye's Syndrome] in the study were significantly more likely to have used salicylates, and ... this association continued even when the data were statistically adjusted to account for differences in cases and controls for the symptoms headache, fever, sore throat, and cough and when cases with 4 or fewer days between the onset of antecedent illness and the onset of RS were eliminated.

At the same time that the CDC initially concluded that aspirin should be avoided, an even stronger recommendation was made by the prestigious American Academy of Pediatrics' Committee on Infectious Diseases (known as the Redbook Committee). In December 1981, having just completed a review of the state studies, the Redbook Committee recommended that pediatricians be alerted to advise their patients not to use aspirin during the winter flu season but instead use a non-aspirin substitute containing acetaminophen—which amounted to a recommendation to use Tylenol. This warning was initially scheduled to be published in the February 1982 issue of the Academy's newsletter *News and Comment*.

In "Stalling for Time," a 1985 review of the battle over Reye's Syndrome and aspirin, *San Francisco Chronicle* reporter K. Patrick Conner describes how these first alerts were received in the boardrooms of the nation's aspirin companies:

> Those recommendations deeply troubled the nation's aspirin manufacturers. Ever since the 1960s, when Johnson & Johnson's Tylenol was made a non-prescription drug, aspirin manufacturers have

watched their share of the $1 billion analgesic market steadily decline. In 1973 Tylenol possessed just 7 to 8 percent of the market; by 1981 Tylenol commanded 37 percent, only slightly less than the combined share of Anacin, Bayer, Excedrin and Bufferin, the four leading brands of aspirin.

With profits at risk, the aspirin manufacturers attacked the validity of the state studies, pressuring the CDC to withdraw its warning and the FDA to do nothing. The aspirin manufacturers also went after the American Academy of Pediatrics, forcing it to withhold publication of the Redbook Committee's recommendation. Just before the February 1982 issue of *News and Comment* was to be mailed, the executive director of the Academy ordered the paragraph with the warning deleted, even though it meant reprinting all thirty thousand copies of the newsletter. Asked why, the executive director stated on national television that one of the main reasons he had ordered the reprinting was his concern that Schering-Plough, which made St. Joseph's aspirin, might sue the Academy. Of course, the fact that the Academy received a lot of its funding from the drug industry might also have accounted for the switch.

In mid-April 1982, Wolfe sent a letter proposing specific wording for a warning label and urging the agency to move immediately. Still nothing happened. On May 17, the Litigation Group filed suit in federal district court to compel the FDA to require manufacturers of aspirin products to include in the labels of those products a warning that they should not be given to children with the chicken pox or flu, because of evidence linking the use of aspirin to the development of Reye's Syndrome. A few weeks later, the American Academy of Pediatrics published the following statement in its monthly newsletter:

> [I]nasmuch as salicylates are over-the-counter preparations, education of parents to their avoidance in influenza and chicken pox requires a total community effort. We urge that the appropriate governmental agencies undertake appropriate review and necessary action to inform the public at large.

Then, on June 4, 1982, the secretary of Health and Human Services (HHS), Richard Schweiker, announced that "medical experts have concluded that the use of salicylates such as aspirin in children with influenza ... has been sufficiently associated with Reye Syndrome to warrant warning physicians and parents." He also announced that he had made a determination that warning labels must be placed on aspirin and directed the FDA (which is an agency within HHS) to move at once to mount a public information campaign about the dangers of giving aspirin to children with the flu. Six weeks passed and not even a draft regulation appeared. Meanwhile, the lawsuit Wolfe had filed in May continued. Litigation Group attorney Kathy Meyer was tagged as lead counsel in the case. Over the summer she worked on the briefs and prepared for oral argument.

Shortly after Meyer's brief was filed, the FDA submitted draft regulations to the HHS secretary. On October 4, the FDA sent an official letter to Wolfe, reiterating Schweiker's June 4 direction to the FDA to require a labeling warning. It said that on September 20, the secretary had signed proposed regulations that were sent to the White House Office of Management and Budget (OMB) for review. At a hearing before a House subcommittee on September 29, the "general substance of the proposed regulations was made public," including that non-prescription drugs containing aspirin would bear the following label:

> Warning: This product contains salicylate [aspirin]. Do not use in persons under 16 years of age with flu or chicken pox unless directed by your doctor. The use of salicylate to treat these conditions has been reported to be associated with a rare but serious childhood disease called Reye's Syndrome.

Learning that the rule was sent to OMB raised new worries for Meyer and Wolfe. Now the problem they faced was not just delay but a potential derailment.

Throughout the 1960s and 1970s Congress had reacted to the public demand for laws to curb air and water pollution, clean up toxic waste dumps, ensure the safety of products such as cars and baby cribs, and clean up the election process. The solutions to many such problems demanded scientific, medical or engineering expertise beyond what members of Congress possessed. Moreover, often the solutions were unknown, politically controversial or so costly to corporations that Congress could not, or would not, spell out clearly what to do. Instead, Congress delegated power to the executive branch to find solutions and put them into operation.

This delegation, resulting in a vast transfer of legislative power to the executive, was once considered suspect under our constitutional design of separation of powers. But now courts uphold such delegations, reasoning that the executive branch expertise is needed to carry out the will of Congress if given sufficient guidance in the law.

Nader and others soon discovered that when an agency acted under these delegated powers, it was difficult to hold anyone accountable. Much power was being exercised behind closed doors. The Freedom of Information and Sunshine acts were supposed to open up the process so that citizens could know what was going on, and the courts played a powerful role in ensuring that agencies followed the law and the administrative procedures that allowed citizen involvement. Regulated industries generally disliked openness because it required that defensible, rational arguments—not political muscle—govern the rulemaking process.

Then along came Reagan. By far, the most overwhelming change in the rulemaking process was brought about by executive orders. The first was Executive

Order 12291; the second, Executive Order 12498. Together these orders directed that no agency could issue a proposed rule, final rule or regulatory impact analysis until it was reviewed by OMB, an office run by political appointees of the president. The review, according to the executive order, was intended "only to improve the internal management of the Federal government" and "nothing in [the OMB review requirements] shall be construed as displacing the agencies' responsibilities delegated by law." Reality soon proved quite different.

OMB is an agency within the White House that is intended to provide advice and counsel to the president on budgetary, management and other matters. Although OMB is generally subject to the Freedom of Information Act, its status was less clear when acting as an arm of the president, as the two executive orders contemplated. As a result, OMB's review process was not easily discovered. It did not take long, however, for the media and watchdog groups like Public Citizen to figure out that industry and big business were finding a sympathetic ear at OMB. Many, including Morrison and Nader, believed that OMB's new power was not authorized by Congress, but short of a court ruling saying so, agencies followed the president's orders. OMB axed and gutted regulations. Adding OMB as a player enabled Reagan to close the door on public access to the regulatory process while holding it wide open to the powerful business interests, many of which helped fund his campaign.

For the most part, proving that political decisions within OMB were overriding the expertise of regulatory agencies was difficult if not impossible. But in the case of the FDA's proposed aspirin labeling rule, OMB officials publicly bragged about their role. OMB's review was supposed to be a "cost-benefit" analysis, and the aspirin rule "flunked the test," according to Jim Tozzi, the OMB official responsible for deciding that the labeling rule was unwarranted. "Without OMB's involvement," Tozzi stated, "the rule would have gone out." He later told a *Boston Globe* reporter that "[p]rocedurally, that was the best decision I ever made." Soon after his aspirin rule reviews, Tozzi left OMB to represent companies seeking regulatory relief. "OMB's role in the aspirin case was the most disgusting action" in a long list of OMB horror stories, says Litigation Group's Meyer. Delay in getting the word out to parents about the dangers of using aspirin for children sick with the flu resulted in hundreds of needless deaths. Why someone would think or, worse yet, proudly proclaim a decision that led to this end as his "best decision" was hard to fathom.

What prompted OMB's actions? The story was eventually revealed through investigative journalism and the Litigation Group's court case. When HHS Secretary Schweiker announced the new labeling requirement for aspirin on June 4, 1982, the Aspirin Foundation, a Washington-based lobbying arm of the aspirin manufacturers, turned to Tozzi, who had been successful in killing other health and safety regulations. That fall, a group from the Aspirin Foundation told Tozzi the studies Schweiker was relying on were flawed and warned that the labels would cost the aspirin industry $100 million in unsold aspirin.

The hearing in Public Citizen's lawsuit was held on November 8, 1982, before District Judge John Garrett Penn. There was much confusion about the status of the proposed labeling rule. As the plaintiff's attorney, Meyer was first to argue, but she had not seen a copy of the full proposed rule, only the wording of the warning label from the House subcommittee hearing. The government attorney said the OMB was still reviewing the rule, and he did not know how long it would remain there.

Meyer was asking the court to rule that aspirin products became "misbranded" under the Food and Drug and Cosmetics Act "from the moment it became apparent that the risk of Reye's syndrome was significantly increased with the use of aspirin and the current label on the products did not warn about that risk." That Act provides that a drug is "misbranded and thus cannot lawfully be sold to the public unless its labeling bears ... such adequate warnings against use ... by children where its use may be dangerous to health." The law also states that a drug is misbranded if its label "fails to reveal facts [that are] material with respect to consequences which may result from use ... under the conditions of use prescribed in the labeling or advertising thereof or under such conditions of use as are customary or usual."

The law does not require proof that it is dangerous, merely that it *may* be. Meyer argued that misbranding took place "no later than the Secretary's announcement on June 4th [1982] which was five months ago and yet five months have gone by and the FDA has yet to issue any requirement that the products warn about the association between Reye's syndrome and aspirin." She argued that this delay was unreasonable, much like the delay in the ethylene oxide and hazardous communication standards. Yet in those cases, years had passed with no action. Meyer had to make a case that five months was excessive under the present circumstances. She fired away:

> First of all, the nature of the problem is severe and the FDA does not contest that. Children with the flu or chicken pox who are treated with aspirin significantly increase their risk of getting this disease.

> Secondly, the longer the FDA delays the more likelihood there is that more children are going to suffer and in fact, we have recently learned from the CDC that between Dec. 1, 1981 and October 31 of this year there have been 170 confirmed cases of Reye's syndrome including 57 deaths. [All of these cases occurred after the CDC's first warning.]

> Third, the flu season is now upon us and the risk of Reye's syndrome is significantly increased for children who take aspirin during the flu season.

> Fourth, the situation with Reye's syndrome and aspirin, the risk the

children experience, can be avoided simply by warning parents not to treat their children with aspirin if they have the chicken pox or flu.

Also, she argued, the aspirin industry "is using the fact that FDA has not required a label warning to encourage physicians to continue to treat children with aspirin regardless of whether they have the flu or chicken pox." Her Exhibits 16 and 17 were examples of form letters from major manufacturers of aspirin encouraging physicians to feel confident to treat children with aspirin when they have flu or chicken pox. The basis for their recommendation was that the FDA had not moved to require a warning label. The association between aspirin and Reye's had been known for over a year, she pointed out, and "there has been no new evidence since June 4, 1982 to dispute the Secretary's finding."

Then Meyer went after the drug manufacturers. Just compare the FDA's delay, she said, "with the speed with which it has acted to issue final regulations governing tamper-resistant packaging for over-the-counter drugs." It took "barely one month after the first incidence of Tylenol poisoning, the first death!" Here she was referring to the rush to reassure the consumers after cyanide was first found in a Tylenol bottle. The drug companies immediately repackaged their products and added labels warning against using the product if the tamper-proof seal was broken. Not only were new labels required, but a full redesign of the packaging was necessary, and the FDA had no trouble setting up a short and specific timetable. The drug industry was delighted to comply, delighted to have the government use its good name to quiet public concern. FDA waived the notice and comment requirement of the Administrative Procedure Act and moved full-throttle toward a final rule. Meyer noted that these new regulations had appeared in the *Federal Register* just the week before. She went on:

> Here, in contrast, the problem is much more severe than in the Tylenol cyanide poisonings. There was a case where you had seven deaths by independent action not caused by the drug itself, but caused by someone injecting cyanide into the drug. Here we have a situation where the drug itself and aspirin products, causes the problem. We have had 57 deaths [all children] and many more illnesses occurring in children and again the remedy here is much simpler.

An education campaign would be helpful but not as effective as a warning label, Meyer argued. When a mother picks the bottle off the bathroom shelf and prepares to give a dose to a sick child, she checks to see what the right dose is, and that is when a warning hits home. The companies were doing nothing voluntarily to inform consumers. Instead, they were taking advantage of the absence of a labeling rule to urge that their products be used for children with flu or chicken pox. Finally, the judge asked about the OMB review, to which Meyer responded that the reason her brief had not addressed this issue was that "this is the first time that the Government has rested on the claim, on the fact that it has done everything it can do, and the regulations are sitting over at OMB." She would be happy, she noted, to file a memorandum quickly addressing the issue.

All of her best efforts did not win the day, though several events that played out between her oral argument and the court's decision may well have had a great deal to do with how the court decided.

On November 8, the same day Meyer was presenting her oral argument to the court, the executive board of the American Academy of Pediatrics made a surprise announcement: "Labeling aspirin-containing preparations as contraindicated in the treatment of influenza or chicken pox should be delayed until more conclusive evidence of the association of aspirin administration and Reye's Syndrome is shown by further investigation." The executive board had acted at a hastily arranged telephone conference without consulting its own scientific committee. An Academy official phoned C. Boyden Gray, counsel to the president's Task Force on Regulatory Relief. Now OMB had a powerful weapon with which to club HHS Secretary Schweiker into line.

Ten days later, on November 18, Schweiker reversed himself, basing his change of heart solely on the concerns raised by the American Academy of Pediatrics. This was the first time such "concerns have been raised by an independent body," Schweiker noted, "and it is critical that they be resolved." He asked the FDA to set up new government-supported studies to resolve the scientific dispute. With that he withdrew the rule, which still had not been approved by OMB, stating that any new proposed rules would have to rely on evidence from new studies and from testimony taken during an advanced notice of proposed rulemaking—a pre-proposal phase.

The next day, November 19, the "independent body" cited by Schweiker suddenly flip-flopped again. "The American Academy of Pediatrics continues to be concerned about the possible association of aspirin and Reye's Syndrome and has alerted physicians to use caution in recommending aspirin for treatment of influenza and chicken pox symptoms." The announcement further stated that the Academy believed "that the current labeling [on aspirin] which includes 'flu' among those conditions which may be treated with aspirin is inappropriate," and recommended "deletion of the flu indication from labeling of children's aspirin-containing products." But the damage was done; the proposed rule had already been killed.

What on earth would cause such a prestigious group of medical experts to behave so preposterously? Meyer and Wolfe certainly suspected pressure from the aspirin industry, but proof was another matter. Proof came quickly, but it did not help obtain a warning label. And again, it was the power of a lawsuit that exposed the truth.

In a confidential letter marked "not sent to any public official," Edward A. Mortimer, a professor of community health and pediatrics and chairman of the Department of Community Health at Case Western Reserve University, on November 17, 1982, resigned from the Committee on Infectious Diseases (the Redbook Committee) of the American Academy of Pediatrics. Mortimer had served as director of the Redbook Committee since 1966 and was the person most responsible for its investigations on the aspirin-Reye's Syndrome link.

In his letter of resignation, Mortimer charged that the executive board had made its decision recommending the labeling regulation be delayed "in cursory fashion without adequate examination of the facts" or consultation with its own expert advisory committee. The executive committee had "overstepped its bounds." He reminded the Academy that the Redbook Committee had recommended only that children not be given aspirin for flu and had not taken a position on labeling. "Without adequate study and knowledge, the Academy took a position on something which I think was not its business."

Most of all, Mortimer was clearly troubled by the fact that "the Academy has now set a most unfortunate and potentially dangerous precedent for itself and for other public or quasi-public advisory bodies in terms of responding to outside pressures. ... Suppose that it becomes a generally accepted and effective policy for industries affected by recommendations made by such advisory bodies to intimidate those bodies by threats of lawsuits, withholding financial support, legal investigations of those responsible for the recommendations." This was precisely what had happened: an independent, scientific body had succumbed to threats. Mortimer wrote of the danger if this were to become the norm:

> If such becomes the case, imagine the position of the American Heart Association which, upon recommendation of its Committee on Rheumatic Fever, has said that treatment of streptococcal pharyngitis with the tetracycline group of antibiotics is not recommended because it doesn't work. Can Upjohn sue the American Heart Association? Could it have the Dr. subpoenaed or otherwise belabored the late Charles H. Rammelkamp, whose studies showed the lack of efficacy of these drugs? Can the American Cancer Society be intimidated or sued by the tobacco manufacturers because of its position on cigarettes? ... We have, in effect, opened Pandora's box because the Academy, one of the most respected voluntary health-related organizations, has set a precedent by acquiescing to such pressures.

> Mortimer raised another concern. The Academy had sent a warning to pediatricians "which no doubt will be communicated to parents who can afford optimum pediatric care." The Academy thought the problem critical enough to warn its members, but who would warn

those too poor to have a regular doctor? It looked altogether as if the Academy was "endorsing a double standard of care."

His resignation concluded, "I believe that the Academy has also compromised or tarnished its reputation with other groups who have long held it in respect, including the FDA, the NIH, the CDC and the many epidemiologists who have studied this matter in detail. The Academy simply should have stood pat with its prior, conservative and cautious recommendations, rather than backing off under pressure." Just two days after Mortimer handed his resignation letter to the Academy president, the Academy publicly returned to its original position on the danger of using aspirin for children with flu and other viral diseases.

Meyer submitted a supplemental memorandum to the district court on December 2, 1982, responding to the secretary's withdrawal of the rule and the American Academy of Pediatricians' contradictory statements. Attached to her memorandum as Exhibit 27 was a copy of Mortimer's resignation letter, which she had obtained as a result of her lawsuit. Once again, she argued, "all of the government officials, agencies and expert advisory groups that had studied the evidence concluded that there was an association between aspirin and Reye's." Reliance of the secretary on the American Academy of Pediatricians was inappropriate, because it was not the Academy's responsibility to determine if a label was required under the law. Furthermore, the secretary's withdrawal of the proposed rule was "completely lacking of any claim of new scientific evidence to support his abrupt changed position." Moreover, the Academy had announced its new position supporting the evidence connecting aspirin and Reye's Syndrome just the day after Schweiker's announcement of the withdrawal of the proposed rule. Even if it were a proper basis for his decision then, it clearly was not now. There was quite simply no rational basis for supporting the secretary's action. In addition, though an educational campaign was certainly welcome, the law, she argued, "simply does not provide the Secretary or FDA with the option of conducting a public education campaign in lieu of requiring a labeling warning." Indeed, the secretary had stated that because label changes take time and quickly alerting consumers was a priority, he was conducting the education campaign.

On December 28, the FDA published an advanced notice of rulemaking in the *Federal Register* stating that the agency was considering a variety of rules on aspirin and Reye's Syndrome. This notice set no specific rule or timetable. Action could be years in the future. Officials at the time estimated it would take three to four years to complete the studies. But the notice did provide evidence that the agency intended to move forward on some sort of labeling rule—the sort of reassurance that the court could see as reason to defer to the FDA. On March 14, 1983, Judge Penn upheld the agency's delay, relying on the fact that the American Academy of Pediatricians had raised concerns about the advisability of a labeling requirement and on the secretary's assurance that careful and expedited consideration would be given to the matter. As to the misbranding claim Meyer had raised, the court ruled that it was not yet ripe for review, because the FDA had not issued a final decision on whether there would be a label change.

The aspirin industry had won all the rounds so far. When the rule was withdrawn in November 1982, the flu season was starting. Wolfe went into high gear on the publicity front, issuing press releases and going on TV and radio talk shows to warn parents. Working with an organization of pharmacists, he also had warning labels printed and distributed throughout the United States, and he urged pharmacists to put them on bottles of aspirin. And though the rule had been withdrawn, HHS, FDA, the surgeon general and the CDC continued their own education campaigns, distributing consumer brochures and radio public service announcements.

An organization called the Committee for the Care of Children (CCC) filed suit against the HHS, FDA, surgeon general and the CDC in U.S. district court in Boston. The CCC had been formed by a Boston lawyer named Neil Chayet with funding from two of the largest aspirin manufacturers, Schering-Plough and Sterling Drug. The group claimed membership of some twelve hundred people, including pediatricians. Chayet also served as attorney for the group. His suit charged that the government had "engaged in a massive action warning the public and medical professions of a possible relation between the use of aspirin and Reye's Syndrome ... contrary to [its] publicly stated decision not to proceed with a labeling regulation." These campaigns, he claimed, were misleading and causing vast confusion. But it was not just the government he was after. He angrily denounced Public Citizen, "this so-called public interest group." Chayet's brief failed to mention the fact that his own group was funded by two major aspirin manufacturers. Chayet asked the court to enjoin any further distribution by Public Citizen of such warnings in print or on the air— the First Amendment be damned.

Not satisfied with the pace of the legal process for stopping these public education campaigns, the Aspirin Foundation resorted once again to political pressure. On October 7, 1983, representatives of the Aspirin Foundation met with the assistant secretary for health and a handful of other top HHS officials. Shortly after that meeting, the pamphlets—all four hundred and seventy thousand, printed at public expense—were quietly stashed in an FDA warehouse in Rockville, Maryland. The same fate met HHS plans to send out public service announcements to radio stations and newspapers. Public Citizen continued its campaign, but with a small budget there was no way it could match the federal government's intended effort. In a nation with a population of more than two hundred and thirty million, even the government's larger education campaign was a drop in the bucket. Labeling was the only really effective way to get the word out to the parents who needed to hear it.

By November 1983, nearly two years had passed since the CDC's panel of experts had concluded that aspirin should not be given to children with the flu or chicken pox. Three hundred and sixty cases of Reye's Syndrome had been reported, and one hundred and thirteen children had died. The government went on studying, Wolfe went on warning, Meyer went on litigating, and the aspirin industry went on lobbying and doing its own version of an education campaign.

* * * * *

There were many other things on Meyer's desk at the time, including a challenge to the Department of Agriculture's responsibility to see that food products are not misbranded and do not endanger health. Like the aspirin case, this one concerned providing information to the public so that citizens could make informed decisions. The issue, in what is known as the "deboned meat case," was not as life-threatening (though for some individuals it could be health-threatening) as aspirin, but it was very much about the use of government power to protect the financial interests of industry over consumers' right to accurate information about what they buy.

Prior to the late 1960s, meat was cut by hand off the carcass of an animal. The remaining skeleton, with whatever meat and tissue was left, was typically ground for feed, fertilizer or other such purposes. Then in the early 1960s, the Japanese developed a mechanical process that pulverized the bones that remained after the hand-cutting process into a mash. The mash was pushed through a fine sieve that held back any larger pieces of bone that had not been thoroughly ground. The end product consisted of skeletal muscle and tissue, bone and bone marrow, something called "mechanically produced beef product."

In 1976, the U.S. Department of Agriculture first proposed allowing this process to be used in the United States for red meat and its product to be used in processed meat foods such as hot dogs, bologna, pizza sauces, chili and similar foodstuffs, without any special labeling requirement. The label could just say "beef." This new regulation was quickly challenged in federal court by four consumer groups. Their motion for a preliminary injunction to prevent Agriculture Secretary Earl Butz from enforcing the rule was filed on September 1 and granted (*Community Nutrition Institute v. Butz*, September 10, 1976). The court ruled that the Agriculture Department had failed to determine whether the added product "*may* render it [the meat] injurious to health," and that, although the parties to the case had not fully argued the point, it "appeared to the Court that the interim regulation permits misbranding of product labeled, for example, 'all beef franks.' " The judge also ruled that the regulation had been issued without notice, public participation or a thirty-day delayed effective date (all requirements of the Administrative Procedure Act).

Following the court's injunction, the Agriculture Department withdrew the regulation and began a new rulemaking process to address the health, use and labeling issues. Following the notice and comment period, the department issued regulations requiring that any product including mechanically deboned meat would have to be labeled as containing "mechanically separated beef product" or "mechanically separated pork product," etc. The new rule also required that the label state the percentage of powdered bone in the product and limited the amount of mechanically separated meat to 20 percent of the total meat in a product. The industry preferred the term "mechanically deboned meat," but the Agriculture Department found this to be false or misleading to consumers since the term deboned would tend to imply that there was no bone, just meat. The reasons the secretary insisted that the label state that bone was included were: (1) bone contains calcium and some people must limit their intake of calcium; and (2) bone often contains significant amounts of lead—a health hazard, especially to children.

Although the meat industry did not challenge the regulations in court, the next year the Pacific Coast Meat Association petitioned the department to amend the regulations because the "negative labeling and unrealistic standards" effectively precluded its members and other companies from producing and selling mechanically deboned meat. The industry wanted the label to list the percentage of calcium content in a product rather than the percentage of powdered bone content, which was required. Further, the petition requested the deletion of the requirement to label products as containing mechanically separated beef products. In May 1979, the Agriculture Department denied the petition. The 1978 regulation, the department noted, "was an attempt to accommodate this widespread desire to avoid the product, while still permitting it on the market." In June of that year, the meat association resubmitted its request. The department replied that there was no new evidence to support or permit a change.

In February 1981, the meat industry was back again. But this time things had changed. The Reagan administration was now in charge. In support of its new petition, the industry submitted data from eight consumer focus groups it had commissioned.

Focus group studies are often used by advertisers before releasing a new product and by political candidates to get a feel for how a new position or political ad will play with the public. No claim is made that they are representative of the population as a whole. Participants are not selected randomly, and there is no claim that they are statistically valid. The focus group approach involves gathering a group of citizens (often for pay) who are asked questions by a professional group leader about some issue. In the case of the deboned meat focus groups, the sessions were filmed, and the group's responses were analyzed by the Market Survey Research firm. Later, the Agriculture Department hired another firm, Arthur D. Little Inc., to review this assessment. Arthur D. Little concluded: "For the most part the report reasonably reflects the focus groups. There are, however, a number of instances of omission, inappropriate emphasis, or misuse of terms." One of these was that the professional group leader repeatedly used words like "confused," "misleading" and "fair." Instead of asking questions like, "How do you feel about these label requirements?" she tended to ask, "Do you feel this is misleading?"

One would think consumers' resistance to a product containing mechanically separated beef product would lend support for continued labeling or even strengthening the labeling requirement. That, after all, is the point of truth in labeling—to enable consumers to make informed decisions. But the Agriculture Department apparently was convinced that these focus group studies supported the petition, and it proposed new regulations in July 1981 that did just what the meat industry wanted.

In August 1982, a month after the new regulations became final, Meyer filed suit in federal court. She lost, then appealed. "When I heard that our appeals court panel was to be Judges Wilkey, Scalia and Bork," Meyer recalls, "I knew we were doomed." It was about as conservative a panel of the Appeals Court for the District of Columbia as was possible at the time. "I knew we would lose, but still we put our all into it." Meyer went through the usual grueling moot court, but nothing could have prepared her for what she would experience at oral argument on October 19, 1983.

"I got up and began my argument, but before I got even a minute into it, Judge Wilkey leaned over and asked, 'Well Ms. Meyer, what about horseradish?'" Meyer continues:

> Well I was stumped. Horseradish? So I said, "I don't know, your Honor, what about horseradish?" He replied, "Well, it doesn't have any horse in there." Well that set these three judges off on a one-upmanship game of one-liners. What about hot dogs? What about hamburg? And on and on. After a bit they let me get back to my argument. Then Wilkey leaned forward again: "What's the big deal about bone. You see dogs chomping on them." I decided that I might as well play along. "Sounds like my father-in-law!" That cracked the three judges up. At least they let me finish the argument, though I well knew it fell on deaf ears.

A couple of years later, when Public Citizen was fighting Reagan's nomination of Robert Bork to the Supreme Court, the Litigation Group did a thorough analysis of the judge's opinions, articles and speeches, and published it in a book called *The Judicial Record of Judge Robert H. Bork*. One day, while Meyer was poring over some Bork speeches, she discovered one about using humor in oral argument and discovered this: "I'll never forget this young woman ..." and then Bork went on to tell all about the deboned meat oral argument. She had amused the judges, but had not persuaded one. On December 5, 1984, the court unanimously ruled for the secretary of Agriculture. Meyer had to read no further than the opening sentence in Judge Antonin Scalia's opinion to know that it was only the humor that made it through:

This case, involving legal requirements for the content and labeling of meat products such as frankfurters, affords a rare opportunity to explore simultaneously both parts of Bismarck's aphorism that "no man should see how laws or sausages are made."

* * * * *

Meanwhile, in the aspirin case, Meyer appealed the district court's decision upholding the agency's delay in the labeling rule. More than a year later, on July 27, 1984, the court of appeals issued its decision, agreeing that the misbranding claim was not yet ripe for review. However, the appeals court was disturbed about the delay: "the record strongly suggests that the pace of agency decision-making is unreasonably dilatory," especially since "[a]ll the scientific evidence in the record points to a link between [aspirin] and Reye's Syndrome." Moreover, the court was clearly troubled by the evidence of the industry's role in the delay, finding it particularly troubling "in that the pace of agency decision-making may jeopardize the lives of children." Thus, the court of appeals remanded the case to the district court, instructing that court to hear evidence concerning the agency's justifications for the delay in requiring a warning label, and, after doing so, to rule on whether that delay was unreasonable.

Over the next few months Meyer prepared for the case on remand, conducting extensive discovery on the basis for the secretary of agriculture's November 18, 1982, decision to reverse his previous determination that a warning label was required. By deposing officials at the American Academy of Pediatrics and the FDA, she found evidence to show that the secretary had relied solely on the Academy's announcement that labeling should be postponed. She also discovered that the Academy's executive board had misunderstood the legal requirement for a warning label, believing a cause and effect relationship had to be proved. Legally, a warning label is required if a drug "may be" injurious to a child's health.

Meanwhile, the Committee for the Care of Children, the industry front group, began sending out its own "public service" announcements: "We do not know what causes Reye's Syndrome. We do know that no medicine has been proven to cause Reye's." The ads went on to say that the disease was being studied, but in the meantime parents should call their doctor if they thought their child had Reye's. Journalists tracked down Mortimer for his comment on the ads. "Misleading, irresponsible and dangerous," was his response. Soon thereafter, the assistant secretary for health at HHS offered a similar sentiment: "grossly misleading." Then, on December 13, 1984, the Public Health Service announced preliminary results of the pilot study phase of the study that the secretary of HHS had directed it to do when he withdrew the original aspirin warning rule. The announcement was made at a secret meeting involving a National Academy of Sciences (Institute of Medicine) committee that had been monitoring the study. Wolfe got wind of the meeting and through the efforts of Representative John Dingell managed to get a copy of the study. It showed a strong relationship, even stronger than the state studies, between taking aspirin for the flu or chicken pox and the development of Reye's Syndrome. Since the FDA's "Advanced Notice of Proposed Rulemaking" had stated that labeling regulations would immediately be issued "if warranted by new scientific information," Wolfe had some hope that a rule would come soon. Still, with the normal bureaucratic foot-dragging and the Reagan administration's anti-regulation stance, he was taking no chances.

On January 9, 1985, Wolfe asked FDA Commissioner Frank Young to:

> Immediately seize or require warning stickers to be placed on all previously manufactured bottles of children's aspirin. Such bottles now say "fast effective relief of fever and minor aches and pains of colds and flu" (St. Joseph's Aspirin for Children) or "Effective, gentle relief for painful discomforts, sore throat, fever of colds and flu" (Bayer Children's Aspirin). In view of the accumulated evidence linking aspirin and Reye's, such a label is an invitation for parents to unwittingly injure or kill their children.

Wolfe asked that a warning regulation be immediately promulgated, noting that "such a regulation was proposed 2 1/2 years ago, but dropped due to aspirin industry pressure filtered through OMB. HHS said, 'another study' is needed. This is the study." He also asked the FDA to strengthen the public education campaign to explicitly state, "Do not use aspirin to treat chicken pox or flu symptoms in anyone 19 years or younger." Wolfe then noted that, despite the absence of warning labels, there had been some decrease in the use of aspirin to treat chicken pox and flu. In the 1980-81 studies, 95 to 100 percent of the children who contracted Reye's had used aspirin, while 70 percent of the children in the control group, those who did not get Reye's, had used aspirin. In the new Public Health Service study, 96 percent of the children with Reye's had used aspirin, but only 45 percent of the non-Reye's control subjects had used aspirin. Though education campaigns had clearly helped some, clearly they were not enough.

The same day that Wolfe sent his letter to the FDA, the new HHS secretary, Margaret Heckler, made public the results of the pilot study. But instead of issuing a new aspirin warning regulation, Heckler called on the industry to use a warning label "voluntarily" and promised to expand the department's education campaign. On January 11, she announced that the major aspirin manufacturers had agreed to cooperate with the FDA to develop new labeling for aspirin products. The result of that "cooperation" was that, by the fall of 1985, all medicines containing aspirin would bear a new warning. The industry version made no mention of Reye's or the terrible danger to children. It said, "Warning: Consult a physician before giving this medicine to children, including teenagers, with chicken pox or flu."

Needless to say, this was not a sufficient warning. Both Wolfe and Meyer knew, though, that it would be hard to win in court, because the FDA had at least done something. Wolfe and his Health Research Group (with help from Public Citizen's Congress Watch) turned their attention to Capitol Hill. If the executive branch would not act, maybe they could get Congress to do so. There they found help from Representative Henry Waxman, who was chairman of a House subcommittee with jurisdiction over the HHS. He wrote a letter to Heckler urging her to "implement swiftly your stated intention to use the Food and Drug administration and the mass media to alert the public of this serious health hazard" and warning her that his subcommittee would be following her actions closely. Lest she not get the message, he added:

> If it appears from your report to the Subcommittee or other evidence that a voluntary approach is not adequate, I intend to pursue legislation making warning labels and other informational measures mandatory.

In March, Waxman's subcommittee held hearings on H.R. 1381, the "Emergency Reye's Syndrome Prevention Act of 1985." FDA Commissioner Young testified in opposition to the bill. Why was he opposed? "First, the definitive scientific data are still not available." Although the pilot study had found "that nearly all Reye cases had aspirin exposure, as opposed to only about 45% of controls ... the relatively small size of the pilot project means its findings should not be considered definitive. The larger more dispositive, full scale PHS study is now underway." His advice: wait for more proof. "Second, there is currently a voluntary labeling and extensive public education program underway."

At the same congressional hearing, representatives of the American Academy of Pediatricians testified that the results of the pilot study gave "more reason than ever to warn the public and especially young adolescents about the association between aspirin and Reye's Syndrome." But the proposed law got no further than the hearing stage, though that at least forced the executive branch to defend its actions. It also provided more public visibility for the aspirin-Reye's Syndrome connection. Most important, though, it let the administration know that someone besides the Health Research Group and the president's OMB were watching.

On April 9, 1985, Meyer filed a motion for summary judgment (asking for a decision based on a reading of the law where no material facts are in dispute), arguing that the decision to seek voluntary labeling amounted to a final decision not to require a label and, therefore, the challenge under the misbranding provisions of the Food, Drug and Cosmetic Act was now ripe for review. Young's testimony before the congressional committee provided some useful evidence that the department did not intend to move any further at this point on a warning rule. On September 30, Meyer was once again arguing before the district court, but then it was back to the waiting game. Finally, on March 7,

1986, with the flu season almost at an end, and no new evidence in hand, the FDA issued a final rule requiring this warning label on aspirin:

> WARNING: Children and teenagers should not use this medicine for chicken pox or flu symptoms before a doctor is consulted about Reye's Syndrome, a rare but serious illness.

Their long fight was at an end. Four and a half years had passed since the Centers for Disease Control had reported the strong evidence linking Reye's Syndrome to aspirin use by children ill with chicken pox and flu. Since that time, more than six hundred cases of Reye's Syndrome were reported. One hundred and ninety-four children died, and many others suffered permanent brain damage. It was a lot fewer cases and deaths than would have been expected, based on past statistics. Prior to 1981 the average number of cases was between six hundred and twelve hundred per year; the average number of deaths was one hundred and eighty to three hundred and sixty per year. Much of the decline, no doubt, was attributable to increased public awareness. That is not much consolation for those parents who did not hear the educational messages and whose children were forever lost or permanently damaged. But, Wolfe said, "I think about the lives saved because change has finally come as a result of our efforts—if we had not acted, these too would have been lost." The precise causes of Reye's Syndrome remain unclear, but by 2004 the disease had been virtually eradicated in the United States.

17

Separation of Powers
and the Gramm-Rudman Act

In 1981, the total federal debt surpassed the $1 trillion mark. Four years later it stood at nearly $2 trillion. It had taken almost two hundred years for the United States government to accumulate the first trillion in debt, but the second trillion took only four years. By 1985, as President Reagan began his second term, the deficit had become a political minefield in Washington. Who was to blame? Reagan pointed his finger at Congress. Members of Congress pointed back at him.

The terms deficit and debt, often misunderstood, are key to understanding the budget debate. The federal *deficit* is the shortfall in a single budget year between what is spent by the government and what is raised in taxes and other revenue. The government borrows money to fund this shortfall by issuing interest-bearing bonds that are purchased by investors. The federal *debt*, on the other hand, is the total accumulation of those annual shortfalls—the amount the government owes to investors at any particular time. Every annual budget includes a line item showing the cost of servicing this debt. The percentage of the annual federal budget that is paid out as interest on the debt has increased dramatically as the debt has grown, cutting into the funds available for government programs.

Prior to 1970, some budget years ended with surpluses. When this happened, the government could pay off some of its debt. By the mid-1980s, though, there had been nothing but deficits since the last surplus in 1969, and so the debt grew larger. In the early 1980s, deficits suddenly spiraled higher. The reasons for higher deficits were many: Reagan's huge 1981 tax cuts; big increases in defense spending pressed by the Reagan administration; rising costs in Medicare and other health programs as medical science advanced and the population aged; lower tax revenues because of higher unemployment; increased costs of servicing the federal debt because of high interest rates; and higher costs for Social Security and other federal programs that included cost-of-living increases. After Reagan's first term, the total federal debt had ballooned from $1 trillion to $1.9 trillion—a startling 91 percent increase. Average deficits under the first four Reagan-era budgets were $183 million, nearly triple the average deficit of $63 billion over the previous four years.

When members of Congress returned from their August recess in 1985, they faced the need to pass legislation to increase the federal debt ceiling. Congress had chosen to limit how much the U.S. Treasury Department could borrow to cover expenses when tax income fell short. Having made this choice, Congress had to deal with the issue each time total borrowing neared the ceiling. There was really no choice but to raise the debt ceiling. Without an increase to allow the government to borrow more, the government would simply have to shut down. But with all the attention focused on the issue in the fall of 1985, no one wanted to go on record favoring more debt; nor was there support for the alternatives—raising taxes or cutting spending. Members of Congress wanted a way to hide from the blame, some way to prove their fiscal responsibility without having to make difficult choices.

Phil Gramm, a freshman Republican senator from Texas, had just the device in mind. When the bill to increase the debt ceiling reached the Senate floor in late September, Gramm was primed for action. On September 25, he and two co-sponsors, freshman Republican Senator Warren Rudman of New Hampshire and a more senior Democrat, Ernest Hollings of South Carolina, offered a deficit reduction amendment that, they claimed, would solve the deficit and debt problems by 1991. The Gramm-Rudman-Hollings deficit reduction amendment, usually known as Gramm-Rudman, established maximum deficit targets for each of the following five budget years, with the aim of eliminating the deficit by October 1, 1990. The targets were to be set in stone with no further congressional votes required. Based on their economic forecasts, the White House's Office of Management and Budget (OMB) and the Congressional Budget Office (CBO) were directed to evaluate whether the government would meet the targets.

Economists at OMB and CBO were to make their best estimates about the next year's inflation rate, interest rates, unemployment rate, gross domestic product growth, tax income and expenditures for any programs that depended on these factors. In the past, predictions by OMB and CBO about these fiscal indicators rarely had matched subsequent reality, and often the agencies disagreed. The amendment provided that if the two agencies disagreed, an average between their figures was to be used. This evaluation would be done at two different points in the congressional budget process. A first "snapshot" would be due in mid-August, and a final evaluation would be due in early October, just after the start of the federal budget year. If the second evaluation showed that the budget bills passed by Congress and signed into law by the president would exceed the deficit targets, the president would be forced to cut spending to meet the deficit target. Initially, it was envisioned that all federal programs would face such spending cuts. Political reality quickly led to exempting Social Security, and before the bill passed, many other programs were exempted.

The *Christian Science Monitor* called Gramm's legislation the "Balanced Baloney Act of 1985," a "perilously unbalanced ... fantasy." Columnist George Will charged that congressional pleas in support of it sounded "like the notes that a homicidal maniac sends to the police: 'Stop me before I kill (spend) again!' " *Time* magazine termed it "a statutory act of desperation, an admission that Government is incapable of governing itself." *BusinessWeek* said the act was "hopelessly impractical and violates the spirit, if not the letter, of the Constitution." The Gramm-Rudman act was, said Walter Heller, who served as President Kennedy's chief economic adviser, "economically capricious, socially unfair, militarily risky, constitutionally questionable, politically irresponsible, procedurally perverse and administratively outlandish." These derogatory assessments, coming from both ends of the political spectrum, mirrored Ralph Nader's initial reaction. He also worried that the budget ax, as it would be wielded by the sitting president, would become a dangerous weapon that most likely would fall disproportionately on the poor and the politically weak.

Morrison also read in disbelief about Gramm's scheme. His litigator's nose smelled a potential constitutional challenge. After all, power over the federal purse had been of paramount concern to the framers of the Constitution, and control by the elected representatives in Congress had been their clear choice. The Constitution is explicit about this. Article I, Section 8, says, "The Congress shall have the power to lay and collect taxes, duties, imposts and excises, to pay the debts and provide for the common defense and general welfare of the United States." Article I, Section 9, says, "No money shall be drawn from the treasury, but in consequence of appropriations made by law." The Constitution does not say that anyone else can pass appropriations laws or amend them after they are passed, and *Chadha* made clear that for Congress to exercise its power it had to follow the dictates of the Presentment Clause. But if somehow a court were to see the vast delegation of lawmaking power in the Gramm-Rudman amendment to be an acceptable delegation of power to the president, then both *Chadha* and *Buckley* made it clear that Congress could not share in the execution of the law once passed. It is unconstitutional to allow one or both houses to share in the execution of the law through the use of the legislative veto or sharing in the appointment process. The CBO is a mere creature of Congress. Its director is appointed by Congress and its job is to advise Congress. Surely it would be a breach of the Constitution for a branch of Congress to do what one house or even both acting together were prevented from doing. Morrison could see no way that OMB and CBO acting together could order the president to alter existing appropriations law.

On October 9, the Senate voted 75-24 vote to pass the amendment. Prior to the vote, there had been no committee hearings or discussions on the deficit reduction amendment, and thus no formal economic, procedural or legal analyses were available for senators to review. Debate had to rely largely on speculative statements about what the measure would do and proceed while key provisions were constantly altered as the bill's sponsors and the Republican leadership negotiated for votes. Pressure for passage was immense. The Republican Senate leadership held the Senate in session on both Saturday and Sunday (only the eleventh time in history that a Sunday session had been held in the Senate) and refused to allow a separate vote on the debt ceiling bill. The leadership was browbeating its troops with the Treasury Department's warning that the government would run out of money by October 9 and with the threatened public spectacle of a government shutdown.

Morrison's inquiries about the legislation brought him into contact with Representative Mike Synar (D-Oklahoma), who shared his opinion about the amendment's constitutionality. Synar impressed Morrison as "both politically shrewd and constitutionally principled." While the Senate raced to pass the deficit reduction amendment, Morrison worked with Synar and his staff to shape the law to accommodate a quick legal challenge. Synar was willing to be a plaintiff in a challenge, and Morrison was ready to represent him at no charge. To that end, they fashioned an amendment to provide standing for members of Congress and an expedited judicial review process.

Expecting the Senate-passed version to reach the House floor quickly, Morrison had a final version of the proposed expedited judicial review amendment and a seven-page floor statement of explanation and support prepared for Synar's use by October 10. But action did not move next to the House floor.

Congressional pressure to fight the deficit was so strong that House Democratic leaders feared a stampede in support of the Gramm-Rudman amendment. To buy some time and avoid an immediate floor vote, the House leadership asked for a conference between the houses, hoping that, if they could not kill the legislation, perhaps they could at least shape it into a more acceptable form. Nine senators and forty-eight representatives were appointed to the conference committee. On October 31, conferees declared the conference deadlocked. House conferees wanted the CBO to have sole responsibility for the economic analyses that could trigger a sequester order, wanted more of the cuts to fall on the defense budget, and wanted more protection for Medicare and other health programs. In a show of party unity the next day, House Democrats voted almost unanimously in support of the House conferees' version of the amendment, which had been rejected by the Senate conferees. The Senate followed suit, voting for its own version the following day. It was back to conference.

The second conference was made up of sixty-six conferees. Over the first week, many changes were put on the table, one of which raised a potential stumbling block for Morrison's intended constitutional attack on the bill. In an effort to overcome the constitutional problem raised by CBO's participation in the process, the Senate proposed adding a new player, the General Accounting Office (GAO) and its head, the comptroller general, to the CBO/OMB team, setting up a troika of economic wizards to crunch the fiscal numbers. CBO's involvement was the clearest and most immediate constitutional problem, as Morrison well knew, making an attack on the constitutionality of the process a relatively easy task. The addition of the GAO complicated the issue. Morrison did not believe, however, that it solved the constitutional problem.

Just where the GAO fit into the three constitutional branches was open to debate. Its head is chosen by the president from a list of nominees suggested by Congress and appointed to a fifteen-year term, with confirmation by the Senate. The GAO's major role is to ensure that the executive branch follows the law as it spends money appropriated by Congress. Its reports are directed to Congress. Members of Congress can ask for and order the GAO to undertake specific program investigations. Its expenses are paid out of money budgeted for Congress. On the other hand, since its creation by the Budget and Accounting Act of 1921, it has exercised many functions that resemble executive functions. It is independent, yet dependent on Congress; the president has no control over it other than his appointment of the comptroller general. Congress can remove the director by joint resolution—a process that requires bicameral passage and presentment to the president, or a two-thirds vote over a presidential veto—but has never made any effort to do so. The president cannot remove the comptroller general "for cause" as he can remove the heads of other so-called independent agencies such as the Federal Trade Commission (FTC), the Federal Energy Regulatory Commission (FERC) or the Securities and Exchange Commission (SEC). The GAO simply does not fit well in the constitutional design of three separate branches.

The proposed addition of the GAO to the trigger process made no practical sense, Morrison argued, as it would be given only ten days to review and make determinations about the report from CBO and OMB before it had to report a sequester order, if one were needed, to the president. Moreover, the comptroller general would be given little latitude to change what CBO and OMB recommended. The GAO's role would be little more than symbolic.

By November 10, the Senate had also proposed adding a fallback provision to the law: if a court were to declare unconstitutional any part of the triggering mechanism (including the role of any of the three players and/or that appropriations law could not be changed in this manner), then the sequester report would be delivered to a joint congressional committee for review. To be accepted then, the report would have to be approved by both houses and presented to the president. This process, Morrison noted, clearly would pass constitutional muster. Why not just do it that way from the start? The reason, of course, was that this approach would force members to vote on sequestering funds, an action that would inevitably hurt a lot of their constituents. By November 10, there were also two expedited judicial review provisions before the conference committee. The Senate version limited expedited review to members of Congress. The House version included expedited review for members of Congress but also provided expedited review for other adversely affected parties. The Senate version provided review by the D.C. Court of Appeals sitting *en banc*. The House version, as Morrison had set it up, provided for review by a three-judge panel of the D.C. district court. Both versions provided for appeal directly to the Supreme Court under an expedited schedule.

Bargaining and political maneuvering continued through November, but most of the action, after the first week, happened in a sub-group of twenty-nine conferees working in private. In the end, most of the compromises were forged by an even smaller working group of congressional leaders. Finding out what was going on was virtually impossible for anyone outside the secret meetings. Synar had some access to the process from his position on the House Government Operations Committee. Still, no one knew for sure what would emerge. In mid-November, most members scurried off to their home districts for the Thanksgiving recess.

The compromise amendment, all one hundred and fifty-eight pages of it, was finally plopped down in front of the conference at 5 p.m. on December 10 "for a vote, without an explanation or even a summary," as one conferee later charged. With no time for anything more than a cursory read, if any, the conferees adopted the proposal and sent it to both houses for action. The conference committee changes included: (1) adding the GAO to the process; (2) forcing the first round of automatic spending cuts to occur in March 1986 (not after the 1986 elections, as the Republican Senate wanted); (3) forcing half of the cuts to come from defense spending and the other half from programs that were not specifically exempt, thus preventing presidential discretion; (4) exempting additional programs, including veterans' pensions, Medicaid, Aid to Families with Dependent Children, WIC (a food program for women and infant children), Supplemental Security Income, food stamps and child nutrition; (5) limiting the cuts in five health programs, including Medicare; and, (6) providing for expedited judicial review for any member of Congress and adversely affected parties to challenge the trigger and sequester process before a three-judge district court with expedited appeal to the Supreme Court. Democrats in the House had been successful in protecting some of their favored programs, but that meant other programs would be hit harder by the automatic spending cuts.

In the almost $1 trillion federal budget for 1986, $627 billion would be totally exempt from the spending cuts, and $82 billion in health care programs would be mostly exempt. Just $265 billion would be available for cutting under any sequester order. Half the cuts would have to come from the $175 billion representing the defense budget. Half would have to come from the remaining $90 billion, which included the expenses of all other federal agencies and programs not exempted. These included the departments of Education, Energy, Justice, Transportation, Commerce and Agriculture, and the Environmental Protection Agency. Also subject to cuts were independent agencies such as FTC, FERC and the SEC, as well as housing and urban development programs, foreign aid, the federal judiciary and federal corrections, Congress and the Executive Office of the President. By December 1985, the estimated deficit for FY 1986, which was predicted to be $171 billion just three months earlier, had risen to $200 billion. A few weeks later, the estimate would be ratcheted up another $20 billion. It did not take a mathematics wizard to see the problems that would follow from such a large deficit and the narrow pool of federal spending available for cutting to reach the deficit reduction targets.

The day after the conference vote, the Gramm-Rudman amendment was scheduled for floor action in both houses. For Morrison, the House and Senate debate provided useful evidence to show that Congress knew perfectly well how constitutionally suspect the automatic spending cuts were and knew equally well that it was doing this to avoid its own constitutional responsibilities. What follows are excerpts from comments delivered in the House. It is worth noting that recognition of the bill's negative features and of its constitutional problems comes from both Republicans and Democrats. Those who intended to vote in favor were as apt to express negative comments as those voting against the measure. Very few seemed much enamored of Gramm-Rudman, yet in the end the amendment passed by a wide margin.

> **Trent Lott:** Mr. Speaker, this has been an interesting conference experience. I wonder how many of our colleagues know, really, what was in the final agreement. ... Here we are, talking about the most monumental, indeed, revolutionary of budget process changes in over a decade—how we will order our national priorities and enforce fiscal discipline on ourselves. And yet, this conference process has treated this like some sacred rite of some secret order that can only be performed in seclusion by a few high priests.

***

> **Dick Gephardt:** Is this the best way to take care of the deficit? Absolutely not. Gramm-Rudman is going to tie the Congress in knots. If you do not believe that, read the bill. It could be a disaster. But the question is not that. The question is not: is this the best polity? The question is, can you let this madness [the deficits] go on? My answer is "no." ... I think tonight is a watershed occasion. It is the Congress asserting leadership. A committee of 535 people, disparate people, with different views and different values saying, "Enough is enough." ... I am proud of the Congress, I am proud of the House, I am proud of the changes made in this bill.

***

> **Joe Barton:** I rise today in strong support of the Gramm-Rudman Emergency Deficit Control Act. ... This simple yet powerful measure will impose on Congress the discipline which we have so amply demonstrated we do not possess. ... Our actions speak louder than our words. It is obvious that Congress is incapable of exercising

budgetary restraint.

***

Henry Waxman: I am sad that the Congress thinks so little of itself. It is our job to look at each government effort—each tax incentive, each subsidy, each grant—to evaluate its success, and to choose to continue it, revise it, or end it. It's politically painful work, especially in a time of limited public resources, but it should be done ... [R]ather than facing up to this responsibility, we are today adopting government by automatic pilot. We are establishing a financial doomsday machine. ... This is a shameful bill. It is unworthy of this House. It is unworthy of the trust that the American people have placed in us. We are betraying this trust by handing our jobs over to bureaucracies, triggers, and automatic decisions. ... Ironically ... the nation may be rescued from this bill when the U.S. Supreme Court holds this proposal next to the Constitution of our land and finds it violative of that document. ... Fearing the elections ... advocates for Gramm-Rudman have handed the government over to agencies that few of us know well and that no constituent can find.

***

Michael Barnes: I have only been here seven years. Many of you have been in the House far longer than I. But in my seven years in the House I have not seen a piece of legislation as clearly unconstitutional ... or as clearly fiscally irresponsible as the bill that is before us tonight.

***

John Williams: The founders of this nation wanted the members of Congress to make the spending decisions. They did not turn those decisions over to unelected staff at OMB or CBO, and they prohibited the president of the United States from making those decisions. Tonight, we are about the business, after two centuries, of eroding our own requirement to prioritize as the founders intended we should do. We are about to turn the picking and choosing over to someone else.

***

Barney Frank: We are going to do this instead of thinking.

327

Courting Change

***

Silvio Conte: The legislation before us would have Congress concede ... that [it] simply lacks the ability—or the will—to control federal revenues and expenditures on its own. Instead, that power would be delegated to bean counters—unelected officials. ... I am not ready to surrender my vote to a bureaucrat's red pen.

***

Henry Hyde: Mr. Speaker, the vice of Gramm-Rudman is it confines to a mindless, unfeeling, unthinking, bloodless formula the judgments—the sensitive, hard judgments—that we were elected to make. When we go [to] the voters and we say, "Trust us, we'll exercise our judgment based on our conscience and our experience," and then we lateral over to a computer the judgments on defense and on so many important issues, that is cowardice, and I cannot buy it.

Comments in the Senate that day were much the same. Those of Senator Bennett Johnston of Louisiana are illustrative:

Bennett Johnston: We got here because of the failure in the process—because of the failure of the president of the United States, in my judgment, to do his duty; because of the failure of the Congress, in my judgment, to do its duty; because of the failure of the people of this country to understand what it is all about. ... In a word, Mr. President, we got here because the people, the Congress, the president, and the press all want that which never was and never can be. That is, they want a balanced budget without cuts, without pain, without taxes, without taking the blame, without taking the responsibility, without measuring up to those duties of statesmanship which require occasionally that we say "no" to our most profligate desires to spend and to avoid pain.

That evening, after nine hours of speeches, the Senate passed the conference agreement on the amendment by a vote of 61-31. At 10:15 p.m. the House of Representatives followed suit by a vote of 271-154. The next day, at 10:19 a.m., without ceremony, the president signed the bill into law. There were no television lights, no beaming politicians, no souvenir pens. *Newsweek* called it "the Case of the Missing Signing Ceremony." Despite the fact that Gramm-Rudman was the most far-reaching deficit reduction legislation in postwar history, even the president was not anxious to be associated with it too closely. The stealth signing, as *Time* magazine noted, was "understandable. ... [T]he force that drove it through Congress was an embarrassment, not something to crow about. ... [The amendment] is a statutory act of desperation, an admission that Government is incapable of governing itself."

Fully aware that passage was inevitable, Synar and Morrison had spent their time preparing to move the battleground to court. With the expectation that court action would proceed swiftly, Morrison assigned Litigation Group attorney Kathy Meyer to help with the briefs. Synar had insisted that they file suit the same day the president signed the bill into law. "We had everything ready to go, all the court documents for filing in order," Morrison recalls. "We had someone stationed at the White House and someone at a public phone booth near the U.S. district court ready to file as soon as a call came saying that the president's signature was on the page." As the first to file (other members of Congress soon followed), the case became known as *Synar v. U.S.* Having eschewed publicity for the signing ceremony, the president had left an empty stage, which Synar quickly commandeered. Not only did he enjoy a packed news conference all to himself, he was able to focus public debate on the constitutional issues.

It was clear that the court was taking the expedited process seriously. On December 19, the same date that Morrison filed an amended complaint, U.S. District Judge Oliver Gasch issued an order directing the administration to respond to Synar's challenge by December 30. The order also provided that if the House or Senate wanted to intervene, their pleadings also would be due by December 30. The court gave Morrison and Synar until January 6 of the new year to reply to the briefs filed by the government and scheduled the oral argument for January 10.

In the three weeks between the court's initial order and the oral argument, motions and pleadings flooded into the court. Both the House and Senate moved to intervene. The House's motion did not appear until just the day before oral argument, but it was granted in spite of its tardiness. Comptroller General Charles Bowsher moved to intervene to defend the GAO's role in the process, a role the Justice Department was attacking in its brief. That too was granted. On December 31, the National Treasury Employees Union, representing one hundred and twenty thousand active and retired federal employees, filed a separate case attacking the constitutionality of the law, noting that its members were injured because a cost-of-living adjustment due federal retirees on January 1, 1986, has been withheld. On January 2, 1986, the court consolidated this case with Synar's challenge. That order indicated for the first time which judges would serve on the three-judge court. In addition to Gasch, a senior judge appointed by President Johnson, the panel included U.S. District Judge Norma Holloway Johnson, a Carter appointee, and U.S. Circuit Judge Antonin Scalia, whom Reagan had appointed to the D.C. Circuit Court in 1982.

* * * * *

Motions to intervene, motions to exceed page limits, motions to dismiss, motions for summary judgment, opposition motions, memoranda, reply memoranda and court orders responding to each all flew back and forth between the parties and the court from January 2 to the scheduled oral hearing on January 10. Argument before the three-judge panel went on for nearly three hours, with six lawyers presenting arguments for the various parties. Assistant Attorney General Richard Willard argued that the law was unconstitutional because it would make the president subservient to the comptroller general, a situation he termed "repugnant to the Constitution." Morrison argued that the law was an unconstitutional delegation of authority to unelected officials, but comments from Judge Scalia suggested that he did not accept that argument. "Congress often delegates to the executive difficult questions that it would rather not grapple with," Scalia said. "I don't see how you can say that Congress hasn't made the tough judgment. They've made a judgment to balance the budget." Morrison knew that it was unlikely he would win over Scalia on that ground, but he still hoped his argument might resonate with the other two judges or at least that the court might be more receptive to ruling against the role of the comptroller general.

After argument, the motions and supplemental briefs (ordered by the court to address the fallback provision) continued to pour in. By the end of January, the court granted two motions of the U.S. Senate to include in the court record the initial joint report of OMB and CBO that the law had directed. The same day, the court granted permission for the comptroller general's report to be added as well. On February 1, the president issued the first sequester order, cutting $11.7 billion in spending, and this too was added to the record. A few days later, on February 7, the court announced its ruling. It was a win, of sorts, for Synar and Morrison. If upheld by the Supreme Court, it would force Congress to revert to its constitutional role of voting for the cuts, as required by the fallback provision. Synar penned a note to Morrison and Meyer: "Alan and Kathy, I know it is only round 1, but damn what a round! Thanks, Mike."

Like the lower court ruling in *Chadha*, though, the three-judge panel's reasoning was narrowly drawn, dismissing entirely what Morrison believed to be the most basic argument—that the law had impermissibly delegated the central power of Congress to make the budget decisions. Instead, the trigger process was declared unconstitutional because an otherwise permissible delegation had been made to a non-executive agency—the GAO. "It is unquestionable," the court notes, "that some of the Comptroller General's powers ... consist of (in the words of *Humphrey's Executor*) 'specified duties as a legislative ... aid,' in the performance of which he cannot in any proper sense be characterized as an arm or an eye of the executive." However, the comptroller general's "powers under the automatic deficit reduction process ... do not come within that category." Rather, the court concluded, after a thorough review of the law's provisions concerning the comptroller's role, they are "executive powers in the constitutional sense." In so concluding, the court seemed to place particular emphasis on the fact that the comptroller general's report to the president (specifying which budget items were to be reduced and by how much) is *"made binding upon the President in the latter's application of the law"* (emphasis in the decision). Moreover, the comptroller general was directed by the law to report to Congress on the extent to which the president followed his instructions. Since "it seems entirely clear that under the recent landmark decision in *INS v. Chadha* ... that if the present statute had not inserted the Comptroller General between the President and the report of the Directors of the CBO and the OMB, and if the determinations to be made under the Act by the Comptroller General had been assigned instead to the President himself, Congress could not constitutionally provide for a legislative veto of those determinations." Having concluded that Congress could not have used a legislative veto to control such a delegation, the court continued: "It seems no more constitutionally permissible to achieve the same result *ex ante* instead of *ex post*, prescribing in advance the exercise of executive power, instead of invalidating its exercise." It was a convoluted application of the *Chadha* decision, but it at least embraced Morrison's separation of powers argument to some extent. Having "proved" that executive power cannot "constitutionally be exercised by an officer removable by Congress," and having concluded that the powers delegated in the Gramm-Rudman law were executive in nature, the court ruled that the automatic deficit reduction process "cannot be exercised."

Two things were obvious about the decision. First, though the opinion was *per curiam*, Scalia was clearly its author. Second, the reasoning in the opinion was specifically aimed at protecting presidential power. Any concern about protecting the legislative branch, even from itself, was totally absent. There would be no problem with this abdication of the constitutionally mandated power over the budget if the abdication had been to the president or to a clearly executive branch actor like the OMB. Writing for the *Wall Street Journal*, Michael Kinsley attacked the decision as the "most sweeping assertion of judicial power in years." Explaining Scalia's reasoning as an "attempted executive-judicial mugging of the legislative branch," he argued that it is all part of conservative strategy. Conservatives "think they will always control the executive branch, and they're boyishly eager to break down all the (inherently conservative) barriers to strong presidential action."

After admitting that it was "strictly unnecessary for us to reach [the delegation issue], since we hold ... that the challenged provisions of the Act are unconstitutional on other grounds," the court went on for fourteen pages to give its opinion about the matter anyway, claiming it was doing so to provide the Supreme Court with the benefit of its wisdom in the event that court wanted to address the point. As to the notion that the appropriations function is a "core function" of Congress, the court concluded that there was no reason to believe that appropriations was any more important than Congress's other powers. Even as *obiter dicta* (that which is not necessary to the decision and thus not binding as precedent), which the opinion admits that it is, the complete dismissal of virtually every argument Morrison had raised challenging the deficit law as an unconstitutional delegation did not bode well for his success on that point on appeal.

Interestingly, as the courts considered the constitutionality of the law, the first sequester order included a $40.5 million cut in federal judicial expenditures. Cuts of that magnitude would lead to employee layoffs and a deterioration in court security. They could also exacerbate case backlogs, one court spokesperson noted. If Congress did not restore some of the judicial funding, sixteen thousand secretaries, law clerks and other federal court employees faced the possibility of being laid off for a week at the end of the fiscal year. In addition, expenditures for security would be cut by $1.4 million nationwide. Jurors wouldn't be reimbursed for their parking fees for the rest of the fiscal year. Nonsequestered jurors wouldn't be provided meals. Spending would be reduced for renovations, law books, office furniture and equipment, staff travel and for attorneys representing indigents. "If the Gramm-Rudman cuts continue as projected in fiscal year 1987, the Midwest's Seventh Circuit probably will close some courthouses," said Collins Fitzpatrick, a Seventh Circuit administrator. In the judiciary, only the federal judges would be exempt because of constitutional restrictions against reducing their salaries.

* * * * *

The day the court decision was announced, both houses of Congress and the comptroller general filed notices of appeal to the Supreme Court. On February 18, all parties to the case joined together to file a joint motion setting forth a proposed schedule for briefing and oral argument and seeking to consolidate the appeals. Senate attorney Michael Davidson performed the lead role in organizing this joint effort. On February 24, 1986, the Supreme Court noted "probable jurisdiction" and allotted a total of one hour to each side for oral argument, which it scheduled for April 23.

Synar and Morrison intended to challenge the lower court's *dicta* on the delegation doctrine and to make a separation of powers argument based on the participation of the Congressional Budget Office. The Justice Department disagreed and planned to join the House and Senate in supporting the lower court's reasoning on the delegation doctrine issue. The Justice Department also planned to challenge the portion of the district court's judgment granting standing to one or both of the plaintiffs.

While the briefing process proceeded, the parties attempted to negotiate a mutually agreeable division of the time allotted for oral argument and the topics each counsel would address—a process that appears to have been quite contentious. Included in the Litigation Group files is a handwritten note by Morrison, obviously jotted in frustration and handed to one of the other counsel during a meeting. "Is it your view that the most difficult issues in the case are who is going to argue on each side, and for how long? Are there any neutral principles on which those questions can be decided?" A letter from Davidson to all counsel on March 27 gives further evidence of the difficulty this issue presented. Davidson concludes, "I will be leaving tomorrow morning for a week's vacation, and so, if the motion [to divide the oral argument] is not filed today, I'll happily turn over the coordination of it to someone else." No one else wanted the job. Accommodation was finally reached. Lloyd Cutler would go first, arguing on behalf of the comptroller general for twenty-four minutes. Steven Ross would then get eighteen minutes to argue on behalf of the House. Davidson, for the Senate, would go last and argue eighteen minutes. Cutler would reserve a portion of his longer time and present rebuttal on behalf of all appellants. On the appellee side, Solicitor General Charles Fried would argue first, for twenty-four minutes, on behalf of the administration. Morrison would go next, making the delegation and separation of powers arguments and defending standing for members of Congress, for eighteen minutes. Finally, Lois Williams, counsel for the National Treasury Employees Union, would get eighteen minutes. The joint motion requested the court to waive its normal limit of two counsel arguing on each side, citing the importance of the case and the court's allowing for six counsel to argue in *Buckley v. Valeo*. Again the Supreme Court agreed to accommodate all of their requests.

Oral argument in the case, known on appeal as *Bowsher v. Synar*, began at 10 a.m. on April 23, 1986. By early morning, a long line of Washington spectators—attorneys, congressional and government staffers and members of the public—began forming on the Supreme Court steps. By the time the doors opened to admit the few who could be squeezed in, the line stretched for nearly a block. The historic significance of the case, called by one law professor "of towering importance to the nation's political system," was well understood by Washington insiders, but there were comparatively few available seats for spectators. In the end, seventy-five lawyers, more than one hundred reporters and about three hundred other people, mostly Washington insiders, were able to squeeze in for the show.

At last the moment came, and in came the Justices. Cutler approached the podium and the argument began. It was nearly 11:30 before Morrison got his turn. Reporter Lyle Denniston had this to say:

> The plainest, most direct language against Gramm-Rudman came from Alan B. Morrison, counsel to the 12 congressmen challenging the bill. The public interest lawyer began by bluntly accusing Congress of "trying to create an elaborate mechanism under which it could obtain a reduction in the budget deficit without having either to increase taxes or to cut any of the spending programs, because it was unable to muster the votes needed to do that under our lawmaking provisions of the Constitution." In Gramm-Rudman, he said, Congress sought to "accomplish through the back door that which it could not accomplish through the front door."

Morrison warmed to his oratory: "I suggest to you that the very reason that Gramm-Rudman was enacted was because the Congress found that it was not making the hard choices. It wanted to have defense, it wanted to have social programs, it wanted to have clean air, it wanted to have transportation and it couldn't pick and choose among them." So it passed off the chore, he said, and "that kind of abdication goes to the very heart of our system of government, and it changes all of the dynamics around in our legislative process."

Morrison gave it all he had. But judging from the justices' questions to him—mostly from Chief Justice Burger and Justice Rehnquist—it seemed his argument was not falling on receptive ears here any more than it had in the court below. Burger's questions were particularly interesting, considering the next big separation of powers case that Morrison would take, *Mistretta v. U.S.* In that case, Congress had set up a special commission made up of three circuit judges and four private citizens, called the Sentencing Commission, which was delegated the responsibility for reviewing all federal criminal laws and establish new guidelines that U.S. judges would have to follow in sentencing criminals convicted of federal crimes. It was both an enormous undertaking and a delegation of Congress's responsibility. Though the case did not yet exist, the Sentencing Commission did and was already exercising the powers given to it. At two points in the argument, Burger asked questions that seemed more directed at how a decision would affect the Sentencing Commission, though he did not mention the commission by name. "I've noticed that over the last fifteen years Congress has authorized special judicial panels," Burger noted. "Would your argument be what Congress did here would be as though we assigned this function to judges?" And then later: "Your conclusion is that it would be just as improper to assign these functions to judges for much the same reasons?" Both questions undoubtedly gave Morrison a clue as to Burger's likely position on the delegation doctrine. But as to how the rest of the court would rule, he was less sure.

On July 8, the last day of its 1986 term, the court ruled 7-2 to overturn the automatic trigger process of the Gramm-Rudman law, declaring that the comptroller general could not exercise the power given to him because he was not an executive officer. The majority opinion, the last one written by Burger before retiring, relied on the joint removal provision as proof that the comptroller general was a creature of Congress. Burger then looked at the responsibility given under Gramm-Rudman and determined that it was executive in character and thus could not be exercised by a legislative actor. The two dissenting opinions would have allowed the law to stand but for different reasons. Justice White's dissent, just as it had in *Chadha*, focused on the need to give Congress the flexibility to do its job. His analysis relied more on the necessary and proper clause and a separation of powers argument that aimed to protect the legislative branch, in contrast to the majority's emphasis on protecting the executive branch. Justice Blackmun's dissent was directed at the joint resolution removal power in the 1921 Budget Act; to defeat this more recent law on the basis of a sixty-year-old provision that had never been used was inappropriate. When and if Congress tried to remove a comptroller general, then the court could declare the removal provision unconstitutional; until then it was a non-issue. None of the opinions embraced the excessive delegation argument that was the centerpiece of Morrison's argument.

The constitutional design of the government and its powers was not intended simply to protect the legislature from the executive or the reverse. It was intended to protect the people from the possibility of an overbearing government. In Gramm-Rudman, Congress openly admitted that it could not do its job; it needed something other than the lawmaking process to solve the problem. It seemed to Morrison that it was so obviously unconstitutional. Why was the court so unwilling to see it that way?

But the fight in court over Gramm-Rudman was over, and the automatic deficit reduction trigger process was dead. Since that was the primary goal, it is fair to conclude that Synar and Morrison won. There is no doubt that Morrison's *Chadha* case played a critical role in the majority opinion, and, though Morrison's delegation argument did not persuade even one justice or judge, his argument showed what was at stake in the delegation to the comptroller general and gained a wide audience both in the legal community and the media. In the never-ending game of constitutional interpretation, where doctrines are constantly being tweaked this way and that, the trick to moving the court in new directions is to try out new arguments and if they fail, modify and try again. Morrison soon would be back with his delegation argument, and though he also would lose the next time (*Mistretta v. U.S.*), there would always be more opportunities ahead.

As for the deficit battle, it went on and on. Indeed, it still goes on. After the Supreme Court's decision, Congress managed to pass the first sequester, the $11.7 billion spending cut, under the fallback provision, and the president signed it into law. But, as many members predicted it would do, Congress managed to ease the sting of the cuts through the back door, passing supplemental appropriations bills to restore some of the funds. In the years to come, Congress would try many variations of the gimmick: giving the sequester power to OMB and the president; spreading the targets out over more years; increasing the targets; failing to pass appropriations bills on time so that OMB could not realistically project costs and thereby make it appear for the "snapshot" moment that the budget would meet the targets; and passing supplemental bill after supplemental bill to add expenditures after the sequester process for the year was over. In the early 1990s, admitting defeat on the Gramm-Rudman process, Congress tried yet another shortcut to congressional responsibility, pyramiding yet another budget process onto existing ones. Pay-as-you-go, as it was termed, gave up on containing the expenses of existing programs. Instead, it focused attention on any new suggested expenditures. No new program or addition to an existing program could be added unless there was specific new tax revenue to support it or a specific cut in something else to cover its costs. This pay-as-you-go gimmick did not last long either, though it fell of its own weight, not a court challenge. Budget deficits remained high throughout the rest of the 1980s and into the mid-1990s. Finally, toward the end of the 1990s, tax increases introduced by President Clinton and a booming economy helped shrink deficits and eventually bring four straight years of large surpluses. But then the stock markets tumbled as the technology investment bubble burst and widespread corporate fraud was revealed. The economy took a nosedive, and President George W. Bush pushed huge tax cuts through Congress and then embarked on a costly war against Iraq. It was back to big deficits and a galloping growth in the national debt once again. Budget deficits under Bush had reached $375 billion in 2003, and the national debt had grown to $3.9 trillion.

The politics of blame avoidance inevitably will encourage inventive minds in Congress and the executive branch to seek solutions like the automatic trigger-sequestration process and the legislative veto in the future. Whether the Supreme Court will continue its role as umpire between the branches, with special concern for protecting the executive branch, remains an open question.

Afterword
Alan B. Morrison
March 2004

Chapter 17 ends in July 1986, which is less than half the life of the Litigation Group. When Barbara Craig embarked on this project, she planned to take the book all the way through the mid-1990s. She researched cases and compiled files far beyond what is in this volume. And she interviewed a number of people who do not even appear in the book. Fortunately, she has given Public Citizen all her files, including priceless tape recordings of twenty-one lawyers who worked at the Group and a number of others who know its work well. All of these will be available for scholars or anyone interested in what the Group has done for the quarter of a century that she covered. There are more than a thousand case files and other documents that will also prove fruitful to those interested in digging deeper into public interest law and the role of the Public Citizen Litigation Group.

But that kind of in-depth inquiry will have to wait for another day. For now, something more should be said about what the Litigation Group did in the intervening eighteen years, a task that falls to me as the director through early January 1993 and then again at various times through September 2003 before my retirement from Public Citizen on February 29, 2004. It is worth exploring some of the cases on which we worked in the past eighteen years, although not in the detail, and with none of the personal touches that this book contains.

Before looking at the subject areas in which the Litigation Group made its mark, it seems to me that the unwritten part of its history can be summed up in three words: continuity, evolution and change. Each of the subject areas discussed in the book and below has some of each in it, although not all in equal proportions. Then at the end I will introduce three new areas that were not present in 1972: (1) preemption, by federal law, of state law claims for money damages; (2) free speech issues over the Internet; and (3) assisting other lawyers with little or no Supreme Court experience with their cases in the High Court. The reasons for their later arrivals are obvious: there was almost no federal preemption of this type when we began; the Internet was just an idea that no one save a few computer scientists had heard of until two decades later, and at our outset we were in no position to give anyone advice about Supreme

Court practice since our first case in the High Court was in 1974.

Openness in Government

Our Freedom of Information Act (FOIA) docket continues to be a significant part of our workload. Many of the same agencies have continued to refuse our requests over the years, and presumably if the next chapter in this story is written twenty years from now, the same will be true. And we continue to do cases involving FOIA's first cousin—the Federal Advisory Committee Act (FACA)—as well as occasional Privacy Act cases and suits under state open government laws.

The major evolution in our FOIA work came in the 1990s when we took over the litigation to prevent the Reagan administration from destroying all of the tapes on which were saved the e-mail records of the White House. These tapes included e-mails from the National Security Council (NSC) for the period covering Iran-Contra and other historic events. The ACLU filed the case, *Armstrong v. Bush*, literally on the eve of destruction, obtained a temporary restraining order that prevented the case from becoming moot, and then decided that our expertise and staff were needed. Kathy Meyer handled the first round in the district court, persuading Judge Charles Richey that the government's claims—that there was nothing on e-mails worth saving because everything of substance had been printed out—should not be accepted at face value. Our clients, who were vitally interested in gaining access to these e-mails and in seeing that they were preserved for historical purposes, had claims under FOIA and also under the Federal Records Act and the Presidential Materials Act, which require that agencies and the president preserve all their records unless specifically authorized by the National Archives to destroy them. Since no one at the Archives had ever considered the issue of preservation of electronic, as opposed to paper records, there was, in our view, no authorization of the kind that the law required.

Although Judge Richey refused to dismiss the case, as the government requested, he allowed the government to ask the court of appeals to review his refusal, which it agreed to do. By this time, Kathy and her then-husband and Litigation Group attorney Eric Glitzenstein had moved on to other public interest work (and now have their own public interest firm), and so it fell to me, as her co-counsel in the district court, to defend the ruling on appeal. We emerged largely, but not entirely, victorious, and so the next round began with our basic case (and the backup tapes of the e-mails) still intact. As the case began to heat up on remand, it was clear to me that I did not have the time, and as I would subsequently learn, the understanding of electronic records and computers, to be the lead counsel. In a stroke of amazing good fortune, Michael Tankersley came to work for us at precisely the right moment, and he was given the case.

If ever there were a lawyer made for a case, he was it. With no disrespect for any other lawyer who ever worked at the Group, no one could have done the job Michael did in sorting through and keeping straight the massive amount of information and ever-changing government theories on why we should lose. The story of this case could easily take up nearly an entire chapter by itself, and in the end we won on the key points. In doing so, we revolutionized the way the federal government thinks about, maintains and retains electronic records. Some of the agencies still have a long way to go, and presidential records are, at least in most cases, not subject to court supervision. But the basic mechanisms of responding to FOIA requests for electronic records and preserving records in electronic form are now firmly established. Along the way, we obtained thousands of e-mails that were not found among any of the printed records and that contained vital information about the way that the White House and the NSC worked—disproving the claims that the e-mails that the White House so much wanted to destroy had nothing useful on them. We recognize that no system of records preservation is perfect, but the basics are now in place so that nothing like what almost happened in the final days of the Reagan administration should ever happen again.

The vice presidential records of President Nixon were at the center of an early FOIA case (*Brandon v. Sampson*), and the presidential papers and the secret tapes of Richard Nixon continued to be of concern. Congress had passed a law to recapture the Nixon tapes and papers that he had tried to give away with enough strings attached so that no one would see or hear them in his lifetime without his permission. The statute transferred the tapes and papers to the National Archives for processing. As some of the papers became ready for release, President Reagan issued an order that would have allowed the former president to decide for himself whether any or all of the materials were privileged, and if he made such a claim, the incumbent president would have to honor it. We took the archivist, who was designated to carry out this order, to court, with Glitzenstein as lead counsel. The court of appeals agreed with us that the order was inconsistent with the statute and would allow Nixon the very control that Congress sought to eliminate when it enacted the statute (*Public Citizen v. Burke*). One of the great lessons that we have learned is that most battles are never over. Under the Presidential Records Act, all records are supposed to be made public twelve years after a president leaves office, with a few exemptions that generally follow those that apply under FOIA. There is one important exception to the exemptions: the exemption for internal agency documents does not apply. Thus, once the required time passes, memos to and from presidents and their top aides will become public—a great boon to historians and others. But despite the law, the opening of the records scheduled for January 21, 2001, the twelfth anniversary of the end of the Reagan era, did not occur because President George W. Bush, whose father was Reagan's vice president and whose own presidential records would become public four years hence, decided that he had to review them and that he also needed more Reagan input.

Once again we went to court, this time with Scott Nelson in the lead, claiming that this president, like his predecessors, had violated the law and given too much power to ex-presidents (*American Historical Association v. National Archives*).

Unfortunately, the case languished for two years before Judge Colleen Kollar-Kotelly. In fairness, she also was assigned to the retrial of *U.S. v. Microsoft* and was a member of the panel hearing the massive challenge to the McCain-Feingold campaign finance reform act of 2002, which we had a role in successfully defending. In the meantime, the vast majority of withheld records were released, for the stated reason that all reviews had been completed. The legal principle at stake, however, had yet to be resolved. In March 2004, without resolving the issue, Judge Kollar-Kotelly dismissed the case for the stated reason that because of the passage of time and the release of the materials, the injury that had originally prompted the lawsuit was no longer "redressable." At this writing, the propriety of the administration's action remains to be decided, either through an appeal of Judge Kollar-Kotelly's order or in some future litigation.

In between these two presidential papers cases came the Nixon tapes case, *Kutler v. Carlin*. Our client, Stanley Kutler, is a professor of history at the University of Wisconsin. He had written a book about Nixon and Watergate, and he was very anxious to gain access to the tapes. Under the law, the National Archives was supposed to process the tapes promptly, giving precedence to Watergate materials. The statute also gave the former president the right to review the materials that were proposed for release, and he exercised that right with vigor. His objections were not just to individual determinations, but that the Archives had done a poor job overall so that a complete re-review was needed. Kutler was of the opposite view—that the Archives had bent over backward to placate the Nixon family and that the tapes, or at least the Watergate batch, should have been released long ago. Not surprisingly, when we sued the Archives in 1992, Nixon came in to defend the Archives' work— just what we had expected.

Patti Goldman was in charge of the case for us, and she served written discovery, took and defended depositions, and was preparing to move the case ahead when Nixon went on the offensive. The law required the Archives to remove and return to Nixon all personal materials, such as those relating to his family or medical information about those whom he knew or whom served in the White House. With papers, there was no problem once the personal nature of the material was determined: the Archives simply gave back the original. But tapes presented a different problem because the personal was mixed with the official; the tapes recorded everything, with one conversation often immediately following or being interspersed with another.

Until our lawsuit, Nixon had never made much of a fuss about the return of personal materials—he just wanted no disclosure. But now his lawyers took a different tack, claiming that the Archives was violating the law by not returning the personal portions and that until it complied, it should be enjoined from processing and releasing the non-personal material. Much to our consternation, and the government's, Judge Royce Lamberth agreed, placing a significant barrier in our path. But the move did have one salutary effect: the government concluded that the real problem was Nixon and that we were really on the government's side, more or less. As a result, we began to consult with the Justice Department about what to do next, although we reached no firm conclusions, in part due to the departure of Patti Goldman, who took at job with the Sierra Club Legal Defense Fund (now Earthjustice) in Seattle. Once again, the case fell into my lap.

The situation changed when Nixon died in April 1994. His will provided that his two executors would be a New Jersey lawyer and John Taylor, a former aide who was by this time in charge of the Nixon library in California. Nixon's lawyers moved to substitute the executors as defendants, and we asked to see the will. In it, I discovered a matter of great interest: virtually all of Nixon's estate would go to his library, after the payment of his legal bills, including those relating to this case. I speculated that John Taylor had not made the connection between the legal bills he was paying and the fact that they were literally coming out of the endowment for the library he ran. And so I asked to take his deposition, and was not asked why. After some preliminary questions, I asked him to read the key passage of the will, and it was as if a light went on: this lawsuit was costing his library big money. I did not think that he would sell the Nixon family down the river, but I did think that there might be an opening to discuss settling the case, a concept that would have been unthinkable had Nixon still been alive.

It took a number of months before the parties could even agree to the idea of a mediation process and a period after that before we agreed on the parameters and had our first session with the incredibly patient Clifford Hendler of the law firm of Crowell & Moring, who took on the task, which took over a year, on a *pro bono* basis. Court rules forbid discussion of the process, let alone its details, but I think I breach no confidences when I say that it was very hard to reach agreement on principles and equally hard to find a way to express them to everyone's satisfaction. Perhaps the one hurdle that we surmounted that loomed very large was the issue of a fixed schedule for review and release of the documents. Quite naturally, in view of the delays that were now in the twentieth year, Kutler wanted immediate action, and quite naturally, the Archives was reluctant to commit to a firm schedule. The Nixon people, who were to review all proposed releases, also were concerned about specific time limits for them. In the end, we had no fixed timetable. Instead, we adopted a series of goals that we hoped would be met—and they were and still are, more or less.

One other issue nearly caused a collapse of the talks but was eventually resolved. The Nixon family did not want the world to be able to make copies of the tapes once they became available; we took the opposite view, but since

Kutler wanted the tapes for a book on Watergate and was prepared to listen to the tapes and have them transcribed, that was not his main concern. Public Citizen was also a plaintiff (just in case for any reason Kutler dropped out), and we would not have agreed to an order forever forbidding the duplication of the tapes. We also believed that a no-copying order was unlawful, but we agreed to one for a limited duration after each batch of tapes was made public, breaking a difficult impasse. One issue had to be litigated between the Archives and the Nixon estate (the latter prevailed), but its resolution did not hold up the processing, which would not have been true if the case had to be litigated. No court could ever have issued an order like this (what law could have been cited to reach such a multifaceted compromise?) and any court case would have dragged on for years. Most of the tapes are now public, and in addition to the Kutler book (*Abuse of Power*, Free Press, 1997), John Dean, former counsel to Nixon, has used the tapes to write a fascinating story of how William Rehnquist became a nominee to the Supreme Court (*The Rehnquist Choice*, Free Press, 2001).

There is one other open government area in which the Litigation Group had a substantial involvement, beginning in the mid-1980s. In a typical tort lawsuit, a plaintiff sues over injuries from a defective product, and discovery occurs, but with all materials kept secret by a protective order. Eventually, there is a settlement but on the condition that all evidence is returned to the defendant, and the plaintiff and her lawyers are forbidden from discussing anything about the case with anyone else.

Two specific harms result from that kind of a deal. First, the lawyers for other victims have to start from scratch, making the case more costly and more difficult, and some of the candor from some company witnesses disappears in later rounds of litigation. Second, most of these cases involve widely used products, many still on the market, yet the secret settlement prevents consumers from learning of potential dangers and often keeps the regulatory agencies in the dark about significant problems. That is why silicone breast implants remained in use for so long and why Firestone tires were not recalled until far too many people had been killed or injured from their defects.

In a number of cases, we intervened after the case was closed, to try to unseal documents filed with the court and release the plaintiff's lawyer from the order that required him to keep everyone else in the dark. We met with mixed success in the courts, but the issue is one that is of much more concern to the courts, the bar and the legislatures than it once was. The practice of keeping other lawyers, representing other clients, in the dark has largely disappeared because of the advent of clearinghouses and other information-sharing devices where there are a large number of cases. In addition, there is an increased willingness of many defendants to allow sharing of information, so long as the second lawyer agrees to the protective order.

Criminal law is not generally our area of endeavor, but one part of the criminal process intersects with open government: access to historically important grand jury minutes, which are sealed by law and can only be opened by a court order in limited circumstances. One of the most controversial prosecutions during the Cold War era was of Alger Hiss, in part because then-U.S. Representative Richard Nixon was a major witness before the grand jury that indicted Hiss. A group of historians approached us about unsealing the Hiss grand jury records. Lucinda Sikes took on the task with David Vladeck, but she and her family left for California before the case was argued, and so it fell to David to do that portion. The result was an almost complete victory. The records have been judged significant for what they show and what they do not show, but equally important is the precedent that it will provide for other historians who wish to try to crack the almost impenetrable wall of grand jury secrecy.

The Legal Profession

Issues surrounding lawyer advertising and solicitation continue to this day, and are unlikely to go away, largely because the bar has never made peace with the notion that the First Amendment protects that kind of speech at all, let alone in all the ways that lawyers have tried to use it. We won (mostly) two Supreme Court cases in this area. *Zauderer v. Office of Disciplinary Counsel* allowed a lawyer to advertise with a picture of a defective intrauterine device known as the Dalkon Shield, while *Edenfeld v. Fane* upheld the right of an accountant to engage in in-person solicitation of business clients. In another case, David Vladeck worked with local counsel in Mississippi to knock out restrictive and unnecessary advertising rules, and just recently we filed extensive comments on a proposal by the Kentucky Bar that would forbid much advertising that is commonplace today. Our suggestion that the rules might violate not only the First Amendment but also the federal antitrust laws seems to have slowed down the process quite a bit.

Our efforts to loosen the restrictions on what non-lawyers can do is one of the areas where we have been able to make the fewest changes in the legal profession. The Florida Bar continues to go after paralegals like Rosemary Furman, refusing even to allow them to call themselves paralegals, but insisting on the inaccurate label of legal secretary. We had a major constitutional challenge to the Florida rules as they affected low-income individuals, primarily women who wanted a divorce but could not afford a lawyer and could not get legal services to give them the assistance they needed even to be able to fill out the forms. Our due process case was based on the theory that, because the state has a monopoly on divorce and on what only lawyers can do, it cannot both restrict the services of paralegals and not provide help to those who require it for a divorce. Our case survived several motions and was set to go to trial when the Florida Supreme Court amended its rules to allow paralegals to fill out court-approved forms. Given what appeared to be a significant change in the rules, and the absence of any record under the changes, we dismissed the case and declared victory. But the court and the bar had out-foxed us. The forms were few and late in coming, and they have done very little to help those most in need. And so far, we have not found the right case to start the process again, especially since some intervening decisions have made our legal theory more tenuous. From time to time, we help out a paralegal in distress, but our efforts at reform have been a serious disappointment to us and others who see the need that paralegals can fill.

One of the issues on which I had hoped to make progress when I started the Litigation Group in 1972 was the insistence by most states that lawyers live in that state to be admitted to practice. Once admitted, lawyers could move out of state, so that the partners of many New York law firms could reside in Connecticut or New Jersey. The rule appeared to be almost entirely a protection device to keep out-of-state lawyers from taking more than one bar exam and having a multistate practice.

We found a case raising this precise issue right in the District of Columbia. Our client wanted to take the Maryland Bar, but she lived about three hundred yards on the wrong side of the state line and was forbidden from doing so. She filed her case *pro se*, and then John Sims and I took it over. We lost in the district court, but meanwhile John got another case that was going to be heard in the New York Court of Appeals—the state's highest court—and he won it unanimously on the ground that we had chosen: the rules violated the not-often used Privileges and Immunities Clause of Article IV of the Constitution. That provision forbids one state from discriminating against citizens of another state, which is exactly what was happening with these rules.

Maryland changed its rules while the case was on appeal, and another case from New Hampshire reached the Supreme Court before any of our cases got there. We filed a brief supporting the challenger, who prevailed 8-1 (*New Hampshire v. Piper*), and Litigation Group attorney Con Hitchcock subsequently won a number of other cases involving various related discriminations, including one applicable to federal courts, to which the Privileges and Immunities Clause does not apply. Of these, our only loss was in Virginia, where the rule was that if you were admitted to practice in another state and wanted to avoid taking Virginia's Bar exam, you had to live in Virginia (which was later struck down), and you had to promise to practice in Virginia full-time. Our client, Ron Goldfarb, no relation to our minimum fee schedule client Lew Goldfarb, lived in Virginia but wanted to continue to practice part-time in the District of Columbia, where he was admitted and where his law office had been for many years. Virginia said he had to take the Virginia Bar exam, which he did not want to do, and we sued to strike down what we called the "full-time victimization rule": if you promise to victimize Virginia clients on a full-time basis, then you don't have to take the bar exam, but if you only want to practice on a part-time basis, then we need to check your knowledge of Virginia law. Silly as it seems, Virginia defended its rules and won in the Fourth Circuit. Our *cert* petition was denied, with only Justice White dissenting.

Afterword

Policing the Regulators

One other constant, besides FOIA denials, has been the need to take regulatory agencies to court for not doing their jobs properly. Democratic administrations were less problematic than Republican ones, but both have consistently produced litigation in which we have alleged that the agency did not follow the required procedures, misread the statutory mandate, considered irrelevant factors, based their decisions on unsupportable factual conclusions, and/or made policy choices that were arbitrary and capricious, not to mention occasional constitutional violations.

Our principal agency defendants have largely remained the same: the National Highway Traffic Safety Administration (NHTSA), the Food and Drug Administration (FDA) and the Occupational Safety and Health Administration (OSHA). For NHTSA, even the parts of the car are the same: frontal air bags in the 1970s and 1980s, side impact airbags in 2002, uninformative tire quality grading systems in the 1980s, and ineffective tire pressure warning systems in 2003. At FDA, the drugs change over time, but the consistent pattern of resolving doubts in favor of industry has not. And at OSHA, it was cotton dust and ethylene oxide in the early years, and our latest suit was over hexavalent chromium; the constant is that, but for pressure in the form of lawsuits, the agency, which is supposed to protect the health and safety of workers, would do nothing and when it would finally act, the industry would win in all close cases.

Among the lessons we learned from our agency litigation is how necessary litigation is, and how important it is not to assume that a problem is ever resolved satisfactorily. Keeping an eye on an agency is a job for long-distance runners; if you slow down or take another path, the agency will be back where it started. We have also learned that it matters that we have the proven capability and willingness to litigate. Agencies do not like to be sued, even if they often win, because, among other reasons, they have to explain what they did and why, and sometimes that is the most embarrassing part.

When we first sued agencies, we often won when they simply did not follow the law because they never imagined that anyone would sue them for not holding a hearing, as the statute required, or not allowing the public to comment on a new rule. Unfortunately, those easy victories of the 1970s are long gone, as agencies assume they may be sued by anyone and everyone and at least purport to adhere to their governing statutes. Even worse for us, the law on standing has become much more difficult over the past thirty years. Some cases, where the injury is to the taxpayers or citizens at large, cannot be brought. In many others, we have to be much more precise in our allegations and must also obtain factual support for our allegations on injury, particularly when we sue on behalf of the members of Public Citizen. And even when we satisfy the legal requirements for standing, doing so takes time and money and very often we have to litigate the issue, which slows down the case and delays

345

final relief.

There is one other obstacle that loomed large for almost twenty years, but may be diminishing in significance. In 1984, the Supreme Court in *Chevron v. NRDC* instructed the lower courts that they should give considerable deference, in most cases, to the agency's interpretation of its own statutes, rather than the court deciding on its own what the law means. In many cases, this gave the agency a big leg up on questions of law, making our task even harder. However, in 2001, the court in *United States v. Mead Corp.* backpedaled a fair amount from its *Chevron* ruling, and directed the lower courts to be more cautious in accepting the agency's views, especially in situations where there is reason to believe that the agency's consideration of the issue was not made by its top officials and did not show the kind of careful consideration to which courts should defer. Some courts had started to question *Chevron*, at least in some situations, but it remains unclear how much of a change *Mead Corp.* will make.

One area of change has been the formalization of control over agency rulemaking by the Office of Management and Budget (OMB), sometimes through executive orders, and other times by legislative directives from Congress. Initially, we fought the notion of OMB involvement as a matter of principle and under the law. When it became clear that we could not win that battle, we shifted ground and were able to press for many changes that at least ensured a fair degree of openness in the process, which at least eliminated its worst aspects. But statutes like the Paperwork Reduction Act, the Regulatory Flexibility Act and the Data Quality Act have definitely made it more difficult for agencies to get their jobs done, and sometimes have made it close to impossible to issue rules that they think are the proper ones. In some administrations, these laws are used as excuses, but the reality of the barriers cannot be overstated. None of this means that we cannot or will not litigate, or that we should not; it means that our job is that much more difficult, even if the federal courts had nothing but sympathetic judges, which is decidedly not the case.

Separation of Powers

The Litigation Group's unique role in separation of powers litigation continued through the 1990s and into the twenty-first century. No other non-governmental organization has had a role remotely comparable to ours, and because of our status as outsiders, we are not obligated to defend the position of one of the three branches, but can decide which position to support based on our assessment of the merits of the case.

The year after the Gramm-Rudman case, we filed an *amicus* brief supporting the constitutionality of the independent counsel statute, which the court sustained, and also began our efforts to have the U.S. Sentencing Commission and the guidelines that it wrote declared unconstitutional. The statute that Congress enacted gave the commission enormous discretion in determining what the range of sentences for each offense should be, what factors could or could not properly be taken into account in deciding on the precise sentence for the defendant, and how the sentences for a crime like tax fraud should compare with those for a crime such as assault or drug possession. In addition, the commission was composed of three federal judges and four non-judicial presidential appointees, whose job it was to write what looked like rules that an administrative agency would issue. Patti Goldman and I undertook to challenge these guidelines, first in a civil case on behalf of a federal defender office that was dismissed for lack of standing, and then in a series of criminal cases around the country, representing individuals whose sentences under the guidelines were much harsher than they would have been under the old law—as was almost universally the case (although not in itself a ground for overturning the law). We argued both that there was excessive delegation and that the unique mixture of judges and non-judges appointed to carry out this mission violated separation of powers. We did not expect to win any cases on the former ground (and we did not), but it served as a launching pad to explain why the separation of powers argument really mattered—federal judges were making sentencing law on a wholesale basis, unlike the case-by-case sentencing practices that they had always performed.

The statute provided that the commission was in the judicial branch, which caused the Justice Department great consternation, since it saw the function being performed as an executive one. And so it defended the law by asking the court to uphold the commission as an entity performing executive functions, despite Congress' contrary designation. The Sentencing Commission was thus forced to hire its own lawyers to defend the statute as written, but Congress and the Justice Department agreed that what was being done did not violate principles of excess delegation and that federal judges could perform these functions, even in conjunction with non-judges.

I have never done a tally of how the district court judges in these many cases voted, but it was clear that they did not like the guidelines because they significantly reduced their discretion in sentencing, and perhaps that is why so many agreed with us. Only one court of appeals ruled on the issue before it got to the Supreme Court, and it agreed with us. But chaos was about to reign, and so the solicitor general, with our consent, used a special procedure under which a party can ask the Supreme Court to take a case from a court of appeals before it has ruled, when there is a great need for a final resolution, as there was here.

Our victories in the lower courts did not predict the response of the Supreme Court, which upheld the commission and the guidelines by a vote of 8-1, in an opinion by Justice Blackmun (*Mistretta v. United States*). The opinion fairly stated our claims, acknowledged that they had some merit, but came down the other way. It seemed that we simply could not persuade the court that federal judges should be imposing sentences on individual defendants, instead of passing sentencing guidelines applicable to everyone, under our system of separation of powers. They could do the latter without hurting their ability to do the former, the court concluded. Only Justice Scalia accepted our arguments, decrying the whole system as one establishing a "junior varsity Congress," instead of having Congress do the job itself.

Goldman had much more success in her case challenging the scheme that Congress has set up so that it could use a small group of members of Congress to control the major decisions of the supposedly independent authority that Congress had established to operate Dulles and National (now Reagan) airports. To us, and eventually a majority of the Supreme Court, this seemed like the legislative veto and Gramm-Rudman all over again. In the end, with a merits victory in the first case (*Metropolitan Wash. Airports Auth. v. Citizens Against Aircraft Noise*), and a denial of *cert* on the second round, Congress was told in no uncertain terms that the only way it could affect the work of the authority was to pass a law, which is not what Congress wanted to do.

Our separation of powers work began in 1972 with presidential impoundment cases, which ceased in the mid-1970s after the Supreme Court decided one case and Congress passed a law severely limiting the president 's power to hold up spending. The law did allow the president to defer spending within a given fiscal year but allowed Congress to exercise a one-house veto over any such deferrals. Deferrals were not as powerful as outright cancellations of spending, but they were a tool that presidents liked to use, even with the possibility of a legislative veto.

After *Chadha* was decided in 1983, an issue arose as to whether the right to defer still existed now that the veto was invalidated. Not surprisingly, Reagan and his lawyers contended that the two powers were severable, and the Litigation Group and David Vladeck took the opposite position. Not only did we win the case (*City of New Haven v. United States*), but one of the judges who agreed with us was Robert Bork, who was rarely on our side in any case, let alone one involving the president. That vote did not save him several years later when he was nominated to the Supreme Court and the Litigation Group, for the only time in its history, took a position on a judicial nomination by writing a short book—*The Judicial Record of Robert H. Bork*—that examined his decisions and destroyed the claim of his supporters that he had a consistent judicial philosophy that had nothing to do with what he wanted the outcome to be in a given case.

There were several other separation of powers cases along the way—and at this writing, I am preparing to argue another in April 2004 involving the Federal Advisory Committee Act and the Cheney Energy Task Force—but the most significant one was a challenge to the line-item veto. For decades, presidents have complained that Congress sent them massive appropriations bills, late in the session, and that they were forced to accept many provisions for wasteful spending because they could not, as a practical matter, veto the entire bill. They wanted what more that forty governors had in one form or another—the authority to pick and choose among the provisions of an appropriations bill, vetoing those they did not like and keeping those they did.

Afterword

There were two obstacles to a federal line-item veto. Congress had steadfastly refused to grant the president such a power (and after the impoundment controversy, no president would exercise such a power on his own), and the Constitution seemed to require that the president sign or veto the entire bill, and not parts of it. When the Republicans took over both the Senate and House of Representatives in 1995, one of the top items on their legislative priority list was the line-item veto. They assumed a Republican presidential victory in 1996 and delayed the effective date of the law so that only the new president, who turned out to be Bill Clinton, would be able to use it.

That solved one problem, but it left the Constitution in the way. The device Congress hit on was to have the president sign the whole bill, and then, within ten days, to "cancel" those spending items and certain tax breaks that he disapproved. Congress then would have a limited period to override his cancellation by passing another bill, but since the president could veto that also, it would effectively take two-thirds of both Houses to override his cancellations. Everyone knew that there were serious doubts about this attempted end-run on the Constitution, and so a special judicial review provision was included that allowed members of Congress, whose power would be significantly undercut by the line-item veto, to sue in advance of any specific veto, to test its constitutionality.

A number of lawyers and law firms were anxious to undertake the challenge. Among them were our office (Colette Matzzie and I); Wilmer Cutler & Pickering (which had represented the comptroller general in the Gramm-Rudman case); former Senate Legal Counsel Mike Davidson (who had been a lawyer for the Senate in *Chadha*); and Chuck Cooper, a former Reagan Justice Department lawyer with impeccable conservative credentials. We joined forces to file suit, with Senator Robert Byrd of West Virginia, the Senate's greatest defender of congressional prerogatives and separation of powers, as our lead plaintiff.

The case moved very quickly in the district court, and we emerged with a clear victory in a strongly worded and well-reasoned opinion by Judge Thomas P. Jackson. He saw the cancellation device for what it was: an attempt to evade the requirement that a president approve all of an appropriations bill or veto it all, which the judge said could not be done. The case went immediately to the High Court under the special statute that Congress had included, and I was chosen to argue. The government had urged the district court not to decide the merits because it said that members of Congress lacked standing, despite the statute and the obvious harm to them in their legislative capacities. The district court disagreed, perhaps because it would have to declare the special review provision unconstitutional in order to accept that position. But the Supreme Court had no such hesitation, as it held that members of Congress must show a direct personal injury to themselves, not just in their capacities as legislators, in order to be able to bring such an action. We had made separation of powers law, but not the kind we wanted or in an area that we planned to do so

(*Raines v. Byrd*).

So back we went to the drawing board. Clinton, to the surprise of some, did not hesitate to exercise his cancellation power. Quite quickly, two other cases were filed, with the lawyers from Wilmer taking the lead on one, and Chuck Cooper on the other. We stayed involved, offering assistance, and filing an *amicus* brief, but most of the work (except for another round of standing arguments) had been done on the first round. A different district judge reached the same conclusion as Judge Jackson, and this time the court did not back away from the merits, ruling 6-3 that the law was unconstitutional for substantially the reasons that we had urged from the start. Perhaps the most unusual aspect of the case was the lineup of the dissent: Justices O'Connor, Scalia and Breyer. This meant that there were liberals and conservatives on both sides, strict constructionists on both sides, and pragmatists on both sides, proving that figuring out votes in advance, at least in separation of powers cases, is a risky business.

Representing Workers

Through our work with the Health Research Group on occupational health, we have always represented workers. We also have had a long history of helping truck drivers and others in the Teamsters union obtain a safer workplace and fight for their rights in their union. Although historically the Teamsters were our primary focus, we also represented workers in other unions when their rights were being violated.

In recent years, our union democracy and other work in the Teamsters has become a much smaller part of our litigation. Part of that is due to the Justice Department's suit against the union, which alleged massive corruption and undemocratic practices and resulted in a consent decree that significantly improved the state of democracy there, including ending the delegate system of electing national officers and replacing it with a secret ballot in which every member is allowed to vote. Many factors contributed to the government's decision to bring that suit, but among them was our work (and that of our client, Teamsters for a Democratic Union, or TDU) in bringing the situation to light through litigation and other means.

The filing of the lawsuit and the agreement to settle by making major changes in the union's governance were only the beginning of the matter for TDU and us. For the rank-and-file members, the consent decree created almost as many issues as it resolved, and so it was necessary for us to devote considerable resources to ensure that how the decree played out did not vary too markedly from the promise of democracy that it offered. To do this, we had to battle not only the Justice Department and the union, but also a senior federal district judge (David Edelstein) who had his own ideas as to what should and should not happen. Although the election process and other aspects of the consent decree's operations were far from perfect, our presence improved the situation substantially.

Afterword

Today, we do very little of the kind of union democracy work that we once did, but we still litigate to protect workers in a number of contexts, including the use of the Internet (discussed below) and, most recently, taking up an issue that was one of the first on our truck driver agenda: the number of hours per day and per week that drivers are allowed to be behind the wheel and the length and timing of mandatory breaks. The Department of Transportation (DOT) had refused to make significant changes in the late 1970s, and the courts did not come to our rescue. After Congress ordered new rules, the DOT did very little to help overworked drivers and those in other vehicles who are generally the victims when fatigue causes a truck driver to get into an accident. We are now in court challenging the failures of the new rules, aiming to protect workers and the rest of us who encounter large trucks with fatigued drivers on the highways.

Other Consumer Litigation

In a broad sense, almost all of our work is "consumer" litigation since we generally are trying to protect the interests of ordinary consumers. But to help sort through the cases, we have broken out agency cases, legal profession cases and open government cases. There remain a number of very significant areas that are yet to be discussed under this quite broad topic.

For consumers to be effective, they must be able to band together to achieve their goals, and they must be able to raise money to operate. When Public Citizen began, it chose to seek an exemption from federal income taxes that would enable it to lobby Congress freely (under section 501(c)(4)), but by doing so, it could not accept grants from foundations, and its contributors did not receive a tax deduction for their gifts. To obtain those latter benefits, a charitable organization would have had to agree not to engage in any "substantial" lobbying activity—a limitation to which Public Citizen would not agree.

But we also believed that the lobbying restriction, which then did not apply to business lobbying, was unfair, and so we set out to challenge it. John Sims took the lead in making a variety of First Amendment and Equal Protection challenges, including one claim that the statutory test was so vague that it unduly inhibited the right to petition the government, which is protected by the First Amendment. While that initial case was pending, Congress responded by allowing charities (broadly defined) to elect to limit their lobbying under rules that avoided the vagueness problem, thereby eliminating one of the worst fears of the old law, and creating a safe haven that allowed substantial lobbying that would make it possible for most groups to do what they needed and not lose their exempt status. We then filed a second case, which we won before the full D.C. Circuit on equal protection grounds—veterans and other groups could receive favorable tax treatment with no restrictions on their lobbying—but the Supreme Court did not agree (*Regan v. Taxation with Representation of Washington*). One of the reasons that it upheld the law was that an organization could readily set up a lobbying and a non-lobbying arm, and if it kept them separate, the ends could be achieved with only a modest additional amount of paperwork, burden and added cost. It did not solve all the problems, but it was good enough so that Public Citizen was able to set up parallel groups with no great problems from the IRS.

Another related area in which we have been active for many years is state regulation of fundraising by charities, especially those from out of state. Every year, there are stories of frauds committed by charities in raising money, and the response has been to impose paperwork burdens or tell charities how much they or may not spend on fundraising, with little thought given to the burdens those rules impose, especially for groups that solicit throughout the United States. Over the years, we participated in a series of cases but became more active in 2000 when local governments, as well as states, started insisting that we register with them, fill out their forms and abide by their rules. We first filed suit against the county in which Louisville, Kentucky, is located, but almost as soon as it received the complaint, the county decided that the law was not worth defending, and so a new law was swiftly enacted that requires only that we send the county a copy of our tax return that we file with the IRS—an unnecessary requirement but hardly worth litigating over. Now we are engaged in a major First Amendment litigation against Pinellas County, Florida (Clearwater/St. Petersburg area), over an extremely burdensome and largely useless law (because no one does anything with the forms except put them in a file cabinet). The case (*Public Citizen v. Pinellas County*) has been fully briefed and a decision is expected shortly.

Another consumer case illustrates how what starts out as a seemingly small and perhaps unique problem can result in a significant change in consumer protection. David and Maria Caplan owned a home outside New York City, on which the Village Savings Bank held a mortgage. Like most other mortgages, the lender required the homeowner to pay an estimate of the amount of real estate taxes each month along with the principal and interest due on the mortgage. In the area where the Caplans lived, there were five separate taxes that fell into the category covered by their mortgage, each due at a different time. The bank decided, with no basis in the mortgage, that it would require the Caplans to use what it called the "fully accrued" method for calculating the size of the monthly tax payment. Under this method, each of the separate taxes had its own account, and the bank insisted that each separate account be fully funded to pay those taxes, even if there was plenty of other tax money in the account.

When Mr. Caplan discovered that the bank was keeping something close to $2,000 more of his money, on average, than was needed to keep his tax payments current, he wrote the bank in protest. This was in the late 1970s, when inflation was going through the roof and banks were loaning money at mortgage rates of about 15 percent while paying the customers only 1 percent or so on their tax deposits. The bank refused to budge, but the Caplans decided to send in only the proper amount of their mortgage and taxes, as they calculated it. The bank refused to cash their checks and instead foreclosed on their home. They defended the case on their own in the trial court, where they lost, at which point they came to Public Citizen, and I agreed to help out.

After a victory on the appeal, which sent the case back for further proceedings, the case took a number of twists and turns as the bank dug in its heels. Eventually, the bank agreed not to charge more than the Caplans had always said was proper and also paid the Caplans a modest settlement because it had impeded their ability to sell their home. Fortunately, the case of *Village Savings Bank v. Caplan* did not sink away into obscurity. Other plaintiffs in various places brought similar suits, and a number of state attorneys general became involved in what they saw to be a form of consumer fraud, even where the mortgages themselves appeared to allow this special type of accounting. Congress held a hearing at which I testified, and eventually the Department of Housing and Urban Development issued rules making these and other related practices unlawful. It was a long ride, and there were many people besides the Caplans involved, but it all got started with two people who stood up for their rights, even when they almost lost their home because of it.

Perhaps the most significant consumer work that we have been doing since about 1990 is in the class action field, principally by objecting to unfair and often collusive settlements in which the class members get very little and the attorneys for the class get very large fees. We have always recognized the importance of class actions and their first cousins—stockholder derivative suits—and have filed some of our own and filed *amicus* briefs in cases supporting them. In fact, our first venture into this area was in the 1970s when we filed the first two shareholder cases seeking to require corporate officers from American Airlines and 3M to pay back to the company the money that they had illegally paid out from the company's treasury to support candidates for political office. In the 3M case, we established that the amounts of illegal contributions far exceeded the amounts alleged by the Watergate special prosecutor, and our settlements in both cases energized the Securities and Exchange Commission and set a pattern for repayments by officials in other companies.

Our work in opposing what we considered to be unjust settlements began with one of these corporate contribution cases involving Phillips Petroleum, where our principal objection was to the excessive fees being paid for what was a quite modest settlement, especially in light of our cases that had come before this one. Objecting to settlements, and especially to the fees for attorneys, is always an unpopular activity, but in this case the other lawyers were from another non-profit group, which made the matter even more contentious. Our objections led to some modest improvements in the settlement, but the fees were largely unchanged. From that beginning, we did a few other cases of a similar ilk in the 1980s, mainly because we feared that bad settlements and large fees would provide ammunition to those who opposed class actions because they understood what a powerful instrument they were for redressing small grievances that applied to thousands of people. This work also fit in with our efforts to ensure that legal services were affordable and available, and because, as we found out, almost no one else would take on these cases.

One of the first steps we took in this area was in the A.H. Robins bankruptcy reorganization case. Robins had sold the Dalkon Shield, an intrauterine device that turned out to cause serious problems in many women who used it. With an ever-increasing number of lawsuits to defend, and losses coming in those it were litigated, Robins filed for bankruptcy, which put an automatic halt to all litigation. Eventually, the company came up with a reorganization plan that was supported by the committee of tort claimants who were the major creditors of the company. A number of lawyers who represented individual claimants believed that the plan was unfair and asked us to represent them in opposing the plan. Although the forum and the procedural rules were different, the situation was in many respects like a class action settlement, and our opposition to it was met with the same reaction—annoyance by the court, the company and many claimants and their lawyers. We did not succeed in stopping or even changing the plan, and our other subsequent efforts to prevent what we and others saw as distortions of the plan also largely failed. But we learned a great deal about bankruptcies with tort claimants as major creditors, which we put to use in the later Dow Corning breast implant reorganization. We did have one important accomplishment. We managed to obtain a court order ensuring that all the records of the claims process would be preserved so that lawyers in future cases with similar problems could learn from what happened here.

The full story of the evolution of class actions and the role that we and other objectors played is much too long to tell here. Our efforts were led by Brian Wolfman, who was named director of the Litigation Group in 2004. We learned quite early that the courts would not be willing to overturn a settlement on the grounds that the deal was so unfair as to be unreasonable, except in a few extreme cases. Thus, while unfairness was always a theme, our main attacks were on the non-compliance with the class action rules, in particular those focusing on whether the named plaintiffs and their lawyers could adequately represent the class or whether inherent conflicts within the class as designed by the plaintiffs made that impossible. In all, we have challenged about three dozen nationwide settlements, including many of the most important mass tort settlements of the 1990s.

A major cause of the need to object to class settlements was that these new cases stretched the notion of class actions far beyond the basic idea of joining many individuals with small claims into a single action that could not economically be brought by each claimant. Many of the classes, such as the *Amchem* asbestos settlement, involved tort claims based on product liability, which traditionally had been filed as individual cases. These settlements, which were often driven by the desires of the defendants to achieve what they liked to call "global peace," sometimes included future claimants, *i.e.*, those who had been exposed to the product (asbestos) or had the product inserted in their bodies (breast implants and other medical devices), but at the time of settlement had no symptoms, in some cases because the disease had a long latency period. Finally, in some cases, defendants sought to place a limit on the amount they would pay to all claimants and to forbid anyone from going outside the fund and suing on their own.

Our work in this area prevented a number of ill-advised settlements from going ahead and produced changes that benefited the class members in a number of others. In some cases, fees were reduced, and in others we had limited or no success. In one case involving a fund created for victims of an unsafe pedicle screw that was supposed to set broken bones, there can be no doubt of our value to the class. The court had set a deadline for filing claims, which it strictly enforced, even though there was no harm to the class from late-filers, most of whom found out about the settlement after the deadline had passed. Wolfman challenged these decisions and won a victory in the court of appeals for the Third Circuit (*Sambolin v. Acromed*). As a result, two hundred and eight claimants obtained approximately $4.5 million in damages when class counsel supported the decision cutting them out entirely while also precluding them from bringing their own cases, on the theory that they were part of the class but were too late to be paid anything.

Perhaps our greatest influence in class actions was not what happened in particular cases, but what our sustained efforts did to change the way that courts (and the federal rules) looked at class actions and, in particular, the role of objectors, who are themselves class members but who could not hope to be effective without lawyers who are willing to take on these cases with little chance of being paid. Courts have now come to realize that, for the class action process to operate properly, objectors should not be seen as the "skunks at the garden party" but as a necessary part of the process and the one way that the courts can have some assurance that they have the necessary information to decide whether to approve the settlement. But despite these changes, the class action battles are far from over and are likely to remain a significant portion of our work for many years.

Federal Preemption of State Laws

The Constitution is clear that if there is a conflict between federal and state law, federal law prevails or "preempts" state laws. The issue to which the Litigation Group has devoted substantial resources in the past fifteen years is how to resolve the preemption issue when there is uncertainty as to whether there is a conflict. The principal context in which that issue has arisen for us are cases in which an individual is suing under state law, generally seeking money damages for a bodily or economic injury, and in which the defendant alleges that there is a controlling federal law under which the conduct alleged to have caused the harm is lawful. Thus, according to the defendants, the federal law or regulation preempts, and hence invalidates, the state law on which the claim is based, leaving the plaintiff with no remedy.

The theory of preemption law is not new, and insofar as the conflict was over whether a state regulatory agency could undertake particular activities or not, there were relatively few conflicts. Two factors changed the face of preemption law: (1) after the election of Reagan, the federal government began to relax its standards (or at least not keep up with changes to issue newer ones); and (2) defendants began to develop the theory that the preemption that was explicit in some federal laws and implicit in others extended not just to states doing affirmative regulation but also to state common law claims for money damages. To them, preemption became, as my colleague David Vladeck described it, a "get-out-of-jail-free card" because it makes all other issues of fact and law irrelevant, no matter how badly the plaintiff was harmed or how badly the defendant had behaved.

The list of cases, let alone their description, is too vast for this book, but the subject areas in which defendants have claimed preemption and in which we have been involved will give some idea of how popular the defense has become: Labor, banking, airlines, tobacco, medical devices, prescription drugs, automobile and truck safety, pesticides, arbitration, boat safety and jet ski accidents, plus some others that don't come readily to mind. Somewhat to our surprise, the federal courts below the Supreme Court have been willing to accept broad preemption claims, whereas the Supreme Court, while not rejecting them entirely, has been much more willing to find a way for state and federal law to coexist. Unlike most of the litigation in which we are involved, we generally are not lead counsel in these cases but are brought in because of our expertise in this field when the case reaches an appellate court, or we chose to file an *amicus* brief supporting the non-preemption side. With the stakes so high, and the payoffs with a victory so great, we can expect to be in the preemption business for a long time.

One preemption victory is worth mentioning by name because of its combined practical and legal impact. In the early 1990s, medical device manufacturers began arguing, and a steady stream of appellate courts began holding, that state-law claims seeking damages for injuries caused by medical devices were preempted simply because the FDA had approved the product for marketing under the federal Medical Device Amendments of 1976 that, for the first time, required FDA approval for medical devices. We handled many of these cases, hoping that eventually the Supreme Court would take one of them. In 1996, we got our wish in a case involving a defective pacemaker whose failure nearly killed our client. In *Medtronic v. Lohr*, argued by Brian Wolfman, the Supreme Court held our clients' damages claims were not preempted, overturning in whole or in part decisions in eight of the nine federal courts of appeals to have ruled on the issue. The ruling means that device manufacturers cannot escape liability simply because their products are regulated by the federal government, a tremendous victory for consumers. The case has allowed most medical device cases to go forward, including many "mass torts" cases

Afterword

involving faulty bone screws, knee implants, pacemakers and other devices implanted in tens of thousands of patients. Unfortunately, ambiguities in the decision have meant more litigation. We continue to litigate those cases and to seek to extend *Medtronic's* rationale to other cases involving pesticides, hazardous substances and other potentially dangerous products.

Internet Cases

In the late 1990s, we were contacted by a woman who had been sued by the pest-control company Terminex and its parent company for trademark infringement based on the fact that she had set up a Web site very critical of the companies because of a bad experience that she had. She lived in California but the suit was filed in Memphis, where the companies were located. She was a person of modest means, with no access to a lawyer and no experience in trademark law, the First Amendment or the various procedural defenses that might get the case back to California, if it could be brought at all. We saw this case for what it was—a blatant attempt to shut down a consumer critic—and for what it was not—a defense of the company's trademarks. This was precisely the kind of case in which an organization like the Litigation Group was needed, and so we stepped in and Paul Levy began his new career as an Internet consumer lawyer.

Paul was able to mount a massive counter-attack, with the *pro bono* help of some Memphis trademark lawyers. In addition, the *Wall Street Journal* ran a story that was very unfavorable for Terminex. Soon thereafter, the case was "voluntarily" dismissed, and our client kept her Web site. This was just the beginning of a number of similar cases in which trademark claims were alleged but where there actually was no possibility of consumer confusion. After all, who would think that a Web site called "AlitaliaSucks" was actually sponsored by the airline, as opposed to a very unhappy customer? But winning the legal battle was not the reason these cases were brought, and so we also devised a strategy to make these companies pay for attempting to silence their critics, especially in California where there is a special statute that gives victims of such lawsuits the right to recover attorneys' fees. We have now gone beyond the obviously retaliatory suits (although there still are some) to cases in which the plaintiff objects to the Web site because it is misleading and sometimes shocking (pictures of aborted fetuses on a site that has the name of a company such as the *Washington Post* as part of it), and the issue is how to balance the First Amendment rights of the speaker and the company. Our view is that it is appropriate to use such a site to criticize the *Post's* stand on abortion but not to suggest that the paper actually performs abortions or endorses the graphic photos.

The other set of Internet cases involves chat rooms run by the Internet service provider Yahoo! for every publicly listed corporation. These chat rooms are operated on an informal basis, and many of the participants post their com-

357

ments anonymously for a variety of reasons. Not surprisingly, some of the companies, and in some cases company officers, have been displeased with certain comments and have sued Yahoo! to get the names of the posters in order, in theory, to sue the posters for torts such as defamation, theft of trade secrets, or misuse of inside information. Initially, Yahoo! simply turned over the identities. We argued that people who post messages anonymously should be entitled to maintain their secrecy unless the plaintiff makes a strong showing that there is a legal and factual basis for the complaint. A number of these posters are employees of the companies they are criticizing, and their fear is that the motive for getting their name is not to pursue the lawsuit but to take peremptory disciplinary action against them. Our legal efforts have advanced the law considerably so that, in general, there is reasonable protection such that posters who have reason to try to protect their anonymity have an opportunity to do so. Yahoo! now gives notice to posters when their identities are sought.

Our ventures in the Internet are just beginning. But with the changes that are a constant in this area, we will be alert in both our current areas and in new ones so that the Internet will continue to be engine of free speech for all who want to use it.

Supreme Court Assistance Project

In the mid-1980s the Litigation Group received a request to file an *amicus* brief in a welfare case that was about to be argued in the Supreme Court. After reading the draft brief prepared by the legal services lawyers who had made the request, three conclusions jumped out: (1) the Litigation Group had nothing that it could add as an *amicus*; (2) the legal services lawyers were obviously knowledgeable about the substantive issues but not very familiar with the unique nature of Supreme Court litigation; and (3) the request came very late in the briefing process. Indeed, the best help we could have provided would have been at the *certiorari* stage, when the court was considering whether to hear the case, because there seemed to be arguments that might have persuaded the court not to take the case, preserving the clients' victory below. We also concluded that we needed to develop a new approach to helping lawyers with little or no Supreme Court experience with their public interest cases in the High Court.

The Litigation Group had the expertise to deal with this problem. By that time, we had argued more than two dozen cases in the High Court, winning almost 60 percent of them. (By the end of the 2004 term, we will have argued forty-seven cases on the merits, with our winning percentage about the same.) The concept we developed was to become involved in public interest cases as early as possible and to be active in seeking them out, instead of waiting for requests to come to us. We also knew that the project could not succeed unless we were clear that we were not trying to take over the case from the lawyer who had it and that we would not be paid for our services, unless there were court-awarded fees or the lawyer decided to make a donation. Our plan was to identify cases in which we might offer help right after they were filed. To do that, we needed someone to read nearly two thousand *cert* petitions filed each year, identify those cases in which we might be helpful, and then contact the existing counsel to offer our assistance. We concluded that a recent law school graduate could do the job, but it took several years before we were able to securing initial funding (from the Public Welfare Foundation), and the project began in the fall of 1990.

The project has been an enormous success for all concerned. It has provided invaluable services to scores of lawyers and their clients every year. It has provided an opportunity each year for a young lawyer to participate in and observe public interest advocacy at the highest levels. And it has continued to hone the skills of Litigation Group lawyers who provide the assistance at both the *cert* and merits stages, and who do moot courts in approximately fifteen to twenty of the seventy-five cases that the court hears each year. In addition, in seven cases we were asked to take over the argument from the original counsel and in two others we took over from prisoners who had handled the case on their own until then. Quite by chance, the two prisoner cases were argued on the same day, by Allison Zieve and Bonnie Robin-Vergeer, but not actually at the Supreme Court, because the building was shut down for the anthrax scare.

Because of the number of cases in which we provide assistance every year, no sample of the cases could truly be representative. Nonetheless, here are some cases that will provide some insight into the kind of cases in which we have provided help.

- *IOLTA* (Interest on Lawyers Trust Accounts) *Litigation.* We assisted counsel through two Supreme Court battles in upholding the validity of IOLTA programs that provide funds for legal services programs in all fifty states against a Takings Clause challenge.

- *Troxel v. Granville.* In this case, which established the right of a concededly fit parent to prevent the state from second-guessing her decision about the extent to which her children should visit their grandparents, we helped write the parent's merits briefs and prepare the lawyer for oral argument.

- *Connecticut v. Doehr.* We helped a New Haven solo practitioner sustain a ruling that a Connecticut statute, which permitted a prejudgment lien on real property in collection cases before notice and an opportunity to be heard, violated her client's rights to due process.

- *Devlin v. Scardelletti.* In this case, we acted as co-counsel and helped prepare lead counsel for argument, as the court overruled most circuit courts and held that objecting class members have an absolute right to appellate review of a district court's approval of a class action settlement, a ruling that is critical to consumers wishing to challenge unfair, unlawful or collusive class action settlements.

- *Reeves v. Sanderson Plumbing.* We assisted in obtaining a reversal of an appeals court opinion that set aside a jury decision for the plaintiff in an age discrimination case, in a ruling in which the Supreme Court sternly reminded appellate judges of their limited roles in reviewing jury verdicts.

- *Chicago v. Weinberg.* In this case, our lawyer wrote a successful opposition to *certiorari*, thereby sustaining a Seventh Circuit ruling that a ban on the sale of a book critical of a local sports franchise on the public sidewalks within one thousand feet of a Chicago sports arena violated the author-seller's First Amendment rights.

* * * * *

I think I can safely speak for all of the lawyers who have worked for the Litigation Group that our belief that we are making a difference is what brought us and kept us here, in many cases for very long periods of time. We have had many important cases, but the value of our work far exceeds the sum of our lawsuits.

First, the other groups within Public Citizen have also made a major difference, and the expertise of the Litigation Group and its ability to take the government and others to court has been a vital component of their successes. Second, even when we have lost, we have educated the public and policymakers about issues of importance and demonstrated the significant role that public interest litigation performs in our society. Third, the fact that we have sued in the past and will sue in the future is taken into account by those whose actions are likely to get our attention. Fourth, by our willingness to consider new areas of the law, and at the same time continue our work from the past, we have shown that public interest advocacy requires the endurance of a long-distance runner and the ability to see and take on new challenges when government or corporate actions impinge on our freedoms and rights as citizens and consumers.

None of this would have been possible without the vision of Ralph Nader. He understood the possibilities of litigation, both for Public Citizen and for the country. When he hired me, he ensured the Litigation Group enough funding so that we would not have to raise it ourselves. He gave us the gift of his personal backing and the greatest gift of all: the almost complete freedom to pursue the kinds of cases that we (and he) saw as being in the public interest. For

Afterword

all those gifts, and for all his insights and wisdom, I will be forever grateful.

Last, I want to say just a word about the superb group of lawyers with whom I have worked at the Litigation Group. Far beyond their legal skills and their devotion to public interest law, I pay tribute to their spirit, their sense of outrage, their willingness to help each other accomplish our joint goals and their friendship. No one could ever find a better group than those who stood shoulder to shoulder with me for thirty-two years. Despite the book's length, many of their stories were never written, but they are not forgotten by me or by the many people they helped. I also cannot forget our support staff, those who worked for the Litigation Group and others who worked for all of us at Public Citizen. Without them, we could never have gotten our briefs out the door, let alone filed in the right court at the right time. Especially in the years before computers, our litigation literally would not have been possible without them.

If, as I firmly believe, the Public Citizen Litigation Group has made a difference and, I am confident, will continue to make a difference, it will be because of the selfless men and women who have dedicated their lives to its efforts. Yes, it was intellectually stimulating. Yes, it was exciting to work on big cases. Yes, it was better to be David fighting Goliath than the other way around. And yes, it was so much fun that we looked forward to coming to work every day. But in the end, it was because we thought we made a difference that all this was possible. Thanks.

Citations and Notes

Between the winter of 1995 and the completion of this book I interviewed most of the full-time lawyers who have worked at the Public Citizen Litigation Group since its birth in 1972. There were a few whom I could not locate and a couple who were not included because they were there such a short time. Those who stayed for a considerable time have been interviewed on several occasions. All interviews were taped except for two that were conducted on the phone. In addition, I interviewed many other major players in Public Citizen, as well as numerous other individuals who either worked with or against the Litigation Group, were represented by it or sat on courts before which it litigated. Information not otherwise attributed is from these interviews. The Litigation Group's archived case files—containing letters, memoranda, briefs, notes, unreported court decisions and other documents—provided another major source of information. This information is not cited when there is sufficient description in the text to identify the source. Copies of all cited material from these sources are contained in files that I have turned over to the Litigation Group along with the taped interviews and notes. Citations for reported court decisions are provided in the endnotes. The Litigation Group's archives contain the originals of all copies found in my files.

I have relied on many sources for the story of Ralph Nader's early years. The most comprehensive account is Charles McCarry's *Citizen Nader* (New York: Saturday Review Press, 1972). Though McCarry often seems hostile toward Nader and Nader's claim that he speaks on behalf of "the public interest," on the whole the book provides a fascinating look at Nader's life, why he followed the path he did and what the battles from 1966 through 1971 were like. It generally gives the reader a sense of what made the young Nader tick. Other important sources include Connie Bruck, "Will Reaganism Revive Ralph NADER?" in *The American Lawyer*, May 1981; Peter Brimelow and Leslie Spencer, "Ralph Nader, Inc." in *Forbes*, September 17, 1990; various editions of *Public Citizen Magazine*, and innumerable newspaper articles.

Chapter 1

p. 3   Ralph Nader, *Unsafe at Any Speed: The designed-in dangers of the American automobile*, (New York, NY: Grossman Publishers, 1965).

p. 4   The newspaperman's response to Nader's publisher is quoted in McCarry, *Citizen Nader*, p. 8.

p. 6   The excerpt is from McCarry, *Citizen Nader*, p. 29.

Citations and Notes

p. 6   Quotation is from a high school address given by Nader in his home town, Winsted, Connecticut, as quoted in McCarry, *Citizen Nader*, p. 38.

p. 7   Nader's comments about the NHTSA rules are from McCarry, Citizen Nader, p. 96.

p. 7   Nader quoted in McCarry, *Citizen Nader*, p. 211.

p. 8   Nader quoted in Jonathan Rowe, "Ralph Nader Reconsidered," *The Washington Monthly*, 1985 reprinted in the February 1989 issue at p. 65.

Chapter 2

p. 12   The description of the Center is from McCarry, *Citizen Nader*, p. 196.

p. 15   430 F.2d 891 (D.C. Cir. 1970). Citation from *Moss v. CAB*, at 901.

p. 17   The Fallows quotation is from Connie Bruck, "Will Reaganism Revive Ralph Nader?," p. 32.

p. 20   Wolfe's testimony before the Congressional Hearings on Governmental Lawlessness on June 29, 1972 (copy in author's files).

p. 23   The excerpt describing Nader's concerns about formal organizations is from McCarry, *Citizen Nader*, p. 313.

p. 23   Nader's remarks at the 25th anniversary party are from author's notes at the event.

p. 24   Nader's description of his ideal recruit is from McCarry, *Citizen Nader*, p. 212.

p. 25   Robert Fulghum, *It Was on Fire When I Lay Down on It*, (New York, NY: Villard Books), p. 97.

Chapter 3

p. 27   The opening quotation is from an address at Yale Law School by Victor H. Kramer, printed as *Public Interest Law*, Yale Law Report, Sesquicentennial Convocation II. 1824-1974, Vol. 21, No. 3, Spring 1975, p. 24.

p. 27   Joseph Goulden, *The Superlawyers: The Small and Powerful World of the Great Washington Law Firms* (New York, NY: Weybright and Talley, 1972).

p. 27   For more on the Ford Foundation's role see: *Public Interest Law: Five Years Later*, a special joint publication of the Ford Foundation and the American Bar Association Special Committee on Public Interest Practice, March 1976.

p. 28   Burger quoted in Goulden, *The Superlawyers*, p. 352.

p. 28   The term "private attorney general" was first used by Judge Jerome Frank in *Associated Industries, Inc. v. Ickes*, 134 F.2d 694, at 704 (2d Cir. 1943) vacated as moot, 320 U.S. 707 (1943).

p. 29   Louis L. Jaffe, *The Citizen as Litigant in Public Actions: The Non-Hohlfeldian or Ideological Plaintiff*, The University of Pennsylvania Law Review, 116:1033 (1968). The excerpt is from p. 1038.

p. 30   Nader is quoted in Goulden, *The Superlawyers*, p. 352.

p. 30   The former Nader associate quoted is Thomas Stanton who served as head of the Tax Reform Group in the early 1970s, from author's interview.

p. 32   Nader is quoted in Goulden, *The Superlawyers*, p. 348.

p. 33   Mintz is quoted in McCarry, *Citizen Nader*, p. 108-109.

p. 34   Morrison's former associate is quoted in Burt Schoor, *Alan Morrison: Even When He Loses, He Wins*, Juris Doctor, January 1976.

Chapter 4

p. 40   Information for the summary of the political events of February, 1972 comes from a review of *The New York Times* and *The Washington Post* stories for the month.

p. 45   Warren Bennis, *Organizing Genius: The Secrets of Creative Collaboration* (Perseus Books Group, 1998). Some of the quotations from Bennis come from a televised interview with Bennis by David Gergen on PBS, March 26, 1997.

Chapter 5

p. 56   Senator Kennedy quote is from CQ Almanac, 1974, p. 652: statement of Kennedy opening debate on S2543, the 1974 FOIA amendments bill.

p. 57   *Stern v. Department of Justice (also listed as Stern v. Richardson)* 367 F. Supp. 1316 (D.D.C. 1973).

p. 57   Copies of all letters between the DOJ and Stern are in the author's files.

p. 59	The "political spy puzzle" quotation is from "1972 Break-in Clouded Nixon Administration Aura," in *Congress and the Nation*, Vol. III, (D.C.: CQ Press, 1973), p. 978. This source was used as the primary one for summarizing events along with *The Washington Post's* Web site summary surrounding Watergate throughout the chapter unless otherwise noted.
p. 59	Quotation from Dean's testimony is from *Congress and the Nation*, ibid.
p. 60	*Stern*, 367 F. Supp. at 1323-24.
p. 61	*Nixon v. Sirica*, 487 F.2d 700 (D.C. Cir. 1973).
p. 61	Cox's comment is from "Statement Issued by Prosecutor Cox," *The Washington Post*, Oct. 20, 1973, p. A8.
p. 61	Copies of COINTELPRO documents turned over to Stern in author's files.
p. 63	Quote is from *The New York Times*, November 24, 1974.
p. 65	*Brandon v. Sampson*, 569 F.2d 683 (D.C. Cir. 1977).
p. 65	Copy of appraisal in author's files.
p. 66	Data on dated documents transmitted in March 22, 1978, letter from Richard Nixon to Mr. Joel W. Solomon, Administrator, General Services Administration, (copy in author's files).
p. 66	Data on chronology of events from affidavit of Robert M. Brandon, March 25, 1974, copy in author's files.
p. 67	*The Washington Post*, January 19, 1974, p. 1.
p. 68	*Nixon v. Administrator of General Services*, 433 U.S. 425 (1977); 408 F. Supp. 321 (D.D.C. 1976), three-judge district court.

Chapter 6

p. 71	Peter Rutland, "Yeltsin: The Problem, Not the Solution," *National Interest*, Fall, 1997.
p. 72	*Missouri v. Volpe*, 479 F.2d 1099 (8th Cir. 1973).
p. 76	The impoundment case that Jacks argued was *Campaign Clean Water v. Train*, 420 U.S. 136 (1975).
p. 76	Information on the mail cover issue from Litigation Group's files including the letter from Califano to Robertson.
p. 80	*INS v. Chadha*, 462 U.S. 919 (1983).
p. 81	Broder's "Getting Returns From Tax Gripes," *The Washington Post*, April 8, 1973.
p. 84	Nader commentary article on Legal Aid "New Allies for Public Interest Law," *Washington Star*, Jan. 15, 1977.
p. 87	*Williams v. Phillips*, 360 F. Supp. 1363 (D.D.C. 1973) decision of June 11.
p. 88	*Williams v. Phillips* 482 F.2d 669 (D.C. Cir. 1973). p. 89. *Williams v. Phillips*, unreported case on remand in D.C. District Court, decided June 27, 1973.
p. 91	*Nader v. Bork*, 366 F. Supp. 104 (D.D.C. 1973).

Chapter 7

p. 93	Schecter's story is taken from "Why HEW Won't Clue the Public In," *Evening Star*, April 20, 1972, p. 8.
p. 94	*Schecter v. Richardson*, 199 Ct. Cl. 1010 (1972) (this will be referred to as Schecter 1); no appeal was taken from Judge Waddy's decision.
p. 94	Quote is from letter to Schecter from Russell R. Jalbert, the Assistant Commissioner for Public Affairs of the Social Security Administration, November 14, 1972 (copy in author's files).
p. 94	Description of Senate hearings from *Evening Star* article cited above.
p. 94	The administration's rationale for not releasing the documents is found in the transcript of hearings for what is called *Schecter 2* before District Judge George L. Hart Jr. on June 1, 1973 (copy of transcript in author's files).
p. 96	*Getman v. NLRB*, 450 F.2d 670, 672 (D.C. Cir. 1971).
p. 97	Description of the NHTSA process from affidavit of Robert L. Carter, Associate Administrator, Motor Vehicle Program, National Highway Traffic Safety Administration, in the Appendix to *Ditlow v. Volpe*, (also known as *Ditlow v. Brinegar*) 494 F.2d 1073 (D.C. Cir. 1974).
p. 98	Excerpt from Judge Robinson Jr.'s decision in *Ditlow v. Volpe*, 362 F. Supp. 1321, 1324 (D.D.C. 1973).
p. 98	*Weisburg v. DOJ*, 489 F.2d 1195 (D.C. Cir. 1973), *cert. denied*, 416 U.S. 993 (1974);

Citations and Notes

	supercedled by statute as noted in *FBI v. Abramson*, 456 U.S. 615, 628 (1982).
p. 100	Quote is from Robert G. Vaughn, *The Freedom of Information Act and Vaughn v. Rosen: Some Personal Comments*, The American University Law Review, Vol. 23, (1974), pp. 865-66. The results of Vaughn's study of the U.S. Civil Service Commission were published in 1974 by Public Citizen as: "The Spoiled System: A Call for Civil Service Reform."
p. 100	*Vaughn v. Rosen*, 484 F.2d 820 (D.C. Cir. 1973) (this is the case that is referred to as *Vaughn 1*) cert. denied, 415 U.S. 977 (1974).
p. 102	Transcript of oral hearing before Judge Hart in author's files.
p. 104	*Schecter v. Weinberger*, 506 F.2d 1275 (D.C. Cir. 1974).
p. 107	*Ditlow v. Brinegar*, 494 F.2d 1073 (D.C. Cir. 1974).
p. 107	Representative Moorhead quote from *CQ Almanac*, 1972, p. 670.
p. 108	*EPA v. Mink*, 410 U.S. 73 (1973) (Stewart, J. concurring).
p. 110	Colloquy between Senators Hart and Kennedy at 120 Cong Rec. S9330 (daily ed. May 30, 1974).
p. 111	*Robertson v. Butterfield*, 498 F.2d 1031 (D.C. Cir. 1974); overruled and vacated in *Adm'r, FAA v. Robertson*, 422 U.S. 255 (1975).
p. 112	Shaffer's comments about Nader from *Aviation Daily*, Aug. 24, 1970 (quoted in Litigation Group brief filed in District Court, p. 9 (copy in author's files).
p. 113	*Robertson v. Butterfield*, 498 F.2d 1031 (D.C. Cir. 1974).
p. 114	*Administrator, FAA (Butterfield) v. Robertson*, 422 U.S. 255 (1975).
p. 114	Senate Report No. 94-880 (Part I and II) and House Conference Report No. 94-1441 of P.L. 94-409, subsection (b)(3).

Chapter 8

p. 116	Comments of Goldfarb from his testimony before the Subcommittee on Representation of Citizen Interests of the Committee on the Judiciary of the United States Senate, September 23, 1973 (Senator Tunney's hearings).
p. 117	Sample replies from Exhibits 1-20 in the District Court documentation (copies in author's files).
p. 117	Virginia Bar Legal Ethics Opinion No. 170, see 421 U.S. 773, 778 (1975).
p. 118	Copy of letter from Goldfarb to Virginia state attorney general in author's file.
p. 118	Morrison, "Changing the Legal Profession," an unpublished, undated paper written around 1986 (copy in author's files). Quotations that follow attributed to Morrison come either from this paper or from interviews.
p. 119	Figures on Goldfarb's costs from Plaintiffs Proposed Stipulation of Facts, p. 4 (copy in author's files).
p. 121	Motion to Recuse, May 15, 1972 (copy in author's files).
p. 124	Transcript of *Goldfarb v. Virginia State Bar* oral before the district court (copy in author's files).
p. 124	*Goldfarb v. Virginia State Bar*, 355 F. Supp. 491 (E.D.Va. 1973).
p. 125	*Goldfarb v. Virginia State Bar*, 497 F.2d 1 (4th Cir. 1974).
p. 126	*Wall Street Journal*, May 8, 1974, p. 1.
pp. 127-128	Transcript of Supreme Court oral argument in *Goldfarb* (copy in author's files).
p. 128	*Goldfarb v. Virginia State Bar*, 421 U.S. 773 (1975) footnote 16 at 788.
p. 129	*U. S. News & World Report*, September 22, 1978, pp. 27-30.
p. 130	Figures on Tetracycline costs from Joint Appendix to the Supreme Court Briefs in *Virginia State Board of Pharmacy v. Virginia Citizens Consumer Council*, p. App 14.
p. 130	The case closing the door to the Fourteenth was *North Dakota State Board of Pharmacy v. Synder's Drug Stores, Inc.*, 414 U.S. 156 (1973).
pp. 130-131	Information on Bonner's approach to developing the case from an undated memo from the Litigation Group's files (copy in author's files).
p. 131	Department of Justice Report printed in Joint Appendix, pp. 21-27.
p. 132	*Virginia Citizens Consumer Council v. State Board of Pharmacy*, 373 F. Supp. 683, (E.D.Va. 1974).
p. 132	*Bigelow v. Commonwealth of Virginia*, 421 U.S. 809 (1975).
p. 133	April 3, 1975 mandamus petition (copy in author's files).
pp. 134-137	Transcript of oral argument, November 11, 1975. Attorney Troy, pp. 3-19, 49-53; Attorney Morrison, pp. 19-49.

Courting Change

p. 137   *State Board of Pharmacy v. Virginia Citizens Consumer Council*, 425 U.S. 748 (1976).
p. 137   *The New York Times*, May 28, 1976, p. A24.
pp. 137-138 *The Wall Street Journal*, May 27, 1976, p. 22.
p. 138   Morrison quote from "Changing the Legal Profession," p. 38.
p. 138   *Bates v. State Bar of Arizona*, 433 U.S. 350 (1977).

Chapter 9

p. 139   Background and quotations on the ITT affair from Anthony Sampson, *The Sovereign State of ITT*, (New York: Stein and Day, 1973), pp. 199-213.
p. 140   Excerpt, ibid., p. 199.
p. 143   Jurisdictional Statement on Appeal to the Supreme Court, Do. N. 72-823, December 5, 1972 in *USA v. ITT and Hartford Fire Insurance*, 349 F. Supp. 22 (D. Conn. 1972), p. 21.
p. 144   Information on the tax story is from Sampson, p.179-80 and interviews.
p. 146   Copies of flyers in author's files.
p. 146   A copy of the typed account covering the events that day and signed by Barry Wilner is in author's files.
p. 146   Supreme Court case law at the time protecting leafleting: *Schneider v. State*, 308 U.S. 147 (1939); *Jamison v. Texas*, 318 U.S. 413 (1943).
p. 146   Supreme Court case law at the time protecting picketing: *Thornhill v. Alabama*, 310 U.S. 88 (1940); *Marsh v. Alabama*, 326 U.S. 501 (1946); *Shuttlesworth v. Birmingham*, 394 U.S. 147 (1969).
p. 146   Supreme Court case law on public space at the time: *Marsh v. Alabama*, 326 U.S. 501 (1946), *Amalgamated Food Employees v. Logan Valley Plaza*, 391 U.S. 308 (1968).
pp. 146-47 Nader bumping story from Litigation Group briefs and affidavits in *Nader v. Allegheny Airlines, Inc.*, 365 F. Supp. 128 (D.D.C. 1973) (copies in author's files).
p. 147   Memo from Mr. John Jenkins, Regional Director, Ground Services, April 28, 1972 (copy in author's files).
p. 148   Letter from Grossman Publishers to Mr. James L. Ricks, Customer Relations Manager, Allegheny Airlines, Washington National Airport, October 25, 1972 (copy in author's files).
p. 148   Judge Richey's remarks in transcript of trial as printed in the Joint Appendix for the Supreme Court in *Nader v. Allegheny*, 426 U.S. 290 (1976) (copy in author's files).
p. 149   Judge Richey's Order and Findings of Fact and Conclusions of Law in *Nader v. Allegheny* in Joint Appendix to the Supreme Court.
p. 149   *The Wall Street Journal*, October 19, 1973.
p. 149   Letter from Roberson to Robertson, October 26, 1973 (copy in author's files).
p. 149   Story on Thanksgiving weekend leafleting from Litigation Group briefs and affidavits in *Nader v. Butterfield*, 373 F. Supp. 1175 (D.D.C. 1974).
pp. 149-50 Copy of Judge Waddy's orders in author's files.
p. 149   Letter from Morrison to Assistant Attorney General Thomas G. Corcoran Jr., Dec. 14, 1973 (copy in author's file).
p. 150   *Wolin v. Port of New York Authority*, 392 F.2d 83 (2nd Cir. 1968).
p. 150   *Virginia Citizens Consumer Council, Inc. v. State Board of Pharmacy*, 373 F. Supp. 683 (E.D.Va. 1974).
p. 150   Letter from James H. Stark, ACLU staff attorney to Robertson, April 30, 1974 (copy in author's files).
p. 151   Memorandum in Opposition to Motion of Civil Aeronautics Board for Leave to File Untimely Amicus Brief, July 3, 1974, p. 3 (copy in author's files).
p. 153   The past Supreme Court decision is *American Airlines v. North American Airlines*, 351 U.S. 79 (1956).
p. 153   *Nader v. Allegheny Airlines, Inc.*, 512 F.2d 527 (D.C. Cir. 1975).
pp. 153-54 *Nader v. Allegheny Airlines, Inc.*, 512 F.2d 527, 552 (D.C. Cir. 1975) (Fahy, J. dissenting).
p. 154   Robertson's comment from Petition for a Writ of Certiorari to the U.S. Court of Appeals for the District of Columbia, September 22, 1975, p. 6-7 (author's files).
p. 155   *Nader v. Schaffer*, 417 F. Supp. 837 (D. Conn. 1976).
p. 156   Transcript of Oral Argument before the Supreme Court in *Nader v. Allegheny Airlines*, 426 U.S. 290 (1976) No. 75-455, argued on March 24, 1976, Reuben B. Robertson III

Citations and Notes

counsel for Nader and E. Barrett Prettyman Jr. for Allegheny Airlines.

p. 157   *Chicago Daily News*, Aug. 3, 1976, "Ralph Nader has a case of the bumps," p. 16.

p. 157   Information concerning the ATA meeting from affidavits in Litigation Group files (copy in author's files).

Chapter 10

p. 161   Affidavit of Armond M. Welch, member of the OTC Drug Review Staff and panel administrator for Antacid OTC Drug Review Panel, in civil action no. 74-454, p. 2.

p. 161   *Wolfe v. Weinberger*, 403 F. Supp. 238 (D.D.C. 1975).

p. 162   Government defense of OTC panel from Memorandum in Opposition to Plaintiff's cross-motion for Summary Judgment, pp. 3, 7, 9-11.

p. 162   Judge Richey's Memorandum Opinion in *Wolfe v. Weinberger*, 403 F. Supp. 238 (D.D.C. 1975), pp. 240-1.

p. 162   From Reuben Robertson's testimony on May 9, 1976, hearings before the Subcommittee on Reports, Accounting and Management on S2947, the Federal Advisory Committee Act Amendments of 1976, p 141.

p. 162   *Nader v. Baroody*, 396 F. Supp. 1231 (D.D.C. 1975); *Aviation Consumer Action Project v. Washburn*, 535 F.2d 101 (D.C. Cir. 1976); *Food Chemical News v. Davis*, 378 F. Supp. 1048 (D.D.C.) and *Nader v. Dunlop*, 370 F. Supp. 177 (D.D.C. 1973).

p. 162   5 U.S.C. § 552.

p. 163   IRS ruling in letter to Public Citizen from E.D. Coleman, Chief, Rulings Section 2, IRS, Nov. 15, 1974.

p. 164   See Robert Vaughn, *The Freedom of Information Act and Vaughn v. Rosen: Some Personal Comments*, The American University Law Review, Vol. 23, 865 at 873.

p. 165   Case against Agnew summarized from U.S. Attorney George Beall's report to the court in Criminal No. 73-0535, *U.S. v. Agnew*, p. 1. These documents were what were released to Baldwin and Finney in 1975.

p. 166   Judge Green, Memorandum Order, Oct. 8, 1975, p. 2.

p. 167   Copies of all briefs, memorandum opinions cited in *Baldwin* case in author's files.

p. 169   Cohen is quoted in "More Agnew Papers to be Released," *The Baltimore Sun*, March 7, 1978, p. C1.

p. 169   Comments on what was released from *ibid.*

p. 172   Judge Gesell's unpublished order in *Murphy* reproduced in the Joint Appendix of the Appeals documents in Baldwin, pp. 61-63.

p. 172   *Murphy v. Department of the Army*, 613 F.2d 1151 (D.C. Cir. 1979).

p. 173   Wolfe quote from Introduction to *Directory of Local Physicians for Prince Georges County*, 1974, Public Citizen's Health Research Group.

p. 175   Transcript of oral argument before Judge Gesell in author's files.

p. 176   Memorandum and Order of Judge Gesell, April 25, 1978, unpublished (copy in author's files).

p. 176   Memorandum and Order of Judge Gesell, Sept. 25, 1979, unpublished (copy in author's files).

p. 178   *Public Citizen HRG v. HEW*, 668 F.2d 537 (D.C. Cir. 1981) (*Wolfe v. Weinberger*).

p. 179   Copy of "NOTICE" in author's files.

p. 179   Riddles' story from his Affidavit, September 11, 1978 and his testimony before the House Subcommittee on Civil Service of the House Post Office and Civil Service Committee, Oct. 18. 1979.

p. 181   DOJ letter to Betsy Ginsberg, Esq., Civil Division, U.S. DOJ, from Department of Army Judge Advocate General, Oct. 4, 1978 (copy as provided to Cohn in author's file).

p. 183   "New Federal Rules Prohibit Coercing Employees to Give to Charities," *The Washington Post*, December 22, 1980, p. 23.

Chapter 11

p. 188   Copy of the "summons" in author's files.

p. 189   *Bonderman v. Minn. Mining & Manufacturing*, D. Minn. 3-74 108.

p. 191   John W. Johnson, *Insuring Against Disaster: The Nuclear Industry on Trial* (Macon, Georgia: Mercer University Press, 1986). This is an exhaustive and fascinating account of the case, the people involved and background on the nuclear power issue before

	and after the decision. Summary of challenges raised see pp. 22-24.
pp. 191-92	Ibid. p. 81-82 on how case came to the Litigation Group and quotations.
p. 192	Ibid. p. 31 and p. 94 for background on Judge McMillan.
p. 193	Ibid. p. 119 for description of tour and judge's comment.
p. 193	*Carolina Environmental Study Group, Inc. v. United States Atomic Energy Commission*, 431 F. Supp. 203 (W.D.N.C. 1977).
p. 194	Decision reprinted in appendix to *Duke v. CESG* appeal to Supreme Court, Robert Burns excerpt at 457. *Duke Power Co. v. Carolina Envtl. Study Group*, 438 U.S. 59 (1978).
p. 195	Johnson, *Insuring Against Disaster*, p. 155.
p. 195	Letter from Schultz to O'Connell, October 14, 1977 (copy in author's files).
p. 196	Johnson, *Insuring Against Disaster*, for description of oral see pp. 206-207.
p. 197	Johnson, *Insuring Against Disaster*, pp. 250-251 for information on Three Mile Island and Silkwood.
p. 197	*Silkwood v. Kerr-McGee Corp.*, 485 F. Supp. 566 (W.D.Okla. 1979).
p. 197	*Mink v. University of Chicago*, 460 F. Supp. 713 (N.D.Ill. 1978).
p. 197	Copy of letter to Mink from Dr. Bibbo in author's files.
p. 198	"Des Suit Highlights Victims' Plight," *The Los Angeles Times*, May 5, 1977, p. 9 for Mink quote.
p. 198	"Medical Time Bomb Triggers Threat of Cancer," *Three Village Herald*, November 19, 1975, for "morality" quote.
p. 199	"University, Firm Sued over DES Tests in Mothers," *The Washington Post*, April 26, 1977, p. 1.
p. 199	Herb Block editorial cartoon, *The Washington Post*, December 21, 1977.
p. 202	Auto Industry challenge to the air bag rule: *Chrysler Corp. v. Department of Transportation*, 472 F.2d 659 (6th Cir. 1972).
p. 203	Copy of letter from Nader to Claybrook in author's files.
p. 204	*Public Citizen v. Adams*, 593 F.2d 1338 (D.C. Cir. 1979) consolidated with *Pacific Legal Foundation v. Department of Transportation*, 593 F.2d 1338 (D.C. Cir. 1979).
p. 204	Nader's sworn statement (February 22, 1978) detailing November 30, 1977, press conference (copy in author's files).
p. 206	*Pacific Legal Foundation v. Department of Transportation*, 593 F.2d 1338 (D.C. Cir. 1979) (Wright, J. opinion of the court).
p. 209	*Nader v. Allegheny*, 445 F. Supp. 168 (D.D.C. 1978) second Judge Richey decision.
p. 209	*Nader v. Allegheny*, 626 F.2d 1031 (D.C. Cir. 1980).
p. 209	Note from Sims to Nader (copy in author's file).
p. 209	"Texas Judges Bump Back with Lawsuit Against Southwestern Airlines," *Washington Post*, May 6, 1981, p. A14.

Chapter 12

p. 213	Kenneth C. Crowe, *Collision: How the Rank and File Took Back the Teamsters*, (New York: Scribner's, 1993) p. 52.
p. 214	*Fergusson v. NLRB*, 505 F.2d 342 (D.C. Cir. 1974).
p. 215	*Banyard v. NLRB*, 505 F.2d 342 (D.C. Cir. 1974).
p. 215	Judge Wilkey's quotation re "abdication" see *Banyard v. NLRB*, 505 F.2d 342 (D.C. Cir. 1974) at 346.
p. 216	*The Wall Street Journal* article information from Crowe, p. 54.
p. 217	Robert Kennedy, *Enemy Within* (New York: Harper, 1960).
p. 217	John Sikorski, *Teamster Democracy and Financial Responsibility* (Washington: Prod, 1976).
p. 217	See Crowe for Fitzsimmon statement at National Convention.
p. 218	Dan Rodricks, "Meat Mouth in a crusade, sinks his teeth into fat cat." *Baltimore Sun*, date unknown 1977.
p. 219	Landrum-Griffin Act, Labor Management and Disclosure Act of 1950, 29 U.S.C. §501.
p. 219	Title IV of the Employee Retirement Income Security Act of 1974 (ERISA) 29 U.S.C. §1101 *et seq.*, and Labor Management Relations Act, 29 U.S.C. § 186(c)(5).
p. 219	For quotation re "found nothing" see *Baltimore Sun* articles in author's files.
p. 220	Information on Bell's wheeling and dealing from various news articles from the *Baltimore Sun*, Dec. 11, 1977, p. 1, and Jan. 26, 1978.

Citations and Notes

p. 221   *Tinker v. Des Moines Independent Community School District*, 393 U.S. 503 (1969).

p. 224   Jan. 8, 1980 letter to Judge Young (copy in author's files).

p. 226   Transcript of Oral, May 5, 1980, p. 199 (author's files).

p. 226   *Brink v. DaLesio*, 453 F. Supp. 272 (D.Md. 1978) (Young, J. opinion of the court).

p. 226   *The Washington Post*, Aug. 21, 1980, p. A15.

p. 226   Letter from Fox to Brink and Eline (copy in author's files).

p. 227   Copy of letter from Fox to the attorney for the fund in author's files.

p. 229   Copy of letter from Smith to Nader in author's files.

p. 230   NLRB v. Wilson Freight Co., 604 F.2d 712 (1st Cir. 1979), cert. denied in *Smith v. Wilson Freight Co.*, 445 U.S. 962 (1980).

p. 230   Copy of Petition from Wilson Employees to Governor Francis W. Sargent, September 30, 1974, in author's files.

p. 230   *NLRB v. Wilson Freight Co.*, 604 F.2d 712 (1st Cir. 1979).

p. 231   Petition for a Writ of Certiorari filed by Levy, Jan. 28, 1980, p. 3-8 (copy in author's files).

p. 233   Copy of letters from Smith to Levy and from Levy to Smith in author's files.

p. 233   Robert Pear, "Money Bill Decked with Many Plums," *The New York Times*, Dec 20, 1982, p. A1.

pp. 234-35   *Barrentine v. Arkansas-Best Freight System*, 450 U.S. 728 (1981). Facts and history of case from Litigation Group Brief to Supreme Court No. 79-2006 by Vladeck on Nov. 20, 1980.

p. 235   *Barrentine v. Arkansas-Best Freight System*, LR-C-77-85, (E.D.Ak. May 4, 1979).

p. 236   Copy of letter from Vladeck to Barrentine in author's files.

p. 236   *Barrentine v. Arkansas-Best Freight System*, 615 F.2d 1194 (8th Cir. 1980).

p. 236   Copy of letter from Fox to Barrentine in author's files.

p. 237   *Alexander v. Gardner-Denver*, 415 U.S. 36 (1974).

p. 238   *Boys Markets, Inc. v. Retail Clerk's Union*, Local 770, 416 F.2d 368 (9th Cir. 1969) overruled by *Boys Markets, Inc. v. Retail Clerks Union, Local 770*, 398 U.S. 235 (1970); *Buffalo Forge Co. v. United Steelworkers of America*, 386 F. Supp. 405 (W.D.N.Y. 1974), affirmed by 517 F.2d 1207 (2nd Cir. 1975), affirmed by 428 U.S. 397 (1976).

p. 239   *Barrentine v. Arkansas-Best Freight System*, 750 F.2d 47 (8th Cir. 1984).

p. 239   Copy of letter from Vladeck to ABF legal counsel S. Walton Maurras in author's files.

p. 239   Copy of proposed findings from ABF counsel in author's files.

p. 240   Copy of letter from Vladeck to ABF counsel S. Walton Maurras in author's files.

Chapter 13

p. 242   Letter from Furman to Morrison, April 4, 1977. Quotations attributed to Furman unless otherwise cited come from letters from her to Morrison over the long history of this case (1977-1984) (copies of all quoted letters are in author's files).

p. 242   "Jurisdictional Statement to the Supreme Court," by Morrison and Attorney Paul Levy, in *Furman v. the Florida Bar*, 376 So. 2d 378 (Fla. 1979), Nov. 30, 1979, (Furman I) (copy in author's files).

p. 242   Furman's advice from, "Furman's Law: Shootout at the Florida Bar," *Jacksonville Monthly*, Feb. 1984, p. 77.

p. 243   Furman's comments on judges and the bar come from various newspaper articles in Litigation Group files (undated) and from "Furman's Law: Shootout at the Florida Bar," p. 77.

p. 243   ibid.

p. 243   See "Furman's Law" for stories on Judges Santora and Fay, pp. 79-80.

p. 245   Smith's quote is from *Legal Assistant Today: A Quarterly Journal for the Paralegal Profession*, No. 4, Summer 1984, p. 23.

p. 245   Quotations attributed to Hadeed come from letters to and from Morrison over the long history of this case (copies of all letters quoted from in author's files).

p. 246   *Florida Bar v. Brumbaugh*, 355 So. 2d 1186 (Fla. 1978).

p. 246   Excerpts from the hearing from "Jurisdictional Statement," p. 88A-89A for Morrison questioning Furman; 100a-101a for Mahon questioning Furman.

p. 247   Ravels report is unpublished but can be found in the "Jurisdictional Statement," p.s 25a-114a.

p. 249   The European case is the *Airey Case*, see "Jurisdictional Statement," p. 13-14.

Chapter 14

Citations and Notes

	Attorneys' Fees, October 17, 1985, p. 10-11.
p. 273	Copy of the judge's ruling in the fee case in author's file.
p. 273	Vicky Cahan, "The Pressure on OSHA to get Back to Work," *Business Week*, June 10, 1985, p. 56.
p. 274	*United Steel Workers of America and Public Citizen v. Pendergrass, Asst. Sect of Labor* (Hazards Communications Standard case) 819 F.2d 1263, 1269-70 (3rd Cir. 1987).
p. 274	*PCHRG v. Auchter*, 702 2d 1150 (D.C. Cir. 1983)-first ruling of Appeals Court in the Ethylene Oxide case.
p. 275	*PCHRG v. Tyson*, 796 F.2d 1479 (D.C. Cir. 1986)-second ruling of Appeals Court in Ethylene Oxide case (Tyson replaced Auchter at Labor Dept).
p. 275	*Tyson*, 796 F.2d at 1495.
p. 275	*Ibid* at 1504, 1506-1507.
pp. 276-77	*PCHRG v. Brock, Secretary of Labor, and Pendergrass, Asst. Sect of Labor*, 823 F.2d 626 (D.C. Cir. 1987)-third ruling of Appeals Court in Ethylene Oxide case. Excerpts at 629.

Chapter 15

For a detailed account of *Chadha* and other legislative veto cases see: Barbara Hinkson Craig, *Chadha: The Story of an Epic Constitutional Struggle* (New York: Oxford University Press, 1988) and paperback edition (Berkley, CA: University of California Press, 1990). For a detailed account of the development of the legislative veto, particularly its use over regulatory agencies, see: Barbara Hinkson Craig, *The Legislative Veto: Congressional Control of Regulation* (Boulder, Colo.: Westview Press, 1983). Both of these books, by this author, were based on extensive interviews, congressional and executive branch documents, court cases, law and political science journal articles, and books on the topics. Descriptions of the Litigation Group's involvement in the legislative veto cases here are based on this research as well. Where specific quotes are used from these books, citations are given to the pages there. There is ample footnote and bibliographic material cited in the originals for anyone wishing more details.

p. 278	Excerpt is from *Chadha: The Story* ..., p. 60.
p. 279	Excerpt and Morrison quotes from *Chadha: The Story* ..., p. 61.
p. 279	Morrison statement from *Chadha: The Story* ..., p. 70.
p. 280	*Buckley* citation is *Buckley v. Valeo*, 424 U.S. 1 (1976).
p. 280	U.S. Constitution Article II, Section 2 (appointments clause).
p. 280	*Buckley*, 424 U.S. at 176.
p. 280	President Ford's directions see: *Chadha: The Story* ..., p. 69.
p. 281	For statistics on growth of legislative veto see: *The Legislative Veto*, pp. 8-9.
p. 281	Clark v. Valeo, 559 F.2d 642 (D.C. Cir. 1977).
p. 281	For Assistant Attorney General Rex E. Lee's statement see: *Chadha: The Story* ..., pp. 71-72.
p. 282	For Morrison's statements see: *Chadha: The Story* ..., pp. 73-74.
p. 282	For Morrison's statements see: *Chadha: The Story* ..., p. 73.
p. 283	For Morrison's statement see: *Chadha: The Story* ..., p. 84.
p. 283	*Clark v. Valeo*, 431 U.S. 950 (1977) cert. denied, Clark ruling affirmed.
p. 283	*Chadha v. INS*, 634 F.2d 408 (9th Cir. 1980).
pp. 283-84	For Chadha's story see: *Chadha: The Story* ..., Chapter 1.
p. 284	For British Consulate's response to Chadha see: *Chadha: The Story* ..., p. 8.
p. 285	For Chadha's "mind-boggling" quote see: *Chadha: The Story* ..., p. 25.
p. 285	For Pohlmann's comments see: *Chadha: The Story* ..., p. 88.
p. 286	For Justice Department note to court see: *Chadha: The Story* ..., p. 102.
p. 286	For Morrison's comments see: *Chadha: The Story* ..., p. 114.
p. 287	For Morrison's statement and "Legislative Veto Month" comments see: *Chadha: The*

	Story ..., p. 134 and 137.
p. 288	For information on passage of Natural Gas Policy Act in 1978 see: *Chadha: The Story* ..., pp. 136-137.
p. 290	For FERC's response to Morrison's petition and his reaction see: *Chadha: The Story* ..., p. 139.
p. 290	*Consumer Energy Council of America, Consumer Federation of America and Public Citizen v. Federal Energy Regulatory Commission*, 673 F.2d 425 (D.C. Cir. 1982) generally referred to as *The FERC* case.
p. 291	*Chadha*, 634 F.2d 408 (9th Cir. 1980) For a discussion of the Ninth Circuit's decision in *Chadha* see: *Chadha: The Story* ..., pp. 143-146.
p. 291	For Deputy Attorney General Schmults' comments see: *Chadha: The Story* ..., p. 155.
p. 292	For quote from Administration Brief see: *Chadha: The Story* ..., p. 166; for quote from Congressional Brief see p. 167.
p. 292	For excerpt from Congressional Brief see: *Chadha: The Story* ..., p. 169.
p. 294	For Morrison's reaction to winning *FERC* see: *Chadha: The Story* ..., p. 198.
pp. 294-95	FERC, 673 F.2d 425 (D.C. Cir. 1982). For an analysis of the Wilkey opinion in *FERC* see also: *Chadha: The Story* ..., pp. 191-198.
p. 296	For Morrison's role in oral arguments see: *Chadha: The Story* ..., pp. 200 and 211-214.
p. 297	Information and citations concerning the FTC used-car rule see: *Chadha: The Story* ..., pp. 216-218.
p. 298	For Morrison's reaction to *Chadha* see: *Chadha: The Story* ..., p. 224.
pp. 298-99	*INS v. Chadha*, 462 U.S. 919 (1983).

Chapter 16

p. 302	For statistics see: 47 Fed. Reg. 57886. This is the Advanced Notice for Proposed Rulemaking, Labeling for Salicylate-Containing Drug Products, Dec. 28, 1982.
p. 302	Alvin R. Feinstein, M.D., and Ralph I. Horowitz, M.D., "Epidemiologic Research: Double Standards, Scientific Method and Epidemiologic Research," *New England Journal of Medicine*, Vol. 307, No. 26, Dec. 23, 1982, p. 11.
p. 303	Wolfe letter to FDA (copy in author's files).
p. 304	For story and quotes on aspirin industry and AAP: K. Patrick Conner, "Stalling for Time," *San Francisco Chronicle*, Aug. 25. 1985, pp. 7-8.
p. 304	See 47 Fed. Reg. 57896 for AAP statements in June.
p. 304	Ibid for HHS announcement.
p. 305	FDA "second interim letter" to Wolfe, Exhibit 19 in Plaintiff's Supplemental Memorandum in *PCHRG v. Young*, 700 F. Supp. 581 (D.D.C. 1988).
p. 306	Tozzi quoted in *Walter v. Robinson*, "Aspirin industry slowed US on Reye's peril. officials say," *The Globe*, date unknown, copy in author's files.
p. 307	Conner, "Stalling for Time," p. 8.
pp. 307-8	Transcript of Proceedings before U.S. District Court Judge Penn in *PCHRG v. Hayes*, Nov. 8, 1982 (copy in author's files).
p. 309	Secretary Schweiker quoted in Supplemental Memorandum, p. 3.
p. 309	For statement of AAP see Supplemental Memorandum, p. 7.
pp. 310-11	Mortimer's letter to Dr. James E. Strain, Nov, 17, 1982 (Plaintiff's Exhibit 27)—copy in author's files.
p. 311	Supplemental Memorandum, p. 6.
p. 312	For story on CCC actions and court case see Conner, "Stalling for Time," p. 8 and Miller, "Aspirin Industry Slows US on Reye's Peril ...", p. 8.
p. 312	The CCC case is *Eichenwald v. Schweiker*, D. Mass. Civil Action No. 82-3554-N. Excerpts from Amended Complaint of Plaintiffs p. 19-20. Copy in author's files.
p. 312	On fate of pamphlets see Conner, "Stalling for Time," p. 9.
p. 313	Statistics from CDC for 1982 and 1983 surveillance years (Reye's surveillance years run from Dec. 1 to Nov. 30 each year).
p. 313	Plaintiffs Memorandum In Support of Their Motion for Summary Judgment, p. 1. in *Community Nutrition Institute v. Butz*, 420 F. Supp. 751 (D.D.C. 1976), continued on appeal as *Community Nutrition Institute v. Block*, 749 F.2d 50 (D.C. Cir. 1984).
p. 314	*Community Nutrition Institute*, 420 F. Supp. at 751.
p. 314	43 Fed. Reg. 54439 (1977) at 55756.
p. 314	For summary of the Department of Agriculture's actions see *Community Nutrition*

Institute, 749 F. 2d at 53.

p. 315   46 Fed. Reg. 39275 (1981) at 39278.

p. 315   The Arthur D. Little "Report to Food Safety and Inspection Service, US Department of Agriculture, Assessment of the Market Research Services Summary Report on Focus Groups Concerning Mechanically Processed Meat Product," June 1982, (Exhibit H in Plaintiff's Brief in *CNI v. Block* on appeal), copy in author's files.

p. 316   *Community Nutrition Institute*, 749 F.2d at 51 (Scalia, J., opinion of the court).

p. 316   *Community Nutrition Institute*, 740 F.2d at 35-6.

p. 316   For CCC actions see "Stalling for Time," p. 9.

p. 316   For Mortimer's comments see "Stalling for Time," p. 9. For HHS's comments see "Aspirin industry slowed ... ," p. 8.

p. 317   Letter from Wolfe to Frank Young, FDA Commissioner, January 9, 1985.

p. 318   Waxman's letter to Secretary Heckler Jan 11, 1985, copy in author's files.

p. 318   Commissioner Young's "Statement before the Subcommittee on Health and the Environment, March 15, 1985, Department of Health and Human Services copy of testimony in author's files. See pp. 3-4.

Chapter 17

pp. 321-25   Background information on the Gramm-Rudman-Hollings Amendment is from the 1985 *CQ Almanac*, "Congress Enacts Strict Anti-Deficit Measure," pp. 459-468.

p. 322   For reprints of the news articles quoted from see the *United States Congressional Record—Senate*, October 15, 1985, S13599 and S13604.

p. 323   Morrison quote about Synar from Eric Effron, "He's Not Humble—But He Gets Results," *National Law Journal*, March 10, 1985.

p. 325   Representative Lott was the conferee quoted: see *United States Congressional Record—House of Representatives*, December 11, 1985, 11878.

pp. 326-28   Members' comments from *United States Congressional Record—House of Representatives*, December 11, 1985: Lott, H 11878; Gephardt, H 11879; Barton, H 11880; Waxman, H 11881; Crane, H 11882; Barnes, H 11883; Downey, H 11883; Williams, H 11883; Frank, H 11884; Scheuer, H 11884; Conte, H 11888.

p. 328   Senator Johnston's comments from *United States Congressional Record—Senate*, December 11, 1985, S 17383.

p. 328   "1986, The Year of the Lame Duck?" Newsweek, December 23, 1985, p. 22.

p. 328   "Stealth signing ..." quotations from "Look Ma, No Hands," Time, December 23, 1985, p. 18.

p. 329   *Synar v. United States*, 626 F. Supp. 1374 (D.D.C. 1986).

p. 329   For information about court dates and documents see: Joint Appendix, Vol. 1, *Bowsher v. Synar* on Appeal from the United States District Court for the District of Columbia. Copy is in author's files.

p. 330   For comments about oral argument in District Court see Robert Pear, "Court Hears Impassioned Debate Over Legality of New Budget Law," *The New York Times*, January 11, 1986.

p. 330   Copy of Synar's note is in author's files.

p. 331   Michael Kinsley, "Rightist Judicial Activism Rescinds a Popular Mandate," *The Wall Street Journal*, February 20, 1986, p. 25.

pp. 331-32   Information about effect of GRH cuts on the courts from Paul Marcotte, "LawScope: Cheap justice? Gramm-Rudman cuts Loom," *ABA Journal, The Lawyer's Magazine*, June 1986, p. 26.

p. 332   Copy of Morrison's note and letter to court and to other appellees and appellants from Michael Davidson in author's files.

p. 333   "Of towering importance ... " quotation from "Constitutionality of Gramm-Rudman: an argument of 'towering importance,'" *The Washington Post*, April 24, 1986, p. 2A.

p. 333   Statistics on numbers present at oral argument from Lyle Denniston, "A confrontation of power plays a genteel minuet," *The Sun*, April 24, 1986, p 1.

pp. 333-34   Lyle Denniston, *Courtly-Manners* "Gramm-Rudman's 'Trigger' Under Fire," *The American Lawyer*, July/August 1986, p.116.

p. 334   Justice Burger's questions from typed "Supreme Court Question List" in Morrison's files.

p. 334   *Bowsher v. Synar*, 478 U.S. 714 (1986).

Index

Index

Index

Index

About the Author

Barbara Hinkson Craig taught government at Wesleyan University from 1982 until she retired in 2001. She is the author of three previous books: *Abortion and American Politics*, with David M. O'Brien (1993); *Chadha: The Story of an Epic Constitutional Struggle* (1990); and *The Legislative Veto: Congressional Control of Regulation* (1983). She is a graduate of the University of Maine, where she received a bachelor's degree in psychology, and of the University of Connecticut, where she received a master's degree in public administration and a doctorate in political science. Among her commendations are the 1989 Silver Gavel Award from the American Bar Association for *Chadha*, which detailed a Public Citizen Litigation Group case that prompted the U.S. Supreme Court to overturn the legislative veto and strike down more federal statutes than it had in its entire history.